# SHAKESPEARE

## TO BE OR NOT TO BE?

BY THE SAME AUTHOR
*A Study In Foresight*
*Réflexions sur le Grand Théorème de Fermat*
*Proving Shakespeare*
*Nostradamus: The Truth*

# Shakespeare

## *To Be*

## *Or Not To Be?*

### DAVID L ROPER

Copyright © 2010 by David L Roper

All Rights Reserved,
Including the right of reproduction
in whole or in part in any form.

No part of this book may be reproduced, stored in or introduced into a retrieval system, or transmitted in any form, or by any means (electronic, mechanical, photocopying, recording or otherwise), without the prior permission of the copyright holder.

First Published 2010 by
Orvid Editions

ISBN
978-0-9543873-2-7

The right of David L Roper to be identified as author of this work has been asserted in accordance with Section 77 of the Copyright, Designs and Patents Act 1988

Cover design by Vitaly Graphics
Typeset in Palatino by Acumen

British Library Cataloguing in Publication Data
A catalogue record for this book
is available from the
British Library.

*For*
*'Michelle'*

# *Proving Shakespeare*

Roper has, in this book, provided primary evidence relevant to an enigma of over 400 years standing: the actual identity of the author "William Shakespeare". . . . Roper's book is a concise and encompassing study that illuminates a nearly four-century-long controversy.

*Journal for Scientific Exploration*

This book is a 'blockbuster'. Now for the first time, readers have a full-length presentation of definitive, scientifically valid evidence for the true identity of 'William Shakespeare' as recognized by his notable contemporaries.

*Albert W. Burgstahler PhD (Harvard 1953)*
*Professor Emeritus of Chemistry, The University of Kansas USA*

I am most impressed by the analysis of the Stratford monument. To my mind the book unfolds glamorously and cogently.

*Albert C. Labriola, PhD*
*Professor of English and former Acting Dean of the College and Graduate School, Duquesne University, Pittsburgh, Pennsylvania*

In his book Roper presents scholarly, definitive, convincing evidence that E. De Vere, Earl of Oxford, was the man hiding with the pseudonym "William Shakespeare"

*Professor Kurt Dressler*
*Former Professor and Dean of Graduate Programs at the Swiss Federal Institute of Technology, ETH Zurich, and former member of SMN Council*

I think your discovery is one of the wonders of the intellectual world.

*Dr. Bruce Spittle, MB ChB (With Distinction) DPM (Otago) FRANZCP*

The proof that Edward de Vere is the true author of the Shakespeare plays is truly, inescapably, a work of genius.

*Dr. James S. Ferris*

# Contents

Acknowledgements ix

Introduction xi

**1**
Birth and Education 1

**2**
A Marriage of Uncertainties 8

**3**
The Lost Years 15

**4**
Greenes, Groats-Worth of Witte 20

**5**
Venus and Adonis 35

**6**
Shakespeare's Silence 48

**7**
Silent Tongues Give Praise 67

**8**
Predating Venus and Adonis 78

**9**
A Shakespeare First Performance 89

**10**
Shakespeare's Learning Curve 107

**11**
Shakespeare Emerges from the Shadows 127

**12**
Shakespeare Named and Famed 135

**13**
The Artful Lodger 146

**14**
Death of Queen Elizabeth I 151

15
On the Banks of the Avon   158

16
Early Retirement   175

17
The Stratford Years   193

18
The Rival Poet   216

19
The Dark Lady   228

20
A Scandalous Affair   235

21
Will. Shakspere gent. Deceased   258

22
The Stratford Monument   266

23
The First Folio   284

Afterword   301

Appendix A   309

Appendix B   311

Bibliography   314

Illustrations   317

Index   318

# Acknowledgements

I am greatly indebted to those readers of *Proving Shakespeare* that contacted me to further contribute to the advancement of Edward de Vere's eventual acceptance as the poetic genius known as William Shakespeare. I would in particular like to mention Professor Albert Burgstahler for his continued interest and support, and for keeping me up to date with the latest news from across the Atlantic: all of which has been helpful beyond measure. A particular note of thanks most especially belongs to Dr Bruce Spittle for his enlightened observation that the key to unlocking the secret information contained in the Stratford monument occurs in the second line of the Latin distich. This discovery circumvented the mathematics previously used for obtaining the same information, and silenced doubters who had claimed that no such key existed.

My appreciation also extends to Leroy Ellenberger and Dr Richard Desper for their help in bringing my work to a wider audience, also to Arthur Neuendorffer for his recent discovery of the encryption by Leonard Digges, which he has kindly allowed me to include in this book, and to Eric Miller for having made several helpful suggestions that were much appreciated.

Behind these modern names exists a foundation laid by earlier researchers: without their efforts, much in this book would have been impossible. So many times I have leaned upon their backs to see just a little further; their acknowledgement is identified by the contributions they have made within this book. Lastly, so many thanks go to my wife for her endurance during long spells of absence while this work was in progress. To her, I dedicate this book.

*There are two ways to be fooled. One is to believe what isn't true; the other is to refuse to believe what is true.*
                                    Søren Kierkegaard



*Men often applaud an imitation and hiss at the real thing.*
                                    Aesop

# INTRODUCTION

This book was initially intended to be a revised, paperback edition of *Proving Shakespeare*. But while fulfilling this aim, my attention was drawn towards factors in the authorship debate that had previously been neglected or else set aside for lack of space. The opportunity to correct these omissions was soon to take on a life of its own. The result has been that *Shakespeare: To Be Or Not To Be?* continues to retain the four major proofs asserting that the 17th Earl of Oxford wrote under the pseudonym of Shakespeare, and that Will Shakspere, from whom the author's penname was derived, acted as his paid allonym. This has meant that the reason for what became a state-orchestrated deception, as fully described in *Proving Shakespeare*; and, as it would now seem, confirmed by William Camden, is included in abridged form to allow this new material to be presented.

The twentieth century, particularly the latter half, brought with it educational opportunities for the masses. A university education that had once been the privilege of only a wealthy minority became the expected norm of every school pupil who wished to pursue a subject to degree level. Government grants, later supplemented by student loans, meant that wealth was no longer an obstacle to higher education. Secondly, the end of the twentieth century brought with it a rise in the number of households owning a computer. As a consequence of this, an expansion in Internet sites followed. Anyone with a point to make was now at liberty to publish it for a wider audience to read. This has had a significant effect upon the Shakespeare authorship question. Higher education and the ability to freely advertise one's concern to like-minded people, via the Internet, has increased doubts that Shakespeare was the author of the work attributed to him. And if he wasn't that person, then he was a front for the real author. The question this then raises – who did this subordinate, serve?

A university education is meant to furnish students with the ability and knowledge to question facts for themselves, and thereafter to present their thoughts when and wherever former evidence is weakest. If alternative facts provide a contestable theory, then this should be explored. Yet, in the English speaking universities of the western world, with only the rarest of exceptions, the English literature departments steadfastly refuse to apply this principle of scholarship. For these departments, Shakespeare's identity is established by contemporaneous references to that name; which, of course, begs a number of vital questions. Nevertheless, that is the tenet by which authorship disputes are dismissed. Consequently, because of this abject negation of best practice, where most it should flourish, Shakespeare has become equivalent to a cult figure; for he is to be accepted solely upon the dicta of authority, where the reasons given are not to be questioned.

For many centuries the Church of Rome published an Index of banned books that its faithful followers were instructed not to read, for fear these might corrupt their beliefs. Those engaged in Shakespeare studies do not have any such index, but they act as if one existed. These doyens do not read books that pose doubts about Shakespeare; therefore they will not—indeed, cannot discuss what has been newly discovered. Consequently, any question of doubt raised by an inquisitive student is likely to be dismissed with an authoritative sneer, accompanied by the repetition of some out-dated mantra that long ago lost all credibility in logic.

In 2010, Professor James Shapiro wrote a book designed to deal with the growing doubts that continue to be raised about Shakespeare. In the course of writing his book, he made several illuminating statements. The first of which I quote below from page 4 of *Contested Will*:

> There yet remains one subject walled off from serious study by Shakespeare scholars: the authorship question. More than one fellow Shakespearean was disheartened to learn that I was committing my energies to it, as if somehow I was wasting my time and talent, or worse, at risk of gong over to the dark side.

Why should it matter who wrote the works of Shakespeare, so long as that person is known? If there is doubt about the identity of an author, as indeed there most certainly is about Shakespeare, then that doubt should be discussed. How can walling off the authorship question from serious debate benefit Shakespeare and the appreciation of his work? Is it not better to know that that the petulant Bertram in *All's Well That Ends Well* was Oxford's honest portrait of his wilder youth; that Fenton's courtship of Anne Page in *Merry Wives of Windsor* was written from Oxford's memory of his earlier courtship of Anne Cecil; that Prince Hamlet's troubled mind was born from Oxford's own emotional trouble? Yet, these plays, as well as others by Shakespeare, are discussed and studied, but divorced from any contact with the mind that formed them. Instead, they are imagined to have been imagined by a man who had no known connection with the dramatic events occurring in the plays. Could Dickens have written about the plight of his characters without having lived in the hurly-burly of city life? Could Jane Austen have written so eloquently about the class society of George III's England without having lived amongst the people she met? Could Mark Twain have written so naturally about the Mississippi had it not been once a part of his life? Could Chaucer have written the *Canterbury Tales* had he not dwelt amongst the people that live in his verses? In each case these authors wrote about characters they lived amongst. In which case, Shakespeare should be sought in the midst of England's nobility, for 35 of his 36 plays are peopled by upper class citizens.

Shapiro did go some way towards admitting this. In *Contested Will*, he disclosed the reasons why John T. Looney (a teacher of English literature with a Manx surname pronounced low-knee), became convinced that the 17th Earl of Oxford was the pen behind Shakespeare's work. *"His logic is unassailable – but only if you believe that great authors don't write for money and that the plays are transparently autobiographical."* (Shapiro).

Apart from the fact that England's post-feudal ruling class refrained from accepting money for work, three examples have already been cited of plays that contain transparent biographical material; further study would reveal more. Oxford led an eventful life and his many experiences can be found in the plays of Shakespeare. Why are these parallels not remarked upon? Is one to believe that the best brains in English literature are lacking the perspicacity to observe what is in reality quite obvious? Or must one accept that these same minds are so much under the spell of the work they study that they have become oblivious to the one part of scholarship that should always be open to impartial investigation?

The answer probably lies elsewhere. To acknowledge Oxford as the author of work appearing under the name of Shakespeare would interfere with many vested interests; it would threaten others with a loss of face; it would also cause chaos within the teaching world, to history books and to works of reference. Defending Shakespeare is more than a defence of the eldest son from an illiterate family, with illiterate, uneducated children of his own, who died unacknowledged by either men of letters or the theatre, and who left this world with neither a book, letter, nor manuscript to his name; it is the defence of a British tradition; for it would be a sign of national incompetence to admit to an error of such appalling magnitude, as that of mistaking an illiterate nobody for William Shakespeare.

# 1

## BIRTH AND EDUCATION

At some unknown date in the year 1564, or as it now appears, even earlier in 1563, Mary, the wife of John Shakspere or Shaxpere (the names of illiterate people at that time were spelt by clerks to reflect the way the name was pronounced), gave birth to a son whom they named William. The birth took place in a house somewhere in the village of Stratford-upon-Avon in the county of Warwickshire. Currently, a house has been assigned as the birthplace, but there is no substantive proof to support this attribution. On Wednesday 26 April 1564, according to the Julian calendar, baby William was taken to the local parish church: the Church of the Holy Trinity, and baptised by the Reverend John Bretchgirdle.

Nature abhors a vacuum and no more so than in the case of William. He has no known birthday and one must therefore be allocated. The day appointed for this is St George's Day, which occurs on 23 April, just three days before William's baptism. Ian Wilson explains the thinking behind this:

> ... high infant mortality meant that christenings were rarely left later than the first following Sunday or Holy Day, so William almost certainly entered the world no more than two or three days before the 26th, quite possibly on the birthday traditionally attributed to him, 23 April, St Georges Day, which in 1564 fell on the Sunday. (Wilson, 38)

Wednesday, however, was neither a Sunday nor a Holy Day, which were the suggested days for a christening given by Wilson. Midweek may also seem a curious time for arranging a baptism, especially if it was to be witnessed by family members, who would normally be working on a weekday, and some on the mother's side would have had some distance to travel if they wished to attend the celebration. In different circumstances, midweek could suggest some urgency in the matter. Perhaps William's baptism had been neglected, and that a sudden illness had forced the parents to ensure their son was baptised in case the worse should happen, as it often did in those days. However, as we shall see, William's father was not one of those who favoured Sundays or Holy Days for these events. It also seems he had little time for the church, because the monument erected six or seven years after William's death states very clearly that he died on 23 April 1616 aged 53.

Simple arithmetic shows that 1616 minus 53 equals 1563 and not 1564, which was the year of his christening, and not, if documentary evidence written in stone is to be believed, the year of his birth. Quite clearly, there was a not insignificant gap between the boy's birth and his baptism. It may, however, be argued that 1563 refers to the legalistic form of the Julian calendar, which marked 25 March 1564 as New Year's Day. In which case, if William was born in January, February or before March 25th he could then have been born in 1564, in line with the Roman version of the Julian calendar, which accepted 1 January as New Year's Day. One may still, of course, celebrate the birth of this man on each St George's Day, but to do so is as vacuous as visiting the house that claims to be where he was born.

William's parents were illiterate, as were many others of similar status; both signed their names with a mark: John with a + and Mary with an attempt at an 'M'. In the course of their married life, Mary gave birth to Joan, whom they had christened on Thursday 15 September. Her death is unrecorded, but it must have occurred before too long because a second daughter named Joan was christened on Friday 15 April 1569. In that same year Easter Sunday fell on 10 April, a mere five days earlier. It does seem that the father had an aversion to Sundays and Holy Days. Also born into the family was Margaret, christened on Wednesday 2 December 1562: a weekday that fell between the first and second Sundays of Advent. But Margaret did not survive, and was buried five months later on 30 April 1563. On Sunday 13 October 1566, Gilbert was christened: the only child of eight to receive this blessing on a Sunday. He was joined by two more brothers, Richard, baptised on Thursday 11 March 1574, and Edmund baptised on Tuesday 3 May 1580. There was also another daughter, Anne, baptised on Friday 28 September 1571, but she died aged seven, and was buried 4 April 1579. The parish register recorded that the bell was tolled for her parting.

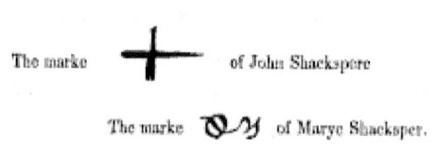

At the head of this expanding family was John Shakspere: a man whose fortunes were to change just at the point when his son William reached the age of ten. By the time William was born, John was on his way towards becoming a prominent citizen within a small community. The village had expanded from a street leading to a ford over the Avon, hence, its name: Stratford-upon-Avon, to a neighbourhood that by the middle of the 16th century boasted about a dozen streets (Wilson, 29), harbouring roughly *"1400 inhabitants'* (Collier, lxx).

> Plague, however, remained the darkest scourge. Just under three months after William's birth, the burials section of the parish register of Holy Trinity Church in Stratford bears the ominous words *Hic incepit pestis*, 'Here begins plague' ... The outbreak of 1564 was a vicious one. At least two hundred people died in Stratford, about ten times the normal rate.
> (Bryson, 23-24)

Much is made of John's elevation in the village where he lived, but within such a small environment, decimated by plague, there was little competition: a willingness to carry out the duties would be seen as the main qualification. In 1561, having previously acted as a constable, he was chosen to be a 'fixer of fines', which referred to matters not covered by existing statutes; this led to him becoming a 'burgess' or village councillor. From 1561 to 1565 he held the position of 'chamberlain': a councillor with one or more special responsibilities; after which, he became an 'alderman': a superior member of the council. Three years later in 1568, he was elected as the village 'bailiff'.

William at this time was five years old, and soon to witness a change in the family's fortune. In 1570, he had become eligible to attend the free school as the son of an alderman. But in the same year, his father stood accused of usury. John had apparently been operating as a loan-shark. Records show that he was indicted four times that year for money lending or illegal wool trading. One of his clients was Walter Mussum, to whom he had made a loan valued at £220, equivalent to £100,000 in today's currency. As Bryson pointed out, those who were found guilty of usury forfeited all of the money lent. Mussum had been a bad risk. At his death, his estate was valued at only £114, barely half of what he had borrowed from John.

In the following year John was again in trouble with the law, perhaps trying to recoup his losses. This time he was charged with illegally acquiring 300 tods of wool. A tod was equivalent to about 2 stones in weight, hence, 300 tods approximates to 3810 kilograms. This high risk strategy, which involved flouting the law, had not paid off, and by 1576 he was finally forced to withdraw from public affairs, which also included church attendance. A surviving record provides the reason: *"for fear of processe of debtte*' (Bryson, 36). In short, he was forced to evade the debt collectors.

Ackroyd (p.62) presents a different picture.

> It cannot be said that John Shakespeare's fortunes in this period were in any way declining. In 1575 he purchased two houses, with garden and orchard, in Stratford for £40.

The fact that, just months afterwards, he was taking evasive action from 'process of debt' suggests that he had been living on borrowed money, and this had financed his property deals. It is not at all unusual for a man, who, having fallen from his pedestal in society, continues life with an air of wellbeing, even if it has to be financed with borrowed money.

John's decline in wealth therefore coincides with his illegal activities, which began in 1570, at the time William had reached school age. As the son of a local dignitary, entitled to free education, one may reasonably suspect that arrangements had already been made for his admission to the free school. Documentary evidence, based upon research undertaken by Thomas Betterton, confirmed this.

> ... tho' he was the eldest son, he could give him no better education than his own employment. He had bred him, 'tis true, for some time at a Free-School, where 'tis probable he acquir'd that little Latin he was master of: but the narrowness of his circumstances, and the want of his assistance at home, forc'd his father to withdraw him from thence and unhappily prevented his further Proficiency in that Language. It is without Controversie, that he had no knowledge of the Writings of the Ancient Poets, not only from this Reason, but from his Works themselves, where we find no traces of any thing that looks like an Imitation of 'em; (Rowe).

This narrative account, gleaned from the heart of Stratford-upon-Avon, and by someone still familiar with the family history, even after a century or thereabouts, suggests that a descendant of Joan Hart, William's sister, was Betterton's informant. Biographers gloss over this report, and they are wise to do so; the reason is obvious. At the beginning of the eighteenth century, Nicholas Rowe was on the point of publishing a six-volume edition of Shakespeare's work, which was why he wanted to include *Some Account of the Life &c. of Mr William Shakespeare*. Already, the First Folio of Shakespeare's collected Histories, Tragedies and Comedies, first published in 1623 had been re-printed in 1632, 1663, 1664 and 1685. Yet, despite the author's obvious literary fame, a local from Stratford-upon-Avon, who knew the history of the man credited as the author, was referring to him as an uneducated denizen of the village he grew-up in. Surely this should begin ringing alarm bells in the mind of anyone with a scholarly outlook.

The modern-day biographer, however, will ignore this report, or else relate it only to dismiss it. Why then did Rowe not do the same? Nicholas Rowe was a barrister by profession, who for two years was engaged as an under-secretary for the Principal Secretary of State for Scotland. His devotion to literature, which he also pursued, was later rewarded, when in 1715 he became England's Poet Laureate. It was as a means for obtaining first-hand evidence of Shakespeare's life that he turned to Betterton, to whom he acknowledged: *'the most considerable part of the passages relating to this life'* came from the enquiries that he had made, when travelling *"into Warwickshire on purpose to gather up what remains he could, of a name for which he had so great a veneration'* (Rowe).

Thomas Betterton was an actor with many Shakespearean roles to his credit. *"Pepys, Pope, Steele and Cibber all bestow lavish praise on his acting.'* As a person, his integrity was never questioned. *"The blamelessness of his life was conspicuous in an age and a profession notorious for dissolute habits.'* He died on the 28 April 1710, and lies buried in Westminster Abbey. (Encyclopædia Britannica, 11th edition).

Against this background of personal integrity, it is peculiar in the least that Betterton was unable to find a better report in Stratford-upon-Avon or its surrounds to counter the one he learned from his informant. There can be no doubt that had such a remembrance, or even a school record been available, it would have been superior to the single voice that went on to relate:

> Upon his leaving School, he seems to have given intirely into that way of Living which his Father propos'd to him; and in order to settle in the World after a Family manner, he thought fit to marry while he was yet very Young. (Rowe)

There are clearly serious conflicting accounts between the biographers' version of Shakespeare's education and that given to Betterton less than a century after the poet's death. The reason for this is because the biographer will mentally approach the subject by thinking backwards in time. This requires the starting point to be a premise that the author of Shakespeare's plays and poetry was the son of John Shakspere. Then, arguing backwards, one can deduce the education required to produce the literature that resulted from it. There is nothing wrong with this practice whatsoever; that is, as long as the evidence continues to support the premise. But on this occasion it does not. The record of pupils admitted to the village school in Stratford-upon-Avon at the time William is thought to have begun his education there, which would include undeniable proof or disproof of his attendance, have been removed, and as we must now believe, have long since been destroyed. This is suspiciously strange. Shakespeare's name was famous in his own time, yet the more one enquires into the man's origins, the more one learns of the lack of awareness that this was the same man. More will be said about this later.

The biographers' response to this absence of school records is to deduce the education needed, and graft it onto the boy's upbringing as a necessary inference: one that is essential to account for Shakespeare's later knowledge and abilities. Once again, this is not an invalid exercise, but only if it is known, beyond reasonable doubt, that William was the author of the plays that were published in the First Folio. Unfortunately, there exists reasonable doubt that this was the case. Not only is there no record of William having received an education: there is no record that he wrote the works bearing Shakespeare's name. Despite Shakespeare having been a prolific writer, not one single word in his hand has ever come to light. Only six childish signatures exist; three of these occur together at the end of his life, and appear on his last will and testament, the other three occur on legal documents, and even these signatures have been disputed, for it has been reliably said, they were not made by the same hand.

Consequently, without substantive proof that William Shakspere wrote the plays that bear the name Shakespeare, biographers are compelled to work on the premise that he was their author. This has an unfortunate consequence, which adherents to the premise fail to realise. Biographies of Shakespeare can no longer be termed factual; they are instead theoretical. Thus, based upon the theory that William wrote the works of Shakespeare, his education becomes inferred *a posteriori*. Thereafter, this inference is then used to both support and establish, *a priori*, the learning that was required for the authorship of Shakespeare's plays. What biographers have achieved by this strategy is an example of circular reasoning: quite worthless as factual evidence and a taboo in formal logic because it proves nothing.

Biographers, however, are not at all deterred from flouting this major principle of logic, because they are confident that the fault will not be held against them by their peers. Biographers well know that no candidate for a university post in an English Department is likely to be employed, unless the applicant has acknowledged, implicitly or explicitly via peer reviewed articles, William's education at King's New School.

Based upon information given to Betterton, and never contradicted by any other informant at the time, young William who was about seven or eight years old at the time of his father's decline in wealth, left school to work for his father. Child labour, even at so young an age, was then and would be for some time to come, a part of English society. It was not until 1867 that the British government took action and passed a law that forbade the employment of any child below the age of eight. Thus, even three hundred years later, Will Shakspere would not have been exempt from working for his father.

There is also another pertinent fact involving the alleged education of William. It concerns a fellow schoolboy of the same age named William Smith. He attended King's New School and made such outstanding progress that he was sent to Winchester College, from where he gained admission to Oxford University. This is in contrast to John Shakspere's son, whose grasp of the classics is held by his biographers to have been the launch pad for his later work. Again, circumstances defy the academics. On the one hand, the education available for their William was of such excellence that it not only primed him for his later work, it also negated the necessity for a university education. On the other hand, in exactly the same period of time, the education available in Stratford-upon-Avon for William Smith was considered too basic for this boy's abilities, and so he was sent to Winchester, from where he gained admission to Oxford.

Essentially, the question surrounding William's attendance at school is one of the pivotal points in the authorship debate. Without a suitable education that can be pinned to his formative years, the early appearance of the plays that are claimed to have been written by him cannot be justified. Attention is therefore drawn, firstly, to the circular reasoning of academics who infer an education from the plays, and the plays from the education; secondly to the evidence collected by Betterton, alleging that Shakspere's education finished almost before it had begun; thirdly to John Shakspere, whose fall from grace required William to forgo an education to help with the family business; and finally to William Smith, an outstanding scholar whose academic promise was beyond what could be offered at King's New School, and resulted in his transfer to Winchester College.

# 2

# A MARRIAGE OF UNCERTAINTIES

From 1570/1, until November 1582, nothing more is heard of William, although records have come to light confirming the social decline of his father. But at the age of eighteen or nineteen, depending upon the year of his birth, he took a wife, or rather she took him.

Details of the marriage were discovered amongst records held at the Bishop of Worcester's office. These referred to an application for a special marriage licence – one that reduced the triple calling of banns to a single call – *"inter Willelmum Shaxpere et Annam Whateley de Temple Grafton"*, that is, between William Shaxpere and Anne Whateley of Temple Grafton (Wilson, 56). It was not until 1836 that Sir Thomas Phillips, a collector of books, discovered a further document dated 28 November 1582, the day after a licence had been issued for the marriage between William Shaxpere and Anne Whateley. The document was found in a different office and written by a clerk who had obviously not seen the licence issued on the previous day. The document was made out for a bond valued at £40, and had been guaranteed by two husbandmen from Stratford, Fulke Sandells and John Richardson. They indemnified —

> the Bishop against any impediment that *'William Shagspere'* on the one part, and *'Anne Hathwey of Stratford in the Diocese of Worcester, maiden'* might *'lawfully solemnise matrimony together and in the same afterwards remain and continue like man and wife'*
> (Wilson, 56)

It is again noteworthy that in an age when seven men out of ten could not sign their names (Bryson, 33), the learned clerks who were required to record those who had business with them, could do no more than enter the names of these three illiterates as they heard them pronounced. In the first instance, the clerk wrote the name as 'Shaxpere'; the second clerk recorded it as 'Shagspere'. In neither case did William correctly spell the name for the clerks. This may be seen as reinforcement for the report given to Betterton, that as a boy, he had been withdrawn from school by his father soon after beginning his education.

What happened during those two days in November 1582 to cause the bride's name and residence to change overnight is never likely to be known for certain. Suffice to say, William Shaxpere or Shakspere emerged with a licence to marry Anne Whateley of Temple Grafton, a village situated some five miles outside Stratford-upon-Avon. And his two companions returned to Shottery having given the Bishop of Worcester a surety for £40 to the effect that if their young companion, who was a minor, married Anne Hathaway, and the validity of the marriage be later tested in court, the Lord Bishop would be exempt from blame.

To add further to the mystery, no record of Will Shakspere's marriage has ever been discovered. It certainly did not take place in Stratford-upon-Avon. But a curious discovery did come to light at a later date. Two leaves were found to be missing, cut out from the registry of St. Martin's Church: both covering the crucial year 1582.

St. Martin's Church was located in Worcester, close to where the marriage licence had been obtained. One is therefore left to wonder what dark secret those pages held that required such drastic action. For, recall, Shakspere's marriage licence was to wed Anne 'Whateley', *not* Anne 'Hathwey'. Whereas, on a different day and before a different clerk, the same three men had obtained a proviso that were William Shagspere to wed Anne Hathwey, and should the said union be declared invalid, the Bishop of Worcester would be indemnified against having had knowledge of this impropriety. For this, the two husbandmen agreed to a bond of £40, a huge amount, presently equivalent to £20,000 by today's reckoning.

What was behind all this? Why the urgency for a marriage licence. It is true that Anne Hathaway was pregnant, but she would not give birth for another six months; plenty of time to prepare for wedding celebrations without requiring Sandells and Richardson to lay down £40 to safeguard the Bishop of Worcester should anything be amiss.

> It was not unusual in this period for couples to cohabit before their wedding. Their Stratford neighbours, George Badger and Alice Court, Robert Young and Margery Field, had a similar arrangement. (Ackroyd, 85)

Some deeper mystery therefore lies behind this incident that biographers have so far preferred to avoid.

Consider, firstly, why was it necessary for these two farmers to take time off from work so as accompany William to Worcester? And why did it require both men, when one would have been sufficient company for a willing suitor? Could it be that William was not that willing to enter wedlock with Anne Hathaway? Let us pursue this possibility and observe where it leads.

In November 1582 it had become apparent that Anne Hathaway was with child, and Will Shakspere was the father. A marriage between the two was the expected outcome. But Anne was seven or eight years older than the father-to-be, and he, still in his teens. Moreover, marriage to Anne was not something Will had contemplated, particularly because of the age difference. Society, even more so then than now, tended to look askance at such unions. Given the situation he was in, there was only one thing to do; he must marry the girl he had been courting, Anne Whateley of Temple Grafton, and he must do it with all possible haste. As a newly married man, or so he may have reasoned, he would escape public censure for his indiscretion with an older woman. The village would blame Mistress Hathaway for conceiving a child out of wedlock. It was therefore with this in mind that he left Stratford-upon-Avon, bound for Worcester, with the intention of obtaining a special licence to marry Mistress Whateley. As to whether he first asked her to marry him before he set off for Worcester, or whether he resolved to ask her, once he had returned with the certificate in his hand, is an open question.

It was in this state of mind that he presented himself before the clerk at the Bishop's office in Worcester. The special licence was granted upon payment of five shillings and a sworn statement that as a minor he had the permission of his father. With the formalities completed, he was free to marry Anne Whateley of Temple Grafton with only one calling of banns. This was most desirable under the circumstances, since it reduced by two weeks the risk of Anne Hathaway discovering his plan, and protesting publicly against the marriage.

For good or ill, as such may be, William's departure from Stratford did not go unnoticed, and his destination and the reason for it were conveyed to Sandells; possibly by Anne, who must have been told what was about to happen. Sandells had been a neighbour of Richard Hathaway, whose death occurred four months earlier, and Sandells had been charged to act as a supervisor to Richard's last will and testament, for which he received one shilling. He would therefore have felt committed towards the welfare of Anne: whose approaching motherhood, as well as knowledge of the father, was undoubtedly known to him. This would be reason enough for him to down tools and set off with Richardson as a companion, in pursuit of Will Shakspere, under the suspicion that he was up to no good.

One may easily dismiss this as idle conjecture. On the other hand, it is safe to conclude that neither Sandells nor Richardson were by Will Shakspere's side when he applied for his marriage licence. It is beyond absurdity to suppose that after accompanying the prospective bridegroom all the way to Worcester, with the express intention of obtaining a licence for William's marriage to the daughter of their friend Richard Hathaway, they then stood silently by while the clerk asked the name of the bride: only to be told it was Anne Whateley. And that they continued to remain dumb when the clerk asked for the bride's place of abode, and heard Will reply: *"Temple Grafton"*.

To explain this away, Shakespeare's biographers repeatedly suggest that the clerk made a clerical error by writing Whateley instead of Hathaway, and compounded the error by entering Temple Grafton instead of Shottery. If this sounds absurd, as many will agree it does, then is it not doubly ridiculous to suppose that when the marriage certificate was handed to the bridegroom (this supposed master of the English language), he failed to notice these errors and raise an objection? There are only two possibilities; either the clerk did make a mistake, therefore the bridegroom was illiterate, or the clerk did not make a mistake, which implies Shakspere was planning a hurried marriage to Mistress Whateley in order to escape fatherhood as the husband of a much older woman. When one is eighteen, twenty-six sounds positively ancient.

Following the line of conjecture set out above, it would appear that the two men caught up with their quarry after the licence had been granted. A row broke out between them when it was discovered that the bride was to be Anne Whateley. A strong protest by the two men was made to the office which had issued the licence. The clerk responded by insisting that if a marriage took place between Shakspere and Anne Hathaway then they must indemnify the Bishop of Worcester against any impediment to the marriage, should some reason against it come to light at a later date. The next day, the three men appeared before a different clerk in another part of the consistory court, and Sandells and Richardson agreed to be liable for the hefty sum of £40, should the marriage between *'William Shagspere' on the one part, and 'Anne Hathwey of Stratford'* be at fault. The enormity of the indemnity reflects the suspicions that had been aroused on the previous day, for it was equivalent to eight years salary for a normal farm worker.

However much one may disagree with this interpretation of the relevant facts, it remains true to say that the three men returned to

Stratford-upon-Avon with William possessing a special licence to marry Anne Whateley, but with the intention of using it to marry Anne Hathaway. After a single calling of the banns, the marriage took place, although the location has never been discovered. Quite obviously, it did not take place at Temple Grafton or any church where Anne Whateley was known, for the marriage licence named her, not Anne Hathaway, as the bride. Mistress Hathaway would therefore have to marry under her rival's name. Thus, in order that this subterfuge should be performed without fear of discovery, a church needed to be found remote from Stratford-upon-Avon where neither woman was known.

Circumstantial evidence suggests that the church in question was St Martin's in Worcester. Not only was it situated far from the neighbourhood of both the bride and groom, and where they were unknown, there was a more sinister reason to support this location. Some unknown person with access to the church's register had, at some later date, cut two leaves from it. The missing pages exactly coincided with the date when the marriage between William Shaxpere (sic) and Anne Hathaway, posing under the name of Anne Whateley of Temple Grafton, were married.

In the nineteenth century, several able scholars with the time, patience and resources to travel across country went in search of documents relating to William Shakespeare, which they intended to find in order to add to the legend of his overriding genius.

> Reputed scholars such as John Payne Collier and James Halliwell-Phillipps, who dedicated their lives to consolidating the legend of the English Bard, are known to have stolen, forged and destroyed numerous documents as they worked their way unsupervised through various libraries and private collections. (Asquith, 282-30)

The problem these scholars faced continues to this day. Apart from church records and legal documents concerning property deals and petty court claims, no other documents appear to exist. Even worse, what has been found, far from adding to the 'legend of the Bard', diminishes it. In a fit of mistaken devotion to his idol, Collier took to forging documents so that others, too, might experience his idolatry. He also believed that by destroying anything he discovered that could diminish his idol in the eyes of others, he was protecting the genius of the man. In later life, when shamed by the public's knowledge of his forgeries, he recanted.

Did Collier remove the leaves from the register belonging to the Church of St Martin in Worcester, when he found, to his undoubted horror, that his idol had married Anne Hathaway under the name of Anne Whateley?

Although one cannot be certain, the quest to discover where William and Anne had exchanged their wedding vows was well within his remit. Moreover, failure to find the missing entries in the registers of churches in the area surrounding Stratford-upon-Avon would suggest the search be extended to the Worcester area, from where the licence had been obtained. If Collier followed this line of thought, it would have eventually taken him to St Martin's, at which point one can only imagine what he may have found there. Certainly, one need be in no doubt that if the record of Shakspere's marriage had been entered in the church's register, this discovery, appalling to Collier's mind, would have motivated him to remove it. The fact that two pages are missing at precisely the time of Shakspere's nuptials is just too coincidental to be due to chance.

There is one further, curiosity that emerged when seeking the location of Will Shakspere's wedding. The Stratford registrar had, some years earlier, entered the marriage of *"Anne Hathaway of Shottery to William Wilson on Jan. 17, 1579'* (Ogburn, 27). That is, less than four years before *"Anne Hathaway ... the daughter of Richard Hathaway of Shottery"* (Fido, 12) married Will Shakspere. Anne would have been twenty-two or twenty-three years old at the time of this marriage: an age when it would have been reasonable for her to marry. But what happened to her first husband remains a mystery; that is, beyond the fact that he must have died, for otherwise, she would not have been free to marry a second time.

Biographers of Shakespeare; that is, those who graft their work onto the life of Will Shakspere, suffer collective amnesia when alluding to Anne Hathaway's first marriage. John Payne Collier would not have been too surprised.

One further curiosity is the absence of any recorded relationship between Shakspere and his wife's relatives. Anne's father, Richard became ill in 1581 and on 1st September he made out his will. He died in July of the following year. We learn from this that his wife Joan was alive (she died in 1599), and that he willed that his legacy be divided between her and his children. He also bequeathed money to his grandchildren, Agnes and Elizabeth, the daughters of his son Thomas, with further amounts going to his godchildren. The will named: William, John, Bartholomew, Thomas, Agnes, Margaret, and Catherine, as his sons and daughters. It omitted any mention of either fifteen-year-old Joan or twenty-five-year-old Anne. Perhaps he believed Anne's marriage to William Wilson placed her under the responsibility of Wilson's family. Shakspere's own will is interesting in this matter, because it makes no reference to his in-laws or to their children, which, by his marriage to Anne, were his nephews and nieces. Nor do we find that any of his business deals involve the Hathaways. A separation between the two families is suspected. In which case, the cause would predate Anne's pregnancy and subsequent marriage to Will Shakspere.

# 3

# THE LOST YEARS

The 'lost years' is a title used by biographers to describe the gap in the life of Will Shakspere during the eight years occurring between 1585, when Judith and Hamnet were born and 1592, when Henry Chettle published Robert Greene's notes, known as *Greenes, Groats-worth of Witte*, in which Shakspere became identified as Shakespeare.

> We don't know when Shakespeare first came to London. Ever a shadow even in his own biography, he disappears, all but utterly, from 1585 to 1592, the very years we would most like to know where he was and what he was up to . . . (Bryson, 55)

There is one very obvious reason why no records exist for a person during a particular period of time; it is because he or she has done nothing worth recording. With regard to the record of Will Shakspere, the parish register for Tuesday 2nd February 1585 records that twins Judith and Hamnet were baptised. Both children took their names from neighbours Judith and Hamnet Sadler, who reciprocated by naming their son, William. The twins, their sister Susanna and their parents were presumably still living with John and Mary Shakspere together with their four children: Gilbert, Joan, Richard and Edmund. Because William had married young, he would not have had the financial means to support a wife and family. It would therefore have been necessary for either his parents or his mother-in-law to accommodate the married couple. For whatever reason, it was to his father's house in Henley Street that William and Anne went to live. This was also used as the family's place of work. But times were hard, with eleven mouths to feed, there was not even money for John to perform his civic duties.

> Soon after [1575] the tide of John Shakespeare's affairs began to turn, and ... he experienced disappointments and losses which seriously affected his pecuniary circumstances. ... At a borough hall on 29th Jan. in that year [1578], it was ordered that every alderman in Stratford should pay 6s. 8d., and every burgess 3s. 4d. towards *"the furniture of three pikemen, two billmen, and an archer."* Now, although John Shakespeare was not only an alderman, but had been chosen *"head alderman"* in 1571, he was allowed to contribute only 3s. 4d., as if he had been merely a burgess: ... In November 1578, when it was required that every

alderman should *"pay weekly to the relief of the poor 4d.,"* John Shakespeare and Robert Bratt were excepted: they were *"not to be taxed to pay any thing,"* ... In March, 1578-9, when another call was made upon the town for the purpose of purchasing corslets, calivers, &c., the name of John Shakespeare is found, at the end of the account, in a list of persons whose *"sums were unpaid and unaccounted for."* Another fact tends strongly to the conclusion that in 1578 John Shakespeare was distressed for money: he owed a baker of the name of Roger Sadler 5l. [5 librae], for which Edmund Lambert, and a person of the name of Cornishe, had become security: Sadler died, and in his will, dated 14th November, 1578, he included the following among the debts due to him: —" *Item of Edmund Lambert and Cornishe, for the debt of Mr. John Shacksper, 5l."* (Collier, lxxix-lxxx).

This lack of money, together with the crowded situation of Shakspere's home life, places his biographers in a dilemma. Writing great literature in such an environment is out of the question; it requires not only a peaceful setting, but also the money to purchase paper and ink. John's ever weakening financial circumstances, coupled with the need to provide for the household, makes it a certainty that no money was available for ink and paper, for these were expensive commodities. How, then, is it possible that by 1593, Shakespeare, if he is Will Shakspere, emerges as such an established writer? Plays by the name of *Titus Andronicus, Henry VI Parts One, Two and Three, Richard III, Comedy of Errors* and *Taming of A Shrew* had by this date already been performed. The lengthy narrative poem, *Venus and Adonis* was about to be set-up at the printers, and the young Earl of Southampton had supposedly taken the poet into his household.

It is by avoiding the pitfalls dug by Shakespeare's biographers, and sticking closely to the known facts, that a very different picture emerges. For example, consider the account learnt by John Aubrey upon his arrival in Stratford to collect material for his book, *Brief Lives*: – *"His father was a Butcher, and I have been told heretofor by some of the neighbours, that when he was a boy he exercised his father's Trade."* (Michell, 59). It was said of Aubrey that he was careful, wherever possible, to seek out and talk with those who had been acquainted with his subjects. In the excerpt quoted above, Aubrey's informants were all in agreement. These were descendents from families where he was raised. Had he been recognised amongst this community as the celebrated William Shakespeare, the villagers would have been more aware of this, than of his trade as a butcher.

This account of Will Shakspere having once worked as an apprentice butcher is not unique. On 10 April 1693, a visitor to Stratford-upon-Avon named Dowdall, wrote to Edward Southwell describing his recent visit.

The clerke that shew'd me this church is above 80 years old; he says that this Shakespeare was formerly in this towne bound apprenti(c)e to a butcher, but that he run from his master to London, and there was received into the playhouse as a serviture, and by this meanes had an oppertunity to be what he afterwards prov'd. (Halliwell-Phillipps, 88)

This coincides with what Aubrey had been told: that when Shakspere slaughtered an animal, he would do it in *"high style, and make a Speech."* The clerk who showed Dowdall the church, and whose early life was close enough to that of Shakspere's last years, can be considered authoritative. Interestingly, he declined to acknowledge Shakspere achieved anything prior to leaving his family for London. What he did admit to, was that Shakspere's fortune changed only after beginning work as a serviture in a playhouse. As a serviture, he would have been one of a body of servants assisting inside the theatre. It is not how one imagines his career as a poet began, especially at the age of twenty-five or twenty-six.

This now brings the total to three accounts; each one of which retells a story obtained from different residents of Stratford-upon-Avon, to the effect that William Shakspere was a normal sort of lad, brought up in the village, much like any other boy of his time, who left school almost before his lessons had begun in order to work for his father, and had thereafter become apprenticed to a local butcher before moving to London. If these accounts are based upon false memories, as is maintained by his apologists, then where are the remembrances of Will Shakspere as the outstanding young scholar of his community, which biographers lovingly write about? There are none. A few stories later emerge to suggest that he wrote a poem lampooning Sir Thomas Lucy, from whom, or so an apocryphal story says, he had been stealing deer; or that later, he composed the epitaph on John Combes monument; another suggestion alleges that he wrote the lines on the stone covering his own grave; if so, his hand in this piece of doggerel is better left unmentioned.

Traditionalists, by and large, dismiss stories of Shakspere the butcher's boy, but only to replace them with stories of their own. They are well aware of the need to prepare the ground for the sudden flow of plays and poetry that flowed into public view as the final decade of the 16th century began. By circular reasoning their idol has been given an education. It is therefore by further circular reasoning that they fill in Shakspere's lost years. Thus, if a play contains detailed knowledge of the law, then the lost years were spent in a lawyer's office; if a play shows detailed knowledge of the hunt, then the lost years were spent in service to a nobleman; if a play describes detailed knowledge of an army camp, then the lost years were spent serving in the army; if a play indicates the author had a detailed knowledge of the sea, then the lost years were spent aboard ship. The deeper one digs, the more one discovers how this polymath of an author has led biographers on a wild goose chase. Amongst other activities which he is supposed to have taken part in during his 'lost years' are horticulture, acting, teaching, forestry, travelling, and printing. Dr Levi Fox was clearly overcome by the sheer variety of what was on offer to fill the 'lost years', for he was compelled to admit —

> Yet in its way, this tantalizing seven-year gap is rather attractive, allowing everyone to construct an apprenticeship to his or her own mind, unfettered by the inconvenience of recorded fact. (Fox, 41)

The frustration felt by Fox is shared by Shakespeare's biographers; how does one explain the acquisition of so much knowledge and such extensive experience in such a short space of time, while also allowing the same time span to be spent in writing the many plays that appeared at the end of those 'lost years'? And this also has to be balanced with the impoverished lives of the ten members of both his and his father's family, left to fend for themselves in Stratford. No biographer has ever been able to reconcile these diverse activities with a single solution. For every activity that has been suggested to fill the 'lost years', numerous other activities are denied a similar time span. Moreover, this seven year gap is also too long. That is to say, if it existed as a learning period, then is should be considerably shortened. The reason for this is tied up with his family commitments.

At the beginning of 1583, William and Anne had been living for one month under the roof of John Shakspere and his family. By February 1585, with the birth of Judith and Hamnet, the family number had increased from nine members to eleven. There is nothing to suggest that the money situation of either family had, by that time, substantially improved. As a married man and father of three children, William had a duty to provide for his family. Leaving them to be fed and clothed by his father, who was in fear of prosecution for debt, was not an option. There is also no evidence that Will had the contacts or the education to do what his biographers claim for him. Once again circular reasoning is called upon to dig the biographers out of a hole.

Scholars may, perhaps, retaliate by claiming that it is not circular reasoning but a legitimate application of *a posteriori* reasoning. This is false. While it is certainly true that one may legitimately infer, *a posteriori*, that Shakespeare's knowledge of the English legal system displayed on stage, meant that he had earlier gained knowledge of the law, and that he had then used this to transfer his understanding of the legal system to a play, the logic fails in the present case. This is because, although the fact that Shakespeare must have received instruction in English law is *necessary* to the conclusion that is drawn, it is not *sufficient*. It only becomes sufficient when it can be proved that it was actually Will Shakspere who received instruction in English law, and not an author who was using Shakspere as a mask, a front man, or an allonym through which to channel his plays and poetry to the public. Without that proof, circular reasoning is being used to fill the lost years; as indeed was the case with Shakspere's education.

Although it is claimed that the seven years between 1585 and 1592 are devoid of any reference to Shakspere, this is to obscure an important record. *"In 1589, William and his father were named in legal proceedings aimed at recovering the property of Mary Arden on which John had failed to lift the mortgage'* (Ogburn, 27). The person, who had provided John with £40 in 1578, to be advanced against property in Wilmcote, was his brother-in-law, Edmund Lambert. This is the same man who, together with an associate named Corniche, had stood surety for £5 owed by John to a baker named Roger Sadler. In 1578 Sadler died, having noted the debt in his will as still owing, and naming the two men who had agreed to stand surety for the loan. One can imagine that Lambert was not best pleased at being asked to pay Sadler's estate for the defaulting Shakspere.

1589 is about the time that William is believed to have left Stratford for the destiny that awaited him in London. Had he still been living with his parents up until then, his absence from the house would leave behind ten members of a family growing in age. Susanna was 6, Judith and Hamnet were both 4, Joan was 20, Gilbert was 23, Richard was 15 and Edmund was 9. William, the eldest of the siblings, celebrated his 25th birthday that year. Perhaps, if his father had repaid the mortgage to Lambert, then William may never have gone to London, choosing instead to manage the Wilmcote estate; thereafter, the story of Shakespeare would be very different.

# 4

# GREENES, GROATS-WORTH OF WITTE

Evidence of William Shakespeare's arrival in London was discovered in a pamphlet published in late 1592 by Henry Chettle. The title was *Greenes, Groats-Worth of Witte, bought with a million of Repentance.* Robert Greene had been a university man who achieved fame by having made a living from writing plays, although what little money there was to be made from this occupation is evident from the fact that he died a pauper. Greene also obtained considerable notoriety for his dissolute life, hence his apparent 'repentance' at its end. What marks this pamphlet for special attention is its reference to a man named Shake-scene: an apparent pun on the name Shake-speare. In an open address to three writers of similar standing, Greene warns them against actors, and in particular one who also has pretensions at being a writer of blank verse.

> Base minded men all three of you, if by my miserie you be not warnd: for unto none of you (like mee) sought those burres to cleave: those Puppets (I meane) that spake from our mouths, those Anticks garnisht in our colours. Is it not strange, that I, to whom they all have beene beholding: is it not like that you, to whome they all have beene beholding, shall (were yee in that case as I am now) bee both at once of them forsaken? Yes trust them not: for there is an up-start Crow, beautified with our feathers, that with his *Tygers hart wrapt in a Players hyde,* supposes he is as well able to bombast out a blanke verse as the best of you: and beeing an absolute *Johannes fac totum,* is in his owne conceit the onely Shake-scene in a countrey. O that I might intreat your rare wits to be imploied in more profitable courses: & let those Apes imitate your past excellence, and never more acquaint them with your admired inventions. (Greene).

On the face of it, the discovery of this pamphlet confirms exactly what biographers have inferred all along, when trying to account for the first twenty-five years of Shakspere's otherwise uneventful life. He is an actor; he turned to writing blank verse, and his name is parodied as Shake-scene. What is more, he is known to Robert Greene, a well known writer, who now insists upon warning his three former companions, with whom he had only recently dined, to beware of this man.

Three questions immediately spring to mind. Firstly, since Greene was addressing three friends with whom he was well acquainted: he, having only a few weeks before dined with him, why is he only now referring to this man? Surely, if the subject was that important, as may be inferred, since Greene raises the matter on his death bed: would it not have been just as important as a topic of conversation over dinner one month earlier? Secondly, what is the nature of the warning that Greene is issuing? A new writer with pretensions at padding out blank verse is a poor cause for issuing a death-bed warning. Thirdly, why did Greene paraphrase a line from 'Shake-scene's' play, *3 Henry VI*. 1. iv; viz. *"O tiger's heart wrapt in a woman's hide:'* and then write to his companions as though the author of this play was unknown to them? Upon a deeper inspection, the letter makes little sense, as we shall see.

In response to the second question, Greene is warning his friends of the man's *pretensions*. He is a 'Jack-of-all-trades', an *actor*, and in his own conceit (*"play of mind"* 2 Hen. 4, 2.iv.231: see Alexander 682), a padder-out of blank verse. But where is the threat in this? Taken at its word, this man is just an actor, an odd-job man, a serviture in the theatre, with pretensions that in his personal conceit he can write blank verse. Moreover, to issue a deathbed warning addressed to three of the most prominent writers at that time, warning them against a person, whom they have apparently never heard of, and who Greene does not even name, is frankly ridiculous.

The third of these questions also merits no sensible answer. One of Greene's companions at the table had been Tom Nashe. He had recently attended a performance of *Henry the Sixth*. This play was entered in Henslowe's diary on fifteen separate occasions in the year leading to the publication of *Greene's Groats-Worth of Wit*; viz. *"harey the vj the 3 of marche 1591 ... harey the vj the 7 marche 1591 ... harey the vj the 11 marche 1591 ... harey the 16 marche 1591 ... harey the vj the 28 marche 1591 ... harey the vj the 5 of ap'ell 1591 ... harey the vj the 13 ap'ell 1591 ... harey the vj the 21 ap'ell 1591 ... harey the vj the 4 of maye 159[1]2".* (At this point, Henslowe began making new entries by changing the year from 1591 to 1592. This was because he had previously used the legalistic form of the Julian calendar in which New Year's Day is 25 March; hence, all years marked 1591 are really 1592, according to the present Gregorian calendar.) *harey the vj the 7 maye 1592 ... harey the 6 the 14 maye 1592 ... harey the vj the 1[0]9 maye 1592* (date was changed) *harey the vj the [17]25 maye 1592 ... harey the vj the 12 June 1592 ... harey the vj the 19 June 1592.* Nashe even referred to the popularity of this play in his *Defence of Plays'* —

> ... remarking how, despite the claims of some 'petitioners of the Council' that plays 'corrupt the youth of the City', there was a great deal both good and patriotic about the revivification of the history of a hundred or so years ago. (Wilson, 121)

Greene died on 3 September 1592. Nashe's pamphlet went to print in the same month with the following review of *"harey the vj'*: believed to refer to *Henry VI Part 1*.

> How it would have joyed brave Talbot (the terror of the French) to think that after he had lain two hundred years in his tomb, he should triumph again on the stage, and have his bones new embalmed with the tears of ten thousand spectators at least (at several time) who, in the tragedian that represents his person, imagine they behold him fresh bleeding.
>
> (ibid)

Shakespeare was therefore already well known to Nashe, for it can hardly be imagined that having so eloquently written about this play, which had already been performed on fifteen occasions that year, he took no interest in the identity of its author. It therefore makes not one jot of sense for Greene to have warned Nashe about an established playwright whose work was both known and admired by him, and for Greene to then warn Nashe as though he were wholly ignorant of this author's existence.

Both Greene and Nashe were leading figures in London's literary circle; they knew the theatre, and of course they knew who wrote the plays that were performed, especially if they were as popular as *"harey the vj"*. Because of this rather obvious fact, Greene's open letter to his three dining companions no longer appears as genuine, or as fortuitous to Shakspere's biographers, as it once may have appeared.

Greene's pamphlet – entered in the Stationers' Register *"uppon the perill of Henrye Chettle'* – was *'Imprinted for William Wright'* and described as *"Written before his death and published at his dying request.'* In fact Greene died alone in the care of two Christian souls, a cobbler and his wife living close to Dow-gate, to the east of St Paul's. They mercifully *"took him, his prostitute mistress, and his illegitimate son Fortunatus, into their lowly and lice-ridden home,'* shortly before his end. (Wilson, 124).

Upon hearing of Greene's death, Henry Chettle, who had recently set up as a publisher, took control of Greene's effects, amongst which were his recent notes for a pamphlet he had apparently been planning to publish. It was these notes that Chettle took away with him as a basis for a publication he would call: *Greenes, Groats-Worth of Witte*. As Chettle later confessed:

> Il written as sometimes Greenes hand was none of the best, licensd it must be, ere it could bee printed which could never be if it might not be read. To be breife I writ it over, and as

neare as I could, followed the copy, onely in the letter I put something out, but in the whole booke not a word in. (Alexander, 404)

So there we have it, the letter was reconstructed by Chettle from scribbled and sometimes undecipherable notes made by Greene. As such, it is fair comment that Chettle did not understand the background to these notes, and that he reproduced their content in a manner that made sense to him, but which Greene may never have intended when he wrote them. Let this be kept in mind, as the identities of Greene's three fellow diners are revealed, for it was to them that the letter was addressed.

> To those Gentlemen his Quondam acquaintance, that spend their Wits in making plaies, R. G. wisheth a better exercise, and wisdom to prevent his extremities.
>
> If wofull experience may move you (Gentlemen) to beware, or unheard of wretchednes intreate you to take heed: I doubt not but you wil looke backe with sorrow on your time past, and indevour with repentance to spend that which is to come. Wonder not, (for with thee wil I first begin) thou famous gracer of Tragedians, that *Greene*, who hath said with thee (like the foole in his heart) There is no God, shoulde now give glorie unto his greatnes.
>
> (Greene)

*Gracer* has been reliably identified as Marlowe; the Privy Council had intervened on his behalf to ensure that he received special grace while at Cambridge in order to receive his degree; the 'Grace Book' held at Cambridge refers (Carroll, 2004, p.284 fn.34). Marlowe was also known for his violent temper, and his subsequent confrontation with Chettle, whom he appears to have recognized as both editor and part-author of *Greenes, Groats-Worth of Witte* led the publisher to afterwards declare: *'With neither of them that take offense was I acquainted, and with one of them I care not if I neuer be.'* (Alexander, 404).

Marlowe had reason to take offence. Greene's pamphlet contained a number of remarks against his character that related to his atheism, which, he thought, made him too easily recognizable. He may also have been persuaded that Greene, who had shared many of his vices and disbeliefs, would never have penned these remarks.

The second member of Greene's trio is also easily identified:

> With thee I joyne yong *Juvenall*, that byting Satyrist, that lastly with mee together writ a Comedie. Sweet boy, might I advise thee, be advisde, and get not many enemies by bitter wordes: inveigh against vaine men, for thou canst do it, no man better, no man so well: thou hast a libertie to reproove all, and name none; for one being spoken to, all are offended; none being blamed no man is injured. (Greene)

Thomas Nashe was known as *"tender Juvenal"* because, like the Roman satirist, Nashe's writing conveyed irony, sarcasm, moral indignation and personal invective. Chettle refers to this as a magnet for attracting enemies; he also referred to his subject's youth: Nashe was 24 years of age in September 1592. Lastly, Chettle mentioned a Comedy they had earlier written together, thus appealing to their former partnership. With two members now identified, we approach the third.

> And thou no lesse deserving than the other two, in some things rarer, in nothing inferiour; driven (as my selfe) to extreme shifts, a litle have I to say to thee: and were it not an idolatrous oth, I would sweare by sweet S. George, thou art unworthy better hap, sith thou dependest on so meane a stay. (ibid)

The identity of the third diner has proved difficult for orthodox scholars, and the much favoured opinion is that it refers to George Peele, another dramatist. Presumably the reference to Saint George has provided the stimulus for this, but the identification remains too weak for certainty. Fortunately, Nashe has rescued the situation by dispensing his own set of clues.

On 12 January 1593, just three months after Greene's death, Nashe published *Strange News*: a pamphlet that included an attack on Gabriel Harvey, for the remarks he had made against the deceased Greene. In mid-flow, Nashe identified himself as one of those who had dined with Greene that summer evening. He also mentioned the third person whom scholars believe was George Peele. But Nashe refers to him by an unfamiliar name:

> I and one of my fellows, Will. Monox (hast thou never heard of him and his great dagger?) were in company with him a month before he died, at that fatal banquet of Rhenish wine and pickled herring (if thou wilt needs have it so. (Nashe)

Nashe has therefore confirmed that he was, indeed, the third member of this quartet, and since *'tender Juvenal'* was his nickname (Ackroyd, 198), and *'gracer'* has been identified as Marlowe, we are left with *"Will Monox"* as *"sweet St George"*.

Will Monox is unknown by name, either as a writer or a member of Elizabethan society. But he was a person, and Nashe knew that Harvey would recognise him, although not by this name. In July 1578, Harvey made a speech addressed to Queen Elizabeth, in which he remarked of Edward de Vere, 17th Earl of Oxford and Lord Great Chamberlain of England: *"In the prime of his gallantest youth he bestowed Angels upon me in Christ's College in Cambridge"* (Ogburn, 542). But in later years Harvey became disenchanted with his former benefactor, and wrote a poem, *Speculum Tuscanismi*, which described Oxford in disparaging terms. Nashe seized upon this fact when reminiscing to Harvey about Greene: *'A good-fellow he was, and would have drunk with thee for more angels than the Lord thou libelledst on gave thee in Christ's College.*' Nashe has reminded Harvey of the kindness shown to him by Oxford during his student days (angels were gold coins with the figure of St Michael on one side).

There was a reason for Nashe to remind Harvey of Oxford's generosity; it was because he wanted Harvey to know that it was Oxford who dined with Greene a month before he died. But because Oxford was a nobleman, and could not be publicly identified as having dined with a reprobate like Greene, the information had to be conveyed by suggestive phrases that Harvey would understand; hence, first there was the reference to '*angels*', and '*the Lord thou libelledst*', then secondly, '*his great dagger*'. This was Nashe being satirical. Oxford's role as Lord Great Chamberlain required that he carry the great Sword of State (his great dagger) before the Queen during special ceremonial processions. But, where does Will Monox fit into this picture? The presence of 'ox' as part of this cryptic name now becomes especially suggestive, for it hints that an anagram may be present; this type of word puzzle being very popular at that time, particularly where secrets of a sensitive nature were concerned.

Treated as an anagram, WILL MONOX becomes M WILL OXON. Oxon will be familiar to every Latin scholar as the conventional abbreviation for '*Oxonia latinized name of Ox(en)ford*' (OED). Hence, M Will Oxon is an abbreviation for Master William Oxenford. But why should Nashe refer to the Earl of Oxford as Master William? And why had Oxford called these three men together for a banquet? The probable answer is given further down. The immediate task is to reconfirm Oxford's identity from the letter appearing in *Greenes, Groats-Worth of Witte*, since this must now refer to Oxford as *"sweet St George"*.

To begin with, the name represents a simple piece of harmless flattery, and in line with the grievance made by Oxford's father-in-law, Lord Burghley. In a letter written to Walsingham in 1587, the Lord Treasurer had complained of '*[Oxford's] lewd friends who still rule him by flatteries*' (Ogburn, 633). Greene, Marlowe, and Nashe would most certainly come under the definition of *lewd friends* in Burghley's estimation. However, the patriotic connotation attached to St George counted for more than just flattery; it also avoided giving offence to a person of Oxford's standing, as some other epithet might have done. For although Oxford occasionally consorted with men like Greene, Marlowe and Nashe, talented writers though they were, it is certain that he insisted upon his own position in society being respected, especially in the class-structured age of Queen Elizabeth's England.

In the summer of 1592, the anonymous play *"harey vj"* was being performed. This play, in parts *One* and *Three*, is well known for the many times it rings out with patriotic cries of Saint George, as does *Richard III*: plays that together with *2 Henry VI* were part of the same tetralogy.

### Henry VI Part I

| | |
|---|---|
| [The English scale the walls and cry '**Saint George**!'] | (Act 2: sc. i) |
| God and **Saint George**, Talbot and England's right, Prosper our colours in this dangerous fight. | (Act 4: sc. ii) |
| **Saint George** and victory! Fight, soldiers, fight. | (Act 4: sc. vi) |
| The thrice victorious Lord of Falconbridge, Knight of the noble order of **Saint George**, | (Act 4: sc. vii) |

### Henry VI Part III

| | |
|---|---|
| Then strike up drums. God and **Saint George** for us. | (Act 2: sc. i) |
| Unsheathe your sword good father; cry '**Saint George**!' | (Act 2: sc. ii) |
| For Warwick and his friends, God and **Saint George**. | (Act 4: sc. ii) |
| Lords to the field, **Saint George** and victory! | (Act 5: sc. I) |

### Richard III

| | |
|---|---|
| God and **Saint George**! Richmond and victory! | (Act 5: sc. iii) |
| This and **Saint George** to boot! What think'st thou, Norfolk? | (Act 5: sc. iii) |
| Our ancient word of courage, fair **Saint George**, Inspire us with the spleen of fiery dragons! | (Act 5: sc. iii) |

Saint George also manages to appear in *The Taming of the Shrew*, said to have been written in 1591, at about the same time as *Henry VI*:

| | |
|---|---|
| Now by **Saint George** I am too young for you. | (Act 2: sc. i) |

The frequency with which an *oath* to **Saint George** is uttered in these plays, must surely link it to the other oath to St George, as mentioned in the Groats-Worth letter; viz. *"and were it not an idolatrous oth, I would sweare by sweet S. George.'* In which case, the missing member of the quorum; that is, according to both Nashe and the letter, is Will Monox, the author of these oaths to St George. As though to draw further attention to this subtlety, Greene's letter has also paraphrased a line taken from *3 Henry VI, I: iv: "O tiger's heart wrapt in a woman's hide.'*

Of further interest is the adjective *sweet*, which the Groats-Worth letter employs to describe St George. It is of particular interest because not only does this word appear 72 times in Shakespeare's Sonnets – many of these poems showing evidence of having been written in 1592 and earlier – but the same adjective occurs almost 1000 times in the works of Shakespeare. However, it is the use of *sweet* in *3 Henry VI* that could be considered most suggestive.

Let it now be understood that St George was intended to refer to Oxford, as Juvenal was intended for Nashe and gracer for Marlowe. Then it must likewise be true that *"sweet St George'* is meant for 'sweet Oxford'. Returning to the source of the oaths mentioning St George, which are found in *3 Henry VI*: we discover these same words: —

King Henry:     **Sweet Oxford**, and my loving Montague,

(Act 4: sc. viii)

Queen Margaret: Thanks, gentle Somerset; **sweet Oxford**, thanks.

(Act 5: sc. iv)

It is more than plausible that Greene had been seeking for a means by which to hint at Oxford's identity as the author of *harey the vj*, without openly revealing it, and Chettle had stumbled across this attempt and quite innocently repeated it in the Groats-Worth letter.

In any event, the mist should now begin to fade as it becomes ever clearer why Nashe referred to Oxford, via an anagram, as *Master* William. It was because he had recently learnt that Oxford was about to publish work under the authorship of *Master* William Shakespeare. When the anagram of Will Monox is solved, it becomes a clever hybrid of Oxford's title and the name of the person who had agreed to become his allonym, *William* Shakspere; that is to say, Master *William* Oxford unites the poet with his allonym in a single name.

It also explains why nothing had been heard before 1592 of William Shakespeare. Before that date he never existed. William Shakspere certainly existed, but his reduced circumstances, the subsequent poverty of his father, the sudden termination of his education while still a child, his years spent in the drab occupation of a boring apprenticeship: these were commonplace at that time, and it led to his departure for London, and his participation in what was destined to become one of the greatest literary conundrums of all time – Who wrote Shakespeare?

When William first arrived in London from Stratford-upon-Avon during his mid-twenties, his greatest priority was to find employment. The account of how he went about this was obtained by Betterton, for inclusion in Rowe's short biography of Shakespeare. Betterton's informant was Sir William Davenant (1606–1668), England's poet laureate in 1638, and son of John Davenant, an innkeeper and former Mayor of Oxford. It was at Davenant's Crown tavern that Shakspere is said to have stayed when commuting between London and Stratford-upon-Avon. And it was during one of these stopovers that he related to the elder Davenant how he began life in London. The account he gave, and which was remembered by his son, William Davenant, sounds appropriate enough for a countryman newly arrived in the capital city. It is quite without airs and graces, and more believable because of that, especially since Shakspere's rural upbringing would have prepared him for the job he described.

> Concerning Shakespeare's first appearance in the playhouse. When he came to London, he was without money and friends, and being a stranger, he knew not to whom to apply, nor by what means to support himself. At that time, coaches not being in use, and as gentlemen were accustomed to ride to the playhouse, Shakespeare, driven to the last necessity, went to the playhouse door, and pick'd up a little money by taking care of the gentlemen's horses who came to the play; he became eminent even in that profession, and was taken notice of for his diligence and skill in it; he had soon more business than he himself could manage, and at last hired boys under him, who were known by the name Shakespeare's boys. Some of the players, accidentally conversing with him, found him so acute, and master of so fine a conversation, that, struck, therewith, they [introduced] and recommended him to the house, in which he was first admitted in a very low station. (Cibber, 12 mo.)

This report is very similar to that told to Dowdall in 1693. The part of London where Shakspere operated as horse attendant was most likely to have been Shoreditch. Both the Curtain, built in 1577, and the Theatre, raised one year earlier were in that vicinity, and the possibility of serving those arriving on horseback at either playhouse was an obvious incentive. In addition, there was a popular watering hole for horses nearby. The added security of having someone like Shakspere to guard against horse thieves would have ensured the demand for his services remained high.

The lack of any alternative account relating to Shakspere's arrival in London places his biographers at an obvious disadvantage. Davenant's narrative account is rejected because it fails to fit in with the premise that governs what is acceptable and what must be discounted. The reader should therefore be aware that it is possible to prove anything when evidence is only accepted if it suits the premise it supports. Shakespeare's biographers are most adept at making this distinction, and will readily insist that Will Monox was George Peele. But ask them how the names are connected, and they will change the subject; lest, instead, it change the colour of their faces.

We must now return to the Groats-Worth letter and discover how well its remaining content fits in with Oxford having been one of the three diners to whom Greene refers. At first glance, one is thrown back to the naïf view taken by orthodoxy. Shakespeare is rebuked for his resemblance to Aesop's crow: the bird that adorned itself with the fine feathers of other birds, so that it might appear like them. The allusion to Shakspere donning the literary garments of Oxford is a more apt translation. By drawing attention to this parallel in his notes, Greene would have been thinking of a play he had written, called *Never Too Late*, in which Cicero employs the same allusion to Aesop's crow. '*Why Roscius are thou proud with Esops Crow, being pranct with the glorie of others feathers?* ' (Alexander, 401).

Roscius was Rome's most celebrated actor during the time of Julius Caesar, and his name has since entered the English language to describe similarly gifted players (OED refers).

Shakespeare also made mention of this actor in *3 Henry VI*: '*What scene of death hath Roscius now to act?* ' (Act V: sc. vi): a play from where Greene had already paraphrased: '*Tygers hart wrapt in a Players hyde* '. It is truly remarkable how the Groats-Worth letter is laden with references to this play. It is understandable, therefore, that with so recent a reference to Roscius and Aesop's crow in Greene's mind, a similar connection between Shakspere and this crow would not have been far from his thinking.

At the same time, it is now easy to see how Chettle had got hold of the wrong end of the stick. Greene had made notes after dining with Oxford, to the effect that by masquerading as a poet and a playwright, Shakspere — or Shakespeare as he was now to be recognized — was really like Aesop's crow: pretending to be someone he was not. Oxford would write the work, Shakspere would adorn himself with the airs and graces of the poet and playwright, as though he were the author; that is, '*in his own conceit* ', which means in his own imaginative play.

As though to confirm this interpretation, Chettle unconsciously allows Greene's letter to state the truth, by noting how this upstart, '*supposes he is well able to bombast out a blank verse as the best of you* ' (Alexander, 400). This indicates that Chettle had managed to decipher Greene's notes with some success, but with no understanding of the underlying story they referred to. He not unnaturally took Greene's words at face value and edited them, believing that what he wrote down was a true account of the matter as seen by Greene before he died. Regrettably, this has had a similar effect upon scholars ever since: each one following the other into the same blind alley. Indeed, the alley has now become so overcrowded that the truth has been smothered in the crush.

With the Groats-Worth letter consistent in every detail, to the effect that Oxford was *"sweet St George"* and therefore the author of 3 *Henry VI*, it is possible to arrive at a reasonable explanation as to why three of London's finest writers were summoned to meet the Earl of Oxford in the summer of 1592.

By calling them together, and treating them to a meal, Oxford had the perfect opportunity of personally explaining to them that an unknown poet and playwright was soon to emerge on the literary scene. Under ordinary circumstances this would give rise to curiosity concerning his educational background and previous work. By telling Nashe, Greene and Marlowe in advance that the so-called poet and playwright was really his allonym, a man known as William Shakspere, but whose surname he had changed to Shakespeare, he was pre-empting their enquiries and the possible ridicule, which was bound to follow, once they learned the truth for themselves that Shakespeare was merely a figurehead: a literary nonentity.

Oxford easily recognized they would be amongst the first to discover this deception, and very likely commit it to a satirical pamphlet. In fact, this happened anyway, when the anonymously written *Willobie His Avisa* appeared in 1594. But in 1592, Oxford still had time on his side. It is also possible that he appealed to the three men dining with him to support his plan, since it would enable his work to be made public for as long as the ruse could be maintained. In those days, an appeal by a senior member of the nobility was as good as a command. Apart from which, Oxford had favours to call in for the collegiate atmosphere he had maintained for writers, when he rented apartments in the Savoy and then transferred these activities to Fishers Folly. He was therefore set fair to begin the first part of his plan: the publication of a narrative poem entitled *Venus and Adonis* by Master William Shakespeare.

It would have been this that worked on Nashe's mind, and resolved itself as an anagram for Master William Oxford. But, even before a single word had been published, the plan began to unwind. Greene unexpectedly died and Chettle published the deceased man's notes, denigrating Shakespeare as an upstart crow, beautified by the feathers of others. For

Oxford's carefully laid plans, this revelation, while being wholly accurate, dealt such a serious blow to the arrangements that were underway, it must have threatened the entire enterprise.

Marlowe responded to Chettle's publication in a manner that left the publisher with the wish never to meet with this man again. Marlowe was renowned for his belligerent temper; he was also an atheist, like Greene had been, and Chettle's publication had rebuked him for his disbelief through the mouth of Greene. Marlowe clearly did not believe the words came from Greene.

Nashe also did not believe the words came from Greene. Some people even thought that he was the author. To refute these allegations, he publicly declared the entire work to be: *"that scald trivial lying pamphlet called Greenes groats-worth of wit"* (Ogburn, 655).

Oxford was faced with a different dilemma. Chettle's letter had totally derailed his plan to launch Shakespeare's career as a fine, upright young poet under the patronage of the youthful Earl of Southampton, the subject of his many sonnets. What could be done to remedy the situation? The solution he chose was to seek an apology from Chettle. The publisher was to be left in no doubt regarding the probity of 'Shakespeare's' character, and the esteem in which gentlemen of the highest rank valued his writing. The strategy worked. On 8 December 1592, an entry appeared in the Stationers' Register, advertising a pamphlet to be published under the title *Kind-Harts Dreame*. This was to be the medium through which Chettle conceded:

> With neither of them that take offence was I acquainted, and with one of them I care not if I never be. The other, whome at that time I did not so much spare, as since I wish I had ... because my selfe have seen his demeanor no less civill than he exelent in the qualities he professes: Besides, divers of worship have reported his uprightness of dealing, which argues his honesty, and his facetious grace in writing, that aprooves his Art. (Alexander, 400)

Who were these two that Chettle referred to, that took offence? Distinguished Regius Professor of English Language and Literature at Glasgow University, Peter Alexander, provided the customary answer.

> It is clear from Chettle's own reply that he is referring to Marlowe and Shakespeare ... Chettle, however, feels he owes no apology to Marlowe ... To Shakespeare Chettle offers a full and frank apology. (ibid)

Certainly, there is little cause to doubt Marlowe's aggressive attitude, which must have frightened Chettle, for he admits that he does not care to meet again with one of the two he mentioned. But, logically, how can the other person be Shakespeare; unless, that is, Shakespeare and Oxford were the same person?

Remember! Greene was supposedly warning his three fellow diners to beware of the *'upstart crow ... the onely Shake-scene in a countrey'*. Had Shakespeare been one of the two diners — to whom Chettle's apology is directed for the offence it caused — then how can Greene have possibly been addressing Shakespeare? For it would then mean that Greene was warning Shakespeare to beware of himself.

To avoid this conclusion, one must accept that Shakspere read the pamphlet, and hurried over to see Chettle to politely point out Greene's error. But why should Shakspere consider Greene's opinion to be anything other than it was? If that was Greene's opinion of him, then he was entitled to express it as such. The correct response for Shakspere to make was to publish a rebuttal, perhaps listing those earlier plays that biographers boast about. Compare Marlowe's reaction to Chettle, or Nashe's. Shakspere, however, remained silent save for a personal plea: relying, instead, upon the reports of *'divers of worship'* to back a request that Chettle refute Greene's words with a published apology. This mysterious ghost squad, which Shakspere managed to conjure up at a moment's notice, promptly vanished afterwards, just as quickly as it had arrived, and was never heard of again.

If Shakespeare was Shakspere, then the reaction he made to the letter, including canvassing for support amongst *'divers of worship'* does not ring true. How could this unknown, unpublished disreputable member of a lower class be able to persuade those of a higher class to write references for him concerning an obscure phrase in a pamphlet, and which did not even name him? Who, amongst those reading the Groatsworth letter would have recognised the object of Greene's reference to *'Shake-scene'*? Even to get an audience for his complaint is doubtful: and were that achieved, a word of sympathy is the most he could have expected before being shown the door. But if Shakespeare was Oxford, his reaction to 'Greene's' criticism was essential for ensuring William Shakespeare's forthcoming arrival on the literary scene was unblemished. And, of course, Oxford's title would ensure he obtained references from the class of person that Chettle refers to.

There is another anomaly associated with Greene's death and the man who wrote Shakespeare's plays. It is clear from the circumstances of his death that Greene had little or no money with which to provide for himself, and it was entirely due to the charity of Isam and his wife that his end came with a modicum of comfort.

Harvey referred to having called at the shoemaker's house in Dow-gate after Greene died, to be told that on his deathbed, Greene had called for '*a penny-pot of Malmsey*', and had then scribbled a final note to his abandoned wife, Doll, begging her to repay the kindness of his two comforters. Harvey, it is assumed, copied the note.

> *Doll, I charge thee by the love of our youth, and by my soul's rest, that thou wilt see this man paid: for if he and his wife had not succoured me, I had died in the streets.*
>
> *Robert Greene.* (Bate, 14)

Oxford, for it could hardly have been 'Shake-scene', the man Greene allegedly raged against in 'his' *Groatsworth of Wit*, committed the dead man's final hours to the pages of *Henry V*. And by doing so, immortalised his former companion's final moments through the mouth of *Sir John Falstaff*.

| Boy: | Mine host Pistol, you must come to my master; and your hostess—he is very sick, and would to bed. | (Act 2: sc. i) |

The *hostess* recalls *Falstaff's* death, but is interrupted by *Nym*.

| Nym: | They say he cried out of sack. | |
| Hostess: | Ay, that 'a did. | (Act 2: sc. iii) |

The *hostess* is referred to by *Pistol* as *Doll* in the quartos, also in the First Folio, but some editors have since changed this to *Nell*.

| Pistol: | Fortune play the housewife with me now? News have I that my Doll is dead i'th'spital Of malady of France, | (Act 5: sc .i) |

Professor Jonathan Bate, an uncompromising advocate of Shakspere's authorship, recognized the connection between Greene's and Falstaff's deathbed scenes, although not without discernible unease.

> Sir John Falstaff—who dies in Hostess Quickly's tavern, calling out for sack and remembering a woman called Doll in an uncanny replication of Greene's death in Hostess Isam's house calling out for malmsey and writing to a wife called Doll. (Bate, 19)

For Bate, this dramatisation of Falstaff's death retains an *uncanny* similarity to Greene's demise. Had Bate, and those of a like mind, not become so mesmerised by the attractive tales that govern Shakespearean study, there would not be the slightest problem in recognizing Oxford's final bow to Robert Greene, with whom he had dined, just a few weeks before the man's death.

Bate was far less uncertain when referring to the death of the other diner at Oxford's table. For Marlowe's death is also referred to by 'Shakespeare' in a passing remark made by *Touchstone* to the unlettered *Audrey* in *As You Like It* (Act 3: sc. iii).

> When a man's verses cannot be understood, nor a man's good wit seconded with the forward child, understanding, it strikes a man more dead than a great reckoning in a little room. Truly, I would the gods had made thee poetical.

Bate saw little difficulty in Shakespeare having written this passage upon recalling that Marlowe had been the one *struck dead in a little room* whilst quarrelling with his two companions over a *great reckoning*. (Bate, 123).

One can therefore see how easily the premise that Shakspere wrote Shakespeare controls what is acceptable and what must be omitted. Greene had insulted Shakespeare; therefore Shakespeare cannot be allowed to honour Greene, especially not with *Falstaff's* death scene. On the other hand, traditionalists believe that Marlowe's work instructed Shakespeare; therefore it is perfectly acceptable that Marlowe's death should be acknowledged with a suitable poetic line. But, compare this with the strong evidence that Oxford was Shakespeare, and that he was immortalising the deaths of two great writers, whose work he respected and with whom he had been acquainted. It is at once apparent that of the two interpretations, it is this latter one that explains the author's intention.

*Greenes, Groats-Worth of Witte* is always cited as prime evidence that in 1592, Shakespeare was already known in London as an actor and a writer of blank verse, and that Robert Greene, known throughout London as a playwright, had taken offence at his arrival, warning other writers to beware of him. Yet, contrarily, Shakespeare's name does not appear on any list of actors in 1592; or, for that matter, on any list in the preceding years. And, at no time in the years that followed is he ever remembered for his acting ability. Chettle admitted he had never heard of Shakespeare, while Greene's letter to his three colleagues makes it appear that Shakespeare was also unknown to them. Nor does the name Shakespeare appear on any published work prior to 1593. In short, Greene's notes can be seen as wholly confusing to anyone without special knowledge of what was about to happen in the year ahead. But when Chettle found them, he blended confusion with naivety and published the result.

# 5

# VENUS AND ADONIS

Oxford's plan to launch William Shakespeare as a penname for his allonym Will Shakspere succeeded. *Venus and Adonis* was published to great acclaim in April 1593, and was followed a year later by *The Rape of Lucrece*. An obsequious letter of dedication from the lower-class 'William Shakespeare' to his supposed patron, Henry Wriothesley, 3rd Earl of Southampton, prefixed the poem, as a similar dedication was to precede *Lucrece* a year later.

> The poem had a growing success with the public as time went on: ten or eleven editions in his own lifetime, twenty before the fatal Civil War struck at culture. Venus and Adonis made its appeal to the cultivated, to the Court and fashionable society; it found its audience especially among the young men of the Inns of Court and the universities, who found it stimulating. (Rowse, 64)

It was not only *Venus and Adonis* that received acclaim: by the year 1616 *Lucrece* had itself gone through six reprints. Yet remarkably, having reached the pinnacle of success as a poet, the name of William Shakespeare disappeared from sight as suddenly as it appeared. The name would not surface again until 1598. For four years the name of Shakespeare was seen no more in print, save as the signature previously attached to dedications appearing in *Venus and Adonis* and *Lucrece*. As for his *supposed* patron, Henry Wriothesley, 3rd Earl of Southampton, he is never heard of again in that capacity.

Shakespearean scholar Marchette Chute was totally baffled by this.

> Whenever any promising young aristocrat made his debut at Court there was a rush of poets dedicating books to him, and a stupid youngster like the Earl of Southampton could hardly come of age before there was a cluster of anxious writers hoping to be admitted to the magic circle of his purse strings. The case of William Shakespeare who succeeded in getting this particular earl for his patron and then abandoned the relationship is so exceptional as to stand alone in the history of Elizabethan letters. (Chute, 58)

Chute had clearly failed to realize that the Shakespeare-Southampton connection was simply a light-hearted hoax, perpetrated by two peers of the realm, and with no thought to its future outcome. Once their ruse was uncovered, the Shakespeare penname was abandoned. No one had been hurt by the deception, Shakspere had prospered, and the literary world was richer by two narrative poems. The subterfuge had simply been a strategy for Oxford to steer his poems into print without giving offence to his peer group: these were members of the ruling class who professed to be aghast at the idea of publishing one's thoughts for the public to read and possibly criticize. The nobility believed that for a member of their class to publish verses, worse still, write plays for public entertainment was a reprehensible indulgence. And it was not only the upper classes that subscribed to this. *'Playwrights, especially in the increasingly Puritan world of the late 1580s, were counted worthless at best.'* (Trow, 82).

It was fear of rebuke that caused John Donne to forego the satisfaction of seeing his verses in print, thus his poems remained unpublished during his lifetime, *'lest he lose his dignity as a gentleman.'* (Kay, 49). Walter Raleigh was another whose poetry remained unpublished while he lived. George Puttenham in *The Arte of English Poesie* (1589) confirmed the unacceptability of a gentleman sullying his reputation as a published poet. At the same time he credited Oxford with an ability that can be construed as sufficient for the authorship of *Venus and Adonis*.

> And in her Majesty's time that now is are sprung up another crew of Courtly makers [poets], Noblemen and Gentlemen of Her Majesty's own servants, who have written excellently well as it would appear if their doings could be found out and made public with the rest, of which number is first that noble gentleman Edward Earl of Oxford. (Ogburn, 621)

Three years earlier, in *A Discourse of English Poetry* William Webbe had made a similar comment regarding Oxford's poetry, defining it as *"most excellent among the rest"*.

> I may not omit the deserved commendations of many honourable and noble Lords and Gentlemen in Her Majesty's Court, which, in the rare devices of poetry, have been and yet are most skilful; among whom the right honourable Earl of Oxford may challenge to himself the title of most excellent among the rest. (Ogburn, 620)

Within these accreditations of Oxford's recognised ability as a poet of the highest order, there may be discerned not only his probable ability to have been the author of *Venus and Adonis*, but also a motive for concealing his identity. Hence, by engaging Will Shakspere, a tradesman's son, as his allonym, and implying that he was the author of both *Venus and Adonis* and *The Rape of Lucrece*, Oxford was attempting to avoid censure from his peer group. What he failed to realize were the long term consequences. For his deception released into the world a genie, whose mischievous activities were to mislead scholars for generation after generation, and there would be no recapturing it in the centuries that lay ahead.

If this, indeed, is what occurred, and the evidence so far supports it, then it is necessary to investigate the relationship between Oxford and Henry Wriothesley, for it was young Southampton who lent his name to the patronage of Oxford's allonym. Confirmation of a relationship between the two noblemen occurs in *Willobie His Avisa*.

> [Willobie His Avisa was] one of the books ... called in by the High Commission in 1599. The poem, first published in 1594, consists of 74 serviceable but uninspired songs and a few other poems. They narrate the unsuccessful courting of Avisa ... by four foreign suitors [after her marriage]. The last of these [identified as H.W.] has a "familiar friend W.S." as a companion; he has been identified with Shakespeare, who is also mentioned as author of The Rape of Lucrece in prefatory verses. (Drabble, 1071)

If the book had been as innocent as implied by this description, there would have been no reason to call it in. But since it was called in, this suggests that the innocent verses expressing chastity and virtue disguised a darker storyline. In the verse below, we see the name Shakespeare, but not as it appeared in *Lucrece* or *Venus* and *Adonis*: here, it has been hyphenated.

Professor Shapiro may have been enjoying a senior moment when he misled readers of *Contested Will:* claiming that in both poems, *"dedicatory letters addressed to the Earl of Southampton and signed 'William Shake–speare' are included in italics.'* (Shapiro, 256). It is easy to verify that in neither poem has the name been printed in *italic font*; nor has it been *hyphenated*. Unaware that he has just dug his own grave, Shapiro continues digging. His next blunder is to claim that hyphenation was simply a convenience by typesetters confronted by *"setting a 'k' followed by a long 's' in italic font – with the name Shakespeare, for example – the two letters could easily collide and the font might snap.'* (ibid). Elizabethan compositors would have smiled at this explanation and shown him the spacer, designed to prevent this occurring. Shapiro also overlooked the title, SHAKE–SPEARES SONNETS, which, with its capital letters, totally negates his explanation for the hyphenated name; as does *Willobie*, in which Shake-speare has been hyphenated in non-italic font.

> *Though* Collatine *have deerely bought.*
> *To high renowne, a lasting life.*
> *And found, that most in vaine have sought.*
> *To have a* Faire *and* Constant *wife,*
>    *Yet* Tarquyne *pluckt his glistering grape.*
>    *And* Shake-speare, *paints poore* Lucrece *rape.*

This reference to Shake–speare represents the fourth known mention of the name, and it has already begun to be hyphenated, as it would in 1623 when the First Folio was published. *The Rape of Lucrece* had been published only months before with the name un-hyphenated. The presence of the hyphen attracts, even sub-consciously, a comparison between the two ways of writing the name, and it suggests that Willobie's poem really did have a darker side to it: enough to alert the censors. Willobie, so it would seem, was allowing the suspicion to take root that Shakespeare was a made-up name. In fact, *Willobie His Avisa* may even have been written in the style of Shakespeare, for Charles Hughes concluded this was the case (*Willobie His Avisa*, London, 1904).

> Apply her still with dyvers thinges,
> (For giftes the wysest will deceave)
> Sometymes with gold, sometymes with ringes.
> No tyme nor fit occasion leave,
>   Though coy at first she seeme and wielde.
>   These toyes in tyme will make her yielde,
>
> And to her will frame all thy ways.
> Spare not to spend, and chiefly there
> Where thy desert may merit praise,
> By ringing in thy lady's ear.
>   The strongest castle, tower, and towne,
>   The golden bullet beats it downe.

The first of the two stanzas above is from *Willobie His Avisa* (XLVII); the second is from *The Passionate Pilgrim* (XIX), which publisher William Jaggard repeatedly maintained were poems by Shakespeare. Modern scholarship, based upon a misunderstanding of William Shakespeare's true identity, asserts that only the first two sonnets (later identified as 138 and 144) in *The Passionate Pilgrim* and three poems that occur in Act 4 of *Love's Labour's Lost* were written by Shakespeare. Others disagree, believing that Shakespeare wrote poetry before his arrival in London, and that poem 19, *When as thine eye hath chose the dame*, was one of his early pieces.

Oxford did write poetry in his youth, although only a few pieces, mostly songs, have survived. William Shakspere, on the other hand, for the first half of his life left nothing at all in the way of literature. Nevertheless, he is denied the poems appearing in *The Passionate Pilgrim* because they are not of the same standard that the mature Shakespeare was later noted for. Readers must make their own judgement about this. Did Willobie copy his style from a poem by Oxford that was circulating before being published by Jaggard in 1599? If so, then Willobie understood that Shake-speare was a pseudonym for the Earl of Oxford; hence the hyphenation.

As the poem progresses, Willobie has more to say about Shakespeare, whom he identifies as W. S.

> H. W. being sodenly affected with the contagion of a fantasticall fit, at the first sight of A, pyneth a while in secret griefe, at length not able any longer to indure the burning heate of so fervent a humour, bewrayeth the secresy of his disease unto his familiar frend W. S. who not long before had tryed the curtesy of the like passion, and was now newly recovered of the like infection ; yet finding his frend let bloud in the same vaine, he took pleasure for a tyme to see him bleed, & in steed of stopping the issue, he inlargeth the wound, with the sharpe rasor of a willing conceit, perswading him that he thought it a matter very easy to be compassed, & no doubt with payne, diligence & some cost in tyme to be obtayned. Thus this miserable comforter comforting his frend with an impossibilitie, eyther for that he now would secretly laugh at his frends folly, that had given occasion not long before unto others to laugh at his owne, or because he would see whether an other could play his part better then himselfe, & in vewing a far off the course of this loving Comedy, he determined to see whether it would sort to a happier end for this new actor, then it did for the old player....
>
> H. W.

This letter, introducing what is to follow, has been initialled by the author of *Avisa*, Henry Willobie; hence, the initials H. W., with which the letter opens, must refer to a different person with the same initials. The connection between Henry Wriothesley 3rd Earl of Southampton and William Shakespeare, whose letter of dedication to this particular Earl appears at the front of *Lucrece* and before that, *Venus and Adonis*, has naturally attracted much attention. It virtually begs acceptance, but there is an obstacle. Willobie refers to W. S. as *'the old player'* and H. W. as the *'new actor'* in this *'loving Comedy'*. Southampton was 19 years of age in 1594. William Shakspere, however, was 30: far too young to be the "old player". Not so, Oxford; in 1594 he was in his forty-fifth year. So, yet again, everything dovetails together, but only if it is accepted that Oxford and Shakespeare were one and the same person. Deny it, and cracks and gaps emerge in the alternative theory that are either papered over or avoided altogether.

*Willobie His Avisa* is a poem concerning five suitors who court a maid named Avisa; four of whom attempt to seduce her after her marriage. The poem has both attracted and intrigued past commentators, because it appears to tell a true story, but does not sufficiently identify those involved. No doubt those who were involved recognised themselves and this caused the poem to be called in.

It is possible that the poem, which refers to five separate events, has been bound together by a single object of desire, Avisa; she being referred to as one woman instead of five, or possibly less if the same woman was involved more than once. The suitors are also said to be foreign gentlemen; thus, H. W. is identified as Henrico Willobego, but this is likely to be the author's ploy to mislead the censors.

Of the five stories, the final one involves W. S. And H. W. and it commences with the introductory address given above. Thereafter, W. S. launches into a series of stanzas designed to instruct his younger companion H. W. in the art of wooing. It begins with their meeting.

> WELL met, frend Harry, what's the cause
> You looke so pale with Lented cheeks?
> Your wanny face and sharpened nose
> Shew plaine, your mind some thing mislikes.
>    If you will tell me what it is,
>    Ile helpe to mend what is amisse.

This opening remark is in complete contrast to the obsequious letter that William Shakespeare addressed to Henry Wriothesley at the front of *Lucrece* earlier in the year. It implies seniority on the part of W. S. combined with familiarity.

In this respect, the 17th Earl of Oxford was not only the elder of the two parties by a quarter of a century; he was also senior in title. Moreover, there was an apparent relationship between the two, as suggested by the air of familiarity being expressed.

W. S. discerns that H. W. is in love, and offers this advice.

> WELL, say no more : I know thy griefe,
> And face from whence these flames arise,
> It is not hard to fynd relief
> If thou wilt follow good advyse :
>    She is no Saynt, She is no Nonne,
>    I thinke in tyme she may be wonne.
>
> At first repulse you must not faint,
> Nor flye the field though she deny
> You twise or thrise, yet manly bent,
> Againe, you must, and still, reply :
>    When tyme permits you not to talke.
>    Then let your pen and fingers walke.

Apply her still with dyvers thmges,
(For giftes the wysest will deceave)
Sometymes with gold, sometymes with ringes.
No tyme nor fit occasion leave,
   Though coy at first she seeme and wielde.
   These toyes in tyme will make her yielde,

Looke what she likes ; that you must love.
And what she hates, you must detest,
Where good or bad, you must approve.
The wordes and workes that please her best:
   If she be godly, you must sweare.
   That to offend you stand in feare.

You must commend her loving face,
For women joy in beauties praise.
You must admire her sober grace.
Her wisdome and her vertuous wayes.
   Say, 't was her wit & modest shoe.
   That made you like and love her so.

You must be secret, constant, free.
Your silent sighes & trickling teares.
Let her in secret often see.
Then wring her hand, as one that feares
   To speake, then wish she were your wife.
   And last desire her save your life.

H. W. continues to remain melancholic, but reinforced by this advice he proceeds to woo Avisa, although to no avail. In a rattling sequence of stanzas, Avisa rejects his advances and remains a faithful wife. H. W. retires from the scene to lick his wounds.

As a parody on the life of Lord Southampton there are unmistakeable parallels. But to understand these one must also understand the position of both earls. After the death of Oxford's father, he was made a ward of court and placed under the protection of Lord Burghley, Queen Elizabeth's chief minister and Lord Treasurer of the nation; Burghley was also appointed by the Queen as a guardian for titled children; that is, those whose fathers had died during their minority. Southampton fell into this category when his father died in 1581. Burghley was therefore responsible for Southampton's education, upbringing, and moral welfare. But Burghley was also related by marriage to Oxford. He was his father-in-law, having also been first his guardian. Living under the same roof as Burghley, Oxford had grown up alongside Anne Cecil, Burghley's daughter, and in 1571 they married.

By the close of 1588, and in the years immediately thereafter, there was turmoil in the lives of Oxford, Burghley and Southampton. Oxford's wife had died in the summer of 1588, leaving three daughters to be cared for by their father in the grip of poverty. Burghley therefore took charge of his granddaughters, the eldest of whom, Elizabeth, celebrated her fifteenth birthday on 2 July 1590; Southampton was then aged sixteen. Nevertheless, Burghley began seeking a suitable bride for his young ward. He appears not to have been very successful. Lady Manners, with a nubile daughter, thought Southampton *"too fantastical"*: the same word used by Willobie in his opening remarks concerning H. W. It therefore fell upon Burghley's fifteen-year-old granddaughter to accept Southampton as her fiancée. As Ackroyd confirmed: – *"At the age of sixteen he had been repeatedly pressed to marry Burghley's granddaughter,"* (Ackroyd, 191).

Agreement was reached by both families concerning the proposed union. The Queen, willingly gave her consent, and then Southampton backed down. He steadfastly refused to proceed with the marriage arrangements. Burghley responded by threatening to impose a £5000 fine if he did not proceed with the marriage. On the basis that £40 in 1582 is equivalent to £20,000 today then £5000 is equivalent to £2,500,000. One can therefore discern, by the crippling enormity of this fine, the measure of Burghley's desperation to force his ward into a marriage. But even this measure failed.

The reason for Burghley's sudden urgency to see his teenage ward wed can be deduced from the portrait of Southampton painted at about the same time as the marriage was being arranged. The portrait shows Southampton attired as a woman. The recently discovered Cobbe portrait shows the young Earl at about seventeen years of age in feminine attire. In fact, for the past three centuries, the sitter was mistakenly thought to have been Lady Norton, the Bishop of Winton's daughter. The portrait, however, is quite unmistakable in showing Southampton wearing double earrings and a Venetian lace collar that was in vogue between 1590 and 1593. The curling tongs have been carefully applied to his hair, which has been styled to give the same appearance as that of Juno, the Roman queen of heaven and of womanhood; a long tress dangles down the side of his left breast and this is held in place by the slender delicate fingers of his right hand. He is also wearing lipstick and rouge colours his cheeks. The eyebrows have been plucked with careful precision and the eyes are bright, from the effects of belladonna (*The Observer Review* 21/4/2002, 5). Burghley's anxiety at attempting to resolve the problem of his ward's transsexual behaviour will be familiar to many parents who see wedlock as the only answer to aberrations in the sexual behaviour of their child. And, of course, Burghley was still responsible to the Queen for Southampton's moral upbringing. This subject is dealt with more fully in chapter 20.

The connection between Willobie's poem in which W. S. advises H. W. in the art of courtship, is not too far removed from the Sonnets of W. S. in which the 'fair youth' H. W. receives similar advise, but in the more elegant style of the iambic pentameter, rather than the hexameters of *Avisa*.

> Look in thy glass, and tell the face thou viewest
> Now is the time that face should form another; (3)

> Is it not fear to wet a widow's eye
> That thou consum'st thyself in single life ?
> Ah ! if thou issueless shalt hap to die,
> The world will wail thee like a makeless wife: (9)

> For shame ! deny that thou bear'st love to any,
> Who for thy self art so unprovident.
> Grant, if thou wilt, thou art belov'd of many,
> But that thou none lov'st is most evident; (10)

The accusal in the fourth line of Sonnet 10, apparently addressed to Henry Wriothesley, is admitted by H. W. in his overture to Avisa.

> Love oft doth spring from due desart.
> As loving cause of true effect.
> But myne proceeds from wounded hart.
> As scholler to a novell sect :
>   I bare that lyking, few have bore,
>   I love, that never lov'd before. (Cant. LI)

It seems evident from this that H. W. appearing in *Willobie His Avisa* is the same Henry Wriothesley who is addressed by William Shakespeare in the *Sonnets*. And it is no less evident from the advice given by Shakespeare that he is also acting as the young Earl's faithful friend. This is especially noteworthy because W. S. too is described as H. W.'s faithful friend in the *Willobie* poem. With such a strong connection between the two, and with the dates also confirming the link, it clearly indicates firm ground exists to continue pursuing this line of investigation.

Burghley was at that time the most important man in England. The Queen referred to him as her *Spirit*. He was also keen to build a dynasty, and any taint of scandal was naturally to be avoided at all costs. His son-in-law's relationship with the effeminate Southampton, who was still legally his ward, must have begun to threaten his ambitions as well as the future reputation of his granddaughters. What is more, any scandal that involved him in his office as principal minister to the Crown, might also pose a threat to the nation's security. But his hands were tied, for he could not take action against either his ward or his son-in-law without implicating himself, which would then damage his family and his ambitions. And so he sought marriage as the simplest solution, together with the censorship of anything suggesting an illicit bond between his ward and his son-in-law. This would explain how *Venus and Adonis* escaped censorship, while *Avisa* was banned.

The subject matter of *Venus and Adonis* and the *Rape of Lucrece*, both with erotic content, would seem to have been part of a more involved plan involving Burghley in his capacity as head of censorship. Only this would explain the astounding fact that William Shakespeare: hitherto unknown as a writer anywhere in England, was immediately, and without difficulty, able to obtain a licence for the publication of two poems whose sexual content would, in different circumstances, have secured the Church's condemnation and censure. *Venus and Adonis* *'was remarkable for what was known as its wantonness. Although it was not half as pornographic as some of the poems then being circulated in manuscript'* (Ackroyd, 193).

> Observing that the printing of Venus and Adonis—which for explicit eroticism can be exceeded by few literary works openly published and sold in the English-speaking world for the next 350 years—was personally authorized by the Archbishop of Canterbury, George Philip V. Akrigg comments, "We have lost a good story concerning Archbishop Whitgift's licence." (Ogburn, 284)

Perhaps not lost, if it is understood that Lord Burghley had explained to Archbishop Whitgift the need for the licence was to achieve the greater good of saving young Southampton from a life of sin and ultimate damnation. In the religious climate of the time: *'sodomy was a capital offence and religious people of all persuasions regarded it as an instant passport to hell.'* (Wilson, 146).

Burghley's anxiousness and his attempt to solve the problem he faced regarding Southampton's sexual behaviour by arranging his marriage, may be seen just as much a desire to save his own skin as his young ward's soul; for Southampton had, to his way of thinking, placed both in jeopardy.

A direct, if circumstantial, link between Shakespeare's verses urging matrimony and the controversy surrounding the teenage Southampton has been the subject of speculation for many years. It has also led to the suggestion that Lord Burghley together with Southampton's mother, Lady Mary Browne, had agreed to their private affairs being made known to a tradesman's son: a man who had recently arrived from the midlands, and was quite unknown to the literary world as a poet, since he had published nothing. This same person was also an actor of bit-parts with a group of players, therefore a member of a sub-class of the population that was frequently associated with prostitution and petty crime. Since neither playwriting nor acting *"was, after all, the profession of a gentleman'* (Ackroyd, 191), the scenario suggested above is true fantasy. Yet, it is against this background that biographers weave their words to entrap readers into believing Burghley did agree to this unknown man, William Shakspere, forming a close relationship with the pampered young earl, and that Queen Elizabeth's councillor then allowed a succession of sonnets to be addressed to his ward, urging him to marry, after disclosing to this low class outsider the young nobleman's aversion to the married state.

In fact, the haste with which this immature young nobleman was being hurried to the altar by Burghley, in order to make his wedding vows, indicates the opposite was happening. Burghley was struggling to avoid rumours getting out into the public domain concerning Southampton's cross-dressing and his preference for homo-erotic poetry, by pressing him to marry. Engaging an unknown, unpublished poet with no background in society to address his ward upon the very personal subject of his marriage is romantic fiction.

Despite the relationship between Southampton and Shakespeare (for which some may prefer to read Oxford), as evidenced by the dedications to *Venus and Adonis* and *Lucrece,* not everyone can believe that the son of a tradesman would be allowed to address the 3rd Earl of Southampton in such familiar language as that adopted by the poet in the Sonnets.

> In the late sixteenth century, however, the impropriety of addressing a young earl in that manner would have been quite apparent; to accuse him of dissoluteness and infidelity, as Shakespeare accuses the unnamed recipient, would have been unthinkable. (Ackroyd, 288)

Ackroyd is perfectly correct. However, by acknowledging the unknown poet of the *Sonnets* to be the 17th Earl of Oxford, the objection he raises is rendered invalid. It would then be perfectly in order for Oxford, as an elder person and senior statesman to have addressed Southampton, or a similar young lord in a critical fashion. Only a person of his high birth could have used the terminology Ackroyd refers to, and directed it at another, if younger, lord.

Alternatively, if Shakspere was the poet of the sonnets, then who was the youth he addressed? Who was this young man he loved and promised immortality to through the virtue of his verse? The lack of any suitable candidate has led some commentators to claim that the sonnets were written as a compilation of imaginative thoughts set to verse. If that were the case, then the impoverished state of Shakspere's family, which he had abandoned in order to travel to London, would surely have persuaded him to publish his sonnets as a follow-up to the triumphant reception received from selling his *Venus and Adonis* and *Lucrece*. The fact that he did not do so points to their content being biographical.

This conclusion is endorsed by the appearance of their having been withheld until making some form of 'escape' in 1609. But this bid for liberty did not last long. As Wilson admitted, *"some form of suppression has to be suspected."* After a very short print run they disappeared for thirty years, despite the First Folio having brought everlasting fame to their author. Compare this absence by contrasting it with *'the altogether lesser sonnets of Shakespeare's exact contemporary Michael Drayton, already six times printed by 1609, [which] went into three further editions.'* (Wilson, 349). It is evident from this that the sonnets held some uncomfortable secret that was best kept away from the public gaze.

*Venus and Adonis* was on the bookstalls by the middle of 1593, published by Richard Field, a former resident of Stratford-upon-Avon. The connection between him and William Shakspere is irresistible. If Shakspere had written *Venus and Adonis* it would be natural for him to have contacted Field. Conversely, if Oxford was employing Shakspere as a front for William Shakespeare, it would also be beneficial for the success of the outcome to employ a publisher from the village where he came from. Therefore, the fact that Field published *Venus and Adonis* cuts both ways, and nothing conclusive can be drawn from it.

'Shakespeare' calls the poem *"the first heire of my inuention"*, as indeed it was, since William Shakespeare did not exist before 1593, except in the mind of 'his' creator. It also seems that Oxford had long term hopes that this subterfuge would continue, so as to allow his 'William Shakespeare' to publish more of his poetry. In the event *Willobie His Avisa* with its candid references to forty-four-year-old Oxford as W. S. *"the old player"* and H. W. as *"the new actor"* – presumably a reference to Southampton's role as the patron of this hitherto unknown William Shakespeare – marked the end of the enterprise. William Shakespeare never published again.

The Shakespeare experts who refuse to accept that this is really what happened have an unanswerable problem to contend with. In a misguided belief that Shakspere wrote *Venus and Adonis* as the *first heir* of his *invention*, an analysis of the poem was conducted to show that it contained dialectic words traceable to the Warwickshire county in which he was raised. Not a single example was found. To an expert witness upon questions of dialect, this can mean only one thing. Shakspere could not have written *Venus and Adonis*. Had he done so, it would rank as a miracle – equivalent to walking on water.

> Circumstantial evidence may be explained away by the testimony of other circumstances. Internal evidence may be upset by context. But words are detectives that never fail to detect, and whose reports cannot be bribed, distorted or gainsaid. No man can write in a language he has never heard, or whose written form he has never learned. (Morgan, 1)

Shakspere grew up in that part of England where an East Midlands dialect was the standard spoken language, yet there is no trace of this dialect in *Venus and Adonis*. While Shakespeare experts wrestle with their 'miracle' of Shakespeare's first heir of invention, they should also consider explaining at the same time, why it is that 'Shakespeare' *"used more than one hundred different types of Essex vocabulary and grammar in 27 of the 37 plays he wrote.'* (Goldstein, 28). The first eleven years of Oxford's life were spent in Essex.

To an impartial scholar, these facts should ring alarm bells and motivate further enquiry. Shakespeare experts are not impartial scholars; they never draw logical conclusions from their investigations when these fail to prop up the premise they operate from. They repeatedly sail against the breath of reason, lest their efforts be swept away in the flood of new scholarship, derived from within the plays and poetry of Oxford. At the back of their minds is a growing unease that centuries of unproductive scholarship, born from imagination, will end up gathering dust in some forgotten archive.

# 6

# SHAKESPEARE'S SILENCE

The enthusiastic reception given to *Venus and Adonis* and *The Rape of Lucrece* is freely acknowledged by Shakespeare's biographers.

> *Venus and Adonis* was immensely popular. ... There were no fewer than eleven editions over the next twenty-five years, and there may have been other reprints that have simply vanished. It was in his lifetime far more popular than any of his plays, and did more to secure his literary reputation than any drama. (Ackroyd, 192-3)

*Lucrece* was also enthusiastically received by the public. And John Harrison was able to publish subsequent editions in octavo rather than quarto format. A second edition duly appeared in 1598, with two further editions in 1600. A fourth and fifth edition was printed in 1607. In 1614, Harrison sold his right to publish *Lucrece* to Roger Jackson who issued a sixth edition in 1616. Three further editions followed in 1624, 1632 and 1655.

Despite the enduring popularity of *Lucrece*, there was a gap of four years before the second edition was published. This is comparable to *Venus and Adonis*, which was published in 1593, followed by two further editions in 1594, and two more before the end of 1596. There was then a gap of three years before William Leake twice reissued the poem in 1599.

Except for a single reprint of *Venus and Adonis* in 1596, nothing with the name of William Shakespeare was published between 1594 and 1598. Yet this was a time when the poet had made his name. It was also the time when he had a number of sonnets available for publication. It was a time when the public would have expected to read more from this new author. Instead, his name slips almost out of sight; retained only on the dedication pages of the two narrative poems that he published in 1593 and 1594: with a reprint of the former in 1596.

The circumstances behind this unprofitable act become even more mysterious when the poet's plays for this period are considered. On 23 January 1594, and on the 28th and again on the 6th February, Henslowe's journal recorded performances of *Titus Andronicus*. Also on 6 February, this same play was entered in the Stationers' Register. When it went on sale, it boasted that it had already been played by three different acting groups: those sponsored by the Earl of Derby, the Earl of Pembroke and the Earl of Sussex. All three noblemen had a close connection with the 17th Earl of Oxford. The 5th Earl of Derby's son married Oxford's daughter Elizabeth in January 1595. As part of the celebration:

> Elizabeth went with Essex to see the first performance of *A Comedy of Errors* and five months later was guest of honour at the celebrations arranged for the wedding between Lord Derby and Lady Elizabeth Vere, when *A Midsummer Night's Dream* had its debut.
> (Williams, 1972: 155)

The Earls of Pembroke were owners of Wilton House where the second Earl's wife, the sister of soldier-poet Philip Sidney, established a college and forum for scholars and artists. We shall later see evidence that Oxford visited Wilton after his wife's death in 1588. The Countess of Pembroke's eldest son, William Herbert, was betrothed to Oxford's daughter Bridget in 1597, but the marriage plans unravelled through Burghley's intervention over the dowry. William's brother Philip was more successful, he later married Oxford's youngest daughter, Susan. Both William and Philip were, of course, *"the most noble brethren'* to whom the First Folio of Shakespeare's plays were dedicated in 1623; and, it is suspected that they financed this hugely expensive enterprise. It would certainly have been beyond the means of grocer Heminge, and of Condell, who was only a player.

Henry Radcliffe, 4th Earl of Sussex (c.1531 - 1593) was a landowner in the county of Essex, where Oxford also owned land: in the midst of which, stood his ancestral home of Hedingham Castle.

Henry's brother was Thomas Radcliffe, 3rd Earl of Sussex with whom it would seem Oxford, at the age of nineteen, saw service as a soldier in the Northern Rebellion of 1569. From 1572 until his death in 1585, Radcliffe served as Lord Chamberlain, which included the task of organising court functions. This would have included plays known to have been written by Oxford for royal performances. Even until recent times, the office of Lord Chamberlain was responsible for licensing plays in the City of London, Westminster, and certain other areas.

Although publication of *Titus Andronicus* referred to the company of players under the protection of the earldoms of Derby, Pembroke, and Sussex, advertising the fact that they had performed this play, there was no mention of the author. This is strange, because the author's name, William

Shakespeare, was on the lips of every person who had bought a copy of *Venus and Adonis*; that this selling point was missed remains inexplicable.

To add further to the mystery, five weeks after the Stationers' Register recorded *Titus Andronicus*, another Shakespeare play was entered in the Register; this has been identified as *Henry VI Part 2*. It will be recalled that by this time, Nashe had already written a rave review of *Henry VI Part 1*, in which he spoke glowingly of Talbot's fight against the French. Also, Chettle had published Greene's letter paraphrasing the quote from *Henry VI Part 3* – *'Tygers hart wrapt in a Players hyde '*. For this reason, the reference made in *Willobie His Avisa* to W.S. as *'the old player'*, can be seen with greater confidence as referring to the author of *Henry VI, Parts One, Two and Three, Titus Andronicus, The Comedy of Errors* and *A Midsummer Night's Dream*. But there is more; much more.

On 6 April 1593 and again two days later, although Henslowe followed the first entry by correcting the year to 1594, he recorded the performance of *King Lear*. One month later he recorded a performance of *Hamlet*. And on the 11 June, the same journal included an entry confirming a performance of *Taming of The Shrew*; Henslowe actually recorded it as *"the tamynge of A shrowe'*, but then his written record of titles was representative rather than exact.

*Willobie His Avisa* was licensed for the press by printer John Windet on September 3, 1594. Before that date, two narrative poems bearing the name William Shakespeare had been published; two pirated editions of the plays *Titus Andronicus* and *2 Henry VI* had also gone on sale, but with no author mentioned. References were also made to *Comedy of Errors, Midsummer Night's Dream, 1 Henry VI, 3 Henry VI, Hamlet, Taming of the Shrew,* and *King Lear*. Shakespearean scholars list still more titles as having been amongst the author's first venture into writing for the theatre, and all of these were written by the close of 1595, just one year after *Lucrece* was published. Among these titles are *Love's Labour's Lost, Two Gentlemen of Verona, Romeo and Juliet, Richard II, Richard III,* and *King John*. (Gervinus, xlix).

By any measure of intelligence, the author of these plays could not have escaped the notice of men like Nashe and Greene; it did not escape the notice of the author of *Willobie His Avisa*. Yet Greene, who had written no more than six plays of note, may be supposed to have called this unnamed author, who by 1592 had written as many plays as he had done, if not more, *"an up-start Crow'*. One can only gape in open-mouthed astonishment at this, for it implies that biographers and their academic mentors alike have failed to count, and thus consider, the number of plays attributed to Shakespeare when Greene supposedly wrote his slur against Shakespeare. Surely, Chettle's hand in Greene's letter must now be acknowledged as an obviously misunderstood fabrication, composed from Greene's scribble?

Academics and biographers will doubtless disagree; they have their own theories to account for these early plays. To be acceptable, all explanations must be based upon William Shakspere of Stratford-upon-Avon having written the plays. *Hamlet* and *King Lear* contradict this theory. In their present form they are too early for an embryo playwright to have been their creator. Consequently, both plays are assigned to the work of another playwright whose identity is unknown.

There is also disquiet concerning the inference that Shakspere began his writing career with the trilogy of *Henry VI parts I, II and III*. And to add to this unease, there is the awkward fact that Shakspere has been guilty of —

> ... lifting or altering 1,479 lines from The Contention [Between the Two Famous Houses of Yorke and Lancaster] for Henry VI., Part 2; and 1,931 lines from The True Tragedy [of Richard Duke of Yorke] for 3 Henry VI., Part 3. (Gervinus, xxxii-xxxiii)

According to this conclusion, Shakspere was a notorious plagiarist who by some unknown means acquired the manuscript copies of several histories. First, there was *The Contention Between the Two Famous Houses of Yorke and Lancaster*, then *The True Tragedy of Richard Duke of Yorke*; this was followed by *The Famous Victories of Henry the Fift*, then came *The Troublesome Raigne of King John*. He is then supposed to have persuaded different theatre groups to perform them under the titles we now recognise as *Henry VI Part One*; *Henry VI Part Three*; *Henry V*; and *King John*; that is, after having revised them by adding his 'master touches'. He then went further, by adding to his plagiarised work, *The Taming of The Shrew*, which some believe he derived from *The Taming of A Shrew*; *Hamlet*, which he allegedly obtained from an earlier play called – Wait for it! – *Hamlet*, and *King Lear* from the earlier play in Henslowe's diary – yes, you've guessed – *"Kinge Leare"*.

Now it is true that Henslowe did sometimes engage writers by paying them to write a play that he thought would draw an audience, and when he did so he entered the details meticulously in his day book.

> Lent vnto Bengemen Johnsone the 3 of decemb.3 1597 vpon a Bocke w$^{ch}$ he was to writte for vs befor crysmas next after the date hereof w$^{ch}$ he showed the plotte vnto the company I saye lente in Redy money vnto hime the some of xxs

But Shakespeare's name does not appear even once in Henslowe's journal, despite its record of day to day business details, which include transactions that involve no less than twenty-seven playwrights, including: Ben Jonson, Christopher Marlowe, Thomas Middleton, Robert Greene, Henry Chettle, George Chapman, Thomas Dekker, John Webster, Anthony Munday, Henry Porter, John Day, John Marston, and Michael Drayton. Tom Nashe also appears in an entry referring to his term of imprisonment in the Fleet, for the part he took in writing the *Isle of Dogs*, but the entry is in different handwriting, which may suggest it was forged; although for what purpose is difficult to answer.

From these details, should we not take the more logical course and conclude that Shakespeare's name does not appear in Henslowe's diary because he was the 17th Earl of Oxford, and would no more accept money from Henslowe than he would from anyone outside his own class? And is it not just as logical to conclude that Oxford revised and rewrote *The Contention, The True Tragedy, The Famous Victories, The Troublesome Raigne, The Shrew, Hamlet* and *King Lear* from his own original manuscripts, than to suppose that they all somehow became available to Shakspere, who plagiarised them?

If we decline to take this more logical course, then by the end of 1594 we are left with Shakspere, now calling himself Shakespeare, who has become famous, and widely seen as an accomplished playwright and poet, but who is also mute. The 'lost years', which were followed by a sudden burst of light in 1593 and 1594, are now followed by the 'silent years'; Shakespeare as a literary figure disappears from the scene until 1598.

The standard response to this is that 'Shakespeare' gave up writing poetry so that he could concentrate on an acting career, while still writing for the stage. There is the usual problem with this explanation. Researchers have toured England searching for his name amongst the visiting players who toured the country during that time and, predictably, have returned empty-handed. In short, there is no evidence to support the standard explanation. Secondly, the briefest look at the chronology of Shakespeare's plays indicates that if the standard response was true, the plays would have been composed at a non-stop rate from the time he arrived in London up until the time he left. It has to be a non-stop rate because there is so much work to squeeze into such a short space of time.

Associated with this frenzy of creative writing is the fact that it was during this same period of time, when 'Shakespeare' was allegedly writing up to three masterpieces a year for the stage, plus the two narrative poems already mentioned, that he was otherwise engaged in the completion of his sonnet sequence; this would eventually result in 154 examples of the most sublime poetry known to man.

To cover these years of obscurity, Shakespeare's image-makers focus upon the ten anonymous plays that appeared between 1594 and 1599, and which became part of the recognised Shakespeare canon. But why should they be anonymous when the name Shakespeare had become so famous? It is futile to protest that writers' names did not always appear on published work. One has to compare like with like. This is the famous William Shakespeare whose name has been omitted, not some Henslowe hack. Conventional thinking has no reliable answer to this, but merely comments upon 'his' plays which, it is supposed, were written during this period. The dates given, however, are nothing more than guesswork. But a consensus based solely upon Shakspere having been the author, together with the narrow margin of time in which reports of these plays appeared ensure this explanation receives the widest acceptance. Moreover, the composition of these plays then accounts for what Shakspere was doing at the time his name disappeared from public view: he was in a state of perpetual motion, writing non-stop.

It was in the midst of this alleged outburst of creativity that Shakspere's name did arise, and on more than one occasion, but never in the context of literature. On 15 March 1595, in the Accounts of the Treasurer of the Chamber, his name was included amongst those having received £20 for performances before the Queen in late December 1594:

> Will Kempe Will Shakespeare & Richard Burbage servants to the Lord Chamb[er]lain ... for two several comedies or interludes shewed by them before her Ma[jesty] ... upon St. Stephens day & Innocents day. (Ogburn, 56)

In the context of Shakspere's role as Oxford's allonym, the appearance of his name as a member of an acting company is not surprising. Existing evidence places him as a member of the theatre group some time after his arrival in London, and following his self-employment as a horse-minder for wealthy visitors to the Shoreditch playhouses. It is argued that because of his previous business acumen and other positive characteristics, he had caught the eye of Oxford, who saw him as a possible front for his plan to publish under the name of someone from the lower classes. Shakspere's connection with Oxford, closely followed by his financial investment in the theatre company, elevated him to the level where it became natural that he would be mentioned along with the recognised names of Kempe and Burbage, for this lent substance to his reputed connection with the theatre.

Coincidentally, in the same year that *Lucrece* was published, Henry Carey, the new Lord Chamberlain, became patron of *'The Lord Chamberlain's Men'*, who were performing at the Theatre in Shoreditch. This gave Oxford the opportunity he needed for his protégé, William Shakspere, to purchase a 10% share in the company. Thereafter, Shakspere's presence in the playhouse was to form a natural reference point for his connection with the plays attributed to him.

It is also likely that Shakspere was required for an occasional part on stage: although there is no actual report of any major character that he played. However, it is in his role as an actor that his image-makers – who subtly change 'The Lord Chamberlain's Men' to 'his company'– commit another contradiction. Marchette Chute explains:

> His company put on about fifteen new plays a year and Shakespeare, as a regular acting member of the company, must have appeared in most of them ... [Dover, on the Kent coast is added to his itinerary because] Shakespeare visited this district more than once with his company. (Ogburn, 56)

But that tireless researcher J. O. Halliwell-Phillipps also visited Dover, expecting to find Shakespeare's name listed amongst the players who visited the harbour town, but it was not there. One can see how easy it is to invent a 'fact' about Shakespeare: in this case, based upon the premise that he was an actor who went on tour with *his* company. What one cannot do is provide evidence that supports the invention; that is, other than by forging it: something, which some of his most fervent admirers have in the past felt impelled to do; so forlorn did they become at the absence of any real evidence supporting their idolatry.

Quite often these assumed 'facts' pass unnoticed, and soon become assimilated into a body of evidence supporting the premise that Shakspere was Shakespeare. But when they are checked, where possible, many so-called 'facts' are discovered to be no more than wished-for assumptions. Consider the following paradox, which is never mentioned by biographers.

An actor's life was a busy one. Everything had to be done in daylight hours. Rehearsals were held in the morning to prepare for the afternoon performance.

The list of preparations was very demanding.

- Wake at dawn, eat breakfast, get to the theatre.
- Learn and run though any fights or dances needed.
  Check you have all your props and costume.
- Perform around 2 o'clock in the afternoon.
- Get your scroll for the play to be performed tomorrow.
- Find your props and costume for that play, and learn
  (or finish off learning) your scroll.

  Ensure that this is done by nightfall, because the poor quality smoky candles afforded by actors would make it difficult or impossible to read at home.

- Visit an ale-tavern (some things don't change).
- To bed, then the same again. (Crystal, 90)

[T]he Henslowe Diary reveals, it was commonplace for a London-based theatrical company to put on six different plays during a working week of six afternoons, and over a period of six months to stage some thirty different plays, about half of these new titles. Many would contain complicated action, sword fights, fits of madness, rapid changes of costume, mood and tempo, etc. As any present-day professional actor will instantly recognize, the pressures of such a programme would have been intense, demanding the strongest concentration, physical agility, personal self-discipline, and closest interdependence between performers.
(Wilson, 75)

Shakspere's engagement as an actor, and the busy schedule that had to be followed for plays he had not written, are quite incompatible with the prolific output that is associated with Shakespeare the author during those four hectic years of composition between 1594 and 1598. For it must be supposed that his copy was written at night by the light of *a smoky candle*, along with the dialogue that his fellow actors would need for their parts: since these were required whenever a new play was to be performed. But his image-makers never dwell upon such practical considerations. Their flights of imagination soar high above matters of realistic fact.

The second reference to Shakspere's whereabouts during his 'silent years', took place close to 11 August 1596, when he may have returned to Stratford-upon-Avon upon learning of his son's death; Hamnet was only eleven years old. Two months later, the parish of St. Helens in Bishopsgate named him on a tax assessment for the sum of five shillings. He did not pay, and in November 1596 he was posted as a tax defaulter. Then, in the same month, his name again appeared, this time alongside that of William Wayte, a stepson of the Surrey gangster and loathed local judge, James Gardiner.

> Be it known that William Wayte craves sureties of the peace against William Shakspere, Francis Langley, Dorothy Soer wife of John Soer, and Anne Lee, for fear of death, and so forth. Writ of attachment issued to the Sheriff of Surrey, returnable on the eighteenth of St Martin [i.e. 29 November 1596]. (Michell, 249)

Gardiner was a Bermondsey leather merchant who had *'enriched himself by criminal dealings, swindling even his own family and oppressing the tenants in his slum properties'* (ibid). Wayte, too, had gained a reputation for being the local bullyboy, and was described as *'a certain loose person of no reckoning or value'* (Wilson, 216).

Professor Leslie Hotson delved into this squalid affair, as far as records permitted, and discovered that *'Francis Langley was an older man who had made his money by crooked means and had previously been charged with violence and extortion.'* (Michell, 249). Some type of feud had clearly developed between these two underworld figures, Gardiner and Langley, and as a result, their henchmen, Wayte on one side and Shakspere on the other, had become involved. The presence of the two termagants on the writ indicates that the altercation between these two gang leaders was for control of the vice trade.

> The most notorious brothels were densely clustered on the Southwark Bankside. These were the 'stews'—so named from the original meaning of a heated room used for hot air or vapour baths, and formally controlled by the Bishop of Winchester (hence 'Winchester goose' the Elizabethan slang for a diseased Southwark whore or an infected client). (Haynes, 62)

The fact that William Shakspere returned to his native Stratford a very rich man is not disputed; the evidence is undeniable; that he made his fortune from pimping is deemed too outrageous for even a moment's consideration. Yet, consider his contemporaries in the theatre, not one of them achieved riches; in fact, the opposite was more often true; Greene, the top writer of his day, with degrees from both Oxford and Cambridge, died penniless in the care of a poor but charitable cobbler and his wife. Tom Nashe also died in poverty. One could barely scratch an existence from the pen unless there was a wealthy patron on hand to lend support. Ben Jonson admitted to having made no more than £200 for his plays. The usual rate was about £6 for a play. But, apart from the two letters that preface *Venus and Adonis* and *Lucrece*, which lack validation from the Southampton archives, and for which an alternative explanation exists, there is neither evidence nor indication that Shakspere ever had such a patron. And, even if it is believed otherwise, no patron ever did more than support an artist; and this is far from being the same as bankrolling him.

> The income from thirty-seven plays would barely have enabled the author to make ends meet over a twenty-year period, and certainly Shakspere did not make sufficient mark as an actor to have prospered in that capacity. The renowned Richard Burbage at his death held property worth £300, in addition to personal possessions. Shakspere put down £440 in one investment, to purchase tithes. (Ogburn, 140)

So, from where did Shakspere acquire his wealth, if not from the vice trade? Could it be that the unknown naval officer, who wrote *The Story of the Learned Pig* in 1786, hit the mark when he referred to 'Pimping Billy'? The author of this book, who referred to himself as *Transmigratus*, tells the story of the transmigration of his soul along the timeline of history. During the course of two thousand years he experienced many reincarnations, these included living as different animals and even insects. However, in the sixteenth century, he was reborn in the body of a man.

> I am now come to a period in which, to my great joy, I once more got possession of a human body. My parents, indeed, were of low extraction; my mother sold fish about the streets of this metropolis, and my father was a water-carrier celebrated by Ben Jonson in his comedy of 'Every Man in his Humour.' I was early in life initiated in the profession of horse-holder to those who came to visit the playhouse, where I was well-known by the name of 'Pimping Billy'. My sprightly genius soon distinguished me here from the common herd of that calling, insomuch that I added considerably to my income by standing 'pander', as it is politely called, to country ladies and gentlemen who were unacquainted with the ways of the town. But this employment getting me frequently engaged in lewd quarrels, I was content to give it up at the expense of many a well tanned hide. I soon after contracted a friendship with that great man and first of geniuses, the 'Immortal Shakspeare', and am happy in now having it in my power to refuse the prevailing opinion of his having run his country for deer-stealing, which is as false as it is disgracing. The fact is, Sir, that he had contracted an intimacy with the wife of a country Justice near Stratford, from his having extolled her beauty in a common ballad; and was unfortunately, by his worship himself, detected in a very aukward situation with her. Shakspeare, to avoid the consequences of this discovery, thought it most prudent to decamp. This I had from his own mouth.

The book is full of allusions, and the extract above occupies just one of many stories recounted by the author. His reference to Ben Jonson and the water-carrier named Cob in *Every Man In His Humour*, presumably contains a subtlety that the author wished to convey. Beyond the fact that Cob admitted to what might be called delusions of grandeur, as did Shakspere, whom he refers to later, this reference need be pursued no further. But it is interesting to note that the speaker identifies himself as a *horse-holder*, whose nickname, *Pimping Billy*, indicated an obvious connection with the vice trade. It also points to his name having been William.

Interestingly, this *Billy* described his first job in London as having been the same as William Shakspere had confessed to, and which Rowe repeated in 1709. The narrator then admits to having struck up a friendship with the *Immortal Shakspeare*. This, again, was concluded as having taken place between Oxford and Shakspere, and which led to Oxford employing Shakspere as his allonym, for which he changed Shakspere's name to the more literary, Shakespeare.

The narrator, although now identified with the same beginning as that of Shakspere upon his arrival in London, continues by referring to him in the third person. The tale of deer poaching as the reason for his having left Stratford is denied. Instead, he says, it was because of an amorous affair with the wife of a country Justice. Thereafter, the narrator reveals what anti-Stratfordians consider validates their belief about Shakespeare.

> With equal falsehood has he been father'd with many spurious dramatic pieces. 'Hamlet, Othello, As you like it, the Tempest, and Midsummer's Night Dream', for five.

Here, written in 1786, we are presented with a straightforward denial that Shakspere wrote the works attributed to Shakespeare, for by extension, the plays named also imply those unnamed. This denial is then tempered by the humorous claim that it was he, the narrator, who had written these plays. However, in denying Shakspere authorship, the narrator provides the same reason that is never far from the authorship debate. Successful authors write about what they know best.

> And that I should turn poet is not to be wondered at, since nothing is more natural than to contract the ways and manners of those with whom we live in habits of strict intimacy.

According to this extract: *The ways and manners of those with whom [Shakespeare] live[d] in habits of strict intimacy*, were those of the Court and to the nobility, for it is these that are described by Shakespeare, and they belong to Oxford: not to Shakspere.

The narrator concludes this part of his life story by continuing to refer to himself and to Shakspere as the author of the plays, which is how these had been seen by different sections of society when they were written. He also admits that comments made about these works have run so wide of the mark, it is impossible to say who has erred most. His story ends in a way long recognised by anti-Stratfordians. He is not recognised as the true author. The glory has been given to Shakespeare.

> You will of course expect me to say something of the comments that have been made by various hands on these works of mine and his: but the fact is, they all run so wide of the real sense, that it would be hard to say who has erred most. ... But, alas! How transient is all human felicity! The preference given to Shakspeare over me, and the great countenance

Gshewn him by the *first* crowned head in the world, and all people of taste and quality, threw me into so violent a fit of the spleen, that it soon put a period to my existence.

It is possible to determine from this storyline that in 1786, when these words were written, the authorship of Shakespeare's plays was already doubted by some. In fact, the same disbelief had already been voiced in Shakspere's village seventeen years earlier, as will be recounted further down. Both Professor Shapiro and Professor Bate seemed unaware of this – a fault shared by the majority of their peer group. *"No one in Shakespeare's lifetime or the first two hundred years after his death expressed the slightest doubt about the authorship.'* (Bate, 73). *"For two hundred years after Shakespeare's death, no one thought to argue that somebody else had written his plays."* (Shapiro, front flap).

This is untrue. Doubts concerning the authorship of Shakespeare's work first emerged a little over a century after Shakspere's death. In 1728, the occasion was Captain Goulding's "*Essay Against Too Much Learning*" (pages 12-15). It was followed in 1769 by Herbert Lawrence with his publication of "*Life and Adventures of Common Sense*" (pages 144-149), and then by "*The Learned Pig*" seventeen years later, concerning *Pimping Billy*.

Pimping would certainly account for Shakspere's unexplained wealth; it also fits the character traits of his life in both London and Stratford; that is, as a tax evader, grain hoarder, moneylender, and debt collector.

We shall discover Shakspere once again in contact with the London underworld, when at the turn of the 16th century he shared lodgings with a known pimp and subsequent brothel-keeper, George Wilkins, in the house of Christopher Mountjoy who, himself, ran several brothels. Against such a background, and as a former associate of Langley, he was unlikely to be seen as a man over-willing to engage in polite conversation regarding the finer points of iambic pentameter.

All of this may sound extreme, but Wayte's appeal to the judiciary for protection must be seen in the context of this man's character, background, and reputation. Wayte was not some simpleton caught up in matters for which he had no part to play. He was a member of a powerful criminal family who were more than capable of taking care of their own. In modern day parlance it sounds as if a contract had been taken out on Wayte's life amidst a mild outbreak of gang warfare. Control of the vice trade would most likely have been the cause.

Shakspere's image-makers naturally blanch at the thought this could be true, and put a wholly different spin on the affair. They believe Langley's quarrel with Gardiner was over a business venture. One year before the writ was taken out, Langley had set up business in the style of Henslowe, and built the Swan theatre on the Surrey shore of the Thames. The south side of the river bustled with 'entertainment' at that time; with theatres, brothels, a bear pit and a bull-baiting arena, all competing with each other. As part of this low life were gangsters seeking control: men like Langley and Gardiner. Shakspere's presence in their midst suggests he was either part of that scene, or at the very least, on its periphery.

On 4 May 1597, Shakspere was again in Stratford-upon-Avon, this time as a wealthy man. His purpose was to acquire two cottages, two barns, and New Place, the second largest house in the district. The purchase price of this alone was £60 (about £30,000 in today's money). The house had once belonged Sir Hugh Clopton, Lord Mayor of London, and at that time Stratford's most illustrious son. It was during the negotiations for this purchase that a further shadow was cast upon Shakspere's suspiciously dissolute character. Prior to his interest in the property, the house had been sold to William Bott, a lawyer and Alderman of Stratford, notorious for having swindled his son-in-law out of his property. Bott had poisoned his daughter inside New Place by feeding her ratsbane which, it is said, he kept concealed beneath a green carpet (Fido, 93). His motive for the murder was to ensure he obtained sole possession of the property.

From Bott, the house passed to William Underhill, *'a subtle, covetous and crafty man'* (Fido, 93-4) whose son, Fulke, had an even worse reputation. Two months after Underhill sold New Place to Shakspere, he was dead:

poisoned by Fulke, to whom he had promised the inheritance of all his lands. The crime was discovered and Fulke was hanged at Warwick. But his younger brother Hercules was suspicious, and he believed that Shakspere had colluded with the murderer in order to secure the £60 purchase price for the property. The matter went to court, but there being no proof of collusion, other than the absurdity of such a low price paid for the house, meant that Shakspere was able to secure a warranty from the court to secure his ownership.

Despite the many researches into Shakspere's background, and in contrast to the defamatory information, which his image-makers set aside almost as soon as it is discovered, since it does nothing to enhance the invented character they are creating, not one single substantive reference to his having written anything between 1594 and 1598 exists. Yet, we are told, not only did he compose many of his most enduring works of literature during that time, he was also regularly acting and directing plays in the daylight hours. Some even believe that he was still in attendance to the 3rd Earl of Southampton, widely regarded as the inspiration for his sonnets.

The problem, of course, is that different writers concentrate upon different aspects of the Shakespeare myth, and it is only when these are all viewed together that the contradictory nature of what is being alleged becomes evident. In short, there was never enough time for Shakspere to have done all that has been claimed for him.

There is also another problem, barely mentioned by his image-makers; it is the dispersion of Shakespeare's plays almost as soon as they were written. Henslowe's Diary reveals that on 3 March 1591 (Old Style), Lord Strange's Men performed *Henry VI* and the receipts taken were £3. 16s. 8d (between £1500 and £2000 by today's reckoning). The play was repeated on 7 March, and again on the 11th, the 16th, and the 28th of the month, after which it was performed in April on the 5th; the 13th, and the 21st. This implies that Shakspere was employed to write plays for Lord Strange. But, contrarily, *Titus Andronicus* was first performed for Henslowe at the Rose for Lord Sussex's Men on 23 January, 28 January, and 6 February.

After a short break, when the theatres were closed because of the fear of spreading the Plague, *Titus Andronicus* was again performed, this time on 5th and 12th of June, but it was then recorded as having been performed by the joint companies of the Admiral's Men and the Lord Chamberlain's Men. One is therefore entitled to ask: Just who was 'Shakespeare' writing for? And why, at the outset of his career, was this unrecorded actor (for he appeared on no lists) so liberally allowed to work as a freelance writer supplying plays for different companies? Freelance writing was at that time more readily available to aristocrats, who naturally received no payment for their work. This would then explain the total absence of Shakespeare's name in Henslowe's accounts, and perhaps the curious inclusion of *'ne'* (Latin for 'not') that Henslowe recorded against certain plays, especially those that are associated with Shakespeare.

These earlier plays also present other problems. *Titus Andronicus*, for example, has Chapter 9 to itself because of the vital information it provides in *proving* that Oxford was the author. Other plays, such as the *Histories* can be examined for the interesting peculiarities exposed in their composition. *Richard II*, for instance, is claimed to have been written in the year following publication of the *Rape of Lucrece*. It is said to be the first of his second tetralogy; that is, *Richard II; Henry IV, Part One; Henry IV, Part Two; Henry V;* According to orthodox dating, which is forced to operate within a very tight timeframe, these four plays were completed between 1594 and 1599. This is not an unreasonable claim to make, until that is: — betwixt these same years, Shakespeare is also said to have completed *Titus Andronicus*, (1594); *The Taming of the Shrew*, (1594); *The Two Gentlemen of Verona*, (1594-5); *Love's Labour's Lost*, (1594-5); *A Midsummer Night's Dream*, (1596); *King John*, (1596-7); *Romeo and Juliet*, (1596-7); *The Merchant of Venice*, (1596-7). And in 1599, when he was putting the final touches to *Henry V*, (1598-9), *Much Ado About Nothing* (1598-9); he then immediately began writing *Hamlet* (1599-1600); *Twelfth Night;* (1599-1600), and *Julius Caesar* (1599-1600). In the midst of this frenzy of activity, he had even begun *As You Like It*, (1596), *The Merry Wives of Windsor*, (1597), and *Troilus and Cressida*, (1597). And this is without mentioning the 154 Sonnets, written, it is said, during the same period.

This exhaustive schedule of work requires the research and writing of each play to be accomplished at the rate of one play every three months: written, of course, during the evening hours by candlelight. It is therefore of some interest to recall what we know of Shakspere during this period of between fifty and sixty months, when all this creativity was supposedly undertaken.

We know that in December 1594 he was involved with the Lord Chamberlain's Men in their production of two comedies or interludes; that in August 1596, he travelled to Stratford-upon-Avon following the death of his son Hamnet; that in October and November he was being pursued for the non-payment of tax; that in the same month of November he was again in trouble with the law, when a writ was issued against him for the surety of the peace; that in May 1597, he was again back in Stratford-upon-Avon, this time negotiating the purchase of New Place, for which he had to obtain a warranty from court to secure ownership of the property. One year later, in 1598, 'his' name, or rather Shake-speare, appears on the cast list of

Jonson's *Every Man In His Humour*. But since the name is hyphenated, one may assume it was *not* Shakspere. In January of that same year, Stratford businessmen, Abraham Sturley and Richard Quiney were discussing together whether Shakspere might be interested in *'the matter of our tithes [10% of the income obtainable from land]'* (Ogburn, 30).

> It semith bi him that our countriman, Mr Shakspere, is willinge to disburse some monei upon some od yarde land or other att Shottri or neare about us; he thinketh it a veri fitt patterne to move him to deale in the matter of our tithes. Bi the instructions u can geve him thereof, and by the frendes he can make therefore, we thinke it a faire marke for him to shoote att, and not unpossible to hitt. (Halliwell-Phillipps, 172)

In that same year famine spread across parts of England, and Shakspere again fell foul of the law. At a time when his name was about to become even more famous as the author of twelve anonymous plays, he was in Stratford. A record of his presence is included in an entry made by the Justices of the Peace, who had been ordered by the Privy Council to investigate those hoarding grain. Concerning this illegality, we learn that *'in the xl$^{th}$ yeare of the raigne of our moste gracious Soveraigne Ladie Queen Elizabethe ... Wm Shackespere of Chapple Street Ward, Stratford [held] x quarters of grain [640 gallons ≈ 2910 litres]'* (Shakespeare Birthplace Trust Records).

> Hoarding drove up the price of wheat and barley (called corn and malt respectively in Elizabethan times) and the shortages led to brawls and open revolt, and the hoarders were condemned as "wicked people in conditions more like to wolves and cormorants than to natural men" (Matus, 38).

This led one enraged citizen to publicly express the wish that – *'God send my Lord of Essex down shortly, to see them hanged on gibbets at their own doors'* (Ogburn, 30). But Essex stayed away and 'Shackespere' was saved from the noose. Irvin Matus attempted to diffuse the situation by comparing 'Shackespere' to other hoarders in Stratford, thus allowing that he was no better than they. Well, yes! But, then we are talking about greedy, opportunistic vermin that preyed on the needy. And, let it not be forgotten that *'in London he repeatedly failed to pay the taxes that supported the poor and aged'* (Duncan Jones, 164). In these two instances, Shakspere can be seen true to life: a dishonourable, greedy man, with no care for those in need; so very different from the *'Sweet Master Shakespeare'* of literary fame.

In October of the same year, having returned to London, Shakspere is once again listed as a tax defaulter: this time for the sum of thirteen shillings and fourpence. Later in the month Richard Quiney arrived in London to conduct some legal business on behalf of Stratford-upon-Avon.

It was while staying at the Bell Inn in Carter Lane that he wrote a letter dated 25 October 1598 – *'To my Lovinge good ffrende & countreymann Mr Wm. Shackespere'* (Laroque, 133), requesting a loan of £30, *'uppon Mr Bushells & my securytee or Mr Myttons with me'* (ibid). But the letter was never delivered. Or, perhaps it was delivered and returned to sender unopened, the messenger having discovered that 'Wm. Shackespere' had already left town. For, several weeks later, his name reappears in the Stratford records, this time in receipt of ten pence for supplying a load of stone. Would it not have made better sense for him to receive money by publishing 'his' sonnets, assuming they were his? This lack of interest in money for 'his' literary work is all the more extraordinary when we read the comments made about him in letters that have survived.

For instance, a letter from Richard Quiney to his son Thomas at the Bell Inn, in London, advised – *'Yff you bargen with Wm. Sha. or receve money ther, or brynge youre money home, yow maye.'* (Halliwell-Phillipps, 175). Another letter dated 4 November 1598; written by Abraham Sturley in response to a letter he received dated the same day that Thomas dated his undelivered letter to Shakspere, warned against borrowing money from their neighbour. *"And that our countriman Mr. Wm. Shak. would procure us money, we. I will like of, as I shall heare when, and wheare, and howe; and I prai let not go that occasion, if it mai sorte to ani indifferent condicions.'* (ibid). Shakspere's neighbours knew their man far better than any biographer has done since.

A further matter of interest with regard to Shakspere at this time concerns the coat of arms that John Shakspere applied for *circa* 1568. The Clarencieux King-of-Arms at that time was Robert Cook, and he refused the application. There the matter rested until October 1596, when William revived his father's request for arms.

The application was founded upon a false claim that the family's antecedents had been rewarded for services to Henry VII. The new Garter-King-at-Arms, William Dethick, approved the grant, and John Shakspere and son became entitled to call themselves Gentlemen; the exact date on which this was approved is unknown. In the event, however, the application and subsequent granting of arms to Shakspere became a key piece of evidence when prosecuting Dethick for fraudulent practices.

> It is an authentic fact that Sir William Dethick, who was Garter-King-at-Arms in 1596 and 1599, was called to account for having forged pedigrees and granted coats to persons whose circumstances and station in society gave them no right to the distinction; the case of John Shakespeare was expressly charged against him. (Gervinus, 467)

Since it is unlikely that John Shakspere travelled four days to London in order to appeal an application for arms that had been turned down more than thirty years earlier, especially when he had then been both younger and more affluent, attention focuses on his son, William. What had changed to instil new confidence that an application this time would be more successful than the last? The answer is the adjudicator. Dethick's reputation for inventing pedigrees in exchange for money was almost akin to Shakspere's role of pretending to write plays in return for payment.

No one other than Shakspere could have revived his father's application for arms, in which case, bribery and fraud have to be added to his growing list of vices: with pretentiousness included for good measure. There is no evidence whatever that Henry VII rewarded Shakspere's great-grandfather with *'lands'* and *'tenements'*, which had been claimed was the reason for the grant of arms; the revised and amended application had been a total fraud, financed and given a spurious legitimacy by what was surely a 'backhander' to Dethick; it is unlikely that he did it for free, or from the kindness of his heart.

Amazingly, Shakspere's adulators actually boast about this acquisition of a coat of arms, thus subscribing to the belief that it had been legitimately obtained. Instead, it is just another part of the mythology attending the sanitized image of 'William Shakespeare', created by his image-makers, and which is vulnerable to the truth.

Shakspere's attempt to achieve the status of a gentleman may have arisen from feelings of inferiority, perhaps related to the esteem that was shown by those ignorant of the fact that he was not the author of the plays and poems attributed to him. Such feelings would be natural for a person living under the false pretence of being someone looked up to in the world of letters, but without any substance supporting it.

Some evidence of scorn at his aspiration to be known as a gentleman is contained in Jonson's play, *Every Man Out of His Humour*. In one scene, a country yokel named Sogliardo is lampooned as being *'so enamoured of the name of a gentleman, that he will have it though he buys it.'* And for his motto, the suggestion made is: *'Not Without Mustard'*. Shakspere's self-acclaimed motto was, *'Not Without Right'*. The joke about mustard is said to refer to the mustard colour of the arms granted to Shakspere.

Jonson's lack of respect for Shakspere, confirmed by the affirmation that he had *bought* the honour was made one year after the hyphenated name, Shake-speare, was given first place at the head of the actors who played *Every Man In His Humour*. It therefore presents a curious contrast to his characterisation of *Sogliardo*; unless, that is, *the* William Shake-speare leading Jonson's cast list was not *the* Shakspere he ridiculed as *Sogliardo*.

This would certainly appear to be the case, according to anecdotal evidence. The story has survived that Jonson had taken his script to the Chamberlain's Men, only to have it rejected. But to Jonson's good fortune, Shakespeare happened to pick it up and saw sufficient merit in it for a performance to be arranged. For Jonson, it was the beginning of his career as a recognised playwright, and his gratitude to Shakespeare would never have allowed him to lampoon his benefactor as Sogliardo.

These years of silence from, 1594 to 1598, have shown two sides to the biographical figure of William Shakespeare. On the one hand, there is documentary evidence indicating that Shakspere was a tax evader, a grain hoarder, a purchaser of honours under false pretences, the confederate of a south London gang leader, and in collusion with a murderer. On the other hand, there is the biographer's undocumented but imaginative version that places their man at the heart of the theatre. It is imaginative because the biographer projects his knowledge of the plays known to have been written by Shakespeare onto the seedy life of Shakspere, when there is no actual, substantive evidence to support it.

Of course, factually, Shakespeare was highly praised by a number of influential people during his time, but that does not make him Shakspere. What guarantees Shakespeare as Shakspere, the Warwickshire poet and dramatist from Stratford-upon-Avon, is documentary evidence that some people, essentially his family, his neighbours, even his business associates, made some passing reference to his being that person while he was alive. None ever did. This was also noticeable at the time of his funeral. Until biographers can provide that guarantee, their work inevitably ranges between historical romance and a rather unconvincing literary theory. Let the buyer beware.

# 7

## SILENT TONGUES GIVE PRAISE

Quite apart from the lack of any documentary evidence in support of Shakespeare's literary pursuits between the years 1594 and 1598, there exist records that specifically refer to Shakespeare's silence.

> To Mr William Shake-speare
> Shake-speare, we must be silent in thy praise,
> 'Cause our encomions will but blast thy bays
> Which envy could not, that thou didst so well;
> Let thine own histories prove thy Chronicle. (Ogburn, 9)

Where has a similar sentiment to this been expressed before? It is, of course, in *The Arte of English Poesie* (1589) by George Puttenham, which bears repeating.

> Noblemen and Gentlemen of Her Majesty's own servants, who have written excellently well as it would appear if their doings could be found out and made public with the rest, of which number is first that noble gentleman Edward Earl of Oxford. (Ogburn, 621)

Is there a connection between these two extracts? There is certainly a common factor. It is one of silence. Puttenham states that silence has been observed where poetry is known to be written by a member of the nobility. He then goes further by adding that Lord Oxford is amongst the first of those to whom this applies. What then do we find in the anonymously written verse? It is a very similar acknowledgement. Do not offer any praise to this man Shake-speare. Now, notice that the unknown author has also refused to write the name in its unbroken form. Instead, he has twice hyphenated it; which seems to be a growing signal of personal awareness that the name is pseudonymous: hence the secrecy, and need for silence.

The second observation is how the author has addressed Shake-speare directly; that is, in the same way a person who is still alive is addressed. Yet, factually, this poem was not printed until 1640, when it was included as an anonymous epigram in *Wit's Recreations Selected from the Finest Fancies of Modern Muses*. Since Shakspere had been dead for the past twenty-four years, and Oxford, half as long again, the epigram makes no sense, unless it was originally written when both men were alive. This may have been the case, as Clare Asquith pointed out: there were manuscripts circulating in the late fifteenth and early sixteenth century, which included *'double and triple meanings within printed texts'* (Asquith, 282-3). Had this verse been written while both men were still alive, it would then account for the author's anonymity.

Let us look again at the hyphenated surname. The name Shake-speare does not appear hyphenated in either *Venus and Adonis* or *Lucrece*, despite Shapiro's assertion to the contrary. But, by deliberately hyphenating it twice, the anonymous author has sent a clear signal to Shake-speare, whom he was addressing, and of course to each attentive reader, that he has inside knowledge regarding the person behind that name. Why else hyphenate it? But in the context of an epigram, that is intended to portray sarcasm or satire, drawing attention to a name that has been deliberately hyphenated was as good as a nod and a wink to all but the blind.

Apologists for Shakspere maintain there was nothing extraordinary in the hyphenation of his name; it was not unusual. Shapiro incorrectly thought it was the type-setter's response to using italic font. It certainly was unusual, because no record exists of Shakespeare's name having been hyphenated in connection with his legal or business dealings. It is only ever hyphenated when someone refers to the name in a literary context, as though to indicate their awareness of the name's pseudish nature.

Since Shakspere's apologists are very quick to excuse the hyphenated surname, what do they say regarding the need for silent praise? This turns out to be another stumbling block for those committed to papering over the cracks in the Stratford theory, for it defies a rational response. Orthodox opinion is struck silent when confronted by this unanswerable question. Quite simply, there is no answer that would account for secrecy where praise for a man of Shakspere's background was concerned. Yet, silent praise for Shake-speare is what the epigram is about.

The next part of the verse has the potential to be even more revealing, because the anonymous author provides the reason for this silence. It is, he states, because our expressions of high praise (encomiums) might *blast thy bays*. What 'bays' are these? The only bays referred to in this context are those claimed by the 17th Earl of Oxford when he offered them to any poet capable of defeating him in a rhyming contest. His challenge appeared in a collection of poems called *The Paradise of Dainty Devices*. Oxford was so adept at impromptu rhyme that he took part in several rhyming duels with other poets, and it is his personal exclamation of triumph that connects him to the anonymously written epigram addressed to Shakespeare.

> A Crown of Bays shall that man wear
> That triumphs over me: (Nelson, 158)

These lines were among those first published in 1576, and the entire collection proved so popular with the public that it was reprinted at least eight times, taking it well into the seventeenth century. This being so, the anonymous epigram writer, to whom we have been referring, can be seen as having alerted Shake-speare to the need for special care, wherever praise is directed at his work.

This warning was necessary because too much praise for Shake-speare would have the effect of an advertisement: it would threaten to blast — blow open, blaze, reveal — Oxford as the rightful owner and wearer of the Shakespeare *bays*.

The epigram writer must therefore have been fully aware Shakspere was Oxford's allonym, and the utmost care was needed, lest praise given to Shake-speare for his work, and which fell upon Shakspere, could become the means of destroying Oxford's efforts to publish his work. A request for silence was therefore of considerable importance.

This epigrammatist then provides further information by disclosing that *envy* had previously failed to *blast* Shakespeare's *bays*. This comment is in keeping with human nature: it being only natural to suppose that some writers amongst the literary elite of the day had grown envious of how Shake-speare's position and talent were being conferred onto Shakspere; who, as a writer, was *'a provincial nobody'* – so-called by a resident in Stratford-upon-Avon at his Jubilee in 1769 (Chapter 21).

Envy of Shakspere had had the very real potential of producing the same effect as praise, since they both placed Shake-speare at the focal point of attention. Either way, the possibility of his secret spilling into the public domain became a serious possibility, and this would have been why the epigram had been circulating in manuscript for so long. To have published it while Oxford lived would have drawn wider attention to its meaning.

The epigram writer concludes with a further expression of the author's wit by suggesting that Shake-speare's *Histories* be examined to prove his own *Chronicle*. In fact, the *Histories* provide a rich source of difficulties for those wedded to the Stratford theory. *Richard II*, allegedly begun in 1595 and completed a year later, was described on 6th February 1601, by

Augustine Phillips, as *'so old, and so long out of use that the house would be poor and the takings thin'*. The Queen, too, was able to recall how *'this tragedy was played 40ᵗⁱᵉ times in open streets and houses'* (Ogburn, 10).

These two references conflict with the suggested date of composition posited by traditionalists, and this is not helped by the further knowledge that the play contains information from two documents that were not in circulation. One of these, *La Chronicque de la Traison et Mort de Richart Deux roy Dengleterre* [The chronicle of the treason and death of Richard II, king of England] was owned by John Stow; the other, *Histoire du Roy d'Angleterre Richard* [History of King Richard of England] was owned by Elizabeth's court astrologer, Dr. John Dee. *'These accounts were not easily come by in England, for their anti-Lancastrian sentiment was not acceptable to Henry the Fourth and his descendants'* (Alexander, vol.2 84).

Oxford knew Dee personally. But how Shakspere could have known the existence of either document, let alone to have acquired access to them, are further examples of the unanswerable questions that befog and vex those committed to explaining the legendary exploits of the mysterious William Shakespeare.

*King John*, a play allegedly begun the year that *Richard II* was finished is another that gives pause for thought. An earlier play called *The Troublesome Raigne of King John*, for which a Quarto edition was published in 1591, is claimed with justification to be the forerunner of Shakespeare's historical drama:

> for its author ... reveals, were he indeed its creator, powers of construction and invention that Shakespeare himself was to acknowledge in what is regarded as his rehandling of the work ... the author of *The Troublesome Raigne* may be fairly held to have anticipated Shakespeare and even to have instructed him; for Shakespeare's *King John* follows *The Troublesome Raigne* almost scene for scene. ... Whatever his deficiencies the anonymous author of *The Troublesome Raigne* must be given high commendation for his constructive powers. (Alexander, vol.2 25)

A more realistic interpretation of this account would suggest that Lord Oxford wrote *The Troublesome Raigne* during the late 1580s and thereafter edited and revised it for the public stage as *King John*; in fact, a clue to its date of composition has been written into the text:

King Philip:  So by a roaring tempest on its flood
              A whole armado of convicted sail
              Is scatter'd and disjoin'd from fellowship.

(Act 3: sc. iv)

By any consideration, this represents an apt description of the fate that befell King Philip's Spanish Armada in the summer of 1588. Nor can the writing of *Love's Labour's Lost* be exempted from an equally early date. The character, *'Don Adriano de Armado, a fantastical Spaniard'*, would have been extremely topical as a figure of fun, especially with a name connecting him to the recently defeated Spanish Armada. Seven years later, the joke would have been so stale as to be barely noticeable.

Moreover, the repeated staging of *The Troublesome Raigne* provides the reason for its publication in 1591. Later, into the mid-1590s, with the leisure to rework his earlier plays, Oxford revised it. After appreciating its strengths, which were left in, and correcting its weaknesses, one of which was to eliminate the play's anti-papist sentiment, it received the shorter title of *King John*. But after Francis Meres reported its attribution to Shakespeare in 1598 (*infra*), nothing more was heard of it, either in performance or print, until it re-emerged in the First Folio edition of 1623.

Turning to another history, with a history of its own, *Henry VI* was preceded by two anonymously written plays: *The Contention Between the Two Famous Houses of Yorke and Lancaster* and *The True Tragedy of Richard Duke of Yorke*. Concerning these two earlier plays, Professor Alexander wrote:

> They treat of the same action as 2 and 3 Henry VI, introduce the same characters, and contain much verse in common with the Folio texts; 3 Henry VI has about 2,900 lines, and of these some 2,000 on Malone's reckoning are found, sometimes word for word, sometimes in various transformations, in the True Tragedy. (ibid 406)

The simplest explanation for what is otherwise blatant plagiarism on a grand scale by Shakespeare is that Oxford wrote *The Troublesome Raigne*, *The Contention*, and *The True Tragedy* as early court dramas during the 1580s, and then revised and updated them for further showing as *King John*, and *Henry VI*. This would explain the two pirated editions of *The Contention*, and *The True Tragedy*: both of which, appeared as 'Bad Quartos' in 1594 and 1595 respectively.

> The Contention, and The True Tragedy belong to the group of texts Pollard called the Bad Quartos and show all the marks of plays put together from memory and odd players' parts.
> (ibid 407)

Neither one of these two plays was challenged legally, nor did the anonymous author come forward to identify himself and exercise his right to 'stay' their publication, if only to protect his reputation against the indiscriminate use of his work—a trait shared by the poet of *Shake-speares*

*Sonnets,* and with the pirated quartos that were printed with Shakespeare's name given as their author. One may therefore reasonably ask: Why this silence? Was there a bond between the anonymous author, who, prior to 1598, never complained, and the author post 1598, who though named, never protested at the indiscriminate use of his name, or the unauthorised publication of his work?

Whatever answer is given, it will always exclude Shakspere. He was a frequent litigant against those who failed to honour their contractual obligations. The number of prosecutions he brought against offenders is so well known that to suppose he would have stood idly by while the fruit of his creative labour was enjoyed by another is absurd. Nevertheless, it is accepted as fact by Shakespeare experts, whose critical ability has become numbed by the slow, steady and unwavering approval they have given to the very many improbabilities that surround Shakspere's supposed genius.

The unknown author of the epigram, with which this chapter began, appears to have been aware of the facts regarding the composition of these *Histories*. Aware that *The Troublesome Raigne of King John* and *King John* were the work of a single author; aware that *The Contention Between the Two Famous Houses of Yorke and Lancaster* and *The True Tragedy of Richard Duke of Yorke* were the same plays that their author rewrote as *2 and 3 Henry VI* and aware that the *Famous Victories of Henry the Fift* was a forerunner to *1 and 2 Henry IV* and *Henry V*.

As a person living when these plays were performed, the anonymous epigrammatist's parting remark: *thine own Histories prove thy Chronicle* would have been intended to relay as clear a signal as possible that he knew the true identity of Shake-speare and the reason why *we must be silent in thy praise*. In which case, this reason need be no different from the one given by Puttenham. The author was a nobleman and a member of Elizabeth's Court.

It is also of some interest that the Histories, to which the epigram writer has referred, were *chronicle plays*. He was therefore indicating that these plays possessed a similarity to the author's own *chronicle*. In the case of the 17th Earl of Oxford, this was perfectly true. His ancestors, Aubrey de Vere and John de Vere, appear as *dramatic personae* in Richard III and 3 Henry VI. To equate the chronicle of both earls with that of their descendent, Edward de Vere, can be seen as the epigrammatist's means of directing attention to Shake-speare's ancestry, and from there to his own identity.

Otherwise, there was the likelihood, as things then stood, that the author would never be acknowledged for his work, especially since silent praise was all he could look forward to.

From this, it necessarily follows that if the person referred to by the unknown epigrammatist was indeed the Earl of Oxford, then as the subject of the epigram, he would have been all too aware that silent praise from those who knew his secret identity as Shakespeare, as well as ignorance from those who did not, must eventually lead to his lasting anonymity. Is there any evidence that Oxford recognised this? There is certainly evidence that Shakespeare did.

In Sonnet 72, Shakespeare wrote: *My name be buried where my body is, / And live no more to shame, nor me nor you.* If Shakespeare *was* the real name of the poet who wrote these words, how can it make sense to claim that this same name will be buried along with his body? What the poet is saying is that his real name will be buried together with his body, but the sonnets he wrote will live on under the name of another author.

Consider also Sonnet 81, in which Shakespeare confessed to his subject: *From hence your memory death cannot take, / Although in me each part will be forgotten.* Once again, the poet is reflecting upon his death, knowing in advance that very soon after his burial, the memory of him will quickly be forgotten, although his work will live on. He openly admits this when he reminded his subject: *You still shall live, such virtue have my pen.* In the same sonnet, he pursued this theme further: *Your name from hence immortal life shall have, / Though I, once gone, to all the world must die.* Repeatedly, the poet is recognising that he, linked to his own name, will fade from the world's memory. But he also recognised the lasting effect his own genius would have: *Not marble nor the gilded monuments / Of princes shall outlive this pow'rful rhyme,* (Sonnet 55).

The evidence that Shakespeare was the pseudonym of an unnamed poet, most certainly a nobleman for the reason given by Puttenham, has been staring academics in the face for centuries. But they have refused to accept that they may have been mistaken; even when their error, in the poet's own hand, is placed before them.

The reason for this is best described as collective denial. Any evidence or argument confirming that Shakespeare was a pseudonym, however strong, is collectively denied by the cohesion of academic resistance. They can always be relied upon to authoritatively declare, *en masse*, that since they *know* Shakespeare to be the author of these plays and sonnets, it is futile to suggest an alternative. Truth dismissed by authority. But enquire further, as to how it is that they know: for the knowledge does not come from the senses, so it must be derived from reason, and their authority appears less certain.

When critically examined, the explanations given by academics are weak, illogical, and puerile. One is even left astounded at the shallowness of their research, and totally bemused that normally intelligent men and women could lend their names to a theory that does not work; and which, in fact, is palpable to refutation by words from the poet's own hand.

In further pursuit of the direction which the links in this current chain of reasoning are joined; from Puttenham to the anonymous epigrammatist, to the sonnets, we arrive at a poet, who is a member of the nobility, and who has concealed his identity behind the name Shakespeare; for that is the logical conclusion to be drawn from the evidence given. In order to be further assured of this silent poet's identity, we turn next to John Marston.

Marston was the son of a gentleman lawyer, and educated in Coventry before attending Oxford University. After being awarded his degree, he joined the Middle Temple to study law. With his education completed, he turned his attention to poetry and playwriting, whereupon, between 1599 and 1601, he became embroiled in a war of words with Ben Jonson. The two men were later reconciled following the dignified Latin dedication he made to Jonson in his play *The Malcontent*. In 1608 Marston was sent to prison for remarks made against King James. After his release, he retired from the theatre and returned to Oxford to be ordained. He spent the remainder of his life in service to the Church, becoming priest in the town of Christchurch in Hampshire. He was buried in London at the Middle Temple.

As poet, playwright and gentleman, Marston was well connected. What unites him to the authorship debate is a quoted reference he made in a poem called *The Scourge of Villainy*. In the midst of Satyre IX, which he prefixes with *'Here's a Toy to mocke an Ape indeed,'* he wrote:

> My soule adores judiciall schollership;
> But when to servile imitatorship
> Some spruce Athenian pen is prentized,
> Tis worse than apish.
> ....
>     Farre fly thy fame,
> Most, most of me beloved! Whose silent name
> One letter bounds. Thy true judiciall stile

> I ever honour; and if my love beguile
> Not much my hopes, then thy unvalued worth
> Shall mount faire place, when apes are turned forth.

Once again there is this reference to a *silent name*. However, on this occasion, Marston has left a clue. The name is bounded by a single letter. Others who have read this verse have found no difficulty in arriving at the name Edward de Vere, observing that it is bounded by the letter 'E'. In fact, there is no viable alternative. The names of Elizabethan poets and playwrights are sufficiently well-known. Consequently, Nicholas Breton is sometimes mentioned as the subject of Marston's verse. But, apart from the obvious fact that there was no reason why Breton's name should remain a secret, it is also the case that in 1598, when Marston published *Scourge of Villainy*, Breton had written very little of note. His best poetry is almost entirely confined to the early years of the seventeenth century; too late to have attracted Marston's attention, apart from which, Breton had neither a gift for, nor much interest in satire, preferring religious subjects and country idylls for themes.

Just for the record there was one other poet whose name was bounded by a single letter. This was Robert Chester. His most noted work, *Love's Martyr* was published in 1601: again, too late to have attracted Marston's interest. However, *Love's Martyr* was accompanied by shorter poems from Marston, Ben Jonson, George Chapman, the mysterious 'Ignoto' (thought to be the Earl of Oxford) and a longer work, untitled, but known as *The Phoenix and the Turtle* by Shakespeare.

By accepting Edward de Vere as the person occupying Marston's ideal, the description he gives falls into place. There is the fervent wish that his subject's fame will *'far fly'*; there is also a reference to his subject's *'judicial style'*, which is evident enough in everything written by Shakespeare, and there is Marston's reference to his subject's *'unvalued worth'* Have we not heard this same complaint before in the Sonnets? Certainly, it is found in Shakespeare's Sonnet 72 (referred to above), which concludes with the couplet: *For I am sham'd by that which I bring forth, / And so should you, to love things nothing worth.* Finally, there is the poet's *silent name one letter bounds.*

Everything in Marston's verse points to Edward de Vere as the silent name and the subject to whom he is referring. Even the words he uses, *I ever honour* can be seen as a deliberate play on E. Ver, an alternative spelling of Vere. Marston also paraphrases Richard III's final cry at Bosworth Field, which, in Satyre VII, becomes: *"A man, a man, my kingdome for a man.* 'For a poet and playwright of Marston's stature to paraphrase the lines of another poet and playwright, must speak of the high regard that he held for Oxford's work, and which he wished to register in his own cryptic way.

It is not surprising therefore to discover Marston's initials beneath a letter of remembrance at the front of the First Folio. In this, it is noticeable that the writer has declined to spell Shakespeare's name as it was written in *Venus and Adonis* and *Lucrece*; preferring, instead, to join with those who wrote it in its hyphenated form, thereby following a pattern that had been set by others, in signalling this to be a penname. Orthodox opinion inclines to the belief that the dedication was written by James Mabbe, a fellow of Magdalen College, Oxford, and a translator with no obvious connection to Shakespeare or the theatre. Yet the memorial poem is full of allusions to the theatre with which Marston was familiar. Marston was also on friendly terms with Jonson, their quarrel having long since been repaired. Jonson's supervision of the preface material in the First Folio is clear from his dismissal of Digges's longer poem, which, as we shall later see, had to wait for a later edition of Shakespeare's work, before it was published.

In summary, we know that apart from the anonymous epigrammatist who addressed *Mr William Shake-speare* by declaring: *Shakes-speare, we must be silent in thy praise:* John Marston also made a similar declaration when he referred to the *judicial style* of a writer *I ever honour, whose silent name one letter bounds.* It is also understood why these references could only apply to Edward de Vere. We know, too, from Marston that the work of this unnamed writer, whom we may refer to as Lord Oxford, was of *unvalued worth* and that Shakespeare also confessed to his work being thought *nothing worth.* We further know from George Puttenham that *Edward Earl of Oxford* was considered to be *first* amongst the noblemen attending Court to have *written excellently well as it would appear* if the work of these gentlemen could be made public. The Earl of Oxford would therefore have needed to ensure that his name remained silent, once his poetry was published, as Marston's verse suggested was actually the case. Hence, for this reason, Oxford could expect only silent praise, as the epigrammatist confirmed was the fate of Shake-speare.

It is therefore impossible to understand how this compilation of factual information can be seen as not pointing to Lord Oxford, and his having used the penname, Shakespeare. Yet academic opinion refuses even to consider this possibility. This is not to say that these academics are in want of intelligence. It rather suggests, instead, that they dwell in Plato's Cave. Inside this insular abode they have before them the works of Shakespeare: and their assessment of his plays and poetry contains all the scholarship one would expect from such a select and qualified group. But Shakespeare himself remains a shadow on the wall. Instead of turning to the light to see who has cast this shadow, they prefer to sit around the fire in discussion, projecting their imagination onto the silhouette before them.

# 8

# PREDATING VENUS AND ADONIS

In 1590, Edmund Spenser published *Tears of the Muses*. The poem bewailed the neglect that writers were then giving to the *Heliconian imps*. This was the name Spenser had applied to the muses in a sonnet addressed to the Earl of Oxford, in which he described them as being most dear to his subject and he to them.

This connection between Oxford and the muses is important, because both *Tears of the Muses* and the sonnet were published in the same year. The occasion was Spenser's publication of *The Faerie Queen*. Several writers had contributed a poetic tribute for inclusion at the front of this book, including one from *Ignoto* (the Unknown). Spenser responded to his admirers by composing seventeen sonnets, the third of which he addressed to the Earl of Oxford (*most probably Ignoto*).

This sonnet later became of special interest, because when composing his dedication to Shakespeare for the First Folio, Ben Jonson paraphrased lines taken from *Ignoto's* poem, thereby suggesting *Ignoto* was connected to Shakespeare. This increases the likelihood that *Ignoto* was a penname used by Oxford, whose rank at Court required anonymity.

Thalia, the Muse of comedy, is addressed by two verses in Spenser's poem that refer to a poet whose identity has intrigued experts ever since.

> And he the Man, whom Nature self had made
> To mock her self, and Truth to imitate,
> With kindly Counter under Mimick Shade,
> Our pleasant Willy, ah! is dead of late:
> With whom all Joy and jolly Merriment
> Is also deaded, and in Dolour drent.
> ...
> But that same gentle Spirit, from whose Pen
> Large Streams of Honey and sweet Nectar flow,
> Scorning the Boldness of such base-born Men,
> Which dare their Follies forth so rashly throw;
> Doth rather choose to sit in idle Cell,
> Than so himself to Mockery to sell.

The clues to this hidden identity are fairly straightforward: the most prominent occurs in the fourth line of the first of these two verses, where Spenser calls him *Willy*. Nicholas Rowe believed both verses referred to William Shakespeare, for he included them in his first edition of the Bard's collected plays; viz. *Some Account of the Life &c. of Mr. William Shakespeare*. But he omitted them when a second edition went to print five years later in 1714. John Dryden never doubted they referred to Shakespeare, and it may have been his influence that caused Rowe to share the same opinion.

The attribution to Shakspere has to be false. In 1590, he was just twenty-six years old, and completely unknown; whereas, Spenser expected his readers, some at least, to know who was meant by *Willy*. A second clue provided by Spenser refers to the man's '*scorn*' for '*base-born men*'. This implies that *Willy* was not from the lower classes. He was therefore highborn: a titled gentleman at least or perhaps even a member of the nobility. This would explain why previous commentators have found difficulty identifying him amongst untitled writers.

We are therefore reminded of George Puttenham and his *Arte of English Poesy*, published just one year earlier, in which he singled out *"that noble gentleman Edward Earl of Oxford"* as being *"first"* amongst the *"Noblemen and Gentlemen of Her Majesty's own servants, who have written excellently well as it would appear if their doings could be found out and made public."* This reference reminds us that it was Spenser, himself, who wrote a sonnet addressed to Oxford: written in the same year that he published *Tears of the Muses*, where he described Oxford's relationship to the muses – the very subject he was writing about – as *"the love which thou dost bear / To th'Heliconian imps— and they to thee."* From this, it may be concluded that the tears, shed so profusely by the muses, were not shed on account of Oxford's writing, for both *Tears of the Muses* and the admiration expressed in the sonnet to Oxford were written in the same year.

Spenser then adds a qualifying remark. The poet whose lines he has likened to '*Large Streams of Honey and sweet Nectar ... Doth rather choose to sit in idle Cell.*' This must refer to the verse before, in which he remarked: *"Willy, ah! is dead of late,"* for it links up with the time his subject spent in idleness, and to which he next refers. The question raised is: Where was Oxford prior to, and including 1590? Does the evidence building up to the conclusion that Oxford was *Willy* still hold true?

If we go back in time by eighteen months, we arrive at 5 Jun 1588, where, at the Queen's Court, Greenwich, the Earl of Oxford's wife, Anne

Cecil, having suffered a debilitating fever, breathed her last; she was aged only thirty-one. Anne was buried at Westminster three weeks later, but her widowed husband was not recorded amongst those attending the funeral.

Less than a month after Anne had been laid to rest, Spanish ships appeared off the English coast, and the grieving husband was called to serve the Queen in defence of the realm. Lord Burghley recorded Oxford's involvement as: *'the Erle of Oxford also in his tyme repayared to the sea co[a]st, for seruice of the Queen in the navy.'* (Nelson, 315). Records indicate that Oxford put to sea during this time, but was recalled to become Governor of Harwich. This was an important harbour town on the eastern shoreline. *'The seacoaste is here and ther furnished with harbours for shipping, whereof the principall is Harwiche.'* (ibid 8). Oxford's role is corroborated by the Earl of Leicester in a letter sent to Walsingham, dated 1 August 1588.

> I did as hir maiestie liked well of deleuer to my Lord of Oxford hir gratious concent of his willingness to serve her. And for that he was content to serve here amonge the formost as he semed, she was pleased that he shuld have the gouerment of Harwich & all those that ar[e] appointed to attend that place which should be ijM [=2000] men. A place of trust & of great daunger. (ibid)

Oxford's active role at Harwich, and its importance, is also suggested by the following report.

> [W]hen old Harbottle Grimston was writing from Bradfield in 1643 asking for £100 to fortify Harwich, he recalled that in 1588, the year of the Armada, new defences were constructed 'with not less than 46 great guns upon them', and there were 17,000 soldiers. (ibid)

With no wish to remain in Harwich once Spain's broken fleet had limped home, Oxford returned to London, with his affairs in ruin, and demands for money he could no longer meet.

> In round sums, Oxford owed the Crown £3000 for his wardship, £4000 for his livery (apparently including a relatively negligible 'fine' for his marriage), a pittance for rents still unpaid from the time of his minority, and £4445 in penalties – in effect, accumulated interest. (Nelson, 334)

In today's money, this would be equivalent to a staggering 5·7 million pounds. Oxford's response was to sell what remained of his estates. Fishers Folly was sold to the Cornwallis family, including an adjoining ten acres of land disposed of separately. At the same time, Vere House in Oxford Place was sold. His company of actors, Oxford's Men, was disbanded, for they disappear from the records after performing at Maidstone in Kent in 1589-90 (Ogburn, 644), and are not heard of again until the mid 1590s. He also disposed of the liability to maintain his ancestral home at Hedingham by assigning it to Lord Burghley in trust for his three children. His abode from 1588 until his second marriage at the close of 1591 is unknown.

It is, however, on record that he attended Queen Elizabeth's Eighth Parliament during February and March of '89. He was also present when Philip Howard was charged with treason in April that year. It is therefore likely that he was dwelling in London or at least within easy reach of the capital. Plaistow House, which he still owned, but was being renovated, even while he negotiated the sale of Fishers Folly, may have been fit for dwelling. Plaistow was then one of several villages lying on the outskirts of London, not far from Hackney, but has long since been absorbed by the capital's expanding boundary.

An alternative dwelling was inside the capital. For it was during this time that Oxford rented accommodation from Julia Penn, the mother of Michael Hicks, Lord Burghley's secretary. Having been forced to vacate Fishers Folly with his school of writers, his idea had apparently been to relocate them in alternative premises, and thus ensure the flow of literature would continue as before.

His old retainer, Thomas Churchyard, was charged with the renting of the premises at the Penn house on St Peter's Hill. The rental was £100 per annum. The house was a large old building that had been the property of *'the Abbot of St Mary in York'*, and fit for the purpose Oxford had in mind. However, it very quickly became apparent that even this tenancy was beyond Oxford's means, and Churchyard was forced to terminate the agreement in fear of being arrested for debt. Mistress Penn responded by writing directly to Oxford: in doing so, she revealed that the tenancy had been a retreat for Oxford's group of writers.

> My Lord of Oxford: The great grief and sorrow I have taken for your unkind dealing with me ... You know, my Lord, you had anything in my house whatsoever you or your men would demand, if it were in my house; if it had been a thousand times more I would have been glad to pleasure your Lordship withal. (Nelson. 329)

Thus, prior to 1590, Oxford was in deep financial trouble: a widower with three daughters to support and no home to call his own. This is not the man that Shakespeare lovers like to believe is the poet they so greatly admire, but it fits the description of Spenser's *Willy*, who *is dead of late*: despondent, alone, possibly contemplating suicide, and with neither the desire nor the inspiration to write again. Or, as Spenser much better explained: *With whom all Joy and jolly Merriment / Is also deaded, and in Dolour drent.*

We shall give the final word regarding Spenser's reference to *Our pleasant Willy* to John Looney (his Manx name is shared by many other people as an Internet search will quickly reveal). In 1920, Looney published *Shakespeare Identified*: it was a book that created a deal of momentum amongst intellectuals when it was published, and which this work, too, is proud to call its ancestor.

Looney drew attention to the possessive pronoun *our* used by Spenser to identify *Willy*. He had not far to look to discover why this was. In 1579, Spenser had published, although anonymously, the *Shepheardes Calender*. It consisted of twelve eclogues representing the months of the seasons, and by the year 1597, five separate editions had been printed. Consequently, in 1590, the year in which the reference to *Our pleasant Willy* occurs, it was still topical.

*Willy* makes his first appearance under the month of MARCH, where he holds a rhyming conversation with *Thomalin*. His second appearance occurs in AUGUST, in company with *Cuddy* and *Perigot*, and it is here that the most important clues are to be found concerning *Willy's* identity.

| | | |
|---|---|---|
| Willye | TELL me Perigot, what shalbe the game, <br> Wherefore with myne thou dare thy musick matche? <br> Or bene thy Bagpypes renne farre out of frame? <br> Or hath the Crampe thy ioynts benomd with ache? | |
| Perigot | Ah Willye, when the hart is ill assayde, <br> How can Bagpipe, or ioynts be well apayd? | |
| Willye | What the foule euill hath thee so bestadde? <br> Whilom thou was peregall to the best, <br> And wont to make the iolly shepeheards gladde <br> With pyping and dauncing, didst passe the rest. | |
| Perigot | Ah Willye now I haue learnd a newe daunce: <br> My old musick mard by a newe mischaunce. | |
| Willye | Mischiefe nought to that newe mischaunce befall, <br> That hath so raft vs of our meriment. <br> But reede me, what payne doth thee so appall? <br> Or louest thou, or bene thy younglings miswent? | |
| Perigot | Loue hath misled both my younglings, and mee: <br> I pyne for payne, and they my payne to see. | (Note 1) |
| Willye | Perdie and wellawaye: ill may they thriue: <br> Neuer knewe I louers sheepe in good plight. <br> But and if rymes with me thou dare striue, <br> Such fond fantsies shall soone be put to flight. | |

| | |
|---|---|
| Perigot | That shall I doe, though mochell worse I fared: |
| | Neuer shall be sayde that Perigot was dared. |

Thus, in 1579, Willy is represented as a happy soul, who upon seeing Perigot's misery, seeks to brighten him with a rhyming game. Perigot accepts the challenge, and Cuddie agrees to officiate.

| | | |
|---|---|---|
| Cuddie | Gynne, when ye lyst, ye iolly shepheards twayne: | |
| | Sike a iudge, as Cuddie, were for a king. | (Note 2) |

| | | |
|---|---|---|
| Perigot. | IT fell vpon a holly eue, | |
| Willye. | hey ho hollidaye, | |
| Per. | When holly fathers wont to shrieue: | |
| Wil. | Now gynneth this roundelay. | |
| Per. | Sitting vpon a hill so hye, | |
| Wil. | hey ho the high hyll, | |
| Per. | The while my flocke did feede thereby, | |
| Wil. | The while the shepheard selfe did spill: | |
| Per. | I saw the bouncing Bellibone, | |
| Wil. | Hey ho Bonibell, | (Note 3) |
| Per. | Tripping ouer the dale alone, | |
| Wil. | She can trippe it very well: | |
| ... | ... | |
| Per. | But whether in paynefull loue I pyne, | |
| Wil. | hey ho pinching payne, | (Note 4) |
| Per. | Or thriue in welth, she shalbe mine. | |
| Wil. | But if thou can her obteine. | |
| ... | ... | |
| Per. | So learnd I loue on a hollye eue, | |
| Wil. | hey ho hollidaye, | |
| Per. | That euer since my hart did greue. | |
| Wil. | Now endeth our roundelay | |

*The Shepheardes Calender* was dedicated to Sir Philip Sidney who died from injuries sustained in 1586 at Zutphen, while fighting against the Spanish who were seeking to regain control of the Netherlands. Sidney had been a frequent visitor to the Continent. In 1572 he travelled to France as a member of the Queen's embassy to negotiate a marriage between England and France in the personages of Elizabeth I and Charles IX's brother, the duc d'Alençon. Afterwards, he wrote a lengthy letter to the Queen detailing the foolishness of the French marriage. But this so angered Elizabeth that he was forced to withdraw from Court. He was certainly in France at the time of the Massacre of St Bartholomew's Day, which began on the night of 23 August, for he took refuge in a house in Paris kept by Sir Francis Walsingham.

It is with these French connections that Spenser would have seen reason to provide Sidney with a suitable French pseudonym for the poem he was writing. *Perigot* is a French surname. In fact, there is even a Perigot Bay in French Polynesia.

Commencing with this tentative association, we can now reinforce it with a revealing comment made by Spenser, see Note 1. *Perigot* admits to *Willy* that "*Loue hath misled both my younglings, and mee.*" Three siblings with love affairs that have caused some heart searching. Sidney's own love affair with Penelope Devereux, which caused him heartache, is well documented, for it became the inspiration to the 108 sonnets and 11 songs that he composed in *Astrophel & Stella*. But this intended love match came to nothing. Sidney was rejected, and Penelope married Lord Rich.

Sidney's younger brother Robert, one of the *younglings*, was also to find himself involved in an affair of the heart: one that had gone against his initial wishes. In 1584 he married Barbara Gamage, a Welsh heiress. The marriage between Robert and Barbara was not a love match. It had been arranged after the death of the bride's father for the sole purpose of preventing relatives from claiming a share in his daughter's wealth.

Another of Sidney's *younglings* was his sister Mary: seven years his junior. She too became involved in a marriage that must have raised eyebrows. At the age of fifteen, she wed Henry Herbert, 2nd Earl of Pembroke, he was then aged forty-three, and had been married twice before; firstly to Catherine Grey, sister to Lady Jane Grey, and then to Lady Catherine Talbot.

The connection between Sidney and *Perigot* is now much stronger. With this in mind, we can give regard to Note 3 above. *Willy* answers *Perigot* with the words '*Hey ho Bonibell*'. It was Looney who first noticed that Sidney had used this same expression in one of his poems; viz. '*Such are these two, you scarce can tell / Which is the dainter bonny belle.*'

This further connection between Sidney and *Perigot* takes us to Note 4, in which *Willy* replies: "*hey ho pinching payne*". It was again Looney who drew attention to the fact that this same expression was used by the Earl of Oxford in one of his poems: '*Patience perforce is such a pinching pain.*' This implies *Willy* was Oxford, quoting from his earlier poem *Revenge of Wrong*.

Looney's other major observation was that Sidney and Oxford had once before both been involved in a poetic exchange.

| | |
|---|---|
| Oxford | Were I a king I might command content, |
| | Were I obscure unknown would be my cares, |
| | And were I dead no thought should me torment, |
| | Nor word, not wrongs, nor love, nor hate, nor fears. |
| | A doubtful choice of three things one to crave, |
| | A kingdom or a cottage or a grave. |
| | |
| Sidney | Wert thou a king, yet not command content, |
| | Since empire none thy mind should yet suffice, |
| | Wert thou obscure, still cares would thee torment; |
| | But wert thou dead all care and sorrow dies. |
| | An easy choice of three things one to crave, |
| | No kingdom nor a cottage but a grave. |

It is this reference each poet has made to being *a king* that was picked up by *Cuddie*, who agreed to act as judge between the two versifiers, see Note 2. For no obvious reason other than to draw attention to their previous conflict in verse, *Cuddie*, who is certainly Spenser, agrees to arbitrate, as *a king* might do: *"Sike a iudge, as Cuddie, were for a king.'*

There can be no better candidate for *Perigot* than Philip Sidney, since everything described by Spenser fits him perfectly. The object of the exercise was, however, to see if *Willy* could be Oxford. That, too, has been established with reasonable assurance. Spenser's reference to *"that same gentle Spirit, from whose Pen / Large Streams of Honey and sweet Nectar flow"* may now be safely referred to work written by Oxford, and acknowledged in his own time by scholars, such as Spenser, Puttenham, Meres and Harvey, but which Shakespeare's biographers prefer to ignore, ascribing them instead to his allonym.

Amongst the works ascribed to his allonym are the Sonnets, which are the subject of separate chapters. However, it cannot be allowed to pass mention that conventional opinion has assigned the bulk of these to the same period in which *Tears of the Muses* was published, with its now familiar reference to *our pleasant Willy*. Bearing in mind Oxford's known excellence for comedy; it should come as no surprise to discover this name has been introduced into SHAKE-SPEARES SONNETS – the name in the title was hyphenated by Thomas Thorpe the publisher, from whom we shall learn more in a later chapter. In Sonnet 136, the poet humorously plays on different meanings suggested by 'Will', as both a name and a word. In the final couplet, he completes the exercise thus:

> Make but my name thy love, and love that still,
> And then thou lov'st me, for my name is Will.

However, as Looney correctly pointed out:

> Had these words been written by a man whose real name was William, like the Stratford man, they would have been as puerile as anything in English literature. Had they contained a direct reference to his nom-de-plume they would have been only slightly better in this respect. We have good reasons, moreover, for supposing that the particular sonnets were written before the "Shakespeare" mask was assumed (1593). Whether this is so or not, the particular words quoted point, no doubt, to some hidden significance. If, then, we are permitted to suppose that Shakespeare was alluding to the "Willie" in the poems of the great contemporary, we shall have in these words nothing less than a direct confession from the great dramatist that he was none other than the Earl of Oxford. (Looney, 293)

In the *Shepheardes Calender,* there is certainly abundant evidence that Spenser had Shakespeare's work in mind, although in 1579 the man popularly thought of by that name was just fifteen years of age, and confined to the environs of Stratford-upon-Avon. Leaving this aside, note how Spenser uses *Willy's* part in the dialogue to repeat the words *Hey ho*; it is one of Shakespeare's catch phrases: and one he seems particularly fond of. Spenser puts it into the mouth of *Willy* no less than seventeen times. Observe, too, how these words recur twelve times in Shakespeare's plays.

> It was a lover and his lass
> With a hey, and a ho, and a hey nonino.
> (*As You Like It*: Act 5, sc.iii)

The second line above is then repeated each time in four verses.

> He that has a little tiny wit —
> With a hey, ho, the wind and the rain.
> (*King Lear*: Act 3, sc.ii)

Beatrice: 'Tis almost five o'clock cousins; 'tis time you were ready.
> By my troth, I am exceeding ill. Hey-ho!
> (*Much Ado About Nothing*: Act 3, sc.iv)

Pandarus: O ho! groans out for ha! ha! ha! — hey ho!
> (*Troilus and Cressida*: Act 3, sc.i)

> When that I was and a little tiny boy
> With hey, ho, the wind and the rain.
> (*Twelfth Night*: Act 5, sc.i)

This second line is then repeated each time in five verses.

Now compare this with the same use uttered by Spenser's *Willy.*

> Willye.  hey ho hollidaye,
> Wil.    hey ho the high hyll
> Wil.    Hey ho Bonibell,
> Wil.    hey ho gray is greete,

| Wil. | hey ho chapelet, |
| Wil. | hey ho bonilasse, |
| Wil. | hey ho the Sunne beame, |
| Wil. | hey ho the Thonder, |
| Wil. | hey ho the Moonelight, |
| Wil. | hey ho the glyder, |
| Wil. | hey ho Perigot, |
| Wil. | hey ho the arrowe, |
| Wil. | hey ho the heauie cheere, |
| Wil. | hey ho pinching payne, |
| Wil. | hey ho gracelesse griefe, |
| Wil. | hey ho the fayre flocke, |
| Wil. | hey ho hollidaye, |

Was Spenser having some good-hearted fun at Oxford's expense? The traditionalist's reply will happily deny this with the response that in 1579, the plays mentioned did not exist. But that is nothing to the point unless; that is, Spenser's *Willy* and Shakespeare were different persons. Only then would it matter which of the two men used this catch-phrase first. In short, Oxford used it first, Spenser copied it, and Oxford continued using it.

Oxford has a well-documented reputation for excellence in writing, but the only evidence of his poetical skill consists in a handful of songs and poems, which were written in his teens or early twenties. His maturity as both a poet and playwright only emerged after his return from renaissance Italy; and it can therefore be no coincidence that many of Shakespeare's plays are set in that country.

It is for this reason that the plays that came to light in the 1590s, are held to be the mature re-editing of former works which Oxford had written and produced for Court entertainment. Chief amongst these must surely be *Love's Labour's Lost*. Even Shakespeare's most fervent admirers accept that this play has been constructed for the amusement of a select audience at Court, or a private house. Yet, it is conceded to be one of the earliest plays by Shakespeare, when thoughts of writing for a private audience at Court would have been far from his mind; that is, if Shakespeare is seen as a recent arrival in London, fresh from the Warwickshire countryside. This argument would not apply to Oxford; in fact, quite the reverse: it is exactly what one would expect from him, given his situation at Court.

With this in mind, recall the rhyming contest between *Perigot* and *Willy* as they jousted with words in Spenser's *Shepheardes Calender*, and then compare this with the rhyming interplay that occurs in *Love's Labour's Lost*. It is persuasive to suppose that Spenser had seen this play performed and used the idea for a rhyming competition he had in mind between *Perigot* and *Willy*, especially if *Willy* was also the author of the play from which the idea had been taken.

| | |
|---|---|
| Berowne: | Your wit's too hot, it speeds too fast, 'twill tire. |
| Rosaline: | Not till it leave the rider in the mire. |
| Ber. | What time o' day? |
| Ros. | The hour that fools should ask. |
| Ber. | Now fair befall your mask! |
| Ros. | Fair fall the face it covers! |
| Ber. | And send you many lovers! |
| Ros. | Amen, so you be none. |
| Ber. | Nay, then will I be gone. |
| ... | ... |
| Rosaline: | Is the fool sick? |
| Berowne: | Sick at the heart. |
| Ros. | Alack! Let it blood. |
| Ber. | Would that do it good? |
| Ros. | My physic says, ay. |
| Ber. | Will you prick't with your eye? |
| Ros. | No point, with my knife. |
| Ber. | Now God save thy life! |
| Ros. | And yours, from long living! |
| Ber. | I cannot stay thanksgiving. (Act 2, sc.i) |

The factors identifying *Willy* with Oxford, and those linking *Willy* with Shakespeare, are sufficiently alike to imply Oxford and Shakespeare are the same person. This would bring the connecting links full circle; that is, according to evidence found in *The Shepheardes Calender* and *Tears of the Muses*: both works having been written by Edmund Spenser, an expert witness to what was occurring during that time.

# 9

# A Shakespeare First Performance

One of the major arguments directed against Oxford's authorship of the Shakespeare canon is that he died in 1604, before three plays bearing his name, either as author or co-author, were written. It will be shown in a separate chapter that this argument is seriously flawed. The reason that it has gained popularity as a counter to Oxford's authorship is because it is backed by authority with a vested interest in maintaining the *status quo*. That is to say, where veridical evidence is lacking, an authoritative pronouncement can be substituted, suitably backed by a few specious statements. The vested interest resides in the simple fact that for centuries, Shakespeare has been venerated as an icon of English culture.

> In Britain politicians of the left and right rely on Shakespeare as a national and quasi-religious authority for their creeds. ... the Shakespeare tourist industry is a vital component of the economic stability of the West Midlands region in England ... There are no figures available for the value of the global Shakespeare economy, but it must run to many billions of pounds per annum. ... His biography, the history of his life and his cultural afterlives, is not only national but triumphantly international. (Holland, 137,139)

Buildings have been dedicated to his memory, history books acknowledge his dominance in Elizabethan culture, reference books repeatedly confirm the basic facts of his existence, and scholarly books are published on a regular, annual basis, delving into every aspect of his plays, his poems and his life story. Expose him as the mask of another and it will be equivalent to releasing a megaton bomb in the midst of the literary world. And that is something to be avoided at all costs; even if that cost is truth itself: the foundation of all genuine scholarship.

In this chapter, it will be shown that the argument against Oxford's authorship; viz. that he died before several plays bearing his name were allegedly written, can be turned on its head. Instead it will be shown that plays bearing his name were written before William Shakspere of Stratford-upon-Avon could reasonably be thought to have authored them.

First amongst those we shall examine is *Titus Andronicus*. It is a tragedy completely out of kilter with his other tragedies. In fact, some scholars have even sought to dismiss it as a Shakespeare play, but the authority of the First Folio, which includes it as a genuine work of the author, together with Meres's *Palladis Tamia*, which also confirmed it as Shakespeare's play, have always blocked attempts to omit it. The reason for scholarly disquiet is because it has been written in the style of Seneca, and is quite unlike anything else that bears Shakespeare's name.

*The Most Lamentable Romaine Tragedie of Titus Andronicus* was first published in 1594 by John Danter as a stitched, unbound pamphlet of 40 quarto leaves. The author's name was not given, but the fact that it was deemed worthy of printing at all, confirmed the popularity it had already achieved. The cover page advertised it as having previously been *'Plaide by the Right Honourable the Earle of Darbie, the Earle of Pembrooke, and Earle of Sussex their Seruants.'* (Adams, 11). Its popularity therefore extended back a number of years.

The first recorded mention of the play may have been made in 1592, when *A Knack to Know A Knave* was acted at the Rose theatre in London. However, there is an alternative suggestion that this allusion refers to a lost play called *Titus & Vespasian*:

> As Titus was vnto the Roman Senators,
> When he had made a conquest on the Goths:
> That in requital of his seruice done,
> Did offer him the imperiall Diademe.                    (ibid 10)

Many years later, Ben Jonson's Introduction to *Bartholomew Fair* (1614) included the following declaration:

> Hee that will sweare Ieronimo or Andronicus are the best playes yet shall passe vnexcepted at heere as a man whose Iudgement shewes it is constant and hath stood still these fiue and twentie or thirtie yeeres. (ibid 9)

Jonson was recalling *Titus Andronicus* as belonging to the same era as Thomas Kyd's *The Spanish Tragedy*: a topical play set at the time of Spain's conquest of Portugal in 1580. Insofar as *The Spanish Tragedy* was concerned, Jonson's memory was accurate. Kyd's play is usually dated between 1585 and 1589. Jonson had previously mentioned it in *Cynthia's Revels*, published at the turn of the 16th century. There, he had referred to *The Spanish Tragedy* as: *'departed a dozen years since.'* (Wilson, 8). In which case, *Ieronimo* had completed its initial wave of popularity by 1588.

This confines the theatrical performances of *Titus Andronicus* to a timeframe commencing in 1584 and reaching to 1594, when the play was published. During that time period, there would have been ample opportunity for it to have changed hands, as the cover of the play confirms had been the case: even naming the acting companies through which it had passed.

Assuming William Shakspere was the author, *Titus Andronicus* must have been written close to the time of his marriage, and the birth of his daughter Susanna. This is not something those educated in the belief that Shakespeare was the Stratford-born poet can easily accept. Conventional biographies place him and his family at home, sharing accommodation with his parents and his brothers and sisters. A house filled with young children, frequent interruptions, and with the embryo playwright having to earn a living from daily manual work under needy sixteenth-century conditions are not conducive to the quiet study and concentration required for writing good drama in verse, especially if it is a budding playwright's first attempt. Moreover, the thought that John Shakspere, as head of the house, would struggle to feed and keep two families, while his son sat idly by, writing a play week after week that might never be performed and would scarcely raise the equivalent of a few months wages if sold, is so unlikely as to cast serious doubt upon the intelligence of anyone proposing it.

Jonson's evidence for *Titus Andronicus* as a play belonging to the mid-1580s, combined with its publication in 1594, which confirmed its previous performances, most definitely requires Shakespeare to have completed it before his arrival in London. Yet, this raises very serious questions. How could this unknown young man, still in his twenties, and with his West Midlands dialect acquired from the rural community wherein he was born, with neither a university education nor any previous attachment to players or the theatre, find such instant acceptance that he was able to successfully transfer his play from one company to another; and then, when it was pirated for publication in 1594, ignore what was happening, and take no action?

Gregory Doran, Chief Associate Director of the Royal Shakespeare Company, and one may assume with vested interests, has no qualms when it comes to explaining how the publication of the play came about.

> The company sold the play to a printer, who rushed it out, and copies were soon to be had at the Sign of the Gun, a bookstall (or station) outside the little north door of St Paul's. Though Henslowe never mentioned his name in the diaries, the play was by Shakespeare, and this was the first time one of his plays had been published. As he was not famous yet, his name did not actually appear on the cover. (Doran, 37)

Firstly, there is no evidence whatever that Henslowe sold the play to John Danter. Henslowe was meticulous when keeping an account of his finances, and there is no indication that he sold this play. In fact, the very same day that Danter entered the title in the Stationers' Record, 6 February 1595, Henslowe recorded a performance by the Earl of Sussex's Men, for which, the second time in nine days, he received forty shillings (about £1000). Henslowe then went on to stage the play on the 5th and 12th of June by the combined Admiral's and Chamberlain's Men. Publishing a play before it had become stale was not the actions of a businessman like Henslowe, because for the price of a single copy, sixpence, the entire drama could be staged by a competitor, bringing in as much as eighty times the amount paid for it.

After Danter had printed the book, he sold the rights to booksellers Thomas Millington and Edward White. But why should Danter have *rushed it out*? One rather obvious explanation is that after entering the title in the Stationers' Register on 6 February 1594, he feared that the author would stay publication, as was the author's legal right at that time. By *rushing it out* the printer was able to pre-empt this action from being taken.

Doran then makes an unaccountable *faux pas*. He claims that because Shakespeare "*was not famous yet, his name did not actually appear on the cover.*" One is tempted to wonder how he could ever become famous if his name was omitted from what he had written. However, as a point of actual fact, Shakespeare's name was extremely famous in 1594. The year before, he had published *Venus and Adonis* to such great acclaim that the poem went through fifteen editions by 1636. Then, in the same year that *Titus Andronicus* went on sale, Shakespeare also published *Lucrece*. Both poems were published containing the unhyphenated name of Shakespeare; not as Shapiro mischievously claims, *William Shake-fpeare*. Why, then, did Danter's copy of *Titus Andronicus* not include the name that was on every readers' lips? The satirical poem, *Willobie His Avisa* had no qualms about using the name when referring to *Lucrece*, which had been published earlier in the year.

Both these narrative poems had made Shakespeare famous. Hence, the name had become highly marketable. Consequently, it is quite inexplicable that in 1594 *Titus Andronicus*, a third work by the great Shakespeare in little more than twelve months, would have omitted the author's name from the title page. But the name was omitted. Therefore some underlying reason for its absence must be suspected.

The reason presently fitting everything learned about Shakespeare so far is that the Earl of Oxford had published *Venus and Adonis* and *Lucrece* under the penname of William Shakespeare. He had also written *Titus Andronicus,* for which his position in the nobility required that he maintain anonymity. Understandably, his authorship would have been recognised by major writers at the time. It was certainly alluded to in *Willobie.*

Against this background, an entrepreneur would have been eager to seize the opportunity this now presented. Since the play was necessarily anonymous, and the author unable to object without revealing his identity, the worst that could happen by publishing it would be to see it stayed. Alternatively by attributing it to William Shakespeare, the penname of the nobleman who had written *Venus and Adonis,* was a step far too dangerous to take, and to be avoided. On the positive side, since the play had been produced many times on stage, hence its marketable value, although the author had never been identified, there could be no harm in publishing it as it had been performed; that is, without naming the author.

This explanation therefore covers other plays of Shakespeare's that were published as anonymous works before 1598: the year when Meres named Shakespeare as the author of twelve anonymous plays. Thereafter, this gave the green light to the inclusion of the name on previously un-authored titles.

This explains why so many unanswered questions remain unresolved when attempting to understand how Shakspere, a country boy with no *known* education and no *known* connections to the theatre, could have written *Titus Andronicus.* And then had it accepted by one company after another, while always remaining absent as an entry in Henslowe's diary. For the 17th Earl of Oxford, with his education, recognised ability, and contacts in the world of literature, the problems facing Shakspere did not exist. But these difficulties were certainly present for others less fortunate, as Juvenal noted in his *Satires. "Difficult is it for those to emerge from obscurity whose noble qualities are cramped by narrow means at home."*(iii, 64). It is only by *supposing* that Shakspere overcame these difficulties with inexplicable ease that he has become the bedrock and starting point for every biographer since Nicholas Rowe.

Fortunately, in the case of *Titus* Andronicus, modern scholarship has been left a vital clue concerning one of its earliest, if not the actual first performance of this play. It is found on the so-called *Titus Manuscript.*

At some time during the second half of the 16th century, a pen drawing in brown ink was made on a folded sheet of paper bearing a watermark in common use between 1523 and 1611. The illustration was that of a scene from Shakespeare's *Titus Andronicus*. Beneath the picture, the artist has included a short excerpt from the play, involving several of the characters taking part. The *Titus Manuscript* presently represents the only known copy of an original Shakespearean production anywhere to be found. But it is also the focus of several mysteries, not least of which is the date.

Unfortunately, the author chose to write this in the style of abbreviated Latin, instead of employing numbers. Normally, there would be no difficulty in interpreting this form of dating. But, in the present case, there is: the author having used a letter that appears to be a 'g' but which others have asserted is a 'q'; someone even suggested it is a '9'. Only one of these choices can be true, since all alternatives have been eliminated.

Another uncertainty is the identity of the author. He has written his name as Henry Peacham. Popular opinion asserts this to be the same author of several books that were published during the early part of the 17th century. But again, this is not certain. Henry Peacham had a father of the same name who was also an author, and as we shall now discover, there are compelling reasons to believe the manuscript was the work of Peacham senior, rather than that of his son.

Consider, firstly, the date. Three letters appear next to the Latin word for 'year' and with sufficient clarity as to leave no doubt as to their intended meaning: **Anno m°q° _ q$^{to}$**, the year **1 5 ? 4** : **m**illesim° (1000); **q**uingentesim° (500) **quar$^{to}$** (4). The inference to be drawn from this is that a person educated in the mid-sixteenth century wrote the date at a time when Latin abbreviations and superscripts were still fashionable.

> In the Middle Ages, when costly parchment was the only available writing material, there was a strong motive for the packing of the greatest possible number of words into each line. As an aid in this compression there grew up a convention of copious abbreviation (the cutting off of the ends of words) and contraction (the omission of medial letters and elements) — devices to which Latin lent itself rather better than English did ... At the opening of the sixteenth century in England the general use of abbreviation and contraction persisted, like so much else that was medieval. (Dawson, 18-19)

This explanation for the late medieval style of dating leads naturally to a consideration of the third letter in the given year. To begin with, the date is presented in conventional form; that is, thousands, hundreds, tens and units. We are therefore seeking a number in the tens column. And since the date refers to a Shakespeare play in the 1500s, the third number must complete a date in the lifetime of 'Shakespeare'. Hence the figure can only be 7, 8 or 9.

However, had Peacham intended this number to be an 8 or 9 he would have written it in conformity with the other abbreviations; that is, 80 = o° for octogesim° or 90 = n° for nonagesim°. Not only did he do neither, he also failed to use a superscript, thus indicating the symbol was not a Latin abbreviation. The logical application of proof by exhaustion, in which 8 and 9 have been eliminated, leaves 7 as the only remaining possibility. If so, there must be an explanation as to why Peacham did not write s° for septuagesim° and why he replaced it with a symbol.

The answer to the first question is simple enough; it is because of the ambiguity involved in using s°, for this is also an abbreviation for 60; viz. sexagesim°. In order to avoid confusion occurring between 60 and 70 an alternative is required. Peacham used 'g'. His strategy was simple: *'G' is the seventh letter of the Roman alphabet.'* (*Oxford Latin Dictionary*) and as the *Oxford English Dictionary* makes abundantly clear: – *'g is used to denote anything occupying the seventh place in a series."* Therefore, with 'g' intended to represent 7, the date on the Titus Manuscript becomes readable as 1574. No other date is logically possible.

This means that *Titus Andronicus* could not have been written by Shakspere of Stratford-upon-Avon; he was barely ten years old at the time. It could have been written by the Earl of Oxford. He was then twenty-four, and about to embark upon a life changing trip to Italy and the ancient world. The play's composition in the style of Seneca is then explained. In 1574 Oxford had no other guide to model upon. It was only after returning from Italy that his transition into the poet that came to be recognised as Shakespeare, received the nourishment that enabled it to fully blossom.

Conventionalist biographers must seek to redeem this turnaround by persuading their readers to accept a different explanation for Peacham's chronogram. Three major players in this controversy have stated their reasons for the date being 1594, even 1604, thus supporting their lifelong belief in Shakspere as the author of *Titus Andronicus*.

Chambers, without providing any explanation, suggested the third figure to be a 9. But this can easily be questioned. Latin letters mixed with Arabic numbers for the purpose of dating a manuscript is an unscholarly practice; the result invariably provides an untidy appearance to the text: apart from which, the symbol bears scant resemblance to a 9. Moreover, if 9 had been the copyist's intention, he would surely have written **n**º as the abbreviation for **n**onagesimº. Or, even more likely, he would have written the date using Arabic numerals throughout. The dispute must therefore be settled between 'g' and 'q'.

To begin with, there are two excellent reasons for rejecting 'q'. Firstly, the symbol is not the same as the first and fourth 'q', which argues its difference. Secondly, the use of 'q' contributes nothing to the date. That is to say, it can neither be 50 (**q**uinquagesimº) nor can it be 40 (**q**uadragesimº, for that would make the date either 1554 or 1544, and a far cry from either Shakspere's year of birth, or even Oxford's.

Finally, a trawl through the Latin dictionary under Q reveals no possibility for which 'q' might form a plausible abbreviation for this third character; the more so, because its emplacement as the third symbol in a date that runs from thousands to units, requires a number in the tens; 'q' must therefore be eliminated. It cannot represent any number that is a multiple of ten and greater than 50. Despite this most obvious conclusion, Professor Herbert Berry claimed otherwise.

> In an analysis appearing in the Spring 1999 issue of Shakespeare Bulletin, Herbert Berry offers what will surely become the definitive reading of this elusive date ... 1594.
>
> (Schlueter, 184)

What is it that Professor Berry has seen that other eyes have apparently missed?

Berry begins by rejecting the third symbol as '*g*', insisting that it is a '**q**'. He supports this opinion by referring to the text, where 'q' occurs twice: in 'conqueror' and 'quench'. Each 'q' has a firm downward stroke, as appears in the chronogram. But the two unquestionable 'q' letters that contribute to the date on the manuscript, **q**º and **q**ᵗᵒ are completed by a downward stroke that turns sharply upwards with a noticeable *convex* arc. Berry argues the same can be seen happening to the third letter. This is untrue. But let Berry speak for himself. *'The upward stroke of the third q rises weakly and peters out about halfway up the downward stroke.'* (Berry, 5) (See picture).

Berry's anxiety to see the third letter as a 'q' has caused him to overlook the glaringly obvious. The copyist has added several flourishes to the letter. One of these is a *concave* arc that starts to the left and well below the vertical stroke of the character in question; the arc then rises to cut across the bottom of Berry's supposed '**q**', transforming what can only have been intended as a '*g*', into what careless observation might easily mistake for a 'q'. In other words, Berry has referred to only the top half of the arc in order to make his case; and even there, the arc is *concave*, not *convex*, as occurs with the second and fourth 'q'.

A second point to observe is that the squiggle beneath this character is similar to the condensed squiggle that now forms part of the typographic '*g*'. Note the barb at the top of an enclosed space, a line dropping down, followed by a squiggle or flourish.

Berry then compounds his first error by committing a second.

> Had the writer (who I assume, perhaps wrongly, was male) written out his abbreviations, therefore, his date would read 'Anno millesimo quingentesimo quinquaginta quadragintaquarto', the English is: 'in the 1594th year [of grace]'. (ibid 5)

Had this been Peacham's intention, he would have written the 9 as nº in conformity with the other parts of the date. But let us consider what his translation actually does say. Literally, word for word, Berry's date reads: *in the thousandth, five-hundredth, a fifty, a forty in the fourth year.*

This is a hotchpotch of absurd mental arithmetic and questionable Latin; the sole purpose of which has been to make the characters add up to 1594. In doing so, Berry mixed ordinal numbers with cardinal numbers. *Millesimo* and *quingentesimo* are both ordinal in the ablative case; *quinquaginta* is cardinal [cardinal numbers other than *unus, duo, tres* and *milia* are never declined], and *quadragintaquarto* is one half cardinal and the other half ordinal.

When Berry wrote *quadragintaquarto*, he presumably meant to say, as is said in English, *forty-fourth* [*quadragintaquarto!*]. But the Romans used their ordinals differently. They would have spoken as Cicero did: '*quarto et quinquagesimo anno post primus consules.*' (cic. Rep. 2.60). Or, as Berry would have said: '*quarto et quadragesimo*'.

Even so, this does nothing to help a cause already lost. It simply allows the translation to read: *in the one thousandth, five-hundredth, fiftieth, forty-fourth year of grace.* This is a nonsensical contrivance; unworthy of a first-class scholar: quite apart from which, the third symbol does not even conform to a 'q', as it is written elsewhere.

Berry does, however, refer to one piece of information that supports the elder Peacham's hand behind the manuscript, rather than that of his son. This occurs when he refers to the superscripts.

> No fewer than eighteen of these occur in two consecutive pages of the elder Henry Peacham's dedication, dated 3 February 1593[/4?], to the second edition of his The Garden of Eloquence (London, 1593[/4?] ... Eight occur in the four pages of his dedication to the first edition (1577). (ibid 6 f.n. 3)

These indicate the Reverend Henry Peacham to have been overly fond of using the type of superscript that occurs in the chronogram on the Titus document.

Professor Jonathan Bate is another supporter of Shakspere's claim to authorship, and eager to date Peacham's chronogram so that it will match his belief. But, like Berry, he, too, is forced to arrive at the date using mental arithmetic; for this, he introduces Roman numerals. He agrees that the letter in question is a 'g' but says: *'I suspect that 'g' is intended to stand for gentesimo: if quingentesimo is 500, gentesimo is 100 (i.e. a variant spelling of centesimo).'* (Bate, 40). Bate has derived this explanation from *quin–gentesimo* (five–hundredth), although the conventional Latin word for 'hundredth' is, and remains, *centesimo*.

At this stage there are two points to be made. Firstly, the 'g' carries no superscript. Had Bate's suggestion been correct, the third character would have been written $g^o$. Secondly, Peacham's chronogram now reads very awkwardly: *In the year 1000 500 100 5* (Bate prefers to read $q^{to}$ as 5 instead of 4). The mental arithmetic occurs when these numbers are added together. In this case, they total to 1605. Bate justifies this hitherto unknown method of dating by referring to the Roman numerals, MDCV, the Roman date for 1605. In other words, M=$m^o$, D=$q^o$, C=$c^o$ (but written as g with an absent superscript), V=$q^{to}$.

Let us now consider some further objections to Bate's dating theory. Firstly, had Bate's explanation coincided with Peacham's intention, then surely, he would have written the date as MDCV, thus avoiding the need for mental gymnastics. Secondly, if 1605 was intended by Peacham, using the Latin abbreviated form, then he would have had no difficulty at all in presenting it as **$m^o$ $s^o$ $q^{to}$** (millesim$^o$ sexcentesim$^o$ quin$^{to}$)? An obvious choice for a Latin scholar! Thirdly, why substitute the Roman numeral C by 'g' and then fail to provide a superscript, even though superscripts appear on the characters either side? Bate's theory fails on too many points of fact. It is therefore unacceptable.

The informed reader of Shakespeare biographies will undoubtedly have encountered the Titus Manuscript before, and will have been made aware that the signature beneath the date is said to be that of Henry Peacham the younger who, in 1594, was a seventeen-year-old student at Trinity College, Cambridge. His handwriting is shown below.

Compare this with the handwriting on the Titus Manuscript.

Even a cursory examination reveals the difference between the two hands. Once again conventionalist thinking is placed under pressure: this time to explain the different handwriting. Peter Croft, former Librarian at King's College Library, Cambridge was *"inclined to think that Peacham was ... using the Longleat manuscript 'as an exercise in 'writing fair' in the 'secretary script' as the emblem books were exercises in 'fair writing in the italic style'.'* (Waith, 25). The problem with this explanation, if one can even call it that, is the same comment can be said about any two examples of handwriting that are penned in a markedly different style. There is no actual justification for it being true. It is an excuse, not an explanation.

The Henry Peacham who copied a page of dialogue from *Titus Andronicus* in 1574 would have had to be the elder of the two bearing that name. His son, Henry, was not born until two years later. Peacham was then curate at St Mary's Church in North Mymms, which is immediately adjacent to Hatfield House, Queen Elizabeth's favourite residence. As a reverend scholar, neighbour and future author of *The Garden of Eloquence* published in 1577, his credentials for receiving an invitation to join the audience for a performance of Oxford's new play, *Titus Andronicus*, is easily understandable. This would then explain how the document came into existence, and where it originated from.

Another member of the audience would have been Michael Hicks, one of Lord Burghley's secretaries. At Court, Hicks was described as *'very witty and jocose'*. He was also a collector of Roman memorabilia, and he filled many notebooks to that effect, for it was said of him:

> [He] was well skilled in philological learning, and had read over the polite Roman historians and moralists; out of which authors he made large collections, especially of the moral and wise sentences out of which he filled divers paper-books, still remaining in the family.
> 
> (Wotton Baronetage)

The attraction of the *Titus Manuscript* to a man of Hicks' taste, with its dramatic Roman content, is at once obvious. It was also amongst Hick's political papers that the document was discovered. Consequently, with Hicks and Peacham at the same performance, one a writer, the other a collector of all things Roman, it does much to explain the circumstances in which the manuscript was copied, and how it came into Hick's possession, with Henry Peacham's name next to the year 1574.

The chapter began by commenting upon the frequent claim that Oxford could not have written the works of Shakespeare because he died too soon: *The Tempest* is always cited to back this up. But this can now be countered by a much stronger and more conclusive argument that exposes Shakspere as having been far too young to have written the earliest of Shakespeare's plays: it being beyond even the imagination of Shakspere's more ardent supporters to believe that *Titus Andronicus* was written by a boy of ten.

Clearly, these arguments are mutually exclusive. In a chapter devoted to plays claimed to have been written after Oxford's death, the weakness of the support given to a belief that *The Tempest, Henry VIII* and *The Two Noble Kinsmen* postdate the possibility of Oxford's authorship will be exposed. This will leave open the overwhelming evidence that *Titus Andronicus* was written before Oxford left for Italy, and that it was later revised by him for performances in the 1580s and early 1590s.

The evidence for these revisions is to be found in the differences that occur between the dialogue that appears on the *Titus Manuscript* and the text of similar passages and scenes printed in the 1594 quarto. Attempts to date the *Titus Manuscript* after publication of the play always come up against the impossibility of correctly placing it between this quarto and those of 1600 and 1611; for all three are consistent with the First Folio.

Conventionalist thinking sees this as a puzzle with no apparent answer: at least, none to satisfy every doubt. But if Peacham's copy is allowed to predate publication of the first quarto, then the *Titus Manuscript* becomes a copy of the original text from which later revisions were made, following Oxford's return from Italy. It is this revised play that was published in 1594, and repeated in the two later quartos, and then again in the First Folio.

Another, otherwise inexplicable Shakespeare puzzle, has therefore been solved by Oxford's authorship.

Although the younger Peacham is always proposed by 'expert' opinion to have been the signatory on the *Titus Manuscript*, he actually refused to recognise Shakspere as Shakespeare. Irrefutable evidence for this occurs in his book, *The Complete Gentleman*. Its publication in 1622 may have been intended to coincide with the First Folio, for this was also planned for publication that year, but delays postponed it until 1623.

In Peacham's chapter on Poetry, the author praised those *'who honoured poesie with their pens and practice,'* "men who had made Elizabeth's England *'a golden age (for such a world of refined wits and excellent spirits it produced whose like are hardly to be hoped for in any succeeding age).'* (Ogburn, 695). He then listed the names of those amongst the recently deceased who exemplified his report. At the very top of the list he placed *'Edward Earl of Oxford.'*

Other poets, such as Sir Philip Sidney and Edmund Spenser are found amongst the names that follow. But Shakespeare is omitted altogether. The author of two best-selling poems, as well as a collection of 154 sonnets, together with a magnificent volume of thirty-six plays, the greatest writer of the English language, and by a man whose stagecraft *'had so taken Eliza and our James,'* is completely ignored by the scholarly Peacham; unless, that is, Shakespeare was merely the penname given to one of the writers he had already mentioned, such as Oxford, whom he named first and foremost, even though he had been dead and forgotten for the past eighteen years.

How easy it would have been for Peacham to have remedied this 'oversight' in his second edition, published in 1627, especially after the reception of Shakespeare's collected plays had been published in the First Folio. But he chose, instead, to ignore making the correction.

In 1634, Peacham published *The Complete Gentleman* for a third time, just two years after the Second Folio of Shakespeare's Comedies, Histories and Tragedies was published. But still, even after twelve years, during which he must have been made fully aware of having omitted any mention of Shakespeare, he still refused to name this man

The reason for this is found at the front of an earlier book he had written called *Minerva Britanna* (the British Minerva). It is an illustration showing an outstretched hand and forearm extended from a man who is concealed behind the arras of a Discovery Space (this is a curtained area occupying an alcove at the rear of the stage); the hand is in the process of completing an inscription in Latin — MENTE. VIDEBOR• *'By the mind I shall be seen'.*

Surrounding this arm and hand is a second scroll. It reads: VIVITUR. INGENIO. CAETERA. MORTIS. ERUNT: *'One lives by means of one's genius, the rest belongs to death'.* Both mottoes were applicable to the man who secretly wrote the works of Shakespeare. This becomes even more evident when it is understood that the declaration occurs on stage, inside the curtained area of the discovery space, and only the writer's hand and forearm are exposed to the audience. Peacham's mystery man is the first emblematic puzzle in a book of emblematic puzzles.

Quite appropriately, Peacham's book *'displays a dazzling preoccupation with word puzzles of various kinds—amongst them, prominently, anagrams.'* (Stritmatter, 11). It is therefore by rearranging the letters: MENTE. VIDEBOR• (BY THE MIND I SHALL BE SEEN) that they become TIB• NOM DE VERE, (NOM is the Latin abbreviation for NOMEN), and then substituting 'I' for '•'; that is, TIBI NOM DE VERE, a perfect anagram is formed, which identifies the man concealed behind the arras, and seen by the mind — THY NAME IS DE VERE.

Perfect anagrams are those in which the rearranged letters are logically connected to their original formation. Terry Ross decried the anagram because Peacham failed to define it as such. Ross also devised a list of words formed from the letters of Mente Videbor, which were intended to demonstrate the flaw in anagrams; e.g., Demon Bit Vere. Vere, Omit Bend. Vere: No Dim Bet. Vere? Be Not Dim! End It, Vere Mob! The intelligent reader will have no trouble in observing that not one of these so-called alternatives is in Latin, nor do they form perfect anagrams.

In the present case, because of the secrecy surrounding Shakespeare's authorship, the phrase: *By the Mind I shall be seen* connects logically to: *Thy Name is de Vere.* The scroll surrounding this epithet, which specifically refers to the genius of its subject, also provides an added reason for this interpretation.

Since Eva Turner Clarke first suggested this rearrangement in *The Man Who Was Shakespeare*, New York, 1937, the anagram has been surrounded by controversy. The dispute centres upon the missing 'I', which is required to complete TIBI. Why, it is asked, should 'I' be especially chosen to fill the gap?

The answer is that the hand, which has just completed MENTE. VIDEBOR• has followed it with a penned dot. This, the argument goes, implies that the letter 'I' was about to be written. But 'videbori' is not a word that exists in the Latin language. Moreover, if Peacham had intended the letter 'I', he could have easily inserted it himself. Thirdly, the letters are all capitals, and a capital 'I' does not need to be dotted. Peacham realised all of this, and so he used a dot, adding a clue: *By the mind 'I' shall be seen*.

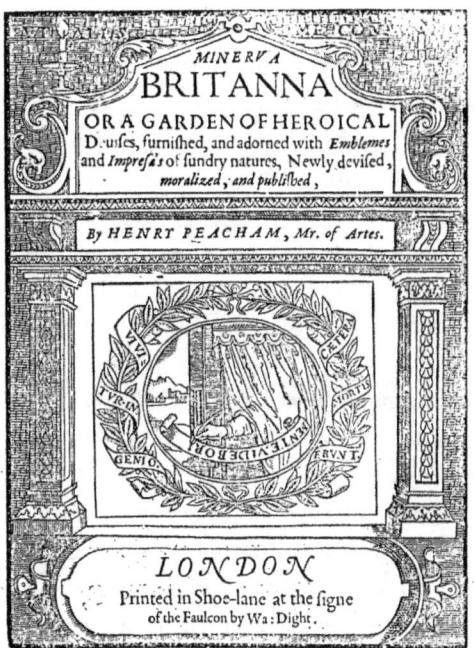

Consider how subtle Peacham has been. First, he has shown a pen held by this mysterious figure, but which is joined to the motto, where it appears next to the last letter of VIDEBOR•, thus forming a dot. This is unusual, therefore deliberate. The dot must be intended to occupy a place in the solution; otherwise it would not be there. Next, by placing the dot into the rearranged lettering, TIB• NOM DE VERE, it is made to stand in for a missing letter. That letter, Peacham says, can be seen by the mind as 'I'.

Hence the sentence: *'By the mind I can be seen'*, identifies the person concealed, because 'I' possess a double meaning. On the one hand, it refers subjectively to the speaker, who is hidden behind the curtain; on the other hand, it refers to the ninth letter of the alphabet. Both of these meanings complement each other in identifying the mysterious figure that Peacham has placed at the centre of this conundrum.

Moreover, if doubt continues to exist, regarding the legitimate use of a dot for the letter 'I', Peacham has resolved this doubt on page 177 of his book. At the top of the page he advertises an anagram of his name in its Latin form. It contains 17 letters. But the rearrangement of these letters to form a Latin motto has only 16 letters: viz.

HENRICUS PEACHAMUS = HINC SUPER HAC, MUSA

To compensate for this inequality, Peacham has inserted a comma to stand in for the missing letter, 'E'.

These subtle, cryptic word puzzles stretch the mind considerably. Word games, especially anagrams, were to that period in English history what computer games, Sudoku, and crossword puzzles are to this. In both eras the requirement is, as it always has been, to challenge solution seekers, by attempting to outwit them with clues that test each person's problem-solving ability. Peacham would have expected his challenge to be met only by the more intelligent reader, confirming to him or her that the First and Second Folio editions of Shakespeare's plays were the product of Edward de Vere's genius.

Strangely, William F. Friedman, who interested himself in Shakespeare codes and ciphers that could be explained away, steered clear of Peacham's cunning device; as he also did by ignoring Thorpe's asyntactic address, and the challenge issued on the Stratford monument. Perhaps he realised that his relationship to the Folger Shakespeare Library would be compromised if he used his expertise in exposing that each of these three, in their own unique way, named de Vere as Shakespeare: the Folger had awarded him a prize for protecting Shakspere's image from the threat posed by Bacon's supporters, who believed the plays contained coded messages identifying Bacon as the pseudonymous Shakespeare. Friedman's commitment to the Folger and the service he provided the Library's administrators may explain his reluctance to embarrass them with the truth.

The Friedmans did however define what makes a successful anagram.

> In the absence of a key, any lengthy sequence of letters with the normal proportions of high, medium, and low-frequency vowels and consonants may be anagrammed in a large number of ways. Hence there may be as many "solutions" as the solver's ingenuity can produce and each will be as valid as any other, but none will carry any objective conviction. There is always room for doubt unless the man who composed the anagram recreates his own message from it; for only he knows for certain what message he intended to conceal.
>
> (Friedmans 113)

The focus is on the word, 'key'. In a book of emblematic puzzles and anagrams, is it so unreasonable to view the suspect illustration as another brainteaser? There are certainly clues to be had: a mystery man; a theatrical discovery space; a hand writing a motto with the pen still on the paper; the slogan 'One lives by one's genius, the rest belongs to death'; and then: 'By the mind I will be seen', with its ingenious double meaning enabling a perfect anagram to be constructed that serves to identify the mystery man. Note too, that by accepting this double meaning, a 'key' is obtained.

Against this, as Ross pointed out, 'nomen' is abbreviated to 'nom'; de Vere is not written in its Latin form, and Peacham has not described it as an anagram.

Firstly, the abbreviation is correct (Capelli, 239). Secondly, it was not strictly necessary to identify de Vere by a Latin translation of his name; therefore the objection raised is of no consequence. Thirdly, for Peacham to have openly declared that the Latin motto was an anagram would be equivalent to identifying de Vere as Shakespeare. This in turn would lead to his relationship with Southampton becoming public knowledge, to the great shame of his family. It would also stain his genius in the eyes of the public, as indeed it may still do. Peacham therefore consigned the truth to a take-it-or-leave-it anagram.

Understandably, Ross, together with many fellow academics, leave it; preferring Shakspere, the *'provincial nobody'*, on which to hang their studies. Others, found amongst Oxford's advocates, opt for incest over paedophilia, by putting together a storyline that Southampton was Oxford's son by an illicit union with Queen Elizabeth, thus allowing the betrothal of young Southampton to his half sister, although while both were still in their mid teens.

In the thoughts of Shakspere's advocates as well as those of Oxford, the power of Shakespeare's genius taking the form of this disgraced earl brings shudders to their minds. It is far more acceptable to the former's belief that this favourite of the Muses was the offspring of uneducated parents, raised in the insanitary conditions of a post-feudal Warwickshire village (some call it a town, which it later became), with no *known* education or cultural background, than it is to countenance the alternative: that Edward de Vere, possessing everything that Shakspere lacked, wrote under the penname of William Shakespeare.

For those who support Oxford, the same revulsion affects their belief. His love for the teenage Southampton must be that of a father for his son. Southampton therefore becomes a changeling, born of the Queen and fostered by Lord and Lady Southampton, following the concealed death of their own son. In both cases, fertile imagination becomes the substitute for historical accuracy. There is no documentary evidence that Shakspere had the education or the cultural background to have written the works of Shakespeare; nor is there any documentary evidence that Elizabeth I was the mother of the 3rd Earl of Southampton. Yet, both are believed by their respective factions; proving only, that truth is sometimes too painful to be accepted.

# 10

## SHAKESPEARE'S LEARNING CURVE

Is there such a thing as scholastic cowardice? One would like to think not; nevertheless, one does wonder why a well-documented event in the life of the Earl of Oxford, which was repeated in a Shakespeare play, is never mentioned in pro-Shakspere commentaries for that play. It is almost an invitation to believe that commentators are affected by collective amnesia; unless, that is, there is something they prefer not to advertise?

The play referred to is *The Famous Victories of Henry the Fift*. It was published in 1598, with no author named, but its appearance coincided with Francis Meres's *Wits Treasury*, which identified William Shakespeare as the author of twelve named but anonymously written plays. *The Famous Victories of Henry the Fift* was an old play, also without a named author. Richard Tarleton had once played the role of Dericke in a performance, and he had been dead since 1588. So, why was *The Famous Victories* suddenly thought to be a marketable commodity? The question appears to have more to do with Meres having brought Shakespeare's name into the public domain, rather than that of meeting an otherwise late and questionable demand.

Three of Shakespeare's plays, *1 Henry IV*, *2 Henry IV*, and *Henry V*, draw upon actions occurring in *The Famous Victories of Henry the Fift*; as happens to be the case with *King John*, *2 Henry VI*, and *3 Henry VI*, which draw upon *The Troublesome Reign of King John*, *The Contention Between Two Famous Houses* and *The True Tragedy of Richard Duke of York*.

In *The Famous Victories*, scenes 1 to 7 correspond to the actions that have been transferred to *1 Henry IV* and the same can be said of scenes 8 and 9, which are found in *2 Henry IV*, while scenes 9 through to 20 are represented in *Henry V*. These earlier plays are therefore ideal, as examples of how the master playwright perfected his art.

There are no comparative examples for Shakspere. The only similarity that does exist can be found in Greek Mythology, where the goddess Athene is plucked fully armed from the head of Zeus. Pro-Shakspere academics prefer to believe this also applies to their man. He arrived in London from an obscure village of less than 1500 inhabitants, having left behind his uneducated, illiterate family, but with a sheaf of plays under his arm, each one word perfect and fully informed about the code of behaviour at court, as well as being near perfect for instant performance on stage.

Those who prefer the reality of an apprenticeship for Shakespeare will find it in the *Histories*. On Thursday 21 May 1573, two of Oxford's former servants, William Faunt and John Wotton (aka Clopton), wrote a letter of complaint to Lord Burghley, concerning an attack with light muskets that had been made upon them the day before at or near Gads Hill, which is situated between Gravesend and Rochester.

> ... wootton and my sealfe, rydynge peasably by the hyghe way, from Grauesend to Rochester, had thre calyvers charged with bullettes discharged at vs by thre of my Lord of Oxenfordes men / Danye Wylkyns Ihon Hannam, and Deny the Frenche man vhoe lay preuylye in a diche awaytynge oure cumminge wythe full intente to murder hus.
>
> (Nelson, 95)

As Professor Bate might be expected to remark, it is uncanny to discover this same scene at Gads Hill, also in the month of May, being exactly repeated in *The Famous Victories of Henry the Fift*, and then found to recur in *Henry IV, Part One*, where this time it involves Prince Hal who is also in company with *three companions*.

Another interesting feature found in *The Famous Victories* concerns the importance given by the author to the role of Richard de Vere, the 11th Earl of Oxford. With no documentary support for the role of this nobleman, he is nevertheless promoted to the position of principal advisor and lieutenant to the King. As Eva Turner Clark astutely remarked —

> [This was] in defiance of Hall, who, on historically accurate grounds, makes Exeter, York, and Westmoreland the principal councillors to both Kings. ... It is especially noteworthy that the organization of the palisade of stakes, which probably did more to win the battle than anything else, is definitely handed over to Lord Oxford. (Clark, 11)

Captain Bernard Ward, writing in July 1928 for the *Review of English Studies* proposed *"that The Famous Victories was based on an account in Hall's Chronicles, published in 1548 ... the source of the historical facts used in the play,"* (ibid 10).

Nor must mention of the controversy surrounding Sir John Oldcastle be neglected. This was a character originally appearing in *The Famous Victories*. The plagiarised version of this play, *2 Henry IV*, also included the character, Oldcastle.

> One of Falstaff's speech prefixes in Act I, Scene ii is mistakenly left uncorrected, "Old." instead of "Falst." In III,ii, 25-6 of the same play, Falstaff is said to have been a "page to Thomas Mowbray, Duke of Norfolk" — which was true of the historical Oldcastle. In *Henry IV, Part 1* i, ii, 42, Prince Hal calls Falstaff "my old lad of the castle." (Wikipedia)

Although the name, Oldcastle, survived unchanged while it remained part of *The Famous Victories*, this was not the case when it appeared publicly on stage in the *Henry IV* plays.

> It may not be improper to observe that this part of Falstaff is said to have been written originally under the name Oldcastle; some of the family being then remaining, the Queen was pleased to command him to alter it, upon which he made use of Falstaff. (Rowe)

By a happy coincidence, the change from Oldcastle was confirmed in an unpublished manuscript written by Richard James in 1625, and addressed to Sir Henry Bourchier. James also confirmed that Shakespeare was the author of *The Famous Victories of Henry the Fift*.

> A young gentle ladie of your acquaintance, having read the works of Shakespeare, made me this question: How Sir John Falstaffe, or Fastolf, as it is written in the statute book of Maudlin College in Oxford, where everye daye that societie were bound to make memorie of his soule, could be dead in Harrie the Fifts time and againe live in the time of Harrie the Sixt to be banisht for cowardice? Whereto I made answeare ... That in Shakespeare's first shewe of Harrie the Fift, the person with which he undertook to playe a buffoon was not Falstaffe, but Sir John Oldcastle, and that offence beinge worthily taken by personages descended from his title, as peradventure by manie others allso whoe ought to have him in honourable memorie, the poet was made to putt an ingonorant shifte of abusing Sir Jhon Falstophe, a man not inferior of vertue, though not so famous in piety as the other.
>
> (Halliwell-Phillipps, 155)

The truth of James's letter is unquestionable, given that Oxford was Shakespeare. To suppose the Queen requested the change is also believable although not for a man of Shakspere's class. For him to have lampooned a real person, especially a former member of the powerful Cobham family, would have been peremptorily dealt with, and the offending author would have been thrown into gaol to dwell upon his misconduct. The position held by the 17th Earl of Oxford in Elizabeth's Court was different. His superior title would have rendered him immune from gaol or physical punishment, but not from being politely asked to spare the Cobham family public embarrassment by this allusion to their ancestor as a figure of fun. It is also against reason to imagine Shakspere would have ridiculed the Cobham family's ancestor by name. And just as much against reason to imagine that a senior member of the irate Cobham family politely asked the Queen if she would be kind enough speak to Shakspere about it, and advise him to change the name to another.

This incident, almost insignificant when set against the larger picture of the authorship debate, is nevertheless a further indication that Shakspere was not Shakespeare. Shakspere's station in life would not have shielded him from the Cobhams in the way that Oxford's position protected him.

Oldcastle had married into the Cobham family in 1408 to become Lord Cobham, which was at the root of the protest. Shakespeare's response was to rename Oldcastle, Falstaff; but he also felt obliged to distance himself from this change, by declaring: *'Oldcastle died a martyr and this is not the man.'*

No Elizabethan was better connected than members of the Cobham family. And the commotion they caused at the time not only secured the character's name change, it also allowed the Admiral's Men to cash in on the rumpus, which had clearly gone public. The result was a new play, *The First Part of the True and Honourable History of the Life of Sir John Oldcastle, the good Lord Cobham*. But, ever careful not to anger the Cobham family, the Prologue explained to the audience: —

> It is no pampered glutton we present
> Nor aged Councellor to youthful sinne
> But one whose vertue shone above the rest
> A valiant Martyr and a virtuous peere.

This brouhaha over Oldcastle's name must have still been in the public mind as late as 1618, because Nathaniel Field referred to it in his play, *Amends for Ladies*, printed that year. In his play, a character says: *'Did you not see the piece in which the fat knight, named Oldcastle, told you truly what was honour?'* This has since been acknowledged as a reference to *1 Henry IV* (Act 5: sc. iii) (Gervinus, 299).

There also exists certain dialogue in *The Famous Victories* to indicate that it had been performed in the privacy of a court performance. Consider the scene occurring at Gads Hill, which is followed in Scene 4, by Prince Hal giving the Chief Justice a box round the ear, and for this, the heir to the throne is sent to prison. In *1 Henry IV* a similar scene at Gads Hill is repeated, but the box round the ears, which Prince Hal gave the Chief Justice, is not performed; it is only referred to, and this only occurs in the sequel, *2 Henry IV*.

> JUSTICE: Your Grace hath said truth, therefore in striking me in this place, you greatly abuse me, and not me onely, but also your father: whose liuely person here in this place I doo represent. And therefore to teach you what prerogatiues meane, I commit you to the Fleete, untill we haue spoken with your father.

| | |
|---|---|
| HENRY 5: | Why then belike you meane to send me to the Fleete? |
| JUSTICE: | I indeed, and therefore carry him away. |

[Exeunt Henry 5 with the Officers.]<br>(The Famous Victories of Henry the Fifth: sc. 4)

| | |
|---|---|
| Falstaff: | ... For the box of the ear that the Prince gave you—he gave it like a rude prince, and you took it like a sensible lord. I have check'd him for it; and the young lion repents—marry, not in ashes and sackcloth, but in new silk and old sack. |
| Justice: | Well, God send the Prince a better companion! |

(2 Henry IV: act 1, sc. ii)

It will not have escaped the reader's attention that the two excerpts are related, in that Shakespeare has referred to a scene that only occurred in the much earlier 'anonymous' play called *The Famous Victories of Henry the Fift*. This, as noted above, was written and performed before Shakspere's arrival in London. Yet, Falstaff's conversation with the Chief Justice in *2 Henry IV*, in which he refers to the *box of the ear* delivered by the Prince, is made with such natural continuity from *The Famous Victories*, it seems more reasonable to believe the same author was responsible for both plays. Alas, not the pro-Shakspere advocates; they hold firmly to the belief that their 'Shakespeare' was a plagiarist, stealing from this anonymous author.

This same disturbing belief also requires that they omit any reference to the fact that their preferred author has dramatised the Gads Hill episode in *1 Henry IV*, from an actual event at that location, undertaken by the Earl of Oxford's servants. For the chain linking the Gads Hill incident in *1 Henry IV*, to its first dramatisation in *The Famous Victories of Henry the Fifth*, back to the original incident at Gads Hill enacted by the Earl of Oxford's servants, is never revealed, beyond the first two links. Biographers are most careful to always omit any connection between William Shakespeare and the Earl of Oxford. They will even deny the third link has any connection with the other two, which is quite illogical. *The Famous Victories* was written by an unnamed author. How, then, can pro-Shakspere academics *know* that this author was not the Earl of Oxford, especially since Oxford's ancestor has been glorified in the play, contrary to what was written down as historical fact?

As for the difference in quality between the two plays, this can easily be explained by the time difference between each composition. The event at Gads Hill occurred in 1573, when Oxford was twenty-two, and before he had embarked upon his mind-bending experience in Renaissance Italy. The later play reflected his greater maturity during the final decade of his life, when in retirement he had the leisure to rewrite, edit, and improve upon his earlier work. Shakspere had no earlier work to improve upon.

In addition to *Titus Andronicus* and *The Famous Victories of Henry the Fifth*, both of which can be dated to before Oxford left for Italy in 1575, we may also add *The Comedy of Errors* after his return. E. T. Clark has drawn attention to the *Documents Relating to the Office of the Revels in the Time of Queen Elizabeth*, published by A. Feuillerat in 1908. These reveal that on Tuesday 1 January 1577 (N.S.) *"The historie of Error (was) shown at Hampton Court on Newyeres daie at night, enacted by the Children of Powles.'* (Clark, 15).

According to Sir Edmund K. Chambers: —

> ... the great choirs of St. Paul's and the Chapel Royal had been at least as conspicuous as the professional companies. ... the Paul's boys appear to have joined ... a composite company, to which Lord Oxford's boys also contributed. (Ogburn, 595)

The Blackfriars theatre was converted from the former monastery of the Black Friars in 1576, and this was where the boy players performed. Oxford acquired the sublease for the theatre in 1583 and passed it to his secretary, causing Gabriel Harvey to comment that Lyly *"hath not played the Vice Master of Paul's, and the Fool Master of the Theatre for noughts."* (ibid).

The connection between Hampton Court Palace, the Children of St Pauls and *A History of Error* has a precedent uniting Hampton Court Palace and Oxford, with *The Comedy of Errors*.

| | |
|---|---|
| Balthazar: | Have patience, sir: O, let it not be so: |
| | Herein you war against your reputation, |
| | And draw within the compass of suspect |
| | The unviolated honour of your wife. |
| | Once this,—your long experience of her wisdom |
| | Her sober virtue, years, and modesty, |
| | Plead on her part some cause to you unknown; |
| | And doubt not , sir, but she will well excuse |
| | Why at this time the doors are made against you. |
| | ... |
| | For slander lives upon succession, |
| | For ever hous'd where it once gets possession. |

(Act 3, Sc. i)

Those aware of Oxford's situation upon his arrival back in England in the spring of 1576, after more than a year's absence, will immediately understand the similarity this has with the passage quoted above.

Oxford's reputation amongst members of the peerage was at its lowest ebb. He had separated from his wife Anne Cecil, believing that despite the many years he had known her for her wisdom, virtue, and modesty, her honour had nevertheless been violated during his absence, and the baby born to her on 2 July 1575 was not his.

He knew, too, that Anne was desperate to be reunited with him, and that she would, as the author of *Errors* made clear: excuse his behaviour, which had since caused the doors to be closed against him. That is to say, he was no longer an invited guest at the great houses that had once welcomed him.

The fault of this unwelcome disruption to Oxford's homecoming is indicated by the final two lines of Balthazar's speech. Anne had been defamed by a false accusation, and the slander made against her had taken root in Oxford's mind. The details of what he had been told, and by whom, were never revealed, and so the identities of the perpetrators remain unknown. However, for a proud young aristocrat descended from one of the noblest families in England, the suggestion that he had been cuckolded proved too much, and he had separated from his wife and child.

Some hint at the efforts made by Anne's family members to placate Oxford can be discerned in the dialogue that follows on from the last scene.

Luciana: If you did wed my sister for her wealth,
Then, for wealth's sake, use her with more kindness:
Or, if you like elsewhere, do it by stealth;
Muffle your false love with some show of blindness:
...
Then, gentle brother, get you in again;
Comfort my sister, cheer her, call her wife:
'Tis holy sport to be a little vain
When the sweet breath of flattery conquers strife.

(Act 3, sc. ii)

Luciana's advice is all the more interesting because no corresponding character occurs in the *Menaechmi* of Plautus, from which *The Comedy of Errors* is derived. (*The Menaechmi* is a Roman comedy with a story of long-lost twin brothers and confused identities.) And, Anne did have a sister, Elizabeth. The suspicion that Oxford had only agreed to marry Anne because of her father's wealth is also apparent. *"Burghley had agreed to provide Anne with a dowry of £3000, which [historian Lawrence] Stone characterizes as a 'record sum'. Oxford's financial condition was nevertheless dire."* (Nelson, 74).

The remainder of Luciana's advice is equally applicable to Oxford. His search for the feminine touch elsewhere, during his separation from Anne is evident from the free-living style of life he exercised when competing with Walter Raleigh for Anne Vavasour's sexual favours in 1580 (Williams, 1962, 21).

It was on 24 July 1579 that John Lyly entered *Euphues and his England* in the Stationers' Register, with its dedication—

> *To the Right Honourable my*
> *very good Lorde and Maister, Edward de Vere,*
> *Earle of Oxenforde, Vicount Bulbeck, Lorde of*
> *Escales and Badlesmere, and Lorde great*
> *Chamberlaine of England, John Lyly*
> *wisheth long lyfe, with en-*
> *crease of Honour.*

On a separate page to itself, immediately before this dedication, is the Oxford coat-of-arms, with the Vere motto, VERO NIHIL VERIVS. Oxford had been maintaining Lyly in his apartment at the Savoy, opposite Burghley House in the Strand. Gabriel Harvey would later remind Lyly of *"thy old acquaintance in the Savoy, when young Euphues hatched the eggs that his elder friends laid."* (Ogburn, 568). Harvey was referring to Lyly's first book, *Euphues: the Anatomy of Wyt*, published in 1578.

Harvey's reference to Lyly's friends, also confirms that Oxford had been operating a school of writers at the Savoy, which would likely have included Kyd, Marlowe, Munday and Lodge. This activity apparently continued when Fishers Folly, with its more spacious accommodation, was purchased by Oxford in 1580.

It was also during this period of separation from his wife that Oxford became the subject for several more dedications. In 1579, Anthony Munday dedicated *The Mirrour of Mutabilitie* to Oxford, describing him as *"his singular good Lord & Patron"* (Nelson, 238). Others who favoured Oxford with their work were Geoffrey Gates, Gabriel Harvey, and John Brooke (ibid). With so much flattery for his vanity to feed upon, Oxford was able to distract himself from the strife of his failed marriage. As Luciana aptly observed: *it is sport to be a little vain, when the sweet breath of flattery conquers marital strife.*

But Oxford remained unmoved: apparently happy with the thought that if a young man married is a young man marred; he, at least, was now free, and intending to remain in that condition. Similar thoughts intrude into the reply Antipholus gave to Luciana.

| | |
|---|---|
| Antipholus: | Your weeping sister is no wife of mine, |
| | Nor to her bed no homage do I owe: |
| | Far more, far more, to you do I decline: |

> O, train me not, sweet mermaid, with thy note,
> To drown me in thy sister's flood of tears:
>
> (Act 3, sc. ii)

Anne Cecil's plight can well be imagined. Her husband had left England to travel abroad, and during his absence she had borne his child. When, after more than a year had passed and he returned, it was to desert her once again, but this time without hope of return. Luciana's weeping sister, drowning in a flood of tears, can have been in no worse state than the Countess of Oxford.

Pro-Shakspere scholars like to date their man's plays by recognising events that have been written into the dialogue. Using the same strategy, *The Comedy of Errors* can be dated to the year of Oxford's return from the Continent. He was therefore able to direct its performance for a royal performance at Hampton Court on New Year's Day, 1577. He initially called it: *The historie of Error*, changing the title later. The Queen would have been especially pleased to note that Oxford had changed the play's location to Ephesius in her honour: a town dedicated to the goddess Diana, with whom she identified.

John T. Looney was the first commentator of *Errors* to draw attention to the similarity between one of Oxford's early poems and a piece of dialogue spoken in the play by Dromio. The style of Oxford in this early piece of verse and that of Shakespeare, which it predates, is quite irrefutable.

> Dromio: She is so hot because the meat is cold;
> The meat is cold because you come not home;
> You come not home because you have no stomach;
> You have no stomach, having broke your fast;
> But we, that know what 'tis to fast and pray,
> Are penitent for your default today.   (Act 1, sc. ii)

> The Grief of Mind
>
> What plague is greater than the grief of mind?
> The grief of mind that eats in every vein;
> In every vein that leaves such clots behind;
> Such clots behind as breed such bitter pain;
> So bitter pain that none shall ever find,
> What plague is greater than the grief of mind.

This verse was originally included amongst Sidney's sonnets, contained in his *Astrophel and Stella*. Many of the poems had circulated in manuscript form before the first edition was printed in 1591, by which time Sidney was dead. When published, it included verses from other poets including the Earl of Oxford. (Wilson, 1931, 168). *The Grief of Mind* was later republished in *England's Parnassus*, in 1600, where it was ascribed to: *'E. of Ox.'* (Clark, 20).

One comedy that a consensus of scholarly opinion attributes to the embryo Shakespeare is *Love's Labour's Lost*, although it was not published until 1598. Professor Gervinus explains the reason for this.

> The reiterated mention of mythological and historical personages; the air of learning, the Italian and Latin expressions, which here, it must be admitted, serve a comic end; the older England versification, the numerous doggerel verses, and the rhymes more frequent than anywhere else and extending over almost half of the play; all this places this work among the early efforts of the poet. (Gervinus, 164)

Two phrases in the extract above strike a nerve; *historical personages* and *Italian expressions*. Neither can be explained by the innate genius of an author. They rely upon personal knowledge from a reliable source, together with an understanding that breeds familiarity. But this play is amongst the earliest written by a young man raised in a cultural backwater. There is no explanation worthy of that description which accounts for this acquisition of special knowledge by Shakspere. Contrarily, Oxford spoke fluent Latin and Italian, and his Court connections allowed him access to the latest news from abroad. Consider, for example, how the content of the play conflicts with the untraveled Shakspere and his culturally barren start in life.

> In the burlesque parts of Love's Labour's Lost we meet with two favourite characters or caricatures of the Italian comedy; the Pedant, that is the schoolmaster and grammarian, and the military Braggart, the Thraso of the Latin, the 'Captain Spavento' of the Italian stage.
> (ibid 165)

Oxford had sought permission from the Queen to travel to Italy, and while there he would have witnessed these *two favourite characters of the Italian comedy*, thus enlivening his desire to share this entertainment in a play of his own, performed before Elizabeth and her Court. No such scenario exists for Shakspere beyond the pale shadow of his advocates' pleaded guesswork.

The historically accurate content of *Love's Labour's Lost* is a feature often remarked upon but never explained by pro-Shakspere scholars, confined as they are to the dim light shed by Shakspere's non-literary life. The play is set in the court of Navarre, which was a kingdom that lay to the south-west of France and adjoining northern Spain. It was ruled over by the King of Navarre, the future Henri IV, who after his succession joined Navarre to France. The scene is therefore set before Henri III's assassination in 1589.

The composition of the play at a date close to this year finds support from Robert Tofte's *Alba* published in 1598. Tofte remarked: *"Loues Labour Lost, I once did see a Play / Ycleped so, so called to my paine.'* (David, xxiii). The phrasing: 'once did see' implies the author was recalling an event that had happened many years past. In fact the basis of the play has been traced to the year 1583, when *"the English ambassador to the court of France reported to Walsingham that Navarre 'has furnished his Court with principal gentlemen of the Religion, and reformed his house'.'* (ibid xxix). This is reflected in the play when Navarre (he is named Ferdinand not Henri) also decides to reform his house by directing the minds of his courtiers away from revelry and the pursuit of women, in preference to a life of contemplation and study. There is a hidden joke in this that would have caused laughter at Court. Henri IV was known as the *"impetuous, outdoor type, full of spirit and humour, keen on hunting and excessively fond of the ladies, he was known as the vert gallant – the gay spark ... and had at least 56 mistresses.'* (Williams, 1986, 215).

Actual historical parallels between Henri IV and Ferdinand of Navarre were discovered by Professor Abel Lefranc. These were found to be characteristic of Henri of Navarre. Lefranc particularly drew attention to the King's *"impetuous style of riding'*, which is repeated in *Love's Labour's Lost*.

Princess: Was that the king, that spurr'd his horse so hard
Against the steep-up rising hill?
(Act 4, sc. i)

Henri of Navarre also had a habit when writing letters that displayed *"his covering of the whole sheet, 'margent and all','* (David, xxx). Once again, this habit of the king finds expression in *Love's Labour's Lost*, when the princess receives a letter from the King.

Princess: Look you what I have from the loving king.

Rosaline: Madam, came nothing else along with that?

Princess: Nothing but this! yes; as much love in rhyme
As would be cramm'd up in a sheet of paper,
Writ o' both sides the leaf, margent and all,
(Act 5, sc. ii)

A passing remark made by Katharine (Act 2, sc.i) proves to be not without some interest. She says of the character, Dumaine, *"I saw him at the Duke Alençon's once.'* Historically, the duc d'Alençon refers to Hercule (later François), the younger brother of Henri III.

Oxford was in Paris in March 1575. Nine months before his arrival, Charles IX died, and his brother Edouard, who was then in Poland as that nation's king, was recalled to accept the French crown; it was then that he chose to be called King Henri III, leaving his former title duc d'Anjou vacant.

Henri III's coronation occurred on 13 February 1575 at Rheims. Oxford would then have been in France, and it is difficult to believe England's ambassador to France would not have arranged for him to be invited to attend the ceremony unofficially. This would then possibly account for Katherine's reference to *Duke Alençon,* for the King's brother did not assume the vacant title duc d'Anjou until May 1576, following the Edict of Beaulieu (Knecht, 54): by which time Oxford was back in England.

Alençon and Katherine are briefly mentioned for a second time, when Katherine is said to be the heir of Alenson. This again proved accurate. [K]atherine, Alençon's mother, became her son's heir following his death from consumption in June 1584. Henri III hated his brother, and declined to benefit from his will. There being no other brothers, the inheritance went to his mother.

Another very interesting connection between the play and historical fact occurs in the exchange made between Rosaline and Berowne:

Rosaline: Did not I dance with you in Brabant once?

Berowne: I know you did.

Rosaline is the Princess's lady-in-waiting, and the inference to be drawn is that she had attended the Princess at Brabant. Historically —

> [Princess] Marguerite had made journeys exactly corresponding to those referred to by the Princess and her ladies in Act II, Scene i, of the play: to Alençon (Marguerite's brother François was Duc d'Alençon) in 1578 and to Liége (Brabant) in 1577. (David, xxix).

Lefranc's researches also disclosed more parallels between *Love's Labour's Lost* and Henri of Navarre. In 1579, Marguerite de Valois Princess of France arrived in Navarre at the town of Nérac with the Queen-mother, Catherine de' Medici. Henri of Navarre had married Marguerite on 18 August 1572, making her Queen of Navarre, but the question of her dowry, which included Aquitaine, was still being disputed. An identical dispute is played out in *Love's Labour's Lost,* also involving Aquitaine and involving the exact sum of money that had led to the dispute.

Boyet: Now, madam, summon up your dearest spirits:
Consider who the king your father sends,

> To whom he sends, and what's his embassy:
> Yourself, held precious in the world's esteem,
> To parley with the sole inheritor
> Of all perfections that a man may owe,
> Matchless Navarre; the pleas of no less weight
> Than Aquitaine, a dowry for a queen.

It was in this regard that Joseph Hunter, (*New Illustrations*, 1845), made known his discovery that in *Chronicles Johnes' translation*, i, 108 (1810), there is a written record of *"an engagement by Charles VI, about 1420, to pay Charles of Aragon, King of Navarre, 200,000 crowns."* (David, 36).

> King:  Madam, your father here doth intimate
> The payment of a hundred thousand crowns;
> Being but the one half of an entire sum
> Disbursed by my father in his wars.
> But say that he, or we, as neither have,
> Receiv'd that sum, yet there remains unpaid
> A hundred thousand more; in surety of the which,
> One part of Aquitaine is bound to us,
> Although not valued to the money's worth,
> If then the king your father will restore
> But that one half of which is unsatisfied,
> We will give up our right in Aquitaine,
> And hold fair friendship with his majesty.
> But that, it seems, he little purposeth,
> For here he doth demand to have repaid
> A hundred thousand crowns; and not demands
> On payment of a hundred thousand crowns
> To have his title live in Aquitaine.          (Act 2, sc. i)

Gervinus confirmed the problem this has for the conventional view of Shakespeare.

> ... it is difficult to explain. No source is known for the purport of this piece, which, however (as Hunter has proved from Monstrelet's 'Chronicles'), in the one point of the payment of France to Navarre (Act II. sc. 1) rests on an historical fact, namely, an exchange of territory between the two crowns. (Gervinus, 165)

Unquestionably, someone had a very detailed knowledge of what was happening across the English Channel at the time this dispute relating to Princess Marguerite's dowry was still under negotiation, and that person was unlikely to be fifteen-year-old Will Shakspere, buried away in the rural environment of a village in the Midlands, with less than fifteen hundred residents (the size of a modern-day UK school). On the other hand, Oxford was twice in Paris during this period: in 1575 on his outward journey, and again in 1576 when he was homeward bound. It would have been within the compass of his position as a senior member of Elizabeth's court to have been kept informed of events relayed back to England by the Queen's ambassador to France.

In Act 5, Scene ii, the lords disguise themselves as Russians. For this, there must have been a reason that was topical when the play was first performed.

> There had been an exchange of ambassadors between England and Russia and in 1583 a special envoy was sent by Czar Ivan the Terrible to ask for the hand of Lady Mary Hastings in marriage. The lady was nicknamed at court the 'Empress of Muscovia' and was much teased about the wooing, which was conducted with elaborate and, on the part of the English, mock ceremony. Sir Sidney Lee was convinced that this incident lay behind the scene in the play. (David, xxvii)

But after the death of Ivan in March 1585 (N.S.), this piece of comedy would have been in too bad taste for it to be included in the composition of the play.

Further evidence of the author's personal acquaintance with French politics is indicated by the names appearing in the *Dramatis Personæ* of *Love's Labour's Lost*. In which instance, it is noteworthy that neither the King of Navarre nor the Princess of France is actually named in the play. The King of Navarre was identified as Ferdinand only because of Rowe in 1709, although no king by that name had previously ruled Navarre. As for the names of those who attended the King, it is these that attract attention. *"The Duc de Biron [Anglicised as Berowne] and the Duc de Longueville [Anglicised as Longaville] were his faithful supporters,'* (David, xxv); these lords are faithfully repeated as supporters of Ferdinand. The third lord in the play, the Duke Dumaine, has been identified with Charles of Lorraine, the duc de Mayenne; the 'i' and 'y' were often interchangeable in Elizabethan English, hence, 'de Mai[en]ne' becomes 'Dumaine'. In addition, *'the names Boyet, Marcadé, and de la Mothe appear in contemporary registers of court officials.'* (David, xxx); thus adding further confirmation of historical accuracy, with regard to the names of those attending the royal couple.

The inclusion of Mayenne is sometimes objected to, because after the murder of Henri III in 1589, Mayenne took up arms against Henri of Navarre to win the right of succession to the Crown. The conflict had resulted from the formation of the Catholic League set up in 1584. The League was opposed to Navarre becoming King of France because he was a Huguenot. Mayenne's opposition can therefore be dated to after 1584.

The composition of *Love's Labour's Lost* from the pen of Lord Oxford may now be confidently dated to a period soon after his return from Italy in 1576, but not later than 1584.

Not all plays written by Oxford after his return from Italy are so easily identifiable. *Twelfth Night* is an interesting example. The composition of this play was originally assigned to 1613-14 upon the basis of internal evidence that had been identified by *scholars* from certain references. Had Oxford been a contender for authorship at that time, he would have been dismissed as easily then, as scholars dismiss him today, and for the same reason: he died in 1604. But in 1831, John Payne Collier published an entry from John Manningham's Diary dated 2 February 1601 (O.S.), reporting that the diarist had seen a performance of *Twelfth Night*. Manningham was a law student at Middle Temple, and the description of the play he gave, leaves no doubt that this was the play he had seen. Scholars were therefore forced to tear up their account of the date when the play was written, and start again. It is now thought to have been written between 1599 and 1601.

Many Oxford supporters believe the date of the original composition is much earlier. The reason for this is found in—

> PECK's "Desiderata Curiosa" [where] there is a passage in which he says that he proposes to publish a manuscript called "a pleasant conceit of Vere, Earl of Oxford, discontented at the rising of a mean gentleman in the English Court, circa 1580." (Clark, 364)

The historical facts surrounding this date can, in fact, be applied to the composition of *Twelfth Night*. It was circa 1580 that Walter Raleigh's star began to rise at Court. An indication of this may be determined from a letter addressed to Lord Treasurer Burghley, dated 15 July 1580, referring to the Acts of the Privy Council.

> Walter Raleigh, gentleman, by the appointment of the Lord Grey is to have the charge of a hundred of those men presently levied within the City of London to be transported for her Majesty's service into Ireland, his Lordship is desired to deliver unto the said Walter Raleigh, by way of imprest, one hundred pounds. (Williams, 1962, 23)

It was at this time that Oxford had cause to be discontented with Raleigh.

> Early in 1580 he was paying attention to a new young lady of the bedchamber, Anne Vavasour, Raleigh showed a protectiveness for her virginity which echoes his reluctance to lay siege to Elizabeth Knollys, and he bravely or foolishly put in writing his warning against the important and wild nobleman. (ibid 21)

This warning, *"Raleigh, advice to Anne Vavasour"* came in the form of a poem of three stanzas of six lines: each commencing with, *"Many desire, but few or none deserve,"* and concluding with, *"farewell the rest ..."* (ibid 22). Oxford's discontent can be imagined at the impertinence of this *mean gentleman* who dared intrude into his personal relationship with Anne Vavasour. But, at the same time, this *mean gentleman* had caught the eye of the Queen, leading Raleigh to believe, misguidedly of course, that she was in love with him and could be wooed into marriage.

Oxford's response can be seen in the characterisation of Malvolio: *"A fantastical steward to Olivia,"* (Rowe). According to Farmer (1767), the name is a transposition of Malivolo. As a figure of fun, he is shown to be *a kind of Puritan*. The advice given by Raleigh to Anne Vavasour, and the poem he slipped into the pocket of Elizabeth Knollys could have some bearing upon this. Despite Malvolio's outwardly moral stance, he is made to look foolish by believing that Olivia is secretly in love with him, and that she has sent him a letter. This allows a capital piece of subtle, bawdy fun to be put into his mouth, effectively mocking his puritan attitude.

Elizabeth, upon seeing the play, would have looked for her own identity in the character of Olivia – *"A Lady of great Beauty and Fortune,'* (Rowe). In Act 3, scene iv: Olivia responds to *'Malvolio's fantastical wooing,"* by referring to it as *'very Midsummer madness.'* Malvolio had been gulled into appearing before Olivia fantastically attired, which may have had something to do with Raleigh's first appearance at Court, dressed as a seaman.

Oxford completes his revenge by having Malvolio declared a lunatic and confined to a dark room. There, in darkness, he is tormented by Feste and Sir Toby into expressing the belief of Pythagoras, with regard to the transmigration of souls. Pythagoras was said to have believed himself the reincarnation of Euphorbus, killed by Menelaus in the Trojan War. The story has been traced to *The Testament of Heraclides of Pontus* and was later confirmed by the biographer Diogenes Laertius, a third century biographer of Greek philosophers. Raleigh later became a central figure for a group of free thinkers investigating spiritualism and discarnate souls. 'The School of Night' is actually referred to in *Love's Labour's Lost*.

It is with these connections: on the one hand Raleigh and Elizabeth, on the other hand Malvolio and Olivia, that when they are viewed with PECK'S *"Desiderata Curiosa"*, concerning Oxford and a *mean gentleman in the English Court*, that a possible unity of purpose can be determined. This would then allow *Twelfth Night* to have been originally begun in 1580, and for Oxford to have sought revenge against Raleigh by mocking him as Malvolio. Certainly, Raleigh believed himself to be at the receiving end of Oxford's annoyance. In a letter he addressed to Burghley dated 12 May 1583, Raleigh does confess, *"myself may be most in danger of his poison and sting."* (Clark, 605).

A quite different set of circumstances surrounds the composition of *Romeo and Juliet*. Commentators appear to be unanimous that when Shakespeare wrote this work, he had by his side, and was indebted to, a copy of Arthur Brooke's edition of *The Tragical History of Romeus and Juliet*. Little of consequence is known about Brooke, other than that this was his only publication before drowning at sea between New Haven and the French coast in 1563.

What is most of interest to supporters of Oxford, is Bandello's version of the story, in which he states Juliet was aged sixteen, 'Shakespeare' unaccountably changed this to fourteen. Fourteen was Anne Cecil's age at the time of her planned wedding to Oxford, scheduled for September 1571. But at the last moment the date was put back to 16 December, the 3rd Sunday in Advent.

It has also been observed that *Romeo and Juliet* contains *"many verbal resemblances'* to the poem of 3020 lines written by Brooke. Research has shown that there was a person named Arthur Brooke, born in 1544. In which case, he would have been seventeen or eighteen years of age in 1562, at the time of publication, and this would account for the poem's description as *pedestrian, prolix, leaden, inert,* and *wearisome*. J. J. Munro, in his introduction to a 1908 edition of *Romeus and Juliet*, stated that *'Brooke's story meanders on like a listless stream in a strange and impossible land.'* It would also explain Oxford's role as the author, were it indeed he, writing under the pseudonym of Brooke, for he would have been barely twelve years old when the poem was published; but a true prodigy in the mould of Mozart.

Oxford's youthfulness and his use of a pseudonym would also explain the need to ensure that any search made for Arthur Brooke would end in failure. His sudden death at sea, with no body recovered, answered that need. It has also been said that he was *en voyage* to take part in France's Religious Wars. This must be doubted. The First War of Religion began in April 1562 and was over in March 1563. Thereafter, Catherine de' Medici, the Queen-mother, took France's boy-king, Charles IX, on a grand tour of the country, which lasted one and a quarter years. During that time France was at peace. The Second War of Religion did not begin until September 1567.

1567 was also the year that George Turberville published a collection of poetry entitled, *Epitaphs, Epigrams, Songs and Sonnets* which included *An Epitaph on the Death of Master Arthur Brooke Drownde in Passing to New Haven*. Turberville is described by Ogburn as a poetical disciple of de

Vere's uncle, the Earl of Surrey, and that by writing this tribute he was providing authenticity for Brooke, thus diverting attention away from the youthful Oxford.

Romeo and Juliet in Shakespearean form, appears to contain two clues, the first of which provides the date of composition, and the second the name of the playwright. The date is alluded to by the Nurse in Act I, Scene iii: *'Tis since the earthquake now eleven years.'* The question is – which earthquake is the nurse referring to? If the nurse is speaking true, then she is referring to the 'earthquake that devastated Verona in 1570. Joseph Hunter described it thus:

> It will not be denied that Shakespeare might make an Italian story allude to an event that occurred in London; but the whole argument is of the most shadowy kind, and it seems to be entirely destroyed when the fact is introduced that in 1570 there did occur a most remarkable earthquake in the neighbourhood of Verona, so severe that it destroyed Ferrara, and which would form long after an epoch in the chronological calculations of the old wives of Lombardy. (Clark, 475)

However, there was also a serious tremor felt in London in April 1580, although its epicentre was thought to be in northern France where greater damage occurred. This earthquake is preferred by conventionalists to the one felt in Verona, because it allows their Shakspere to have written *Romeo and Juliet* in 1591. The truth of the matter is that if Oxford wrote the play, he would have had Verona in mind, and his reference to eleven years dates its composition to 1581. If Shakspere had written the play, it is quite possible he would have been referring to the several accounts written that Easter week, describing the apprehension felt in the capital.

Let us move from this and consider the greatly overlooked importance of an observation made by Admiral Hubert H. Holland in *Shakespeare Through Oxford Glasses*. Interest centres upon a remark made by Mercutio about Romeo in Act 2, Scene iv.

Mercutio: O, here's a wit of cheveril, that stretches from an inch narrow to an ell broad!

Romeo: I stretch it out for that word, broad:

Cheveril is soft flexible kidskin leather, but Mercutio refers to the word, not the skin, and emphasises its part in the wit that he and Romeo are exchanging with each other. So, what is the wit contained in this word?

Holland, to his credit, took Mercutio seriously and narrowed the word 'inche' or 'ynche'; that is, according to Old English spelling, and was left with 'che', which is in accordance with the first three letters of cheveril. He then focussed upon the last two letters, 'il', equivalent to 'ell', since cheverell is an alternative spelling of cheveril (ell is an old English measurement of variable length); *ell broad* is also part of the word play. Thus cheveril stretched from an 'inche' *narrow* to ell, or in this case, 'il' *broad*, becomes: che – ver – il, which rearranged is: IL CHE VER.

'Ver' is a variant form of 'Vere',

> Albericus de Ver married Beatrice, half sister of King William, and they had five sons. He founded Earl's Colne Priory in 1105 ... [His son] Aubrey II was responsible for building the great castle-keep at Hedingham. (www.earlofoxford.com/eo00.htm)

This leaves *che* and *il*, both of which are Italian words. But, much more importantly, *"il che is used to translate 'which' when it represents a whole idea, not just a specific noun.'* (*Italian Grammar*, Alwena Lamping, 2006, p.83).

Consequently, in this piece of dialogue occurring in *Romeo and Juliet*, Mercutio's wit is being used to identify *the thought* behind the middle section 'Ver' of CHEVERIL. What is this thought behind Ver as Romeo? Indeed, what has Ver to do with this play at all; unless, that is, Ver was the author? Most certainly, Romeo accepts that the word should be *broad*; that is stretched out, for he readily agrees with this in his response.

Oxford had, it seems, been leading up to this in the preceding lines:

Benvolio:      Here comes Romeo, here comes Romeo.

Mercutio:     Without his roe, like a dried herring.

As Ogburn observed: Romeo without his phonetic roe is left with ME O. Oxford was wont to identify himself at the foot of his early poems with the initial letter, 'O': a reference to his title. Also, the personal pronoun 'me' occurs in both the accusative and dative cases. This would be seen of significance to the Latin speaker, because it allows 'me' to be the object of Mercutio's banter, with 'O' as the identifier, qualifying the pronoun, 'me'.

Thus, Romeo *without his roe* is 'ME O', which can be understood to be Oxford identifying himself with Romeo, 'like a dried herring'.

Interestingly, it was William Hazlitt who first made known —

> Romeo is Hamlet in love. There is the same rich exuberance of passion and sentiment in the one, that there is of thought and sentiment in the other. Both are absent and self-involved, both live out of themselves in a world of imagination. Hamlet is abstracted from everything: Romeo is abstracted from everything but his love, and lost in it. (Stokes, 282)

Also, Hamlet has long been recognised by Oxford supporters as a self-portrait of its author, surrounded by caricatures of the people closest to him at the time of his greatest, inner, torment.

One can anticipate the pro-Stratford response. Complete disinterest. Yet, consider! The word CHEVERIL exists. The directions exist. Apply the directions to the word; translate this into the language of the play. The result is the solution to Mercutio's wit. Oxford well knew that writing plays fell far below what was expected of his position and high birth. But his innate genius demanded that he release his gift to the world, and this he did, anonymously at first. Later, he used an allonym, whose name has ever since been given credit for the poems and plays that poured from his pen.

Just now and again he identifies himself. Here it is through the wit of Mercutio. In the sonnets, he confessed to the ultimate disappearance of his name after death, while his work lived on. Others took up his cause, like Ben Jonson who revealed the truth of the deception in the inscription beneath the monument at Stratford-upon-Avon. Thomas Thorpe was another, with his cryptogram embedded in the dedication to the Sonnets. Leonard Digges was also amongst this group, with his reference to the 'moniment' confirming the secret it held: and it was he who encrypted de Vere's name into the first sentence of the poem that was originally intended for inclusion in the First Folio.

**This house is the "real" home of Juliet's family (the Capuleti). The building dates from the 13th century (Verona Tourist Board).**

And so, was the teenage Brooke in reality the embryo Shakespeare? Quite probably; the faithful attention that Oxford gave to the childish verse in *Romeus and Juliet* is the love that an older person gives to the fruit of their youth. Did Oxford revise his earlier work written in 1581, eleven years after the giant earthquake struck Verona and destroyed Ferrara? Why not? It was within his power to have done so.

# 11

## SHAKESPEARE EMERGES FROM THE SHADOWS

Having burst onto the literary scene in 1593, by the end of the following year, the name William Shakespeare had just as suddenly disappeared. It was kept alive solely through the two dedications to Henry Wriothesley, which appeared in *Venus and Adonis* and *Lucrece*. Then, in 1598, the name began to re-emerge; cautiously at first, but soon increasing in the number of its appearances.

Its re-emergence began, firstly, as a means of identifying plays that had hitherto been attributed to an anonymous author. Yet, four years earlier, Shakespeare had been at the height of his fame, and this would have been the appropriate time to capitalise on his popularity. The fact that it never happened, suggests some form of censorship had been imposed, and that by 1598, this was no longer operating with the same force. Coincidentally, it was in 1598 that Oxford's father-in-law, Lord Burghley, the man who had for many years been director of censorship, took ill and died.

> As a statesman Burghley saw that his duty was to give the Queen his best advice and then to carry out whatever policy seemed expedient to her. ... His patronage in church and state enabled him to harness the clergy, the gentry, and the nobility to the tasks of administration. His attendance in council and Parliament was constant, and he understood how to manage both. He directed censorship. (Encyclopædia Britannica)

The full explanation of Lord Burghley's role in the suppression and censorship of his son-in-law's plays and poems has been left for later discussion, since it concerns a range of matters that have yet to be introduced. For the present, the important fact to note is that in the spring of 1598, Lord Burghley fell ill. His condition continued to worsen, and on 5 August he breathed his last.

The head of censorship in England was no longer a potent force. Any embargo that he had imposed upon Shakespeare's name appearing in print, beyond the poems that had already been sanctioned by Archbishop Whitgift, was no longer as compelling as it had been while he lived. It is therefore of interest to note that one month after Lord Burghley's death,

Cambridge graduate Francis Meres entered *Palladis Tamia, Wit's Treasury* in the Stationers' Register. Meres was the nephew of John Florio, appointed by Burghley to the Southampton household as a tutor in 1592, where he remained until 1594. Meres has since become famous for having named Shakespeare as the author of some twelve plays, ten of which had already been published anonymously. Meres's family relationship with Florio may explain the knowledge he obtained concerning the nameless author of the plays he identified as 'Shakespeare's', and his reference to the poet's sonnets, circulating amongst his private friends, for these were unheard of until then. *Palladis Tamia*, which means 'Athene's Maidservant', ensured that Shakespeare had been recalled to life.

> The English tongue is mightily enriched and gorgeously invested in rare ornaments and resplendent abiliments by Sir Philip Sidney, Spenser, Daniel, Drayton, Warner, Shakespeare, Marlowe and Chapman. (Wilson, 242)

The name Shakespeare had only thrice before been mentioned in public: once in 1593 and twice in 1594. On the first two occasions it was as a signature on the letters of dedication to Henry Wriothesley. In this respect, the author of the two narrative poems had been shy of drawing too much attention to his name, and had twice omitted it from the title pages of the two poems, leaving it for others to discover by reading the dedication.

This had been a wise but ultimately ineffective strategy, because on the third occasion when the name appeared in print, the anonymous author of *Willobie His Avisa* satirically hyphenated it to Shake–speare, describing W.S. as *'an old player'* (Oxford was then forty-four) while alluding to H.W.'s youth: *'If years I want'* (Southampton was then twenty, rising twenty-one), and had recently been in breach of a marriage arrangement with Elizabeth Vere. The *Avisa* poem declared him to be one *'that never loved before'*.

However, by 1598, given the premise that William Shakespeare had been the pseudonym used by Oxford, it remained essential that the name continue to be mentioned in books like *Wit's Treasury*, so as to allay any suspicions that may have been circulating regarding Shakespeare's true identity. This was especially important because back in 1593-94, within the space of little more than twelve months, Shakespeare's name had been on the lips of every scholar as the result of his two magnificent narrative poems. But, just as suddenly as the name appeared, it faded into the background. Four years were to elapse without a single new publication by Shakespeare. Then, in 1598, the name re-emerged, but no longer as a poet; the man behind the name was now being celebrated for the first time as a playwright, and of having written works that had previously been ascribed to an unnamed author. *Wit's Treasury* made a special point of singling out Shakespeare and listing twelve of his plays, which had previously been known only to a few writers and pirate publishers, but which may have been rumoured as the work of a nobleman.

The apparent suppression of Shakespeare's name on new publications between 1594 and 1598 had finally ceased. But any hint of a connection across the class-divide, between a high-ranking earl and a low class actor, was skilfully avoided. From that moment forward, with Shakespeare now officially named as a playwright, it has become possible to understand how that simple prank in 1592, with Oxford and Southampton joining forces to get the senior Earl's poems into print, had had a knock-on effect. For it had given rise to a situation that would not only befog the literary world for generations to come with imponderable questions and improbabilities, it was also to lead researchers in a merry dance, searching vainly for answers in non-existent records.

Between 1594 and 1598, theatre-goers in London and the provinces had witnessed a number of plays by an unnamed author. These all involved a royal setting, complete with characters drawn from the nobility. The author's connection with the royal court had to be suspected. For it is a dull mind that fails to appreciate questions would be asked regarding the author of these plays. And when questions fail to be answered; and even worse when it seems that nobody has an answer, suspicions are bred and rumours fed.

Meres's timely book allayed any further doubt about the authorship of these Court plays, and it succeeded with panache.

> As the soul of Euphorbus was thought to live in Pythagoras, so the sweet witty soul of Ovid lives in mellifluous and honey-tongued Shakespeare: Witness his Venus and Adonis, his Lucrece, his sugared sonnets among his private friends, etc.
>
> As Plautus and Seneca are accounted the best for comedy and tragedy among the Latins, so Shakespeare among the English is the most excellent in both kinds for the stage. For comedy, witness his 'Gentlemen of Verona', his 'Errors', his 'Love's Labour's Lost', his 'Love's Labour's Won', his 'Midsummer Night's Dream', and his 'Merchant of Venice'; for tragedy his 'Richard II', 'Richard III', 'Henry IV', 'King John', 'Titus Andronicus', and his 'Romeo and Juliet'.
>
> As Epius Stolo said that the Muses would speak with Plautus' tongue, if they would speak Latin; so I say that the Muses would speak with Shakespeare's fine filed phrase, if they would speak English. (Michell, 54-5)

It is noteworthy that Meres included *Love's Labour's Won,* a title lost, or still to be positively identified, while also omitting *Taming of the Shrew,* and

*Henry VI Parts 1, 2 and 3.* Some may also wonder why Meres concentrated so much upon Shakespeare's plays by naming twelve of them. It was an exceptional thing to have done, as Marchette Chute pointed out: *'Meres mentions a great many playwrights in his book ... Shakespeare was the only one he singled out for extended comment.'* (Ogburn, 142)

> There must be a reason for all this, and the only realistic one I can find is that the decision had been reached that the author of the hitherto unattributed dramatic masterpieces was to be 'Shakespeare', and Meres had been selected to launch the artifice unobtrusively.
>
> (ibid 143)

The publication of *Wit's Treasury* settled the question of attribution authoritatively. Shakespeare had been named as the mysterious author of a dozen titles that until then had been performed anonymously: some had even been printed and sold to the public, but always with the author's name absent. These plays would later be referred to by an introductory letter to the First Folio as: *"stolen and surreptitious copies: maimed and deformed by the stealth and frauds of injurious impostors."* Yet, lovers of Shakespeare are still asked to believe that Shakspere, a man famed for his prosecution of those who stole malt from him by not paying for it, was the same man who allowed one after another of his plays to be *stolen, maimed and deformed*, without ever once making the slightest effort to prevent it. This was, of course, the great drawback, brought about by Oxford having appointed an allonym to stand in as the author of his work. When things went wrong, as they did when pirated editions of his plays were published, and later, too, his Sonnets, neither he nor Shakspere, nor for that matter anyone else, were able to intervene without revealing in public the secret of that arrangement.

It may therefore be instructive to glance over events for 1598. On 24 January, Abraham Sturley, a local Warwickshire businessman, wrote to Richard Quiney, enquiring if he thought *'our countriman Mr Shaksper'* would be prepared *"to deal in the matter of our tithes'* (Ogburn, 30). Shakspere's absence from London had been noted in the previous November, when tax collectors in Bishopsgate failed to locate *"William Shackspere'* causing him to be listed amongst the dead – or as one who had left the ward.

On 4 February, *"Wm Shackespere',* living in New Place, in the Chapple Street ward, was reported to be in possession of *'x quarters'* of grain. In other words, he was profiteering at the time of famine. On the 25th of the month, *Henry IV part 1* was entered in the Stationers' Register. It was printed in quarto later that year. The title page included a detailed account of its content, but Shakespeare's name is noticeably absent. This was one amongst *'Eighteen unauthorised versions of his plays [which] were ... published during his lifetime in quarto editions by unscrupulous publishers.'* (www.william-shakespeare.info/shakespeare-play-king-henry-iv-part-1.htm).

In March, Lord Burghley, head of censorship in England, who had recently been noticeably ailing, took to his bed for the final time. That same month a pirated edition of *Love's Labour's Lost* was published. This was the first play to include the author's name. It read: *"Newly corrected and augmented / By W. Shakespere'*. The title-page also claimed the play had been *"presented before her Highnes / this last Christmas.'* The reference to it having been newly corrected and augmented must refer to the play's performance, not the book, for there was no previous edition; also, the book was full of misprints, quite different from the care and attention given to *Venus and Adonis* and *Lucrece*. Furthermore, Shakspere had, some months before the Christmas performance before the Queen, purchased New Place. It was while residing there that he was accused of hoarding grain during a time of famine.

On 22 July, *The Merchant of Venice* otherwise called *The Jew of Venice* was entered in the Stationers' Register by James Roberts, but he declined to go through with the publication. Instead, two years later, he transferred the copyright to Thomas Heyes. The play was finally published at the end of 1600. The title page boldly asserted: *"Written by William Shakespeare'.*

On 4 August Lord Burghley died at his London home and was buried at St Martin's Church, Stamford, in Lincolnshire. Interestingly, his wife and favourite daughter Anne, wife to Edward de Vere, were both buried in London at Westminster Abbey.

One month later, on 7 September, *Wit's Treasury* was entered in the Stationers' Register. Readers were to be left in no doubt that there, set before them in print, was a reference to England's proud master of the written word: a champion amongst poets and playwrights to compete against the greatest minds of the classical world. The villagers in Stratford-upon-Avon had every reason to laud the scholastic son of their former alderman. But, in fact, no one there took any notice. If Meres's Shakespeare was Stratford's Shakspere, then it went unrecognised in the Warwickshire village.

On 1 October, the parish of St Helen's in Bishopsgate listed William Shakspere as a tax defaulter for the sum of 13s. 4d. This remained unpaid. That same month, Richard Quiney wrote a letter addressed to *'To my Lovinge good ffrende & countreymann Mr Wm. Shackespere,'* requesting a loan of

£30, '*uppon Mr Bushells & my securytee or Mr Myttons with me.*' (Laroque, 133). But the letter was never sent.

Quiney was in London representing the affairs of Stratford-upon-Avon at court. He was a well-educated man, and recognised as an obvious choice to make the trip to London on behalf of parishioners, who were seeking a tax reduction for their parish, due to the effects of a recent devastating fire. It is therefore noticeable that Shakspere, supposedly even more educated than Quiney, literate beyond question, a resident in London, and a man most knowledgeable in matters relating to the English legal system, was not asked to perform this important office of representing Stratford-upon-Avon at its time of need. In fact, Shakspere was seen as nothing more than a 'good friend and countryman' who, like his father in the past, had added money-lending to his business activities.

This side of Shakspere's activities was obviously known, and it would seem distrusted in Stratford, for Adrian Quiney, Richard's father, wrote to his son almost immediately, saying: "*If you bargain with Mr. Sha. or receive money therefor, bring your money home if you may.*' (Ogburn, 30). A few days later, Abraham Sturley replied to Richard, having heard of his intended approach to Shakspere. He remarked: "*that our countryman Mr Wm Shak. would procure us money ... I will like of as I shall hear when, and where, and how.*' (ibid). Earlier that year both Sturley and Quiney had consulted together about asking Shakspere to deal in the matter of their tithes. It would seem from their remarks that his response to the offer did nothing to encourage much confidence.

At the time *Wit's Treasury* went on sale, and with the name William Shakespeare soon to become open season for anyone intent upon making money from his work, Shakspere returned home to Stratford-upon-Avon. Soon after his arrival, he collected ten pence at Christmas for the sale of *one load of stone* delivered to the Chamber offices.

Pd. to Mr. Shaxspere for on lod of sion · · · x.d.

If anyone in the village of Stratford had purchased a copy of *Wit's Treasury*, there is no indication that they associated the brilliant mind of William Shakespeare with the ten-penny businessman, 'Mr Shaxspere'. The two men were viewed as being distinct from each other; that is, as far as local records show.

This is not to be wondered at, if documentary evidence is adhered to; Shakspere was the eldest son of a local illiterate family. In order to help support his father, who was going through a difficult period, he left school before any serious lessons had begun. His apprenticeship to a butcher had been short-lived, and his marriage had been a hasty introduction to raising a family. Against this background, it was impossible to believe that he had become the rave of London's literary life.

His modern-day supporters disagree, and to make their point, they cite Meres.

> [T]he best for Comedy amongst vs bee, Edward Earle of Oxforde, Doctor Gager of Oxforde, Maister Rowley once a rare Scholler of learned Pembroke Hall in Cambridge, Maister Edwardes one of her Maiesties Chappell, eloquent and wittie Iohn Lilly, Lodge, Gascoyne, Greene, Shakespeare, Thomas Nash, Thomas Heywood, Anthony Mundye our best plotter, Chapman, Potter, Wilson, Hathway, and Henry Chettle. (Nelson, 386)

Not unnaturally, supporters of Shakespeare's Stratford origins see this as documentary proof that Edward Earl of Oxford could not have been Shakespeare. But proof it is not. Proof has to be both necessary and sufficient to be afforded that highly prized title. Meres's reference to Shakespeare alongside Oxford certainly satisfies the condition of necessity, but not of sufficiency. Several cases are known from the past, where two names appearing on a list have implied they represented different people, but when examined closer, both names have been found to apply to the same individual. (Ogburn, 142)

More to the point, however, is the fact that when an author ceases to write under his or her own name, and thereafter secretly transfers all new work to that of an allonym, both names need to be listed in order to identify which work is assigned to which name. And that is precisely what Meres has achieved. He first acknowledged Oxford for his early Comedies, which were already public knowledge (Puttenham, 1589): he then granted Oxford's allonym, William Shakspere, concessionary title to the work subsequently produced under that name. In this way the allonym was protected. To outward appearances, Oxford and Shakespeare were two different persons, whereas it was Oxford and his allonym, Shakspere, who were the two different persons—all very clever, but also very devious.

It may be instructive to note that some, e.g. Professor Alan Nelson—the only academic, surely, ever to have written a biography of Shakespeare while being entirely ignorant that this was what he had been doing, wrote: *'Meres (for one) knew that Oxford and Shakespeare were not the same man.'* (Nelson, 387) It was, of course, Oxford and Shakspere who were 'not the same man'. Oxford was already known to be a writer of exceptional talent. Puttenham, Harvey and Spenser had made this plain a decade earlier.

Therefore Oxford could not be ignored by Meres. Shakspere, on the other hand, had been secretly engaged as Oxford's allonym. As the allonym of an earl, it was necessary for Meres to furnish him with the work and plaudits of the author, whose role he had undertaken to play. This, Meres did with panache. Nelson's assessment simply displays a typical lack of critical judgement that has become all too common amongst those academics who dwell in Plato's Cave. The Shakespeare authorship question is a complex problem involving logical analysis. It requires far deeper levels of thought, as well as a greater application of intelligence than is currently evident from those defending the Stratford position.

# 12

# SHAKESPEARE NAMED AND FAMED

After four years of absence, during which the name of Shakespeare all but disappeared, the world awoke to discover that the author of *Venus and Adonis* and *Lucrece* was also the author of twelve plays that had previously been anonymous. The fame earlier achieved by Shakespeare for his two poems had never once been used during those years of silence to attract attention to his theatrical work; even the printed quartos of plays he had written failed to, or dared not mention the author's name, although it must have been known. But from 1598 onwards, all this changed. It then became perfectly acceptable to mention the name Shakespeare in print. *Wit's Treasury* can be said to have sanctioned its use by attributing a dozen previously unnamed plays to Shakespeare's credit. And, as for his *sugared sonnets*, these, too, now had a named author. From a poet, having written just two narrative poems four years ago, the name William Shakespeare had been transformed overnight into a famous playwright and sonneteer.

As realisation sank in that censorship of this name was now removed, references to Shakespeare at last began to emerge. In 1598 Oxford graduate Richard Barnfield published *The Encomion of Lady Pecunia*, a poem in praise of money. To this he added *The Complaint of Poetry for the Death of Liberality*. In the final volume, he added a late appendix of *Poems in diverse Humors*. This, together with *Wit's Treasury*, included the earliest praise of Shakespeare ever recorded. It occurs in a piece entitled *A Remembrance of some English Poets*. After the space of four years, someone finally dared to join Meres in offering immortal praise to the poet known as 'Shakespeare'.

> And Shakespeare thou, whose hony-flowing Veine,
> (Pleasing the World) thy praises doth obtain,
> Whose Venus, and whose Lucrece (sweete and chaste)
> Thy Name in fame's immortal Booke have plac't.
> Live ever you, at least in Fame live ever:
> Well may thy Bodie die, but Fame dies never.
> 
> (Rollett, April 1996)

The astute reader may inwardly question the repeated use of the word 'ever'. If Barnfield was aware of Shakespeare's true identity, its deliberate inclusion will have signalled to others who were also in on the secret that E. Ver—an alternative spelling, and phonetically correct pronunciation of E. Vere (rhymes with 'air')—was Shakespeare: the poet to whom he was referring.

In June 1599, Cambridge graduate John Weever also joined in the praise given to Shakespeare, with his publication of *Epigrammes in the oldest cut and newest fashions*. Amongst its one hundred and fifty or so verses, mostly ranging from four lines to twenty, there is one of fourteen lines (Epigram 22). It has been written in the same sonnet form favoured by Shakespeare: whom he names three times.

            Ad Gulielmum Shakespeare

Honie-tong'd Shakespeare when I saw thine issue
I swore Apollo got them and none other.
Their rosie-tinted features cloth'd in tissue,
Some heaven born goddesse said to be their mother:
Rose-cheek't Adonis with his amber tresses,
Fair fire-hot Venus charming him to love her,
Chaste Lucrece virgine-like her dresses,
Prowd lust-stung Tarquine seeking still to prove her:
Romeo Richard, more whose names I know not,
Their sugred tongues, and power attractive beauty
Say they are Saints althogh that Saints they shew not
For thousands vowes to them subjective dutie:
  They burn in love thy children Shakespeare het them,   [heated them]
  Go, woo thy Muse more Nymphish brood beget them.

                                              (ibid)

Weever has drawn upon Meres's reference to Shakespeare's *sugared sonnets* and substituted *sugared tongues*. Then, with a knowing nod to the poet, he has composed the verse in sonnet form. Weever also mentions *Romeo and Juliet* and *Richard II*, both of which had been entered in the Stationers' Register two years earlier. The public could be left in no doubt now that William Shakespeare was a poet and playwright of recognised repute, and greatly admired by Barnfield, Meres and Weever.

In that same year, two editions of *Venus and Adonis* were published by William Leake, who had recently acquired the copyright. The year before, a second edition of *Lucrece* had also been published to coincide with *Wit's Treasury*, and *Poems in Divers Humours*. This was followed in 1600, by two further editions of *Lucrece*. Interest in Shakespeare had revived and was proving to be very profitable.

William Jaggard was another who seized the opportunity afforded by the release of Shakespeare's name from its former restraint. In 1599 he published the first edition of *The Passionate Pilgrim*, ascribing the content to W. Shakespeare:

> ... In fact only five of its 20 poems are Shakespeare's. Two are sonnets from the famous sequence that would be published in 1609 (Sonnet 138 and Sonnet 144). The remaining three poems were lifted from Act 4 of ... Love's Labour's Lost.
>
> (Dunton-Downer & Riding, 458)

And what was Shakspere's reaction to Jaggard having taken this liberty with work claimed to be from the pen of W. Shakespeare? Absolutely none. He ignored what happened, as he had ignored the piratical publications of 'his' plays. It is therefore a fair question to ask, repeatedly, if necessary: Is this really the same man that never once hesitated to apply to the courts for repayment of debts arising from the sale of malt?

Jaggard's publication of sonnets 138 and 144 was the first sight the world had of these poems, although Francis Meres had referred to them in *Wit's Treasury*. It would be another ten years before the complete sequence of 154 was printed. But Shakspere remained quiet about these too, which raises interesting questions concerning his silence: a silence that will bear closer inspection later.

1599 also saw the construction of the Globe theatre on the south bank of the Thames: the work apparently being carried out by carpenter-builder Peter Street and his workmen, using timber transported across the river from the demolished Theatre at Shoreditch. Twenty years later, Heminge and Condell testified at court (*Witter v. Heminge and Condell*) that William Shakespere (sic) held a ten percent shareholding in the Globe: the same as he had held in the Lord Chamberlain's Company.

The circumstances that surrounded the fifty percent shares held equally by Shakspere, Phillips, Heminge, Pope, and Kemp are of some interest. It appears that these were sold to two financiers, William Leveson and Thomas Savage *'who regranted and reassigned to every of them severally a fifth part of the said moiety.'* (Wilson, 253). In short, their holding was returned, but under conditions that left Leveson and Savage with rights to the shares.

The land on which the Globe was built belonged to Nicholas Brend; he had inherited it from his father, Thomas, who died in September of the previous year. Amongst the deceased's assets was listed—translated from the original Latin— *'One house, newly built, with a garden pertaining to the same in the parish of St Saviour's aforesaid ... in the occupation of William Shakespeare and others.'* (ibid 254). Since the list of assets was compiled in May 1599, it is very probable that Shakspere moved in as a security guard at the time of the Globe's construction; some believe the house and the Globe theatre were the same building.

Five months later, and the authorities were again chasing *'Willelmus Shakspeare'* for unpaid taxes in respect of his having dwelt in the parish of St Helen's, in Bishopsgate. Presumably, he had transferred his lodgings from the City, across the Thames, to Southwark: although the tax record reported that he had moved to Sussex; this sounds as though the clerk had misunderstood Shakspere's Warwickshire brogue for Southwark. The tax remained unpaid for another year, and it was not until October 1600, after his debt had been referred for collection to the Bishop of Winchester that the sheriff was able to record a lump sum payment had been received to settle the amount owing.

From this it may be inferred that the tax collector did not associate the tax defaulter *Shakspeare* with the poet and playwright Shakespeare. Had he done so, a visit to the Globe theatre would have quickly resolved the problem.

Before Meres's book was published in 1598, there must have been many enquiries concerning the author of the plays he attributed to Shakespeare. But this can have had no bearing on William Shakspere's sudden wealth. For no known reason connected with either literature or the theatre, he unaccountably became rich enough to return to Stratford and buy two cottages, two barns, and the second-best house in the locality. This can have had nothing to do with publication of Shakespeare's plays, which began to slowly emerge as pirated quartos. Their author always ignored these: neither taking action, nor staying publication; although the latter action was a legal entitlement for any playwright. (Detobel, 39).

In summary, we can compile a list of the events relevant to Shakespeare that took place between 1597 and 1600:

| | |
|---|---|
| 1597 | 29 Aug. Richard II entered in Stationers' Register. |
| | 20 Oct. Richard III entered in Stationers' Register. |
| | 15 Nov. Romeo and Juliet entered in Stationers' Register. |
| | Richard II and Richard III published. |
| 1598 | 25 Feb. Henry IV, Part I entered in Stationers' Register. |
| | 10 Mar. Love's Labour's Lost published, the first of Shakespeare's plays to carry his name on the title page. |
| | 22 July. The Merchant of Venice entered in Stationers' Register. |
| | 7 Sept. Francis Meres's Palladis Tamia entered in |

|      | Stationers' Register, providing a list of at least some of the plays Shakespeare had written thus far.<br>Dec. Richard II (Q2) published. Likewise Richard II (Q2 and Q3) and The Rape of Lucrece. |
|------|---|
| 1599 | June. John Weever publishes an Epigramme with the first allusion to Shakespeare's Sonnets.<br>Oct. Romeo and Juliet (Q2) and Henry IV, Part I (Q2) published. Also Venus and Adonis (Q3). |
| 1600 | 22 July. The Merchant of Venice entered in the Stationers' Register.<br>4 Aug. Henry V, As You Like It, Much Ado About Nothing entered in the Stationers' Register.<br>23 Aug. Much Ado About Nothing and Henry IV Part II entered in the Stationers' Register as 'by Shakespeare'.<br>8 Oct. A Midsummer Night's Dream entered in the Stationers' Register.<br>28 Oct. The Merchant of Venice entered in the Stationers' Register. |

(Wilson, 461-2)

As a result of Meres's publication, or coincidentally if you will have it so, the market became flooded with work by Shakespeare. So great did his reputation become that —

> ... anthologies began to appear containing excerpts from his work. Many extracts appear in three collections all published in 1600 – John Flasket's England's Helicon, John Bodenham's Belvedere or The Garden of the Muses, and Robert Allot's England's Parnassus, whose subtitle was 'The Choysest Flowers of our Modern poets'. (Crystal, 78)

Bodenham's first choice of title is interesting. *Belvedere*, in both modern French and English, is 'a turret': so called, because it provides a fine (*bel*) view (*videre*). However, in the French language, up until Randle Cotgrave's *Dictionary of the French and English Tongues* (1611), 'belvedere' *'is a shrub that grows to a man's height ... full of pleasant green boughs resembling branches of Hysope."* The Italian language also had the word 'belvidere', which is used for the shrub called 'broome'. This may or may not be significant, but 'belvedere' is a perfect anagram for *bel de Vere*. 'Bel' is the French alternative for 'beau', masculine form of the English 'fine'; 'glorious'; 'noble' &c. Hence: 'Noble de Vere'.

Shakespeare's sudden leap into the spotlight of fame also found its way onto the stage as a subject of satirical fun in the Parnassus Plays. These were three dramas produced at St John's College, Cambridge, which had been Edward de Vere's seat of learning. The plays were presented between 1598 and 1602 as part of the students' Christmas celebrations. The first play *The Pilgrimage to Parnassus* is an allegory about student life. The other two plays, *The Return from Parnassus* and *The Second Part of the Return from*

*Parnassus*, describe the two graduates' unsuccessful attempts to make a living.

In the *Return From Parnassus*, Part 2: two characters called Kempe and Burbage—names that are identical to two actors belonging to the Lord Chamberlain's Men—enact the following dialogue:

> Why, here's our fellow Shakespeare puts them all down, I (Aye) and Ben Jonson too, O that Ben Jonson is a pestilent fellow; he brought up Horace giving the poets a pill, but our fellow Shakespeare hath given him a purge that made him bewray his credit. (Ogburn, 94)

Jonson's *Poetaster* was first performed in 1601. It concerns an attempt to defame Horace, whom Jonson identifies with. But, after a trial before Augustus, in which Virgil sits in judgement, Horace is acquitted, and the poetaster, Crispinius, who instigated the attempted conspiracy, is made to take a purge that forces him to vomit his nonsense until he is cleansed (Act v). Exactly what purge 'Shakespeare' gave Jonson that forced him to *reveal* his *credit* can only be guessed. But it has been suggested that Shakespeare had revealed Jonson's sources to the public, and this had been sufficient to deprive Jonson of the credit he would otherwise have received.

In Part 1 of the *Return From Parnassus*, a character—aptly playing the part of a literary critic—with the revealing name of Gullio is introduced to the audience with the words: *'Now, gentlemen, you may laugh if you will, for here comes a gull.'* (Matus, 19). A gull is, of course, someone easily gulled into believing anything they are told. Gullio soon gives voice to his gullibility when he exclaims: *'O sweet Master Shakspeare! I'll have his picture in my study at the court.'* (Wilson, 270). Gullio's naivety was intended to be followed by laughter and applause from the audience; otherwise, as a piece of satire, its inclusion makes no sense. Not only is Gullio made to pronounce Oxford's allonym, presumably in the dialect spoken naturally in Shakspere's native Warwickshire, but Gullio also admits to wanting *his picture to hang at Court.*

There were, of course, no pictures of Shakespeare, nor could there be. A picture of Edward de Vere as Shakespeare would have revealed the nobleman behind the name. A picture of the man from Stratford-upon-Avon as Shakespeare would have brought him to the notice of those aware of his limitations, especially people from his village in Warwickshire who had known him all his life. Either way, the truth about Oxford's penname, which the Court was anxious to keep silent, would have been quickly revealed. Moreover, the idea that John Shakspere's uneducated son, a former apprentice butcher, was London's and the world's great literary genius, as well as being the father of two daughters who could not even write their own names, would have had the whole of Stratford hooting with laughter, quite apart from the audience at St John's College.

As for Gullio suggesting he might hang Shakespeare's picture up at Court. This, of all the places in the world, was the one place that wanted Shakespeare, in the person of Oxford, to remain out of sight. Therefore to suggest hanging his picture in full view of the Court was a brilliant piece of satire that must have rocked the theatre with laughter.

As satire, this scene was perfect. It also tells us that members of the university audience already understood the truth behind Oxford's alias, and this implies it had become an open secret. The strategy of using Meres's *Palladis Tamia* to establish Shakespeare as an accomplished playwright and poet had been given unforeseen licence, and a point of no return had been passed.

This open secret, in which people saw William Shakespeare as either the Earl of Oxford or Will Shakspere depending upon the person's point of view, plays no part in conventionalist thinking. But it does give rise to certain predictions. For example, Shakspere, although now recognised as Shakespeare by theatre-goers, would need to maintain a low profile in London society. It is precisely this that has proved aggravating to his biographers. Records exist of pirated publications of his plays, but the author never once took action to redress the situation. Philip Henslowe kept a journal in which he recorded performances of a number of Shakespeare's plays and the receipts from these performances; he also recorded every penny spent or lent; he bought plays, he advanced money for plays, he commissioned writers to update plays, but there is never a single mention of the name Shakespeare in his journal, even though entries stretch from 1592 to 1609. In other words, look where you will, there are no connections to be found linking the works of William Shakespeare to the day-to-day life of William Shakspere. Every enquiry shows them apart.

Even in death they remained apart, for there was no acknowledgement of his loss to literature from men of letters; not from Chapman, who he had supposedly collaborated with; not from Jonson, who loved the man this side of idolatry. Neither was there any reaction from the theatre, despite Heminge, Condell and Burbage being named as recipients to a bequest in his will. Yet, was this not the man repeatedly called for by Queen Elizabeth and King James? Bill Bryson, who attempted a biography of Shakespeare in 2007, expressed the difficulty in his own unique fashion.

> We don't know if he ever left England. We don't know who his principal companions were or how he amused himself. His sexuality is an irreconcilable mystery. On only a handful of days in his life can we say with absolute certainty where he was. We have no record at all of his whereabouts for the eight critical years when he left his wife and three young children in Stratford and became, with almost impossible swiftness, a successful playwright in London. By the time he is first mentioned in print as a playwright in 1592, his life was already more than half over. For the rest, he is a kind of literary equivalent of an electron – forever there and not there. (Bryson, back cover)

The wariness Shakspere needed to exercise, in order not to be caught out in the role he was playing, may have been the reason why he had no fixed address. Some indication of this wariness can be discerned in a note taken by the scholarly John Aubrey (1627-1697), who amongst several other interests, notably archaeology, wrote about many famous people of his time. In a personal memorandum found amongst his papers, he had noted this memory of Shakespeare provided by one of his informants: *'The more to be admired q[uia] he was not a company keeper lived in Shoreditch, wouldn't be debauched, & if invited to writ[e]: he was in paine.'* (Ogburn, 106)

> N.B. The colon is authentic. This is sometimes omitted, and a comma inserted after the word 'to': thus wrongly implying that he wrote he was in pain. Although why he should want to confess this in writing, instead of saying it: the more especially when he was claiming to be in pain from writing, is totally inexplicable. It is, however, typical of the imaginative editing of evidence, conjured up to avoid embarrassing questions.

Without realizing it, Aubrey has confirmed Shakspere's need to avoid the company of those who, unaware of his true role as Shakespeare, may have sought his acquaintance. It would have been from contemporaneous reports handed down from the previous generation that Aubrey learned of this man's excuse for putting pen to paper, and for never allowing himself to become intoxicated. Both excuses are exactly what one would expect from a man who was hiding the fact that he was only playing the role of a writer. Furthermore, these excuses were still remembered a generation later, which tends to imply they must have been repeated by Shakspere many times, and thought strange, for them to be still recalled after so many years.

Consequently, not only do we have no written letters from Shakspere and no manuscripts, we have an excuse for his not writing anything when asked. This need not mean that he was asked to write anything of a literary nature; it could simply mean that he was asked to write a note, a name, or even his address. According to Aubrey's informant, when asked to write anything at all, he excused himself, complaining that he was in pain. It is an excuse worthy of any illiterate +2 person intent upon hiding the fact.

Despite these excuses, evidence does exist that Shakspere put pen to paper on six notable occasions, although each time it was only to sign a legal document. The first instance was the signature he made in May 1612 on a deposition following evidence he submitted in the Belott-Mountjoie case; this will be discussed in detail later. Concerning this particular signature, Norman Evans of the Public Record Office remarked:

> ... the dramatist's signature appears in the contracted form Willm Shkp. The 'p' is usually regarded as a form of the common abbreviation 'p' for 'per', which would make the signature 'Shakper' ... All six of the known signatures differ from each other in some particular and this example is the most awkward of them all. (Wilson, 361)

A dramatist who cannot properly sign his name? This sounds unlikely, the more so, since conventionalist thinking believes this to be the time that Shakespeare was writing *Henry VIII* and joining forces with Fletcher when contributing his part to *The Two Noble Kinsmen*. Hence, the signatures attempted by Shakspere remain a positive irritant to his biographers.

One year later, in March 1613, Shakspere was one of four men who put up the money for a London property called the Gatehouse; the other three men involved in the conveyance were William Johnson, '*citizen and vintner of London*', John Jackson, '*a Hull shipping magnate*', and John Heminge, a share-holder in both the Globe and the Blackfriars theatres.

Shakspere's signature appears on the deed to the property as *William Shakspē* and is repeated on the form of indenture as *W<sup>m</sup> Shakspē*.

Both Jackson and Johnson were able to sign their names in the normal manner. Shakspere's six attempts at writing his name on various legal documents, without exception each occur after the year 1612, and represent the only evidence we have that this man ever picked up a pen, and even this is suspect. Not surprisingly, all six signatures have attracted expert criticism. Jane Cox of the Public Records Office in London, and an experienced expert in the field of signatories, wrote:

> It is obvious at a glance that these signatures, with the exception of the last two [appearing on the will], are not the signatures of the same man. Almost every letter is formed in a different way in each. Literate men in the sixteenth and seventeenth centuries developed personalized signatures much as people do today and it is unthinkable that Shakespeare did not. Which of the signatures reproduced here is the genuine article is anybody's guess.
> (Cox, 24-34)

Dr. R. W. Leftwich, an authority upon the subject of physical handicaps but not a handwriting expert, accepted the traditionalists' assurances that the signatures were all genuine, in which case he described the hand that wrote them as *'spastic'*.

> In this the pen is not completely under the control of the writer [as is the case with the beginner]. Against his will it makes little jerks, unduly long strokes, or unintended marks; and though a good beginning may be made, the hand very soon tires and refuses to write at all [as is also true when a complete beginner cannot remember what comes next]. [Author's comments] (Wilson, 385)

The signatures and handwriting of 16th and 17th century men of letters – examples of which have survived – pose no similar problem; their hands being neither childish nor spastic. Despite this, and other contrary evidence disputing Shakspere's authorship, Nelson sounded decidedly churlish when he objected to any doubts about Shakspere's authenticity, by raising the rhetorical question – How could Shakespeare experts be mistaken, when they have devoted their careers to the study of Shakespeare and his work?

In the case of the authorship question, it requires a different approach to textual expertise. Apart from which, the evidence for Shakspere's authorship, as put forward by textual experts, repeatedly fails to meet the highest standard of scholarship. Yet, this is ignored, with every unresolved problem excused or explained away. For this to be successful, it requires Shakespeare experts to commit sins of omission and addition, circular reasoning, make specious assertions, adopt shallow conclusions, and use false analogies; there are also rhetorical tricks: such as diverting the reader's attention by circumventing difficult and probing questions, or else introducing some new topic that is related and easier to deal with. And why should they resort to these measures? Because there is a conflict of interest in always ensuring that the *status quo* is maintained. How many scholars would lose face if Oxford was admitted to have been Shakespeare?

William Shakspere's real ability is, nevertheless, much in evidence from the documented history that occurs in Shakespeare biographies. Without a single exception, this concerns the active life of a businessman, albeit with theatrical connections. It is neither more nor less than can be expected from his upbringing. The failure to have discovered any documents confirming that Shakspere was the poet and playwright known as Shakespeare is not only predictable, it is also a consequence of what is known about the man. To search for what does not exist has become the folly of a great many learned men and women, lured on by a chimera in the form of a man of immortal genius, who operated under a pseudonym derived from the name of the non-literary man he engaged as his allonym. Without this understanding, scholars have wasted, and will continue to waste, years of their life in a forlorn search for what doesn't exist.

> Charlotte G. Stopes, Southampton's pioneer biographer, spent seven years or more combing the records of the Earl and his family without turning up a single indication that the fashionable young lord had ever had any contact with a Shakespeare, and for that reason deemed the great work of her life a failure. Two subsequent biographers, Rowse being one, have done no better. (Ogburn, 206-7)

# 13

## THE ARTFUL LODGER

In 1593, the name of William Shakespeare had burst onto the literary scene with *Venus and Adonis*, closely followed a year late by *Lucrece*. But as quickly as the name appeared, it disappeared, and was not heard of again in connection with any work of literature until 1598. This augured a new beginning for work carrying the name William Shakespeare. Meres had given the green light to identifying plays that up until then had been thought anonymous. Before then, pirated editions of his plays had been published, but no one dared identify the author by his penname. This dramatically changed in 1598. Thereafter, one drama after another of 'Shakespeare's', which had previously been presented anonymously, emerged, either as an entry in the Stationers' Register, or as a pirated edition of one of his plays.

It is in the midst of this sudden rise to fame that we find a record of Shakspere's whereabouts. He was lodging at the time in a debauched household on the corner of Silver Street and Muggle Street (later Monkswell Street), inside the walls of the City of London. His fellow lodger was a petty criminal named George Wilkins.

The house lay directly to the east of Aldersgate and south of Cripplegate and was owned by a Huguenot headdress maker and his wife, by the names of Christopher and Mary Mountjoy. *'The Mountjoys regularly took in lodgers and for a number of years one of these was William Shakespeare.'* (Cook, 109).

> His shop was on the ground floor, sheltered by a pentice, which had been a feature of the house for forty years. Upstairs the Mountjoys lived under a pair of gables that covered their end of the building. (Fido, 120)

Apart from his wife, and the lodgers he took in, Mountjoy also had three apprentices, a daughter Mary, and a maid called Joan Johnson. One of the apprentices, Stephen Belott, the son of a French widow, subsequently married Mary Mountjoy, and it was through discussions concerning a prenuptial agreement that the future groom's fellow lodger, Shakspere, was brought into the discussions, for *'they had amongst themselves many conferences about the marriage.'* (Wilson, 360).

> It must have been a lively and somewhat notorious household; for the elders of the French Church in London formally reported that the Mountjoys lived "a licentious life" and that both Mountjoy and his daughter's husband were "debauched". (Cook, 109)

Two years later, the bride's mother died and the Belotts set up a business of their own in opposition to Mountjoy. This not unnaturally resulted in acrimony between the two halves of the family, with the Belotts claiming against Mountjoy for the balance of the promised marriage portion. The dispute was referred to the Court of Requests, and William Shakspere was called from his home in Stratford-upon-Avon to bear witness.

> William Shakespeare of Stratford upon Aven in the Countye of Warwicke gentleman of the age of xlviij [48] yeres or thereabouts sworne and examined the daye and yere abovesaid deposethe & sayethe ... he knoweth the parties plaintiff and deffendant and hathe know them bothe as he now remembrethe for the space of tenne yeres or thereaboutes.
> (Laroque, 131)

Very little was achieved by Shakspere's appearance. The court passed the case over to the French Church in London for arbitration, where Belott's case was partly upheld, and he was awarded 20 nobles, which Mountjoy refused to pay. As for the star witness, apart from not remembering the year in which he was born:—

> Shakespeare also pleaded inability to remember exactly "what implements and necessaries of household stuff" had been given. Nor did he know what sum had been promised to the couple in the event of Mountjoie's death. (Wilson, 361)

At the close of the hearing, Shakspere signed a deposition. It is the first of his six known attempts at writing his name with pen and ink. It is incomplete and displays the inevitable beginner's blot.

*Belott v. Mountjoy* was also instrumental in bringing to the fore another lodger in the house at that time, George Wilkins, with whom Shakspere shared accommodation.

> In touch with the underworld and reputedly a brothel-keeper, Wilkins in his late twenties, clearly had some acquaintance with Shakespeare ... He brutally kicked a pregnant woman in the belly: he beat another woman, and then stamped on her so that she had to be carried home. We know of his behaviour from legal records. (Honan, 328-9)

Wilkins criminal record continued up until his death in 1618. During the eight years previous to this, he was repeatedly brought before the court, charged with assault and battery, mostly due to his connection with prostitutes.

Unsurprisingly, Shakspere's time in the Mountjoy household is one of extreme embarrassment to his image-makers. There is not only his inability to recall either his age or the relevant details of an agreement he had earlier been asked to advise upon, but also the company he was keeping. The Calvinist Elders who were frequently called upon to visit the household, described Mountjoy and Shakspere's fellow lodger Belott, as *'debauched.'*

The Mountjoys' other lodger, Wilkins, was an extremely violent man. Eventually, he obtained enough money from his prostitutes to set up a brothel of his own, which he fronted as a licensed alehouse located in a notorious red light district.

Charles Nicholl also discovered from court records that Mountjoy ran a vice ring, running several brothels to supplement his income. He also acted as surety when three of his clients and a woman were arrested, having been found in bed together. The truth is, *"the Mountjoys were hardly the respectable family they might at first have appeared ... "Mountjoy [had] fathered two bastards and was excommunicated for his dissolute life.'* (Holland, 44).

Compare Shakspere's surroundings and his choice of society with that of his fellow shareholders at the Globe. John Heminge, named in Shakspere's will was born in 1556 at Droitwich Spa in Worcestershire. As a young man, he travelled to London and became apprenticed to a grocer. He prospered in this trade, eventually being admitted to the Company of Grocers as a freeman. The year after his admission he married Rebecca Knell, the sixteen-year-old widow of William Knell, a former actor with the Queen's Men who was killed the year before in a fight with a fellow player. Together the couple had fourteen children, but not all survived. After their marriage, the couple moved from the parish of St. Michael, Cornhill to Rebecca's home in Addle Street, which was owned by goldsmith Thomas Savage; the house was situated in the parish of St. Mary, Aldermanbury, where John Heminge became active in the community, serving in the Church as a deputy churchwarden until his death in October 1630.

Henry Condell, too, arrived in London at an early age, having been born in Norfolk, in 1576: the son of a fishmonger. Upon reaching manhood, Condell appears to have had no occupation worth recording. This supposition is reinforced by the tradition that he was in London in 1592 as a member of Lord Strange's Men. In the same year, it is suggested he took part in *The Seven Deadly Sins*: a play that was allegedly written by Richard

Tarleton. But, Condell's name does not appear amongst those listed that year as a member of Lord Strange's Company.

One fact is known for certain. Henry Condell had the good fortune to win the hand of Elizabeth Smart, the daughter of a wealthy London gentleman who made her his heiress. The marriage took place on 24 August 1596 in the parish of St Mary at Aldermanbury, where Condell was living at the time, and where the newlyweds chose to live afterwards.

Like Heminge, Condell also became a churchwarden at St. Mary's, and it was here that the couple's nine children were baptized, although only three lived to become adults.

In 1605, Henry Condell and William Sly became co-owners of the Globe theatre. We know from a subsequent lawsuit — Witter *v*. Heminge and Condell (1619) — that shares in the Globe had originally been divided up so that Richard and Cuthbert Burbage owned 50% between them with the other 50% allotted equally in 10% holdings to Augustine Phillips, John Heminge, Thomas Pope, William Kempe and Will Shakspere.

Of these named shareholders, only Pope, Kempe and Shakspere (the first an acrobat, the second a dancer and the third a very wealthy man), did not live in a house of their own in London, or its vicinity. One may excuse the acrobat and the dancer, but why should the wealthiest of men in this group of investors not have purchased, at the very least, a *pied-à-terre* in the city? Also, and much to the point, why did he not bring his wife and children to London so that they might too share in his good fortune? Heminge and Condell settled in London; raised families and were known for their community work. Richard Burbage, like his father James, both arrived in London from Stratford-upon-Avon, so it is said (see History of the Globe Theatre's website), and settled in the capital, where Cuthbert was born. Shakspere is the outstanding exception.

Of course, where problems concerning Shakespeare's authorship are concerned, the ingenuity of *Shakespeare experts* seems limitless, especially when it comes to providing answers. However, consider for one moment that Oxford was Shakespeare and that he employed Shakspere to be his allonym. From this there are predictions to be made and these can be seen to have been entirely fulfilled by Shakspere's subsequent behaviour.

For example, he would need to have kept a low profile to protect the role he was asked to play. This explains why so little biographical evidence exists for his time in London. He must also be difficult to locate, which explains why the tax collectors had difficulty finding him. He must not put pen to paper or be *a company keeper*, which explains Aubrey's note to this effect. His family must be kept away from London, lest they reveal his past life. This explains their absence. It also explains why he was forced by circumstances to invest his money in property deals in Stratford from the very outset, instead of in London, where he could have let property very easily and far more lucratively, as well as living on the premises.

Then again, he must not advertise himself as William Shakespeare in Stratford-upon-Avon, where his lack of ability as a poet and writer would be most obvious. This explains why his death was totally ignored by his community, and why the King's Men, the company of actors that is so often described as *Shakespeare's Company*, were paid by the local authority to leave town without giving a single performance: *"To the King's Players for not playing in the Hall. 6/-.'* (Approximately £150 by today's reckoning). It also explains the bust on the monument erected in the parish church seven years after his death, which originally depicted him as a wool merchant (see back cover).

Had Shakspere been free to come to London with his family, he would have been able to enter Hamnet at Westminster School, where Ben Jonson had been educated, and where fellow shareholder Henry Condell had placed his son. A university education may likely have followed, such as that enjoyed by Marlowe, Greene, Nashe, Lodge, Fletcher, Harvey &c. What father would deny his son such opportunity? Instead, the boy was left for most of his life fatherless, and his life cut short by illness at the age of eleven: a price paid for the role his father took. Shapiro also believes that Anne Hathaway would not have had time to contact her *"itinerant husband"* with news of their son's illness and death, and that Shakspere would not have been present at the funeral: *"it would have taken a messenger from Stratford four or five days at least just to find Shakespeare.'* (Shapiro, 15). Moreover, unlike *"Ben Jonson, who left such a touching poem on the death of his young son and namesake Benjamin, Shakespeare left no testimonial for Hamnet."* (ibid); nor could he, were he illiterate. And so, even his son's life and subsequent death, is in line with Shakspere's role as an allonym.

# 14

# DEATH OF QUEEN ELIZABETH I

In March 1603, at the same time Shakspere was apparently living in the Mountjoy household, Queen Elizabeth died.

> The event stirred the Londoners to a flood of poetry. Everyone from Lord Burghley's elder son to the least of Henslowe's hacks rushed into print with combined wails for the death of the Queen. (Chute, 58)

Everyone, that is, except Shakespeare. His advocates are nonplussed. While it is fairly easy to invent situations surrounding Shakespeare; for example, to fill in his education, his lost years, his playacting, etc., using one's imagination coupled with the authority to package it all together as fact, it is quite impossible to invent his poetry. Why, then, did Shakespeare choose to remain silent?

There are several plausible answers for which either one, or a combination, will serve to explain what happened. Firstly, there is no rational explanation as to why Shakespeare — were he truly the poet described by biographers — should have declined to add to the tributes that were being written by a woeful nation. Henry Chettle was fully aware of this at the time, for he remonstrated publicly with Shakespeare over this sad omission.

> Nor doth the silver-tonguèd Melicert,
> Drop from his honeyed Muse one sable tear
> To mourn her death who graced his desert,
> And to his lays opened her royal ear.
> Shepherd, remember our Elizabeth,
> And sing her rape, done by that Tarquin, Death.

*'As most scholars are agreed, Chettle's 'honey' imagery and clear allusion to Lucrece strongly indicate Shakespeare to have been the subject of this rebuke."* (Wilson, 295).

It will be recalled that Chettle had a score to settle with Shakespeare. Ten years earlier he had been gulled into writing an apology in *Kind-Harts Dreame* as the result of a letter he had published in *Greenes Groats-worth of Witte*. In this, he had mistakenly edited Greene's scribbled notes in a way that indicated Shakespeare was an untrustworthy actor with pretensions at writing blank verse. Since then, he had learned the truth. Shakespeare did not actually exist. The name was just a front for Lord Oxford, who had begun writing under this penname shortly after Chettle stumbled across it while sorting through Greene's effects.

As a publisher, Chettle knew that after *Lucrece* had been released in 1594, Oxford never again used this name to publish another work. This meant that Oxford had been forbidden from doing so by higher authority. Chettle's revenge was to publicly rebuke the named author of *Venus and Adonis* and *Lucrece* for his silence at the death of the Queen, knowing that 'Shakespeare' was unable to respond.

How can we be sure that Chettle knew Shakespeare was really the 17th Earl of Oxford? The answer is that Chettle admits it in the first line of his poem, although most careful to cover himself in language too obscure for the uneducated commoner. He calls the subject of his rebuke *the silver-tonguèd Melicert*. Melicertes was the surname of Simonides, whom Plato had described as the best poet of the age. But, more than that, in the mythology of Plato's Greece, Melicertes was the *'the god of harbours'*. (Brewer, 828). By any stretch of the imagination, this latter attribute cannot apply to Shakspere of Stratford-upon-Avon. However, both references fit Edward de Vere to a T.

Oxford's association with harbours occurred at Harwich in 1588. *'The seacoaste is here and ther furnished with harbours for shipping, whereof the principall is Harwiche.'* (Nelson, 8). This was the year when the Spanish Armada set sail to invade England. The battle at sea was fought during July (Old Style), and by the end of that month English ships, aided by gale force winds, had driven the remaining Spanish ships, first to Calais, and then back into their own waters. In the midst of the invasion, Oxford was appointed Governor of Harwich, as corroborated by the Earl of Leicester in a letter to Walsingham, dated 1 August 1588.

In the previous chapter, the law of unintended consequences resulted in a list of events that were liable to affect Shakspere's behaviour, in his day-to-day life, had he been *acting* the role of poet and playwright. Here, then, is yet another. Shakspere could not write a poem mourning the death of Queen Elizabeth, and then submit it as a tribute by Shakespeare. He had not the ability. On the other hand, Oxford could not write a poem that was published as a work of William Shakespeare. The last time this happened it had become a target for satire, appearing in *Willobie His Avisa*. In any case, he would have been aware from the *Parnassus Plays* that his pseudonym was well known in certain literary circles, and to address a memorial poem on the death of the Queen, and then attribute it to his *poet ape* would be an insult to Elizabeth's memory. Thirdly, as a member of the nobility, he was unable to publish poetry under his title. Consequently, because of this impasse, nothing was published by Shakespeare. Chettle must have realised these implications and decided the time had come to repay Oxford for having hoodwinked him into writing an apology for 'Shakespeare': whom he later discovered, amidst some frivolity at the ease with which he had been duped, was no more than an invention.

Instead of publishing a tribute to the Queen upon her death, Oxford chose to write a Sonnet (107), which, it may be concluded, he circulated amongst his private friends. Each phrase in this poem can be applied to events occurring in 1603. It also recalls the relationship between Oxford and Southampton in earlier sonnets, as well as the dedications addressed to Southampton in *Venus and Adonis* and *Lucrece*. These were the poems in which Southampton had agreed to play the part of patron to 'William Shakespeare', to help Oxford seek a new way to get his poetry into print. The ruse proved extremely successful until it was covertly hinted at in *Willobie His Avisa*: after which, no more was heard of it.

In February 1601, Southampton was given a life sentence for the part he played in the revolt against the Crown, led by Robert Devereux, 2nd Earl of Essex, who lost his head in more ways than one. But two years later, Elizabeth died and was succeeded by James I, who proved more lenient. The King released Southampton from the Tower, wherein he had been *confined, doomed* to *forfeit* the rest of his life behind stone walls. The opening words to Sonnet 107 reflect this release, and express Oxford's relief at what he had *supposed* would be Southampton's fate. But in writing the sonnet, he also admitted the young man was his *true love*. This is perfectly in line with the affection and terms of endearment that occur elsewhere in the sonnets.

> Not mine own fears, nor the prophetic soul
> Of the wide world dreaming on things to come,
> Can yet the lease of my true love control,
> Suppos'd as forfeit to a confin'd doom.

Oxford, for it could hardly be someone from a lower class talking so intimately about Southampton, is reflecting upon what had been his *own fears* for the future, and combining them with *the prophetic soul* of the *wide world*; that is, the general population who are constantly given to *dreaming* of *thing to come*. Neither of these, he says can overrule, or *control* the *lease* or charter *of my true love,* whose future, he had *supposed,* would be *forfeit* to a life of *confinement*.

The sonnet then continues with a reference to Queen Elizabeth's recent passing, which he symbolises with her known love for lunar analogies.

> The mortal moon hath her eclipse endur'd,

No one living at that time could have failed to understand who was intended by this, for it was *'Queen Elizabeth I who was often depicted with a crescent moon as her headdress,'* (Wilson, 25). At the height of his attachment to Queen Elizabeth, Walter Raleigh wrote of *The Ocean's Love to Cynthia*. That is, *'Cynthia. The moon; a surname of Artemis or Diana. The Roman Diana who represented the moon was called Cynthia'* (Brewer, 323). Oxford is therefore referring to the Queen's demise, which occurred in the early hours of 24 March 1603.

Some, however, have disputed this meaning: believing that the phrase, *her eclipse endured*, is an inappropriate use of language for expressing a death. Instead, they have searched for an alternative meaning, and have come to believe that *the mortal moon* refers to the Spanish Armada in 1588; which, from an aerial viewpoint can be likened to a crescent. Although why an armada should be referred to by the possessive pronoun *her* and not *its* is left unexplained. Conversely, the plays of Shakespeare use both words, *endure* and *eclipse*, when talking about death, and to find these words repeated in Sonnet 107 is consistent with Shakespeare's use of language.

> Edgar:  Men must endure
> Their going hence, even as their coming hither,
> Ripeness is all.
> *King Lear* (Act 5: sc.ii)

> Talbot:  Then here I take my leave of thee, fair son,
> Born to eclipse thy life this afternoon.
> Come, side by side together live and die;
> And soul with soul from France to heaven fly.
> *1 Henry VI* (Act 4: sc.v)

There is also a special political meaning to the Queen's mortality. *'When she ascended the throne ... the queen's whole being was profoundly altered: her mortal 'body natural' was wedded to an immortal 'body politic'.'* She acknowledged this in her succession speech: *'I am but one body, naturally considered, though by [God's] permission a Body Politic to govern'*. (Encyclopaedia Britannica). When she died, her *mortal* self was *eclipsed* by the immortal Body Politic, which she had occupied during her life, and which emerged renewed as James VI of Scotland, who then became James I of England.

The sonnet continues: —

> And the sad augurs mock their own presage;

This follows logically from the death of Elizabeth. Since the Queen had no children, the succession, while she lived, had been a subject of debate and much concern. Asking Elizabeth to think upon the succession was a touchy subject, and one in which she had refused to participate. Also, England was still at war, and the possible dangers through any change to the monarchy had caused a spread of dire predictions.

> In the mean time several serious deliberations were held in the council, with regard to the succession ... Though there was no great danger in any opposition being made to the Scottish succession, the council thought proper to take every precaution for securing the peace and safety of the kingdom: great numbers of idle and suspected persons, who swarmed in the metropolis and the adjacent villages, were seized and sent to Holland, for the Dutch service. The fleet which lay ready equipped was ordered to guard the mouth of the Thames: the sea ports were all shut, and the lady Arabella Stuart, taken into custody. It was also resolved to summon all the peers to town, and if any commotion should happen on the queen's death, which was now hourly expected, to make the earl of Northumberland general of the forces. (Montague, 84)

What this extract shows, are the *sad augurs* of what was feared when the Queen's death was announced. But once the smooth transition of power had been accomplished, the pessimists were reduced to laughing off their fears, seeing instead, how these former –

> Incertainties now crown themselves assured,

*Uncertainties* were *crowned*, quite literally, in the form of James I, King of Great Britain and Ireland. The King was also repeatedly *assured* of loyalty from the nobility, as he journeyed south from Scotland to the capital.

> James showed his abilities from the first. In the counties through which he passed on his way to London he lavished royal bounty upon the elites who had been starved for honours during Elizabeth's parsimonious reign. He knighted hundreds as he went, enjoying the bountiful entertainments that formed such a contrast with his indigent homeland. (Encyclopaedia Britannica)

The next line continues with a promise:

> And peace proclaims olives of endless age.

In Church affairs, the *Millenary Petition* of 1603 led to the King arranging the *Hampton Court Conference* in which he played a leading role, threatening to *'harry from the land'* those opposed to the established church. At the same time he entered into negotiations with Philip II to end sixteen years of warfare between Spain and England.

James I's efforts proved successful, and the *Treaty of London* was signed in 1604 shortly after the death of Oxford, who, as a member of the Privy Council, would have had prior knowledge of the forthcoming negotiations for peace. This explains the sonnet's continuing lines:

> Now with the drops of this most balmy time
> My love looks fresh, and Death to me subscribes,

The first line picks up the sense of euphoria amongst the people after years of war; it was a *balmy time*. The loss of men dying on the field of battle and the threat of invasion from the sea was finally about to end: brought to a close by a peace settlement between England and Spain.

As part of the King's efforts to bring closure to the politics of the past regime, James had freed Southampton from his life sentence in the Tower. Oxford's reaction to the release of his *true love* was to remark: how *fresh* his *love looks,* despite his time spent in confinement. But Oxford's happiness was also tempered by a grievous confession. He felt his death drawing near. He was to be proved right. Southampton was released from the Tower on 10 April 1603. Oxford died fourteen months later.

Then, in typical fashion, Oxford concludes by remarking that although death is indiscriminate, and treats illiterate and literate people alike, he has a remedy. He will cheat death by living on in his poetry.

> Since spite of him I'll live in this poor rhyme,
> While he insults o'er dull and speechless tribes.

It was this same eternity he promised to Southampton, his *true love*: vowing that his words would outlive the monuments of marble and metal that attempt to preserve the memory of tyrants.

> And thou in this shalt find thy monument,
> When tyrants' crests and tombs of brass are spent.

These are not the words of Shakspere. They are the words of a cultured, well-educated member of the Court. If Shakspere had written this sonnet to Southampton, it would have been at the time he was sharing lodgings with petty criminal and violent pimp Wilkins, in the debauched household of brothel-keeper Christopher Mountjoy. And, as Shakspere admitted to the court in the Belott-Mountjoy case, he had kept company with Mountjoy for *the space of ten years*:

> William Shakespeare of Stratford upon Aven ... sayethe he knowethe the parties plaintiff and defendant and hath know[ne] them bothe as he now remembrethe for the space of tenne yeres or thereabouts. (Laroque, 131)

To continue believing this is sweet Master Shakespeare, the poet and playwright, making the deposition is an offence to common sense. Even more unlikely is the implication that Shakspere was on such intimate terms with the Earl of Southampton that he had left the low life habitants of Silver Street, to make his way over to the home of Southampton, upon learning of his release from the Tower. How else could he have known his love looks fresh? There is also the supposed patronage to consider. This had ended in 1594: if one still insists that Shakspere was Shakespeare.

In any case, a close relationship between the Earl of Southampton and a member of the lower classes, to which Shakspere belonged, is out of the question; it exists only in the elasticised imagination of his biographers, which is often found to stretch to incredible lengths. The class structure of Elizabethan England was extremely well-defined, and the divisions between the different orders strictly maintained.

Then, again, if Shakspere continues to be thought of as the author, what was he talking about when admitting that his death drew near? In 1603 he had still thirteen years of healthy life ahead of him, and according to his biographers, the energy and inspiration for writing many more plays.

Sonnet 107 turns out to be one of the more revealing of Shakespeare's sonnets. It allows both Shakspere and Oxford to be examined and tested to see which of the two contenders fits the poem that one of them has written. The rational answer that ticks every box is the Earl of Oxford.

## 15

## ON THE BANKS OF THE AVON

In late 1603, London was groaning beneath the assault of yet another bout of Plague. King James wisely retreated to the country, passing through Berkshire (Windsor), Surrey (Pyrford via Hampton Court), Oxfordshire (Woodstock), Hampshire (Winchester), Wiltshire (Wilton), and Hampshire again (Isle of Wight), before returning to Wiltshire (Salisbury). We know that during James's progress across this part of southern England, the Pembroke family *'entertained the king at Wilton on 29-30 Aug. 1603 (NICHOLS, Progresses, i.254)*.*"*(D.N.B. Vol. IX: p.679).

We also know that following this brief visit, James travelled to the Hampshire coast, where he and his retinue crossed the Solent to visit the Isle of Wight. Upon his return to the mainland the King changed his itinerary quite unexpectedly by returning to Wilton House. *'We know of this return visit because James' Court ... stayed at Wilton between 24 October and 12 December.'*(Wilson, 299-300). Park Honan agreed, noting that *'after a voyage to the Isle of Wight, James at last reached Wiltshire for a prolonged stay at Wilton House with the young Earl of Pembroke.'*(Honan, 301). What was it that had caused the King to change his schedule?

The answer was the recent arrival of 'Shakespeare' at Wilton House, and the promised performance of As You Like It. Ian Wilson confirms that: *'Shakespeare's company performed ... at Wilton on 2 December is a matter of firm historical record.'*(Wilson, 299-300). Another reason for certainty is the court record, for this confirms that the King's Men had indeed performed for the court on the date mentioned.

> John Heminge, one of his Majesty's players ... for the pains and expenses of himself and the rest of the company in coming from Mortlake in the county of Surrey unto the court aforesaid and there presenting before his Majesty one play. £30. (ibid 299)

Upon the basis of this record, it was Heminge who was the business manager of the King's Men. The financial handling of his grocery business would have qualified him as the most suitable person to handle the company's income. The record thus confirms that the company of actors had been summoned from Mortlake (a village on the Surrey shore of the river Thames), to Wilton House: a journey of about 85 miles (136 kilometres). Prior to this, the men had been settling down to see out the winter after returning from a tour that had taken them away from London and the Plague.

> Provincial account books show Shakespeare's company having done their usual touring during the epidemic, performing in Bath, Shrewsbury, Coventry, and Ipswich on unspecified dates. (ibid 299)

It is unlikely, however, that Will Shakspere was with *his* company during that summer, or indeed any other summer, for not only is his name absent on the lists of players visiting those towns, but *'he spent part of most summers among his family, as the diarist Aubrey reported.'*(Kay, 274).

Given that he spent most of the summer months apart from the King's Men, the busiest time of the year for actors because of the increased number of daylight hours and the warm weather, there was even less reason for him to spend the winter in their company, or so it would follow. We may conclude from this that Shakspere was not one of those who made the journey from Mortlake to Wilton in the winter of 1603. Indeed, he would have had to be in two places at once, since it was his arrival at Wilton House which had prompted the King's Men to be summoned

Was Shakspere really staying at Wilton as a house guest of Lady Pembroke? This, after all, was the reason why James and his court returned to Wilton House, after having arrived back on the mainland from the Isle of Wight. Lord Pembroke, Mary Sidney's son and a favourite of the King with whom he was travelling, had received a letter from his mother inviting the King and his party to return to Wilton, as: *"we have the man Shakespeare here'*.

The letter was later shown to the classical scholar and Victorian poet, William Cory, during his visit to Wilton House in the summer of 1865. He disclosed that it did indeed say that Shakespeare was present in 1603. Apparently, Mary Sidney wanted to cajole the King on Sir Walter Raleigh's behalf. On 17 November, Raleigh was to be tried at Winchester for treason against King James. The dowager countess wished to make her view known on Raleigh's behalf, and urged her son to persuade the King to return, using Shakespeare's name as an enticement. The King came.

Scholars recognise the inconcinnity of the facts associated with this event. They are simply incompatible with the status of Shakspere, and the *milieu* in which his name is mentioned. Consider, Sir Sidney Lee's outburst: *'the 'tenor' of the letter, 'stamps it, if it exists, as an ignorant invention'.'*

E. K. Chambers was slightly more cautious, merely asserting, *'the apparent familiarity with which Shakespeare seems to have been referred to, is noteworthy."* (A New Variorum Edition of Shakespeare, 633-4) Both men realized that Pembroke's mother would not have written to the King in such familiar terms about a man of Shakspere's breeding. Therefore the letter seen by Cory had to be a forgery. Katherine Duncan-Jones wrote in a similar vein.

> Shakespeare was the King's Man, not the Countess of Pembroke's ... he was hardly in a position, either socially or legally to stay at Wilton House as an independent guest, as if for a country-house weekend. (Duncan-Jones, 173)

Then, who was it that made the decision to summon the King's Men to Wilton House in December 1603, and perform *As You Like It*? And what motivated the King to return to Wilton House: a place that he and his Court had left just one month earlier? The answers once again point to the Earl of Oxford. The mere mention of his pseudonym was enough to indicate to King James that there was entertainment to be had, and with the Earl of Pembroke pressing the King to return to his mother's estate, the decision to go back was easily made.

Writing in 1873, local historian, W. Michael, reported how James I —

> ... held a brilliant Court here in November 1603. The Earl was one of the great patrons of Shakspeare (sic) who is said to have assisted in some of his own plays which were performed at Wilton House in the presence of the King. (Michael, 7)

The King's stay at Wilton, which lasted for seven weeks, proved such a memorable occasion for Lady Mary Sidney that it was said she built a 'temple' to commemorate the event. This has been identified as the Holbein Porch. It was originally attached to the House, but was dismantled in 1812 when the Cloisters were added. It was then reassembled fourteen years later at its present location in Lord Pembroke's private garden, where it became known as *Shakespeare's House*.

William Cory's niece, Faith Compton Mackenzie, wrote a biography of her uncle, in which she referred to Wilton House and the visit made by King James I in 1603.

> An interesting entry in his diary when he was staying at Wilton House, Salisbury, tells how Lady Pembroke showed him a letter from her forerunner to her son, urging him to bring the King (James I) from Salisbury to see As You Like It. ... That would have been an agreeable occasion. The excellent play, the author present, and the King lured from Salisbury. To commemorate it a temple was built at Wilton, and known as 'Shakespeares House'.
>
> (Compton Mackenzie, 88)

In August 1887, Edward Rose, a journalist writing for the *Illustrated London News*, who had visited Wilton House for a series of articles he was preparing, reaffirmed the existence of *Shakespeare's House*.

> Straight from the terrace leads a pretty walk, between trees of infinite shades of delicate green; to its right is the great green-house; and to the left the gardens slope gently to the little river.
>
> At the end of the shady walk is a little building which has been christened by Wilton ... Shakespeare's House. For there is a story, in no way improbable, that once upon a time Shakespeare and his actors "gave a play" at Wilton House—before what a company one may imagine!
>
> In memory of this a little temple has been built: classic as to its pillars, feudal as to the devices of arms above, with portrait busts, and an inscription on the wall from the wonderful lines in 'Macbeth'—
>
>> Life's but a walking shadow; a poor player,
>> That struts and frets his hour upon the stage,
>> And then is heard no more:
>
> Close to Shakespeare's House passes one of the three little rivers which pass through the park—not, as it might appropriately have been, the Avon, but the less romantic Nadder. An Avon is, however, the chief of the three streams, the other two being its tributaries; it is ... a pleasant stream—the Upper Avon it is called—which comes through the downs of South Wiltshire, and goes past Salisbury into Hampshire.
>
> (Illustrated London News: Aug. 6th 1887, p.177)

The letter from Countess Pembroke to her son in 1603, urging him to bring the King to Wilton, has since vanished: a fate shared by the school records at Stratford-upon-Avon; which, one way or the other, would have revealed the truth about Shakspere's education, or maybe non-education; likewise, the pages cut from the register at St Martin's Church in Worcester: these too might have confirmed if this was where Shakspere wed Anne Hathaway, and if so, were the vows exchanged under her own name, or that of Anne Whateley?

These are no idle thoughts; 1865, the year that Cory was shown the letter mentioning Shakespeare, was a time when John Payne Collier was still visiting libraries and archive collections that he thought could hold a letter or document referring to Shakespeare. Whereupon, left alone, he was able to destroy or forge entries as he saw fit; his goal being to provide a consistent record of Shakespeare's life and work to fill the void. Shortly before his death, a remorseful Collier confessed to having forged evidence, although he was unable to find the courage to list each misdeed.

> I am bitterly sad and most sincerely grieved that in every way I am such a despicable offender[.] I am ashamed of almost every act of my life ... My repentance is bitter and sincere[.] (Schoenbaum, 361)

James Orchard Halliwell-Phillipps was another Shakespearean scholar of that time, and not above removing documents from collections, if he saw fit. As a result, he was excluded membership of the Library of the British Museum, for having surreptitiously acquired certain manuscripts from Trinity College Cambridge.

Although the Wilton letter may be lost, the circumstances suggested by it have since been confirmed by historians.

Oxford had a particular reason for visiting Wilton House in 1603. His daughter Susan was soon to marry Philip, the younger son of Countess Pembroke, the brother of William who had been responsible for urging the King to return to Wilton. William and Philip Herbert were *"the most noble and incomparable pair of brethren'* to whom William Shakespeare's Comedies, Histories, and Tragedies were dedicated, thereby connecting Susan Vere with her father's work as Shakespeare. In fact, William had once been betrothed to Bridget Vere, Susan's elder sister, but the dowry could not be agreed and the marriage was called off. The relationship between Oxford and Wilton House can therefore be traced back to the sixteenth century.

In the sixteenth and early seventeenth centuries, Wilton House was a place much celebrated for its contribution to literature, learning and scholarship. The person responsible for this was Lady Mary Herbert (née Sidney), Countess of Pembroke. Her husband was immensely rich and well able to satisfy his wife's ambition to *'emulate the liberal culture of the Italian courts,'* something that would have greatly appealed to Oxford, for he was known as *'the Italianate Earl'*. John Aubrey had this to say about her.

> In her time, Wilton House was like a college, there were so many learned and ingenious persons. She was the greatest Patroness of wit and learning of any lady of her time. (Wilton House, official booklet, 33)

Aubrey's description of Wilton House is virtually identical to the place Thomas Nashe wrote about, and from where he had recently returned. Writing in *Strange News* during the period 1592-93, he made the following statement, which was intended for Gabriel Harvey.

> For the order of my life, it is as ciuil as a ciuil orange; I lurke in no corners, but converse in a house of credit, as well gouerned as any Colledge where there be more rare qualified men and selected good Schollers than in any Nobleman's house that I know in England.
> (Ogburn 658)

Earlier in 1592, Nashe had published *Pierce Pennilesse* (the pun in the title is that 'Pierce' is pronounced 'purse'). In the pamphlet he referred to his recent whereabouts, which throws light on its title, for it appears to be connected with the company he was with, viz. *"the feare of infection detained me with my Lord in the country".* Nashe was referring to the Plague, which had forced many to leave the capital, where the close proximity of people rendered the disease most contagious.

Putting together what is known, we have Nashe returning from his stay in the country, and referring to a collegial house that aptly describes Wilton House. He had been admitted to the House because he was in the company of a Lord. Consider, therefore, in this same year, after his return to London, and within weeks of publishing *Strange News*, he dined with Christopher Marlowe, Robert Greene and Will Monox (the abbreviated Latin anagram Nashe gave to conceal Oxford's identity from the general reader).

It is legitimate to conclude from this that to escape the Plague, Oxford had taken Nashe to Wilton House, and there on the banks of the river Avon, which watered the parkland of the Wilton Estate, he employed Nashe as his secretary to write, as well as possibly update, some of the plays that would later be attributed to William Shakespeare.

More than two decades later, when Ben Jonson (a frequent visitor to Wilton House where he collaborated with Inigo Jones in the preparation of Court masques), was preparing his introduction to the First Folio, and searching for parallels between Oxford and his allonym Will Shakspere, he recalled, or was told of the time spent at Wilton House by Oxford, and the composition of some of his plays while a guest of Lady Pembroke. Jonson was therefore able to use this information to describe Oxford as Sweet Swan of Avon; since this met with his search for attributes that carried a double meaning: ones that could be thought to also apply to Shakspere.

In 1592, the seed in Oxford's mind that would bear fruit as Shakespeare had also begun to germinate, for it was upon his return to London, that he and Nashe met up with Marlowe and Greene for a banquet to discuss the 'arrival' of William Shakespeare as a fully fledged poet and author of his forthcoming *Venus and Adonis*. As we shall see, this poem had been on Oxford's mind at Wilton: the clues being in the hints dropped by Nashe in the pamphlet he published upon his return to the capital. *Pierce Pennilesse* was also an apt description of Oxford at that time, for he had lost all his money and property following the death of his wife in 1588.

The clues left by Nashe can now be safely regarded. In the extract from *Strange News* given above, Nashe declared: *"my life, it is as civil as a civil orange.'* This phrase appears in *Much Ado about Nothing*, wherein Act 2: sc. i,

Beatrice exclaims: *"The Count is neither sad, nor sick, nor merry, nor well; but civil Count, civil as an orange, and something of that complexion."*

Civil is a play on Seville and draws its humour from the Spanish city noted for its oranges and their colour. In the play, the colour is likened to jealousy.

In *Hidden Allusions to Shakespeare's Plays*, Eva Turner Clark noticed similarities to the play that were found to have occurred in *A Historie of Ariodanto and Jenevra*, which was performed before Queen Elizabeth on Shrove Tuesday, the 12 February 1583 (Old Style). Hubert Henry Holland, writing in *Shakespeare, Oxford and Elizabethan Times* was also struck by several coincidences: one of which was the number of lines in *Ariodanto and Jenevra*, which appear to anticipate similarly expressed lines in *Much Ado About Nothing*.

However, the *Historie of Ariodanto and Jenevra* was entered in the Stationers' Register in 1565-6, and registered to Henry Wekes. It is a play by Elizabethan poet, Peter Beverley, and was dedicated to the *'Worshipfull M. Peter Reade from my chamber at Staple Inne. The first day of August'*. (DNB). The play is also *"the earliest English translation from Ariosto's Orlando Furioso,"* and includes a sub plot that was to appear in *Much Ado About Nothing*.

If Oxford had picked-up *Ariodanto and Jenevra* in 1592, in order to use it as a source for *Much Ado About Nothing*, this would also help to explain the point made by Philip Johnson, who wrote of similarities existing between *Much Ado About Nothing* and John Lyly's *Endymion*, published in 1591; for both these plays have *"a group of befuddled watchmen given to ludicrous logic."* (Humphreys, 155). In *Endymion*, the watchmen sing:

> Stand: who goes there?
> We charge you, appear
> Fore our Constable here.
> (In the name of the Man in the Moon)
> To us Belman relate,
> Why you stagger so late,
> And how come you drunk so soon
> (Works, ed. Bond, ii. 38)

Now compare this with the watchmen in *Much Ado About Nothing*.

Dogberry: ... This is your charge: you shall comprehend all vagrom (vagrant) men: you are to bid any man to stand, in the Prince's name.

Second Watch: What if a will not stand?

| | |
|---|---|
| Dogberry: | Why then, take no note of him, but let him go, and presently call the rest of the watch together, and thank God you are rid of a knave. |
| Verges: | If he will not stand when he is bidden, he is none of the Prince's subjects. |
| ... | |
| Dogberry: | ... Well, you are to call at all the ale-houses, and bid those that are drunk get them to bed. |
| Watchman: | How if they will not? |
| Dogberry: | Why then, let them alone till they are sober: |

(Act 3: sc. iii)

The similarities between the two plays are self evident. When it is also understood that Lyly was Oxford's secretary from 1580 to 1588, it is not then at all surprising to discover R. W. Bond declare – *'In comedy Lyly is Shakespeare's only model: the evidence of the latter's study and imitation of him is abundant.'* (Ogburn, 569).

But Harvey, a contemporary of Lyly, seems not to have agreed. Five years after Lyly's departure from Oxford's service, Harvey called him: *'the fiddlestick of Oxford, now the very bauble of London'*. (ibid 568). A violin is, of course, an instrument of sound; the bow or fiddlestick is merely the tool used for drawing music from it. To pursue this metaphor, we may judge that Lyly drew his bow across the strings of Oxford's violin in order to elicit his best work, amongst which was *Endymion*.

In support of this interpretation, we may follow Ogburn and observe—

> ... having written nothing before his association with Oxford, Lyly after its end wrote no more plays or anything else of the least merit though he desperately needed the kind of income his writing had brought. (ibid 569)

In which case, *Endymion* is not necessarily a source for part of *Much Ado About Nothing*, but a work that has borrowed from an earlier version of a play written by the Earl of Oxford, Lyly's employer at the time.

Traces of this earlier version were remarked upon by A. R. Humphries:

> That an earlier play lurks behind some of Shakespeare's texts is certain, and some commentators, particularly John Dover Wilson held that
>
> (a) The Quarto's stage-directions introduce characters with no function, either at all or at the point of entry;
> (b) Some stage-directions are eccentric or idiosyncratic;
> (c) In the speech prefixes for iv.ii Dogberry and Verges are named in a variety of forms;
> (d) Verse lines have allegedly been cut or revised;

(e) Loose ends and unexplained allusions occur (e.g. to earlier encounters between Beatrice and Benedick); in particular, explanations are needed for the Borachio-Margaret intrigue.

The 'old play', it is supposed, would have been largely, perhaps, wholly, in verse. The fact that Beatrice is gulled in verse (iii.i) 'shows that Beatrice and Benedick provided a comic underplot in the old play'; the 'surviving' verse is judged to resemble the early styles of *The Two Gentlemen of Verona* and *Romeo and Juliet*; and in revision, it is argued, some of the 'original' verse was cut. (Humphreys, 24)

Clark and Humphries also referred to a letter written by Lord Burghley to Sir Francis Walsingham on 10 August 1586, which calls to mind *Dogberry* and his watchmen in Shakespeare's *Much Ado About Nothing*.

As I came from London homeward, in my coach, I saw at every town's end the number of 10 or 12, standing with long staves, and until I came to Enfield I thought no other of them, but that they had stayed for avoiding of the rain, or to drink at some alehouse, for so they did stand under penthouses at ale houses. But at Enfield finding a dozen in a plump, when there was no rain, I bethought myself that they were appointed as watchmen, for the apprehending of such as are missing; and thereupon I called some of them to me apart, and asked them why they stood there? ... And then I asked who appointed them; and they answered Bankes, a Head Constable, whom I willed to be sent to me. Surely, sir, whoever had the charge from you has used the matter negligently for these watchmen stand so openly in plumps, as no suspected person will come near them. (ibid 22-3)

Apart from the letter's reference to men *standing* about, attention is drawn to the men *standing* under *penthouses* at *alehouses* to get out of the *rain*; for once again we find this also appears in *Much Ado About Nothing*.

| Conrade: | I will owe thee an answer for that: and now forward with thy tale. |
| --- | --- |
| Borachio: | Stand thee close then under this penthouse, for it drizzles with rain, and I will, like a true drunkard, utter all to thee. |
| Second Watch: | [Aside] Some treason, masters; yet stand close. |

(Act 3: sc. iii)

One can easily sympathise with Shakespeare's biographers. Burghley's letter was written on the day that those involved in Babington's treason were arrested. How splendid it would be for their subject's biography if Burghley's letter, involving thoughts of treason, constables, watchmen, penthouses, rain, and men standing about could be the inspiration for *Dogberry* and his watchmen. Alas, the possibility of Shakspere accessing the private papers of Walsingham or Burghley is too far-fetched, and so the connection is cast aside as coincidence. But for Oxford, who was then Burghley's son-in-law, no such difficulties existed. If Oxford did not see the letter, he was just as likely to have heard the same account from his father-in-law.

If, as seems most likely, *Much Ado About Nothing* was completed in 1592 at Wilton, using an earlier Oxford play as its source, then evidence exists to suggest that *The Merry Wives of Windsor* was also written there.

After the death of his wife, and the release of his three daughters into the care of Lord Burghley, Oxford's life fell into a state of collapse, and suicide cannot have been far from his thoughts. The Queen would have been kept fully informed of his condition, for there was a longstanding relationship between the two.

> Elizabeth certainly delighted in his company ... there was something appealing in his eccentric, dissolute ways, and after anger and tears would come reconciliation.
> (Williams, 1972: 152)

The opportunity for the Queen to help Oxford presented itself in 1592. An important guest was due to arrive from Germany, and stay at Windsor Castle, so as to be present for the investiture of knights of the Order of the Garter. Elizabeth therefore commanded that Oxford write a play showing *Falstaff* in love, and that it be finished within two weeks. The time for *sitting in idle cell* was brought to an end. Oxford needed to revitalise himself and begin work immediately. The speed, with which the play needed to be written, and mostly in prose, may account for Gervinus's assessment.

> It is designed without any deeper background, without any merit of idea, without pathetic elevation, and without serious passages; it is almost entirely written in prose; it is the only piece of the poet's in which the plot decidedly outweighs the characterisation, the only one which moves in the stratum of plain, common and homely society. (Gervinus, 378)

It is perfectly understandable why Oxford chose Windsor as the setting for a play commanded by Elizabeth for her guest: as he would be staying at Windsor Castle. It is nowhere near understandable why Shakspere, had he been the author, would not have titled the play *The Merry Wives of Stratford*, and had Falstaff's amorous intentions take place in the Forest of Arden; which is not to be confused with the Forest of Ardennes in France, where the characters: *Amiens, Jaques, Le Beau, Charles, Phebe,* and *Jaques de Boys* are to be found in *As You Like It*. French names, coupled with French locations, are not noticeably strong points amongst Nelson's *Shakespeare experts*. They are prone to believe that this part of France lies close to Birmingham.

Queen Elizabeth had been greatly amused to see the character of *Falstaff* played in *Henry IV* parts 1 and 2, and desired to see how the author would portray him if he were in love. Evidence for the haste in its composition comes from three sources.

John Dennis was first to leave a record of this. In 1702, he produced the play under the title of *The Comical Gallant* and dedicated it to George Granville, to whom he wrote:

> I knew very well, that it had pleas'd one of the greatest Queens that ever was in the World ... This Comedy was written at her Command, and by her direction, and she was so eager to see it Acted, that she commanded it to be finished in fourteen days, and was afterwards as Tradition tells us, very well pleas'd at the Representation. (Oliver, xliv)

Nicholas Rowe repeated the story in his short biography of Shakespeare in 1709.

> [The Queen] was so well pleas'd with that admirable Character of Falstaff, in the two Parts of Henry the Fourth, that she commanded him to continue it for one play more, and to shew him in Love. This is said to be the Occasion of his Writing The Merry Wives of Windsor. How well she was obey'd, the Play it self is an admirable Proof. (ibid xlv)

In the following year another author, Gildon, included in his *Remarks on the Plays of Shakespeare* this observation.

> The Fairys in the fifth Act makes a Handsome Complement to the Queen, in her Palace of Windsor, who had oblig'd him to write a Play of Sir John Falstaff in Love, and which I am well assured he perform'd in a Fortnight; a prodigious Thing, when all is so well contriv'd, and carry'd on without the least Confusion. (ibid xlv)

Shakespearean scholar Edward Dowden, writing in 1911, was in no doubt that this play was given its final touches in 1592. However, it is not difficult to find traditionalist tongues eager to dispute this date. The reason is obvious. Based upon the premise that Will Shakspere was Shakespeare, the year 1592 would mean the plays in which *Falstaff* appears, including perhaps *Henry V*, in which his death is reported, were written sometime earlier. But the composition of these plays would then clash with that of Shakespeare's 'first' tetralogy; for *Henry VI* was already being played in 1592.

Suddenly, there is a logjam of plays, each clamouring for a date of composition that will tie in with the favoured view of Shakespeare's first efforts as a dramatist. To avoid confusion, it becomes necessary to ignore Dowden and posit a much later date for the *Merry Wives of Windsor*. But the evidence for the play's composition in 1592 contradicts this.

> In that year Count Mümpelgart, the prospective Duke of Württemberg, came to London, and the event lent itself to a comic interpolation about 'cosen-germans' and 'garmombles' that depended for its punch on the author's being up-to-the-minute, like a stand-in comedian today; dragged in years later it would have fallen flat. (Ogburn, 436 fn)

Turning to the play, Consider the quarto edition pirated for publication in 1602. In this, the Welsh parson, *Sir Hugh Evans*, makes the following comment: *'there is three sorts of cosen garrmombles, is cosen all the Host of Maidenhead and Readings'* (Oliver, xlviii). In the First Folio this has been edited to read: *'there is three cozen-Germans that has cozened all the hosts of Readins, of Maidenhead, of Colebrook, of horses and money'*. (ibid 125-6).

The word 'cosen', which was a form of address between members of the nobility, has a second meaning, which is to cheat. When Count Mümpelgart visited England in 1592, there was an administrative blunder. Lord Howard had promised to provide a special warrant enabling the German visitors to free post-horses. Consequently, when the visitors set foot in England, they assumed the respective stopovers had been informed, and simply took the horses without payment. Not surprisingly, this caused a minor commotion that resulted in the Germans being branded as horse thieves. Shakespeare included this mess-up as a piece of comedy in the play, and it must have raised a special laugh at Court: but only if the play was performed soon after the event. At a later date the joke would have been so stale as to be pointless.

| | |
|---|---|
| Bardolph: | Sir, the German desires to have three of your horses: the Duke will be tomorrow at court, and they are going to meet him. |
| Host: | They shall have my horses, but I'll make them pay: I'll sauce them.    [Act 4: sc. iii] |
| ... | |
| Bardolph: | Out, alas sir, cozenage, mere cozenage! |
| Host: | Where be my horses? Speak well of them, varletto. |
| Bardolph: | Run away with the cozeners: for so soon as I came beyond Eton, they threw me off, from behind one of them, in a slough of mire; and set spurs and away, like three German devils, three doctor Faustuses.    [Act 5: sc. v] |

These comical allusions to events that took place in 1592 are plain, and would have been out of date and mostly forgotten five years later, which is the preferred date for the play's composition. Consider, also, the places mentioned in the play: Reading, Maidenhead and Colnbrook: all three are towns or villages at which the German party were known to have visited *en route* for Windsor Castle. Eton, which lies close to Windsor, is also referred to in the play.

Consider, too, the reference to 'Doctor Faustus'. Marlowe's play of that title is thought to have been written in 1592. It also includes a scene in which three men who attempt to murder Faustus are dragged through *'a lake of mud and dirt'*. (Oliver, 125, fn 65). This would then have been another topical comment for inclusion in a play performed at court in 1592, where these facts would still have been familiar to many.

Included also in the play is a subtle joke that seems likely to have been aimed especially at Count Mümpelgart, and which would not have been missed by a Court audience.

Caius: I cannot tell vat is dat; but it is tell-a me dat you make grand preparations for a Duke of Jamanie: by my trot, dere is no Duke that the court is know to come. [Act 4: sc. v]

Although *Dr. Caius* is deemed to be a Frenchman (he lapses into this language several times), *'the clipped English of Dr Caius'* (Macauley) is pronounced with a distinct Germanic accent (as verified by a native German speaker and graduate lecturer in psychology). Even *Caius'* grammar conforms to the German tongue, where the infinitive of the verb (in the case cited above, 'to come') occupies the conclusion of a sentence; this is not at all common in French. But it is not only how *Caius* expresses himself that provides the humour, it is also what he says. Despite the preparations made at Court to receive this foreign nobleman, *Caius* claims to know of no such Duke. *Caius* is right. It was a Count that was expected: a Count who had to wait until his return to Germany before becoming a Duke.

Turning attention next to *Evans*, as in the Quarto of 1602, we find: *three sorts of cosen garmombles*. 'Garmomble' is obviously a made-up word derived by phonetically inverting 'Mümpel-gart'; it was subsequently replaced by *cozen-Germans* in the First Folio. By 1623, the pun of turning Mümpelgart's name around had obviously lost its relevance to the visit of the Count in 1592, and so the editor replaced it with the more easily understood, *Germans*.

Noticeably, however, in 1592, Nashe decided to use this reference to Mümpelgart in his pamphlet *Strange News, Of the Intercepting Certaine Letters*. It was while haranguing Gabriel Harvey that he called him a *'fanaticall Phobetor, geremumble ... or what you will'*. (Oliver, 126, fn 72). The word returned in 1599, again from the pen of Nashe; this time it was used as a verb 'geremumble', and occurs in *Nashes Lenten Stuffe*.

The focus of attention for the composition of *The Merry Wives of Windsor* is most decidedly fixed upon 1592. This, we recall, was also the year when

Nashe returned to London, after time spent at Wilton House *in the country* with *my Lord*, having served there in the capacity of Oxford's secretary.

Consequently, there are good reasons to believe that this play was written at the behest of Queen Elizabeth as entertainment for the Court and the arrival of the German Count. In which case, it would have been written in the amenable atmosphere provided by the Countess of Pembroke at Wilton House by the river Avon, with Nashe, acting as secretary. This enabled him to draw upon the punning reference to Mümpelgart's name, which he added to his vocabulary. It would also explain his use of this word, twice, each time in the proximity of Mümpelgart's relationship with England. The first occasion was shortly after the arrival of the Count in England in 1592; the second occasion occurred in 1597, when Mümpelgart, who was then Duke of Württemberg, was granted, *in absentia*, the Order of the Garter; he had requested this honour upon seeing the ceremony at Windsor, but for five years the Queen prevaricated before bowing to political pressure, and investing him with the Garter Order.

This later reference to Württemberg has since become a twig upon which orthodoxy hangs its evidence for dating the play, despite its references to events staled by time. To seek support for this date Mistress Quickly's allusions to the Order of the Garter, which appear in Act 5: scene v. are proposed as evidence. (Oliver, 140-1). However, these allusions may just as easily apply to 1592; especially as the play was to be part of the entertainment ordered by Elizabeth, after the State formalities of the Garter ceremony were concluded.

Tantalisingly, Nashe makes a covert reference to this play and its author in *Strange News*, which was entered in the *Stationers' Register* on 12 January 1593. In his *Epistle Dedicatorie*, he wrote:

To the most copious Carminist of our time, and famous persecutor of Priscian, his verie friend Master Apis Lapis: Tho. Nashe wisheth new strings to his old tawnie Purse.

(Ogburn, 656)

Every comment in this extract is directed at the Earl of Oxford. Earlier in the year Nashe had been Oxford's companion and secretary during their sojourn in the country. Upon their return, Nashe had dined with Oxford at a banquet where they were joined by Marlowe and Greene. Consequently, upon writing, with these past events still fresh in his mind, it is natural to assume any letter of dedication written by Nashe would be directed to his patron, Lord Oxford.

The final phrase seems to leave no doubt this was the case. *Tawnie*, or to be precise, 'Reading Tawny', was the colour of Oxford's livery. Wishing *new strings to his old tawny purse*, at a time when Oxford's purse was all but *penny-less*, is certainly confirmation that Oxford was Nashe's subject. Then there is the play on Oxford's family name, Vere; Nashe calls him *his 'ver(i)e friend*, whom he then refers to as *Apis Lapis*, the *famous persecutor of Priscian*.

'*Priscian was a great grammarian of the fifth century, whose name is almost synonymous with grammar,*" (Brewer, 1008). Nashe seizes upon this fact and uses it as a piece of polite humour that was unlikely to offend Oxford. In *The Merry Wives of Windsor*, there is a comedy sketch involving a Latin grammar lesson (Act 4: sc. i). This involves a Welshman, *Sir Hugh Evans* acting as a schoolmaster, and *William Page* his pupil.

| | |
|---|---|
| Evans: | William, how many numbers is in nouns? |
| William: | Two. |
| ... | |
| Evans: | ... What is lapis, William? |
| William: | A stone. |
| Evans: | And what is 'a stone', William? |
| William: | A pebble. |
| Evans: | No, it is lapis: I pray you remember in your prain |
| William: | Lapis |

The lesson continues in the same vein with further points of Latin grammar introduced, some with sexual undertones, thus adding to the humour. Because it is a comedy sketch and certain grammatical liberties have been taken with the Latin, Nashe is able to accuse his *verie friend*, of being a *persecutor of Priscian*, with a play on the word *Lapis*.

As secretary to Oxford in 1592, Nashe would have likely penned the scene himself at his employer's dictation. In actual fact, the entire sketch was based upon a lesson taken from a book of Latin grammar that Edward VI had commanded for use in all schools; this was *A Shorte Introduction of Grammar* written by William Lilly and John Colet, published in 1549.

> In nouns be two numbers, the singular and the plural. The singular number speaketh of one, as lapis, a stone. The plural number speaketh of more than one, as lapides, stones.
>
> (Crystal, 125)

The connection between *persecuting Priscian*, the scholar upon whose work Lilly and Colet's Latin grammar book was based, and *lapis*, is at once obvious. It requires only that *Apis* be accounted for as part of *The Merry Wives of Windsor* and Nashe's enigmatic reference to *Apis Lapis* will be complete.

For this, we refer to Egyptian mythology. *'Apis, in the form of a real black bull was believed to be the reincarnation or 'glorious soul' of Ptah'*. (Cotterell & Storm, 268). A sacred bull is also the subject, chosen by Shakespeare for another comedy sketch in *The Merry Wives of Windsor*: this time it involves *Falstaff*.

| | |
|---|---|
| Falstaff: | Now, the hot-blooded gods assist me! Remember Jove, thou wast a bull for thy Europa; love set on thy horns. (Act 5: sc. v) |

*Falstaff* was referring to the Latin equivalent of Ptah: both Jove and Ptah were believed by their respective followers to have created the world. Like Ptah, Zeus (the Greek name for Jove) too appeared as a bull: his intention being the amorous desire to carry off Europa. It was this that gave *Falstaff* his idea: he would adopt a similar plan; but instead of a bull, he would disguise himself as a stag: his motive being the same as that of Jove: the amorous desire to carry off Mistress Ford and Mistress Page, who had arranged a tryst with him in the forest of Windsor.

*Master Apis Lapis* is therefore identified as the inventor of the two comedy sketches occurring in *The Merry Wives of Windsor*, involving first *Lapis* and then *Apis*. The fact that Nashe was able to refer to these sketches at the end of 1592, is yet further proof that this play had already been completed by then, and he had knowledge of it. But it also pushes back in time the first appearance of *Falstaff*. He first appears in *1 & 2 Henry IV* with a mention of his death in *Henry V*. The case for Shakspere having been Shakespeare therefore grows ever weaker.

The passage in *Strange News*, where these discrete references occur implying that Oxford wrote *The Merry Wives of Windsor*, yields a further clue. It is Nashe's comment concerning: *the most copious Carminist of our time*. 'Carm/en–inis' is a Latin word, meaning poem, verse, and poetry. Nashe can therefore be seen dedicating his *Epistle* to the most copious poet or versifier of that time, which of course was the man we now refer to as William Shakespeare.

Nashe would have been thinking of Oxford's preparations for his forthcoming publication of *Venus and Adonis*, which went on sale soon after *Strange News*. This narrative poem, hugely popular in its day, consists of 199 stanzas, each containing six lines of rhyme to the pattern of *ababcc*; that is, almost 1200 lines of poetry — *copious,* indeed. *Lucrece,* which followed one year later, has even more, with 1850 lines.

Wilton House; *Much Ado About Nothing; The Merry Wives of Windsor; Venus and Adonis;* Thomas Nashe's reference to his time in the country with a Lord; his description of Wilton House as a college; Oxford's association with the Herbert family resulting in the marriage of his daughter to Philip Herbert, and the planned betrothal of his daughter Bridget to William Herbert; the dedication of Shakespeare's collected plays to two members of Oxford's family by marriage; all of these, occurring at a location next to the river Avon, fully warrants Oxford to have been the person Jonson had in mind when he coined the phrase: *Sweet Swan of Avon.*

**Shakespeare's House at Wilton c.1880**

# 16

## Early Retirement

Francis Meres's *Palladis Tamia Wits Treasury*, published in 1598, opened the floodgates to the naming of Shakespeare as both a playwright and a poet. In the years thereafter, the name enjoyed unprecedented exposure. For biographers of Shakespeare, this is seen as an important development. Their hero, so to speak, is at last receiving acknowledgement for his ability with the pen. And the frequency with which the name appears in print is confirmation that Shakspere was recognised by his peers as Shakespeare.

There are two major problems with this conclusion. Firstly, the references to Shakespeare are all made in praise of his work or his ability as a poet. None connect Shakespeare with what is known about Shakspere's private life. Secondly, assuming that Shakespeare was the penname of a titled gentleman, deliberately concealing his identity as an elite member of England's ruling class, what objection can biographers raise to this, if they also wish to adhere to the known facts?

In truth, beyond a token protest, there is nothing of substance to dispel this alternative as a possibility. Consider, for example, the deference likely to be given to a nobleman who expressed the wish to be known only by his penname. In the class-structured society of Elizabeth's England, it would be expected from those who knew this secret identity to respect that wish. Those who did not share in the secret would express their ignorance by referring to Shakespeare as though this was the actual name of a living person. Consequently, there is nothing positive to be learned about Shakespeare's true identity from the adulation shown to his work by those whose praises have survived long enough to reach modern ears. Experts in the study of Shakespeare's contribution to literature refuse to take this deductive step.

It is also misleading for these same experts to explain that Shakespeare only became recognised for his work after Meres's book appeared. *Venus and Adonis* and *Lucrece* were immensely popular before then: virtually from the time they first went on sale, and well before *Wits Treasury* was even thought of. Moreover, plays we know as Shakespeare's had been pirated for a quick profit based upon their popularity as early as 1594, although always with the author unnamed.

With these objections held in mind, the sudden and repeated references made to Shakespeare by name, after four years of silence, seem more appropriate to a person whose name had been censored, but which emerged in full flood after the censorship was lifted. In this respect, Meres's book came out just after Lord Burghley, the head of censorship, died. And since Burghley was both guardian and grandfather to the Earl of Oxford's three daughters, with the wish to preserve their dignity from the scandalous behaviour of their titled father, he had the motive, the method, and the opportunity to censor Oxford's penname while he lived. If one seeks a parallel for censorship in 16th century England, Stalinist Russia or Ceaușescu's Romania serve as models. Had Professor Nelson lived in either of these regimes, instead of writing with the liberty of free speech afforded him by western society; he would have been more thoughtful before objecting that —

> ... the notion that de Vere could successfully hide his authorship during his lifetime and for more than 400 years after his death would have required the cooperation of so many people as to be transparently preposterous; only those inclined to conspiracy theories could take such an idea seriously. (Waugaman & Stritmatter, 106)

Strict censorship, when applied to all printed matter for a generation, means that memories of the past, in this one respect, will be unavailable to future generations, except by word of mouth; and even that will slowly fade with time. This is essentially what William Camden, Ben Jonson's former tutor at Westminster School, admitted. He referred in his book to the existence of an active conspiracy by the authorities of his time: *'those who think the memory of succeeding ages may be extinguished by present power.'* (Kay, 70). Therefore, when Nelson ridicules *conspiracy theories*, he ignores Camden, a respected historian who, unlike Nelson, lived and wrote about the age in which he lived, which included a conspiracy operated by the *present powers* to deny future generations knowledge of what must, at the time, have been seen as a dangerously, sensitive subject.

In post-medieval England, the political dictum was still that *"every man has a master"*. It would not have seemed fitting, therefore, for a man in Burghley's powerful position to permit his young granddaughters to be publicly known as children of a senior nobleman who laboured for actors, by writing lines they could repeat for their bread. In Burghley's mind it would also have seemed appalling that his son-in-law, to whom he had also been the boy's guardian, was actively associating with public theatres, when the Church was urging their closure: referring to them as centres of moral decadence. This was yet further reason for Burghley to censor his son-in-law's pseudonym.

It can be seen from this that biographers have serious problems with the evidence they possess. However, far greater problems exist with the evidence they do not possess. What they do not have, and which by every consideration possible they should have, is evidence that Shakspere's family knew him to be William Shakespeare, poet, playwright, actor and a favourite entertainer of Queen Elizabeth and thereafter, King James. No such evidence exists, and it would seem has never existed.

New Place, Shakspere's house in Stratford-upon-Avon, remained in the family for fifty years after his death, but never a letter, book or manuscript owned by Shakespeare, or indeed, Shakspere, has ever come to light.

It was not long after this time that the Reverend Doctor John Ward accepted the post of vicar in Stratford-upon-Avon. He was thirty-three years of age and an Oxford University graduate. In his notebook covering the years 1661–1663, he wrote: *'Remember to peruse Shakespeare's plays. And be versed in them, that I may not be ignorant in that matter.'* (Ogburn, 19).

Ward was therefore well placed to furnish his notebooks with stories and anecdotes relating to his parish's famous author. Yet, during the nineteen years that he remained vicar in residence, and though his notebooks increased in number to sixteen, his resolve to discover more about Stratford's famous poet lapsed to a single paragraph. It begins: *'I have heard that Mr Shakespeare was a natural wit'*. This does seem to have been an attractive feature of Shakspere's personality; one may recall how neighbours remembered his speeches being made in high style when slaughtering a farm animal. Ward then continues with a surprising revelation: *'without any art at all,'* for so he was informed.

Even closer to Shakspere was Doctor John Hall, the husband of his elder daughter, Susanna.

> [Hall's] casebooks were to be translated from Latin and published after his death, evidently [he] never found occasion to mention his father-in-law in his writings, though he recorded personal details of many patients, including Michael Drayton, who he called *'an excellent poet'*. (Ogburn, 39)

The plight of biographers becomes even worse when the last will and testament of Shakspere is inspected. There is nothing on this document in the slightest that connects the testator with the life of William Shakespeare. Where are his books? Where, especially, are the manuscript copies of *Timon of Athens, Coriolanus* and *All's Well That Ends Well?* These three plays until 1623 had never before been heard of, making them valuable commodities. If they had previously been sold, why were they never performed? It was not until their inclusion in the First Folio that people became aware of their existence; but it also put them in the hands of any theatre group that cared to perform them, thus depriving Heminge and Condell and the King's Men of potential income.

Added to these previously unknown plays were a further seventeen, which had never been published. This is an important fact because the law protected the author's right to income from them.

> [A]t common law an author of any book or literary composition had the sole right of first printing and publishing the same for sale: and might bring action against any person who printed, published and sold the same without his consent. (Bentley, 15)

Biographers are so stymied by this absence of any reference to the deceased's literary life that they are careful to guide their readers away from the problem. They accomplish this primarily by directing attention to an interlineation on the will. This refers to five pounds being divided between three members of the King's Men with whom Shakspere had been a shareholder while in London. An interlineation is, however, only the testator's afterthought, and this particular afterthought was inserted into the will after it had been almost three months in the drafting: January 1616 through to March. In fact, the final draft is *'unusual among legal documents for its large number of alterations, substitutions and interpolations.'* (Wilson, 385). There is also the fact that the will was written on three sheets of paper, each of a different size, and from different batches, which tends to show how Shakspere may have prevaricated at this time.

In the absence of any literary references, biographers make much of the bequest left to actors, Heminge, Condell and Burbage, meagre though this was. But at what point the interlineation naming them was made, can only be speculated upon. The fact that Heminge and Condell later appear as benefactors and financiers for the compilation and publication of the First Folio could be termed suspicious (Burbage had died before work began). But nothing can be proved. A sceptic would be inclined to believe that the time, education, and finance for such a huge undertaking as the publication of the First Folio was far beyond the reach of two relatively simple men like Heminge and Condell: one a grocer, the other an actor; whereas, Jonson had both the time and the education. Furthermore, his association with the brothers, Lord Pembroke and Lord Montgomery (Oxford's son-in-law), to whom the First Folio was dedicated, ensured the financial backing available to see the project through the printers was in competent hands.

Shakspere's will is also in stark contrast with other actors' wills of that period. Take, for example, the will of Augustine Phillips, one of the King's Men. He, too, had held a ten percent share in the Globe. At his death, he provided for his wife and their four daughters, and then, unlike Shakspere, attended to his friends in the theatre.

> I give and bequeath ... amongst the hired men of the company which I am of, the sum of five pounds to be equally distributed amongst them. I give and bequeath to my fellow William Shakespeare a thirty shilling piece in gold, to my fellow Henry Condell, one other thirty shilling piece in gold, to my servant Christopher Beeston, thirty shillings in gold; to my fellow Lawrence Fletcher twenty shillings in gold; to my fellow Robert Armin... [ditto]; to my fellow Richard Cowley... [ditto]; to my fellow Alexander Cooke... [ditto]; to my fellow Nicholas Tooley... [ditto] ... I give to Samuel Gilbourne, my late apprentice, the sum of forty shillings, and my mouse coloured velvet hose, and a white taffeta doublet, a black taffeta suit, my purple cloak, sword and dagger, and my brass viol. I give to James Sands, my apprentice, the sum of forty shillings and a cittern, a bandore and a lute. (Wilson, 310)

Another problem facing Shakespeare's biographers is the lack of a portrait. Nature abhors a vacuum and so a number of unidentified sitters have been proposed to fill the vacancy. These portraits go by the names of 'Sanders'; 'Janssen'; 'Flower', 'Grafton'; 'Chandos'; 'Soest', and 'Cobbe'. Of these, the 'Flower' portrait is a 19th century fake; the 'Grafton' and 'Cobbe' sitters are wearing the apparel of gentlemen superior to the class that Shakspere belonged to; the 'Janssen' has been over-painted to make the person, now thought to be Sir Thomas Overbury, look balder: it also bears a false inscription; the 'Sanders' portrait is dated 1603 and shows a young man in his twenties, when Shakspere was in his fiftieth year; the 'Soest' picture was painted in the reign of Charles II, and the sitter is unknown. This leaves the 'Chandos' portrait, painted between 1600 and 1610. It shows the sitter wearing an earring, and is in the right age group for Shakspere. However, there is no proof that it is he. According to George Vertue it was painted by John Taylor, an actor. The question this raises is why it was not found at New Place, where a portrait of the famous house owner would be expected to have been proudly displayed?

In fact, there is a picture of Shakspere that is a correct likeness of the man, but it is always rejected by his adulators. This was the original copy of Shakspere's bust inside the Church of the Holy Trinity, drawn by Sir William Dugdale in 1634 during his visit there. It depicts Shakspere as a dour faced businessman clutching a woolsack; Dugdale's original sketch still exists as a family keepsake. The reason for the bust's guaranteed likeness to the features of Shakspere is because his relatives were alive at the time, and what they saw in their local parish church would have met with their agreement. In their eyes, this was the man they knew, and the sack of wool was what they remembered him by. Nor would his family have been alone in making that recognition. The population of the parish was not large, and his neighbours, too, would have acknowledged the bust as sufficiently representative of the person they had known.

Understandably, Shakespeare's biographers completely ignore this, despite the fact that for more than a century after the effigy was put in place other artists repeated the same facial features as in Dugdale's drawing. Nicholas Rowe, for example, sent Thomas Betterton to Stratford-upon-Avon on purpose to identify whatever he could about Shakespeare. The result was that Rowe obtained his own engraving of Shakspere, which is identical in every respect to that drawn by Dugdale. The engraver Reynolds Grignion was another who repeated the same features that were first observed by Dugdale, Betterton, and Dr W. Thomas. Had it not been for George Vertue, the present day monument would not exist. It was he, who in 1723 drew an impression of what the monument *should* look like, and in the process, beheaded the dour faced businessman, replacing it with a likeness copied from the Chandos portrait.

The replacement occurred soon after 1849, after John Britton, F.S.A. had left a record of his interest in the bust of 'Shakespeare'. He recalled that:

> In Dec. 1814 I incited Mr. George Bullock to make a cast of the monumental bust .... He was much alarmed on taking down the Effigy to find it to be in a decayed and dangerous state, and declared it would be risking its destruction to remove it again. (Stopes, 120-1)

This confirmed a report made in the middle of the previous century, which recorded how —

> ... the Curious Original Monument and Bust of that incomparable Poet, erected above the Tomb that enshrines his Dust, in the Church of Stratford upon Avon Warwickshire, is through length of Years and other accidents become much impair'd and decay'd. (Matus, 200)

As a result of this mounting alarm at the monument's precarious decay, Britton was made honorary secretary of a Society engaged to oversee its restoration. A public subscription was raised. Money soon arrived. *'The King subscribed £50, the Borough of Stratford the same. Many sent their subscriptions 'only for the restoration and preservation of the Monument.'* (Stopes, 121). At its close, the total raised was £5,000. But, *'The cost of restoring both the Shakespeare Monument and the Chancel'* was initially estimated to be only £1,210. 12s.

Britton had already referred to the original monument as, *'a small and comparatively trifling tomb ... [that] failed to attract anything like critical or literary notice.'* (Stopes, 121). What emerged from this surplus of available funding has been described as a fine:

> ... polychrome sculptured monument set on the chancel's north wall, within a few feet of his grave. Set against a background of white marble, with black marble Corinthian columns, and black touchstone panels, surmounted by the earliest surviving example of usage of the Shakespeare arms, appears a painted bust of Shakespeare, made of Cotswold limestone.
>
> (Wilson, 397)

No longer is the dour-faced, ageing figure of a businessman on view, grasping a sack of wool. In its place is a bust modelled upon the sketch made by Vertue, although the head is neither that of the Chandos portrait, nor the one which appeared in Dugdale's *Antiquities of Warwickshire*.

Biographers and academics can be assumed to have joined forces with the Stratford committee of the 19th century in condemning the original appearance of Shakspere, preferring to believe that Vertue corrected the errors of the past. Nelson, so often a prominent voice in support of Shakspere, even claimed the monument has *'survived unchanged from the original except for its surface paint,'* (Nelson, 154-5). Is it not remarkable how challenges made to Shakespeare's identity can very quickly metamorphose an acknowledged authority on drama, into a self-proclaimed expert on the science of material decay?

This review of the problems to be overcome when writing a biography of Shakespeare is made still worse when further research reveals —

> For almost fifty years after Shakspere's death nothing personal was written about him. No one appeared in Stratford, notebook in hand, to find out what locals thought about the great man commemorated in their parish church. Shakspere's sister, Joan Hart, outlived him by thirty years, his younger daughter, Judith, by forty-six years, and his last descendant, granddaughter Elizabeth, lived on to 1670. Yet no writer interviewed them, and no one from Stratford who had known William Shakspere recorded any statement about him.
>
> (Michell, 56-7)

The plight of biographers receives another setback when, having seen Shakspere reach the pinnacle of acclaim following *Wits Treasury*, he retired from the theatre, changed his occupation, and left London to concentrate his energy on farm management, property speculation, and usury.

Documentation is the life-blood of history, and history is composed of the biographies of those who have risen to prominence. We shall therefore concentrate upon the documentation available for Shakspere, following the reference to 'Shakespeare' in *Wits Treasury*.

**1599** Shakspere is recorded as owing thirteen shillings and fourpence for unpaid tax. He is also listed as occupying part of the Globe theatre in which he had a 10% holding. This required him to pay £1. 9s. 0d to Nicholas Brend for his share of the ground rent.

William Jaggard published *The Passionate Pilgrim* by W. Shakespeare. This was an anthology of twenty poems of which only five are said to have been Shakespeare's.

Cuthbert Burby published a second quarto of *Romeo and Juliet* with the author's name hyphenated as William Shake-speare.

John Weever published his *Epigrammes in the oldest cut and newest fashions*. In the midst of some one hundred and fifty poems, he referred to *"Honie-tong'd Shakespeare when I saw thine issue"*. Further references were also made to Shakespeare in the *Parnassus Plays*, performed as part of the Christmas celebrations at St John's College, Cambridge.

The free use of Shakespeare's name in association with his newly acquired acclaim as a playwright as well as that of a poet, compared with its virtual absence in previous years, had begun to show. It is therefore natural that Shakespeare's biographers should seize upon this and unite references to Shakspere's theatrical interests with those of Shakespeare's poetry and plays. But as part of a broader picture, it raises the question as to why this popular poet of six years standing, with more than a dozen plays of the highest quality to his name, had to wait for Meres's *Wits Treasury* before he could be publicly recognised? Biographers avoid this question: all too aware that any explanation they offer will sound feeble.

**1600** A court record shows John Clayton had been indebted to *'Willelmus Shackspere'* since 1594 for the sum of £7. This was the result of a loan, which Clayton acknowledged had taken place in Cheapside, but which he had failed to repay. After six years, Shakspere finally got his debtor into court. 1594 also coincided with the period when Shakespeare's name appeared as the author of *Venus and Adonis* and *Lucrece*. It is natural to suppose he had been paid for this by Oxford, and it would then account for his venture into money lending: an occupation he had learned from his father as a quick way to riches. A separate record for October refers to *"Shakspeare'* being referred to the Bishop of Winchester for his unpaid taxes.

In the same year, the Stationers' Register recorded Shakespeare's name for the first time, when Andrew Wyse and William Aspley *"entered for their copies vnder the hands of the wardens ... Muche a Doo about nothinge ... Wrytten by master Shakespeare."* Also entered in the Stationers' Register that year was *Henry V* (this first quarto, turned out to be a garbled version of the play); it was accompanied by *A Midsummer nights dreame*: yet another first quarto copied from 'foul papers'. *The Merchant of Venice*, which had been previously entered in the Stationers' Register in 1598 by James Roberts as *The Marchaunt of Venyce or otherwise called the Jewe of Venyce*, but without naming an author, went to the printing house two years later. On that occasion, it was re-entered by Thomas Heyes and given the title, *The Most excellent Historie of the Merchant of Venice*. *"As you like yt a booke"* was also entered in the Register on 4 August, but was *"to be staied"*. No more was heard of this until it appeared in the First Folio in 1623.

**1601** *The Phoenix and the Turtle* made an appearance in the midst of a collection of poems produced by Robert Chester in *Loves Martyr or Rosalin's Complaint*. The *Phoenix and the Turtle* bears Shake-speare's name, although in its hyphenated form, but this attribution to Shakespeare is doubted by some academics. It may also have been in this year that Gabriel Harvey made a marginal note in his 1598 edition of Chaucer: *'The younger sort take much delight in Shakespeare's Venus and Adonis; but his Lucrece, and the tragedie of Hamlet, Prince of Denmark, haue it in them, to please the wiser sort.'* (Chambers, volume II; 197).

Once again, there is a temptation to see Harvey's note as a defining piece of evidence that Shakspere was Shakespeare. But it is not. Consider a comparison, say: 'Mark Twain's *Tom Sawyer* and *Huckleberry Finn* have it in them to please the wiser child.' It is common knowledge that Mark Twain was the penname of Samuel Clements, but using his penname in the above context is perfectly natural, since it was the name he used for his literary work. And so it would have been for Shakespeare, were that Oxford's penname.

Also published in 1601 was a book of Latin poems and epigrams. The author was the Reverend Charles Fitzgeffrey, and the title of his volume was *Affaniae: Sive Epigrammatum*. Biographers of Shakespeare never refer to this book because at the height of their subject's fame, Fitzgeffrey – *"lauded the big names in contemporary English literature: Samuel Daniel, Michael Drayton, Ben Jonson, George Chapman, Thomas Nashe, John Marston, Edmund Spenser, and so on. Glaring in its absence, however, is even the slightest mention of Shake-speare.'* (Anderson, 336). But, as Mark Anderson rightly indicated: *"Fitzgeffrey does include a series of couplets addressed to a writer he cryptically calls 'The Bard'.'*

<blockquote>
To The Bard<br>
You have been cautious, saying, "I will publish verses after my death."<br>
I would not so hurriedly crucify yourself, O Bard.
</blockquote>

(Anderson, 337)

Once again, one is reminded of that *silent name one letter bounds*, or that *crew of Courtly makers Noble men and Gentlemen of Her Maiesties owne seruauntes, who haue written excellently well as it would appeare if their doings could be found out and made publicke.*

**1602** On 18 January, *"Io Busby'* entered in the Stationers' Register *"A booke called An excellent and pleasant conceited Comedie of S.' Io ffaulstof and the merry wyves of windesor."* It was then transferred to *"Arthure Iohnson"* who engaged Thomas Creede to print it. This first quarto of The Merry Wives of Windsor appears to have been copied from hastily made notes, and is imperfect. On 26 July, the Stationers' Register recorded *"The Revenge of Hamlett Prince Denmarke as yt was lateli acted by the Lord Chamberleyne his servantes.'*

Elsewhere, amongst Stratford-upon-Avon's records, a legal document dated 1 May, recorded the conveyance of *"107 acres in common fields of Stratford.'* This was purchased from William and John Combe for £320 (approximately £160,000 today). Interestingly, Shakspere used his brother Gilbert to make this purchase, thus concealing his personal involvement in acquiring the land. On 28 September, another document recorded that *"Shakspere'* purchased a cottage close to New Place on the chapel side, in *"Walkers Street alias Dead Lane'*. At the end of the year, with the disputed ownership of New Place finally resolved in Shakspere's favour by the court, *"Willielmum Shakespeare'* was described as *"generosus".* Does this hint at bribery one wonders?

This was also the year that an officer from the College of Heralds wrote to complain that the grant of arms to *'Shakspeare the Player'* lowered its status. It would appear from the officer's concern that when the letter was written, he did not have in mind Shakespeare the poet and author of two narrative poems, and the playwright of more than a score of histories, comedies and tragedies, which had been performed before her majesty the Queen. None of this was included in the reply that sought to justify the grant. Instead, it merely pointed out that the grant of arms had been to Shakspere's father, who had once been a justice-of-the-peace, and that he had married an heiress.

Taken overall, the events occurring in 1602 appear to indicate that Shakspere had no further interest in London, and he was making plans to establish himself in Stratford-upon-Avon, with the long term intention of staying there.

**1603** On 7 February, an entry in the Stationers' Register granted a licence to James Roberts for *"the booke of Troilus and Cresseda as yt is acted by my Lord Chamberlens men, to print when he hath gotten sufficient authoritye for it.'* The authority was not obtained. Instead, in May, the first quarto of *The Tragicall Historie of Hamlet Prince of Denmarke* was published, with the author's name hyphenated as William Shake-speare. Once again, the book sold to the public was similar to those referred to above, in that it was *"an imperfect reproduction of the play, printed from a manuscript surreptitiously obtained (Camb. edrs.)'* (Stokes, 135).

The death of Queen Elizabeth on 24 March motivated Henry Chettle into casting a jibe at Shakespeare in his *Mourneful Dittie,* for not lamenting her passing. The fact that Shakespeare was almost alone in failing to write a poem in memory of the Queen was predictable, as Chettle must have known. For, whereas Shakspere could barely write his own name, a poem by Oxford given to Shakspere would be considered in very bad taste.

John Davies, a Hereford teacher of penmanship (Bate, 70) wrote in his *Microcosmos* three lines of verse — *"Players, I love ye, and your Quality, / As ye are Men that pass time not abus'd: / And some I love for painting, poesy.'* In the margin are written two sets of initials: W.S. and R.B. Bate sees this as proof that Davies knew Burbage and Shakspere were actors, and that the latter wrote *poesie*. It is certainly one possibility. Another possibility is that Davies was not in the 'loop'. Alternatively, if he did know that W.S. was code for the Earl of Oxford – after all, the same initials, W.S. occur in

*Willobie His Avisa,* published eight years earlier and called in by the High Commission in 1599 – then the continued appearance of these initials in 1603 is not necessarily remarkable.

The succession of James VI of Scotland to the English throne was accompanied by the abolition of all troupes of players; this was intended as a concession to the Church's complaint against actors. However, the King reserved for himself the right to choose one company of players for his entertainment, who thereafter were to be known as the King's Men. *"The plum appointment was, however reserved for Shakespeare's company. Through what can only have been a special recommendation by someone of influence."* (Wilson, 296-7). Because King James referred to Oxford as *"Great Oxford",* because he appointed him to the Privy Council, because he agreed to the continuation of his £1000 annuity with no accounting; because he restored to him Havering Park and the Forest of Waltham; because of all these royal favours, the identity of the person of influence, to whom Wilson referred, is not difficult to discern.

> Wee ... doe licence and aucthorize theise our Servauntes Lawrence Fletcher, William Shakespeare, Richard Burbage, Augustyne Phillipps, John Heninges, Henrie Condell, William Sly, Robert Armyn, Richard Cowly and the rest of theire Associates freely to use and exercise the Arte and faculty of playing Comedies, Tragedies, histories, Enterludes, morals, pastorals, Stageplaies. (Laroque, 73)

It will be noted that Lawrence Fletcher heads the list of men licensed by King James.

> Lawrence Fletcher had been the King's favourite actor in Scotland. He had to receive the perquisites of royal patronage in the new kingdom, and so, although Fletcher never acted with Shakespeare and his fellows, he was officially numbered among them. (Fido, 115)

This leaves open the suggestion that Shakespeare's name was also included on the list of actors for appearance's sake. He was a shareholder in the Globe: the theatre named by the King as the place where his Men were licensed to perform. The public had also been given an assurance in Meres's *Palladis Tamia* that Shakespeare was the author of a dozen plays, previously thought to be anonymous: it therefore followed that his name would be expected to appear amongst members of the company that staged 'his' plays. But it does not necessarily follow – as with Lawrence Fletcher – that he actually played a major part or, indeed, any part in the Company's performances.

1603 was also the year that William *'Camden completed his Remains of a greater Work concerning Britain, in which he listed William Shakespeare, together with his fellow-dramatists Ben Jonson, George Chapman, and John Marston, among 'the most pregnant wits of these our times'.'* (Bate, 70). Bate believes this confirms Shakspere's identity as Shakespeare. It does not, because Bate has failed to inform his readers that Camden also acknowledged the existence of a secret plot, put in place by the government, to deny future generations any knowledge of the censorship imposed upon some matter. This *matter*, orchestrated by Burghley as Head of Censorship, could well apply to his son-in-law, Oxford. Very wisely, Camden confessed that *'things secret and abstruse I have not pried into".* (Kay, 70).

Camden had been Jonson's schoolmaster at Westminster, and the two men became friends afterwards. Camden would therefore have known through Jonson that the memory of succeeding ages was being erased by the transfer of Lord Oxford's work to Shakspere, and that this was one of the *secret* and *abstruse* matters that it was better not to *pry into*.

Shakspere's intention to return to Stratford-upon-Avon and begin a new life away from the theatre is also implied by Max Reese: *"he does not appear on any of the surviving actor-lists after 1603.'* (Reese, 252). In fact, even the appearance of his name on a list in 1603 is open to doubt. It refers to Ben Jonson's *Sejanus* performed that year. Appearing on the list of actors is the name WILL. SHAKE-SPEARE. That Jonson would have hyphenated the name of the man he otherwise praised as Shakespeare (unhyphenated) in the First Folio, occasions the strongest doubt possible that he had in mind Will Shakspere as the person listed. But then Jonson had written SHAKE-SPEARE before in its hyphenated form when printing the cast of *Every Man In His Humour*. To add further doubt: – are we not told it was Shakspere who was lampooned by Jonson in *Every Man Out of His Humour*? This occurred in a scene where a country yokel named Sogliardo is ridiculed as being, *'so enamoured of the name of a gentleman, that he will have it though he buys it'*. And for his motto, it is suggested: *'Not Without Mustard'*: this was the colour added to the Arms. Shakspere's actual maxim was: *'Not Without Right'*.

From this, it can be discerned that a serious difficulty arises. It is to suppose that Jonson, who was about to make his mark on the stage, would mock the true 'Shakespeare': the actor and acclaimed poet and playwright who had honoured him by agreeing to perform in his next play, *Every Man*

*In His Humour*; and who had been responsible for giving him his first break in becoming a recognised author.

> A theatre legend first recorded in 1709 by Nicholas Rowe has it that Shakespeare advocated production of the play at a point when the company was about to reject it. (Wikipedia).

At the end of 1603, a year in which London was again affected by a serious outbreak of plague, Lady Mary Herbert, Countess of Pembroke, received 'William Shakespeare' as a guest at Wilton House. Upon learning of his arrival, King James and his Court returned to Wilton from nearby Salisbury, and the King's Men were summoned from their winter retreat in Mortlake to give a performance of *As You Like It*.

Although the main facts of the King's visit are documented, and beyond doubt, it is impossible to understand how the arrival of a person belonging to Shakspere's class could have been used as an inducement for the Court to change its itinerary, and return to a place it had only recently vacated.

**1604** In many ways this can be seen as a pivotal year. But first, it is necessary to ask why should Shakespeare choose making preparations for retirement in 1602, when his work had only recently raised him to the pinnacle of success?

After what has been said about Oxford's connection with the stage, and with Shakespeare, it is there where the answer appears to lie. At the time of Queen Elizabeth's funeral in April 1603, Oxford wrote a letter to his brother-in-law Sir Robert Cecil, in which he confessed: *'for by reasone of myne infyrmite, I cannot come amonge yow so often as I wishe.'* (Nelson, 418). Two months later, he followed this with another letter to Cecil, admitting that *'I am growne owlde and spent the chiefest tyme of myne age.'* (ibid 421). Oxford's failing state of health had also been noticed and commented upon by Sir John Peyton, who reported on the murmurings of dissent accompanying the likelihood of James VI of Scotland inheriting the Crown of England. He dismissed Oxford as of no significance because, as he said, *"I knewe hym, to be so weake in boddy, in friends, in habylytie [ability].'* (ibid 415).

Given both the increasing poor state of Oxford's health, and his past literary and theatrical pursuits under the name of Shakespeare, retirement became an unavoidable consequence. But the implication this would have upon Will Shakspere's life is foreseeable. His occupation in London would become redundant. Moreover, without Oxford providing a steady flow of plays for Shakspere to take credit from, and he having neither residence, family, nor business to detain him in the capital, there was no longer any reason for him to stay. The time had come for Shakspere to return to his native environment and begin the remainder of his life according to his finances and ability. His preparation for this can be observed as having gathered pace in 1602, with the purchase of land and property close to the family home.

As part of James's appointment of the King's Men, Shakspere, together with fellow members of the group, was called upon to collect his issue of scarlet cloth to be worn for the procession scheduled for the 15 March, when the King ceremonially entered London. The royal accounts record leading members of the King's Men having each been allocated 4½ yards of scarlet cloth for their part in the intended procession. As a shareholder, Shakspere's presence in the parade would have been obligatory.

On 24 June Edward de Vere died. The parish register at the church of St Augustine in Hackney, which recorded the burial, also contained a number of deaths at that time caused by the plague. Some biographers of Oxford believed this was the cause of his death. But subsequent enquiries have failed to confirm this was true.

It was also during the same year that Anthony Scoloker published his book of poetry, titled: *Diaphantus and the Passions of Love*. Its interest lies in the reference made by the poet to – *"friendly Shakespeare's tragedies, where the comedian rides, when the tragedian stands on tiptoe. Faith it should please all, like Prince Hamlet."*(Matus, 290).

This reference does nothing to suggest who Shakespeare was, for like all other literary references concerning this name, the connection is between the name and the work. Nevertheless, Scoloker does mention *friendly Shakespeare*, although friendly was not an adjective that Philip Rogers, an apothecary working in Stratford-upon-Avon, was likely to agree with. In July, Rogers was sued by *'Willielmus Shexpere'* for an outstanding debt of £1. 15s. 10d; this was in respect of malt purchased in March that year. It will be recalled that March was also the month when Shakspere was due to parade through London in his scarlet cloth.

The death of Oxford in June appears to have had repercussions. King James had been extremely generous towards his Lord Great Chamberlain, as noted above, and it is arguable that his recognition of Oxford's greatness – the King having referred to him as *Great Oxford* – was acknowledged at the end of the year. It came in the form of a series of plays that James requested for the Court's Christmas Revels. These were: *Othello; The Merry Wives of Windsor; Measure for Measure; The Comedy of Errors; Henry V; Love's Labour's Lost* and *The Merchant of Venice* (played twice). Three other plays were called for: two of which were Ben Jonson's *Every Man Out of His Humour* and *Every Man In His Humour*. Both plays were connected to William Shake-speare, and in the former of these, Shakspere is ridiculed as Sogliardo. Interestingly, the only other play requested by the King was *The Spanish Maze*, which Richard Malim believed was the title first given to *The Tempest*, since *maze* is mentioned several times in the text, and Spain has an interesting connection with the play's content. (Malim, 284).

If King James's admiration was for Stratford's William Shakspere, it was not conveyed to Edmund Tilney, who kept account of the expenditure for putting on these plays. He was Master of the Revels between 1577 and 1610, and responsible for censoring plays. He therefore knew very well who had written *The Merchant of Venice*, and it wasn't 'Shaxberd'. *Entries in the Revels Accounts of 1604-5 recording performances by the Kings Men ... 'Shaxberd' is one of the more striking variants of Shakespeare'.* (Fido, 118)

The name 'Shaxberd' has been written twice: each time against *The Merchant of Venice*. No other named author appears on that page. If we look for the reason why it was written in this form, then it is likely that Tilney despised the man who had been given credit for plays he had not written, especially at a memorial performance for the real author. It may therefore have been revulsion that lay behind the distorted version of the name.

Compare this with Tilney's successor, Sir George Buc, who succeeded to the post of Master of the Revels in 1610, where he remained until his death in 1621. Much has been made of a note that Buc copied into a book called *George a Greene* published in 1599. It reads: *'Written by ................ a minister, who ac the pinners part in it himself. Teste W. Shakespea'.* Buc wanted to know the name of the author, which was why he left a space. Henslowe had put on this play four times between 29 December and 22 January 1593/4, which suggests that he would have been the best person to ask. Instead, Buc asked W. Shakespeare.

The facts leading to Buc's information are unknown. The most likely explanation is that the incident took place at Court, for it was where Buc assisted Tilney with the plays of 'Shakespeare', amongst others. Meeting Oxford at Court would have been a natural event. Referring to Oxford as Shakespeare was no different to the Countess of Pembroke asking her son to bring King James back to Wilton, because *"we have the man Shakespeare with us."* Oxford had apparently acquired an *alter ego* concerning all matters theatrical. It was this, the promise of a first-class play by Shakespeare that caused the King to change his itinerary. Had Lady Mary simply remarked that Lord Oxford had arrived, it would not have conveyed the same message.

After Oxford's death in 1604 —

> The ablest defender of his character was Sir George Buck, poet, historian, and Master of the Revels at the royal court. However Buck died insane, and the book in which he championed Edward de Vere was not published as he had written it. His *History of the Life and Reign of Richard the Third* was printed after his death with the passage concerning Oxford left out.
> (Feldman, 106)

During this festive season a second quarto of *Hamlet* was published. *Hamlet* is best understood when it is viewed as a dramatisation of Oxford's life, with characterisations of those who were at one time closest to him. It is therefore noteworthy that King James's royal coat of arms is imprinted on the title page of the 1604 second quarto. In fact there were two editions over the New Year period, and these are dated respectively, 1604 and 1605. But the later 1605 edition has been given a different title page to distinguish it from the tribute paid by the King in the actual year of Oxford's death; otherwise there are no differences between the two printings.

In summary, the period between October 1598 and 1604, represented a high point in Shakespeare's career as both a poet and a playwright, and whose genius was now being acknowledged by his contemporaries. Yet, the brief but detailed accounts provided above, while crediting the praise that had been lavished on his work, failed to elicit any response from the man himself. Shakspere simply prepared himself for early retirement and a change of career in rural England, while still only thirty-eight years of age.

It was into this culturally dead environment, away from the theatres, the gilded halls of Elizabeth's palaces, and the great houses of the nobility where the newly formed King's Men were performing 'his' plays that biographers take up the story of their subject's retirement. His role in life would now be dominated by the sale of malt, wool, and the collection of tithes. They see no contradiction in this, governed as their thoughts are by a premise that has led to so many other contradictions.

Somehow, the thought of, say, Mozart in the midst of composing a composition, and having to break off in mid-flow to collect tithes from the local farmers, or being interrupted to deal with a delivery of wool or barley does not ring true. And for the same reason, the thought of *Anthony and Cleopatra* being written under the same circumstances does not ring true either. A person with the gift of genius does not easily abandon that gift as 'Shakespeare' is said to have done. Illness, whether physical or mental, is the only likely reason, but since Shakspere was still in his late thirties and apparently in the peak of health, it represents yet another reason why this Shakspere was not William Shakespeare.

Some idea of the environment Shakspere was returning to can be ascertained from his defaulting neighbours.

> *\* Presenmentles made this 8th of Januarie, 1605, by the juriers holdenn by Mr. William Wyeatte Bailieffe within the burroughe of Stratford att the Quartler Sessions.*
>
> Item, for Paulle the dier for leavinge mucke before his doore.
> Wyddoe Roggers att the Bullringe for leavinge mucke in Swyenne streitt.
> Goodmane Sannes for leavinge mucke in Swyenne streytte.
> For Mr. Abraham Sturlie nott makinge cleane his soylle before his barne in Rather markett and mud waull in Henlie streytte.
> Richard Burman for makinge a muckhill before his doore.
> Edward Cottrill for makinge a muckhill in Rather markett.
> Edward Bromlie for nott makinge cleane the churche waye before his barne by the water side.
> Nicholis James for makinge a muckhill att the sheip streytts end.
> Roger Marshalle for nott makinge cleane his soille before his door in the Sheip streytte.
> Hamnett Sadler and George Warrane for nott makinge cleane the soille in Sheip streytte.
> Henrye Smythe for nott makinge cleane the water couarsse before his barne in Chapple laine.
> Johne Perrie for a muckhill in the Chapple laine.
> Henrye Smythe for keipinge his swynne and duckes in the Chapple yarde.
>
> **(Halliwell-Phillippes, 285 fn).**

Even in the middle of the 18th century, the well-travelled actor David Garrick, having recently celebrated Shakespeare's Jubilee in a community that had since expanded to become a small town, was compelled to admit it was *"the most, dirty, unseemly, ill-pav'd, wretched looking town in all Britain.'*

# 17

## THE STRATFORD YEARS

Biographers in recent years have been made aware of the difficulties surrounding their subject, and the growing force of argument behind Oxford's credentials as the pen behind 'Shakespeare's' work. To counter this, they have been forced to employ two main strategies. The first is to deny that Oxford's surviving work, which bears his initials or has been acknowledged as his, meets the standard of Shakespeare's mature work. The second strategy is to lay claim to plays that they say were written by Shakespeare after Oxford's death.

In both these arguments, there are serious flaws. In the first place, although Oxford was known to be a playwright, none of his plays survive; that is, unless they are those attributed to Shakspere. In the second place, the only verses that survive with Oxford's initials are his juvenilia. These are a small number of poems and songs, written when he was in his teens or early twenties, and before he travelled to Italy where his artistic talent came under the influence of the Renaissance. In short, it is impossible to compare like with like. Shakspere has no juvenilia with which to compare with Oxford's, and Oxford has no plays assigned to him that can be compared with those attributed to Shakspere.

The second objection to Oxford can easily be countered by pointing out that *Titus Andronicus* was performed in 1574 when Shakspere was ten years of age. This must disqualify him from authorship of that play. Hence, by extending this to the plays that accompany *Titus Andronicus* in the First Folio, Shakspere is denied authorship of these as well.

Another counter to the claim that Shakespeare continued writing after Oxford's death is to emphasise that the sources used by 'Shakespeare' can be traced from 1516 through to 1603, one year before Oxford's death; and then, with one exception that will be dealt with next, they cease (Sobran, 156-7).

This single exception is a letter written by William Strachey. It describes the voyage of the *Sea Venture*, which became separated in a storm from a fleet of nine ships carrying colonists to Virginia. On 25 July 1609, the *Sea Venture* was driven towards the Bermuda shore, where it became lodged between rocks.

This disaster, so it is maintained, furnished Shakespeare with details of a shipwreck, enabling him to recreate it in *The Tempest*. For this reason, composition of *The Tempest* is dated after Strachey's letter, which was written after Oxford's death.

So let us consider Strachey's description of what happened on that July day in 1609:

> Sir George Summers being upon the watch, had an apparition of a **little** round **light**, like a faint Starre, trembling, and streaming along with a sparkeling blaze, halfe the height upon the **Maine Mast**, and shooting sometimes from **Shroud to Shroud**, tempting to settle as it were upon any of the foure Shrouds: and for **three or foure houres** together, or rather more, halfe the night it kept with us, running sometimes along the **Maine-yard** to the very end, and then returning [Author's emphasis]. (Vaughan, 291-2)

The importance of this extract, as was pointed out by Peter Moore, concerns the number of parallels found from earlier voyages: notably two that appear in Richard Hakluyt's *Principal Navigations, Voyages, Traffiques and Discoveries*, Volume III (London 1600).

> And straightaway we saw upon the shrouds of the Trinity as it were a candle, which of itself shined, and gave a **light** ... which appeared on the **shrouds**.
> (Account of Francis de Ulloa, p.405)

> In the night, came there came upon the top of our **mainyard** and **main mast**, a certain **little light**, much like unto the light of a little candle ... This light continued aboard our ship **about three hours**, flying from **mast to mast**, and from top to top: and sometime it would be in two or three places at once. (Account of Robert Tomson, p.450), (Moore, 6).

Since Strachey's letter has so much in common with Hakluyt's 1600 volume that it actually repeats the most important parts, it can no longer be sufficient to claim that Strachey's letter was the source of the storm scene in Shakespeare's *Tempest*. Instead, all that can be said is that both the play and the letter have enough in common to suggest that both of these may very easily have benefited from Hakluyt, and quite possibly from Ulloa and Tomson as well.

There is also another important aspect to the allegation that Shakspere borrowed from Strachey's letter. Shakspere died in 1616, and Strachey's account of the shipwreck was not published until 1625, two years after *The Tempest* appeared in the First Folio: time enough for Strachey to have copied from the play — not the other way round.

The response to this is that Strachey wrote a letter, dated 15 July 1610, which was sent to an unnamed *'noble Lady'*. In this, he described the ship's misadventure. Somehow, exactly how, no one knows, Shakspere was shown this letter by the unnamed *noble lady*, and he used it as his source for *The Tempest*.

Admittedly this book is partisan, nevertheless, this explanation sounds ridiculous. Who can say what was seen, or not seen, by Shakspere in 1610? The records we have confirm only that he was in far-off Stratford-upon-Avon in that year and the one following: immersed in various commercial enterprises. Is one to believe that a messenger arrived in Stratford, all of a sweat, to deliver to the resident of New Place a copy of Strachey's letter? Of course not, the Lady's letter would have remained her private property. And so the situation would likely have remained until several years after the death of Strachey in 1621. It was then that Samuel Purchas discovered the content of Strachey's letter from among Hakluyt's papers, following his death five years earlier. The letter was later published in 1625 as a dramatic tale of a shipwreck, together with other matters concerning the colony in Virginia, to which the *Sea Venture* had been bound.

However, the discovery by Noël Hume of a 19th century *copy* of a *rough draft* of the letter proved it had been edited for publication. One may reasonably suspect some 'borrowing' went on. And since Hakluyt's role in editing Strachey's epistle seems evident, especially since it was in his possession: his memory of the earlier account he wrote in 1600, in which he described a similar shipwreck, could very easily have influenced his input: especially if he was seeking to dramatise the event for future publication. In this respect, there are also noticeable signs of 'borrowing' from Ulloa and Tomson.

Is there now anything that definitely connects the shipwreck in *The Tempest* to the foundering of the *Sea Venture*? True, there are occasional phrases in Strachey's published account of 1625 that are descriptive of what 'Shakespeare' wrote many years earlier, when describing a ship battling against a storm. But Hakluyt's editing of Strachey's letter, based upon what he had written in 1600, easily accounts for these similarities.

The sequence of events would therefore have begun in 1600, with Hakluyt's book; Oxford read this before writing *The Tempest* in 1602. At some time after 1609, Hakluyt obtained Strachey's letter and edited it for literary effect, recalling what he had earlier written in 1600. Purchas later acquired Hakluyt's papers, including the details in Strachey's letter, and published an account of the incident involving the *Sea Venture*. Consequently, there is no proof whatsoever that *The Tempest* was written after 1609.

There is, however, another factor to be considered. It is Strachey's connection with plays and the Jacobean playhouse, for this is confirmed by his name being included amongst those supporting Jonson's play *Sejanus*.

> The publication of Sejanus, equipped with dedication, preface, argument, and commendatory verses, gives some insight into Jonson's standing at that time. Chapman for instance wrote a long poem of one hundred and ninety lines ... Many others of Jonson's well-born or scholarly friends also rallied round to contribute some line of verse to launch the publication on its way: Hugh Holland, Marston, William Strachey, 'Th. R.', 'Philos' and 'Cygnus', among others. (Miles. 99)

Strachey's connections with the theatre and the dramatists of that time would have provided him with an opportunity to see a performance of *The Tempest*, or to even have read it, if a prompt copy was available. In which case, the play's vibrant, nautical expressions can be seen as an alternative source for embellishing the letter he wrote in 1609, with its account of what happened to the *Sea Venture* off the coast of Bermuda.

Actual evidence for *The Tempest* having been written before Oxford's death exists in a different direction: there being parallels between *The Tempest* and a German play called, *Die Schöne Sidea*. The author of this piece, Jakob Ayrer, was well known for his adaptations of English plays. It is therefore probable that *Die Schöne Sidea* was his version of *The Tempest*, which he translated and adapted for the German tongue. And since Ayrer died in 1605, one year after Oxford's demise, the original version of *The Tempest* would fall into line with the chronology of the German version.

References to *The Tempest* cannot be left without mentioning *Ariel's* usage of the word, *Bermoothes*. It occurs only once (Act 1: scene ii) in reply to *Prospero's* enquiry.

> Prospero: Of the King's ship,
> The mariners, say how thou hast dispos'd,
> And all the rest o' th' fleet.
>
> Ariel: Safely in harbour
> Is the King's ship; in the deep nook, where once
> Thou call'dst me up at midnight to fetch dew
> From the still-vex'd Bermoothes, there she's hid:
> ...
> and for the rest o' th' fleet,
> Which I dispers'd, they all have met again,

> And are upon the Mediterranean flote [sea],
> Bound sadly home for Naples;

Astonishingly, *Bermoothes*, becomes the island of Bermuda in the North Atlantic, known as the Somers Islands after Sir George Somers settled there in 1609.

Although the island home of *Prospero* and his daughter *Miranda* is unnamed in the play, the dialogue locates it somewhere between the north coast of Africa and Italy. To relocate it to Bermuda seems hardly credible until one realizes that these are the same minds that believe the son of illiterate parents, raised amongst illiterate siblings, and with illiterate children of his own was the very same person who wrote the works of Shakespeare. Presumably, the appetite for imagination where Shakespeare is concerned grows by what it feeds upon.

In the play, *Prospero* had once been the Duke of Milan, but his brother conspired with the King of Naples to replace him. As a result of this *coup* the Duke and his daughter were carried several leagues out to sea and set adrift in—

> A rotten carcass of a butt, not rigg'd,
> Nor tackle, sail nor mast; the very rats
> Instinctively have quit it:     (Act 1: sc. ii)

They survived, thanks to provisions secretly supplied by a friendly counsellor. Eventually, their boat drifted on to the shore of an uninhabited island. It was from here that *Prospero* was able to exact his revenge. Twelve years later, he learned that the King of Naples was returning home from Tunisia, where he had been attending his daughter's wedding. Using magic, *Prospero* summoned up the tempest, which gives the play its title, and the King's ship was driven onto his island.

Now, according to the Strachey-Bermuda theory *Prospero* and *Miranda* first drifted in their rotten and unrigged tub across the Tyrrhenian Sea into the Mediterranean, whereupon prevailing currents carried them to Gibraltar and out into the Atlantic Ocean, eventually drifting to Bermuda, eighty-seven degrees west of Naples, and just three degrees short of a quarter the distance to circumnavigate the globe: a trip that would have taken a good sized bite out of their water and provisions and the dozen years that *Prospero* was absent from Milan. It was also, we are told, a voyage that *Caliban's* mother, *Sycorax* had made many years before. Because *Ariel* confirmed that *Sycorax* had been born in Algeria (Act 1: sc. ii).

*Prospero* then recounts how *'This damn'd witch'* had, for her sorcery, been banished *'from Argier'* (ancient name for Algeria) and marooned by sailors on the island where he now dwelt. But she had died before he and *Miranda* arrived. Common sense suggests the island lies somewhere in the Mediterranean, between Italy and the north coast of Africa, and has nothing whatever to do with the island of Bermuda.

In the early nineteenth century, Joseph Hunter was of a similar mind, and proposed the unnamed island to be Lampedusa, which is situated in the Mediterranean east of Tunisia. This would have allowed *Prospero* to discover the King of Naples' departure from Tunisia on board a ship bound for Italy. To suppose otherwise is to assume the storm continued unabated for many months, and always following the fleet until it had forced the ships across the Mediterranean, and then across the Atlantic Ocean until reaching the shores of Bermuda.

Bermuda plays no part in the play, and is mentioned just that once. Its inclusion appears to have been no more than a bawdy piece of humour for the private amusement of the players, who would have understood its meaning. In fact, the *Bermoothes*, or Bermudas was a notorious part of London north of the Strand, situated between St Martin in the Fields and Covent Garden —

> 'The Bermudas' (and variations of that spelling) was also a section of London notorious for harbouring thieves and prostitutes; Ben Jonson implied the Bermudas' nefarious character in Bartholomew Fair (6.57-8). (The area was apparently named for the islands because they attracted fugitives from justice during the early years of English settlement.
>
> (Vaughan, 165 & 229 fn)

Shakespeare's description of it as, *still vexed* would be appropriate to the continued depravity of that area, and not directed at the North Atlantic Island of the same name.

The reason for proposing 1602 as the likely date of composition for *The Tempest* is because, in the play, *Miranda* is fifteen years of age. Oxford's daughter Susan was born in 1587; therefore she, too, was fifteen in 1602. This is important because *Prospero* repeats a truth about *Miranda's* mother that is equally applicable to Susan's mother. Neither of the two girls knew their mothers. Anne, Countess of Oxford, died a month after Susan's first birthday. *'Thy mother was a piece of virtue,"* Prospero tells his daughter. Oxford's first wife exactly fitted Prospero's description. *'This Anna lived ever a modest maiden and a chaste wife, faithful in her love, a daughter wonderfully devoted to her parents in all exigencies, exceedingly diligent and devout in her devotion to God.'* (Nelson, 309).

There is also a second reason to conclude that 1602 was the year in which *The Tempest* was begun; it is the air of finality in the plays closing speech. At the time of its composition, Oxford had not an able body, nor had he long to live. In April 1603, he wrote of his ill health in a letter addressed to Robert Cecil: *'for by reasone of myne infyrmite, I cannot come amonge yow so often as I wishe,'* (Nelson, 418). This infirmity conveniently coincides with *Prospero's* farewell speech, which appears to have been the author's valediction.

> Now my charms are all o'erthrown,
> And what strength I have's mine own,
> Which is most faint:

Before making this speech at the end of Act 5, *Prospero* again alludes to his approaching end: *'Every third thought shall be my grave.'* To which, *Alonso* replies: *'I long to hear the story of your life, which must take the ear strangely.'* Oxford's life would indeed fall strangely upon the ear. The same cannot be said for Shakspere. His life was plodding dull, enlivened only by the 'imagined facts' that embroider what is written about him. One such 'imagined fact' is that *Prospero* is a caricature of Shakspere. An unseemly odd suggestion, especially since *Prospero* was at pains to educate *Miranda*, whereas Shakspere never lifted a finger towards that end for his own daughters. Yet, this same man allegedly wrote: *'ignorance is the curse of God / Knowledge the wing wherewith we fly to heaven.'* (2 Henry VI 4: vii).

Wherever belief in William Shakspere's humble, Stratford, upbringing is imagined as a springboard to his genius, it is commonplace to find those attempting a biography of the man to lead the faithful: – like *"Blind guides, which strain at a gnat, and swallow a camel."*

Having thus shown it to be without impediment for Oxford to have written *The Tempest*, the resolute objector will next turn to *Henry VIII*, declaring this to have been penned after Oxford's death. But, once again, alternative explanations exist that tie in with the evidence available.

Let us begin by considering the argument proposed by Jonathan Bate, for this continues to resurface as though it were both *necessary* and *sufficient* to quell all doubt about Shakspere being Shakespeare.

> Henry VIII was described by at least two witnesses as a "new play" in 1613. How de Vere managed to write from beyond the grave is a profound mystery indeed. ...

> Henry VIII was one of Shakespeare's three collaborations with John Fletcher, who subsequently took over as house dramatist of the King's Men. (Bate, 66)

Apart from Bate's quirky comment about writing from the grave, there is nothing in the above statement that disqualifies Oxford from having written *Henry VIII*. All that is needed are the *complete* facts, together with the application of sufficient intelligence to see how they naturally combine.

The first thing to look at is the piece of evidence provided in Sir Henry Wotton's letter to Sir Edmund Bacon, dated 2 July 1613, from which I quote: *'The King's Players had a new Play called All Is True, representing some principal pieces of the reign of Henry 8.'* (Foakes, xxviii). There is nothing conclusive to be drawn from the phrase *new play*; the same could have been said about a number of Shakespeare's plays that had not previously been performed, and which only became known seven years after Shakspere's death, when the First Folio advertised their existence in its list of contents. Wotton's letter goes on to describe the play: —

> ... which was set forth with many extraordinary Circumstances of Pomp and Majesty, even to the matting of the Stage; the Knights of the Order, with their Georges and Garter, the Guards with their embroidered Coats, and the like.

Very clearly, Wotton was treated to a most lavish spectacle. And it is these remarks that open the way to accepting Oxford's authorship. As R. A. Foakes, editor of the Arden edition of *Henry VIII*, commented: *'reference to the 'Knights of the Order, with their Georges and Garter, the Guards with their embroidered coats' [are observations] for which the play provides no evidence.'* In other words, the play *All Is True*, seen by Sir Henry Wotton in 1613, with its principal pieces concerning the reign of Henry VIII was not the same play published in the First Folio under the title, *The Famous History of the Life of King Henry the Eight*.

This disparity is easily explained. Three days before Wotton wrote his letter; that is, on 29 June, the Globe theatre burnt to the ground. In less than an hour the flames had consumed everything that had been abandoned in the rush to evacuate the theatre, and this included the theatre's wardrobe with its *'few forsaken Cloaks'*.

> Out run the Knights, out run the Lords.
> And there was great ado;
> Some lost their hats, and some their swords —
> Then out run Burbage too;
> The reprobates, though drunk on Monday
> Prayed for the Fool and Henry Condye,

...
Oh sorrow, pitiful sorrow, and yet all this is true.

The periwigs and drumheads fried
Like to a butter firkin
A woeful burning did betide
To many a good buff jerkin;
Then with swollen eyes, like drunken Fleming's
Distressed stood old stuttering Heminge.

(Wilson, 377-8)

This *Sonnett upon the pitiful burneing of the Globe playhouse in London* was entered in the Stationers' Register the next day. Noticeably, it refers to the *Knights and Lords* of which there were 3 dukes, 1 earl, 4 lords and 4 knights participating in the later version of *Henry VIII*; and these quite apart from the titled extras.

With the loss of the valuable costumes, what could Henslowe do in order to produce the play in the future? He could order a new set of costumes to be made, but that would be very expensive, and the profit from the play would be unlikely to justify the cost. An alternative solution was far simpler and would have been more to his liking. He could engage Fletcher to rewrite the play, taking care to avoid the scenes requiring an extravagant display of robes.

This would then explain why the actual text of *Henry VIII* is so much better than that of others, and why it is accompanied by a most unusual display of act and scene divisions, together with a comprehensive set of stage directions—Fletcher must have begun rewriting *All Is True* shortly before work on the First Folio began. Thus, Cyrus Hoy's analysis of *Henry VIII*, the play that appears in the First Folio, concluded Fletcher's style was discernible in 1:iii; 1:iv; 3:i, and in 5:ii, iii, iv. These must be where Fletcher substituted his major revisions to the play.

Once again, those within the pro-Shakspere lobby, motivated by a desire to dismiss Oxford as Shakespeare, have failed. Guided by a false premise, it has led to the unnecessary conclusion that John Fletcher *must* have collaborated with Shakespeare to write the play in 1613. What they then fail to mention is that the writing of plays depicting English history was forbidden by law in 1613. Oh sorrow, pitiful sorrow, and yet all this is true.

Another play supposedly written jointly in 1613 by these same two playwrights is *The Two Noble Kinsmen*. Unlike *Henry VIII*, this play was not included in the First Folio, which argues that in 1623 it was an unfinished work. In fact, it was not published until 1634, when the title page claimed it had been written by Fletcher and Shakespeare. Subsequent analysis has indicated that the hands of both men may have been responsible for the play. If that is true, although it continues to be debated, then the reason for this is that Fletcher obtained the incomplete manuscript that Oxford had once been working on, and completed it. A similar occurrence occurred in the following century when Franz Süssmayr completed Mozart's *Requiem*, which the composer had left unfinished when he died.

To claim that Shakespeare collaborated with Fletcher is no more than a belief. It is not a fact, since the evidence is insufficient. In every case where collaboration is proposed as 'fact', an alternative explanation is available: one that allows Oxford to have been William Shakespeare: with Fletcher, if anything, the jackal who fed from the lion's share.

The composition dates of the remaining plays are extremely arbitrary and largely governed by the date they were first mentioned in performance or via the Stationers' Register. There are exceptions, such as *Hamlet* and *King Lear*. Both plays are recorded in Henslowe's diary as early as 1594 alongside *Titus Andronicus, Henry VI* and *Taming of a Shrew*. At this point, pro-Shakspere biographers resort to 'cherry-picking'. *Titus Andronicus* and *Henry VI* are allowed; *Taming of a Shrew* is a 'perhaps'; *Hamlet* and *King Lear* are definitely rejected. If Shakspere is to be seen as William Shakespeare, then his garments must be made to measure. *King Lear* and *Hamlet* do not fit the model of an embryo playwright who has only recently arrived in the capital, and so these two plays must be rejected.

How, then, does the Shakespeare biographer explain these plays? The solution is surprisingly simple and agreeable to those who are like-minded. Shakspere took these anonymous plays when he had matured enough as a writer, and rewrote them as *his* compositions, even retaining the titles given by the anonymous author. But this raises the question: why did that author not come forward and claim part authorship of the plays for himself. After all, it is as much collaboration as if the two men had sat down together and worked through the plot and verse together?

In the case of *Hamlet*, where Thomas Kyd has been elected to fill the vacancy of anonymous author, the answer would be that Kyd died before *Hamlet* was rewritten. But this cannot be said of all cases. Take for example *The Troublesome Raigne of King John*, where *'Shakespeare's King John follows The Troublesome Raigne almost scene for scene.'* Or alternatively, The Contention

# THE STRATFORD YEARS

*Between the Two Famous Houses of Yorke and Lancaster* and *The True Tragedy of Richard Duke of Yorke.* These two plays *'treat of the same action as 2 and 3 Henry VI, introduce the same characters, and contain much verse in common with the Folio texts; 3 Henry VI has about 2,900 lines, and of these some 2,000 on Malone's reckoning are found, sometimes word for word, sometimes in various transformations, in the True Tragedy.'* (Alexander, 406).

The simplest resolution to this puzzle, using *Occam's Razor*, is that the plays mentioned are by the same author. This book shares a similar feature: it deals with the same subject and contains many lines, often word for word, that are found in *Proving Shakespeare*. This is because both books are by the same author. The premise governing the thought patterns of pro-Shakspere biographers refuses to allow this obvious solution.

Factually speaking, Shakspere was born to illiterate parents; his two daughters could not even write their own names (Judith's mark occurs in between her name). After Susanna's marriage to Dr Hall, she alone did learn to write her name. As for her father, there is no actual evidence that he attended school long enough to acquire an education; no letters received by him, or correspondence sent by him, has ever been found; no manuscripts or books of his were mentioned in his will; no one from the world of theatre or literature paid any notice to his death when it occurred; no one in his family or in the little town where he lived acknowledged him to be anymore than a businessman. Yet, it is onto this barren landscape that Shakespeare experts project their thoughts, beliefs and speculations. The result is that excuse follows excuse as they attempt to fill the absence of facts with *what might have happened.* Yes! There are factual reports about Shakespeare the poet and playwright whose work was admired by his contemporaries, but nothing that was said or written identifies this poet with Shakspere.

It is with this that we return to the facts known about this man after his return to Stratford-upon-Avon which occurred shortly after the turn of the century. Although there is no evidence to support the belief that he wrote any of the plays he is credited with, biographers continue to speculate, basing their conclusions on premise that governs their thinking. However, a strict adherence to the facts that have been uncovered reveals that on 24 July 1605 —

> 'William Shakespear' purchased for £440 [equivalent today to £220,000] half the corn and hay tithes of three hamlets in Stratford parish – Old Stratford, Welcome, and Bishopton. (Following abolition of the monasteries under Henry VIII, the tithes formerly paid by the tenants on the vast monastery lands were made over to civil authorities and were leased out for collection.) Shakspere agreed to pay £5 a year to a creditor of the former leaser of the tithes and £17 to the Stratford Corporation. In 1611, his interest in the tithes was valued at £60 [£30,000] annually. (Ogburn, 32)

We can see from this that Shakspere's shrewd use of what must have been available capital was guaranteed to recoup his outlay within the space of seven years, while still preserving his asset. The purchase of these tithes can also be seen as his commitment to remain in Stratford. By 1605 the theatrical life in London has definitely been abandoned for his new venture as a tax collector. The equivalent of £30,000 p.a. had to be earned. He could not sit at home writing two plays each year, for £6 each, as his biographers maintain, for this would entail regularly travelling back and forth between London and Stratford (a four day trip each way) to direct performances. Tithes had to be collected from three hamlets. Tenants were not going to queue up outside New Place, while Shakspere, pen in hand came to the door to receive their money. Records also had to be kept; this was no casual undertaking.

For the next three years no more is heard of him. There were, instead, reports of what was happening to close members of his family. In May 1606, Susanna was named as a recusant – one who refused to attend the Church of England when it was legally required – her failure had been to attend the Easter Sunday service on 24 April at the parish church of the Holy Trinity.

Susanna's name emerged again in the parish church records when, on 5 June 1607, the marriage of *"John Hall gentleman & Susanna Shaxpere'* was recorded. Hall was a university man who received his graduate and postgraduate degrees from Queen's College Cambridge. His father had been a wealthy physician, and this appears to have directed his son's future, for Hall set up a medical practice of his own in Stratford-upon-Avon, and although being neither a member of the Royal College of Physicians, nor having a licence to practice medicine, he achieved notable success. His case book was later translated from Latin by surgeon, James Cooke, and published in 1657.

Six months after Susanna's wedding, her uncle Edmund may have died. Edmund was the youngest child of John and Mary Shakspere, having been born in 1580. It is said that he too travelled to London with the intention of becoming an actor. Nothing supports this claim. At some time *circa* 1600, a man called Edmund Shakespeare, living in London, fathered a son by a woman whose name has not survived. The child was christened Edward at a ceremony held at St Leonard's church in Shoreditch on 12 July 1607, but it died a month later, and was buried at St Giles church in Cripplegate, on 12 August. The father was described as from *"morefilds'* (Moorfields). Four months later this Edmund, born in 1579, also died. He was buried on 31 December at St Saviour's Church in Southwark. It is recorded that the burial cost £1 *'with a forenoone knell of the great bell.'*

William Shakspere's whereabouts remain unknown. Had he been in Stratford-upon-Avon, knowledge of his brother's death, were it he, would have arrived too late for him to have travelled to London in time for the funeral: as was likely to have happened before, when his son Hamnet died in Stratford, while he was in London.

As Bronson Feldman pointed out in *Secrets of Shakespeare* (page 98), there was another Shakespeare with London and theatrical connections. This was Matthew Shakespeare, the brother-in-law of George Peele. Matthew had married Isabel Peele in 1569, although it is not known if Edmund was their son, or otherwise related.

Seven weeks later, in Stratford, Susanna and her husband attended the christening of their daughter Elizabeth. It was close to this time that Shakspere re-entered official records. On 8 August 1608, according to a *"testimony given in 1619 by John Heminge and Henry Condell ... Blackfriars Theatre was leased by seven men:"* one of whom was *"William Shakespeare'*. (Ogburn, 32). The lease ran for *"twenty-one years"* (Wilson, 464).

In 1635, testimonies were again taken relating to the Globe theatre. On this occasion it was Cuthbert Burbage who testified to the Earls of Pembroke and Montgomery, when petitioning for financial aid to cover the expenses involved in running the Globe. In making this appeal, Burbage referred to the Blackfriars Theatre, for which he had *"purchased the lease remaining from Evans with our money, and placed men Players, which to ourselves were joined those deserving men, Shakspere, Heminge, Condell, Philips and other partners.'* (Ogburn, 31, 33). King James had terminated the Children of the Queen's Revels in 1608, causing Henry Evans, the lessee of the theatre, to sell the remaining part of the lease to Richard Burbage. Burbage retained one seventh, and sold the remaining six sevenths to Shakspere, Heminge, Condell, Will Slye, Thomas Evans and Cuthbert Burbage.

Ogburn thought it strange, and rightly so, that when Cuthbert Burbage made his plea for assistance to Pembroke and Montgomery; that is to say, when he petitioned *'the incomparable brethren'* to whom the First Folio of Shakespeare's collected Comedies, Histories and Tragedies had been dedicated twelve years before, he referred to Shakspere as no more than one of seven shareholders who had staked money in the Blackfriars theatre. Given that this was also the playwright William Shakespeare, so much admired by Pembroke and Montgomery as *soul of the age*, how could this be the same man? Excuses will be offered; but the truth is that no other man of such recognised greatness would have been referred to as ignominiously as Burbage did when he lumped Shakspere in with the other shareholders.

Wherever Shakspere was during that week in August, it is certain that he was in Stratford-upon-Avon one month later. On the 9th of the month his mother, described in the parish burial register as *'Mayry Shaxpere wydowe'*, was laid to rest in the church of Holy Trinity. Shortly before her death, *'William Shackspeare'* had begun legal proceedings against John Addenbrooke, a neighbour, by having him arrested for a debt of £6 plus £1. 5s. 0d costs. Addenbrooke was released on the surety provided by his friend T. Hornby, but realising his inability to repay the debt, he left Stratford. *Shackspeare* therefore sued Hornby instead.

The proceedings begun in September 1608, between Addenbrooke, *Shackspeare,* and Hornby continued for ten months, and it indicates the measure of Shakspere's resolve and business attitude towards those who tried to outmanoeuvre him where money was concerned. Biographers praise his good business sense, but fall silent when they are forced to compare the Addenbrooke case with what happened in the midst of these proceedings.

On 20 May 1609, a book of *Shakespeare's Sonnettes* was entered in the Stationers' Register. Yet, strangely, these poems, undoubtedly the labour of so many memorable hours spent in their composition, were utterly and completely disregarded by Shakspere who was still intent upon recovering his £6 with added costs. Shakspere treated the publication of these poems with the same disregard that he had previously displayed over the plays that bore his name; which, according to Heminge and Condell in their letter *'To the Great Variety of Readers'* at the front of the First Folio, had been *"maimed and deformed by the frauds and stealths of injurious impostors that exposed them.*' None of this makes the slightest sense; it is wholly contradictory.

It seems perfectly evident from this alone that *Shackspeare*, the legalistic businessman of Stratford-upon-Avon, was not, and never had been, the poet, playwright and author of the sonnets and plays that were repeatedly stolen for profit by piratical publishers? Had he been Shakespeare and:

> ... who else would have such a complete collection of the sonnets in manuscript? They were an enduring project, continued over several years. No one else would have owned all of the material available to the poet himself. (Ackroyd, 453)

Then how can it be seriously believed that this complete collection of Shakespeare's 154 Sonnets secretly made its way across country into the hands of a London publisher, while their supposed author in Stratford-upon-Avon was involved in some trifling legal matter?

Is it reasonable that upon learning of what had happened to his poems, this legalistic businessman did nothing about it? Of course not! *"But there is no record of Shakespeare's protest, and there is no sign that they were withdrawn from sale or subsequently 'corrected' for an authorised edition."* (ibid). Despite these contradictions, biographers close their eyes, shut their ears, and nod their heads to admit: *'t was so.*

A more realistic explanation for the acquisition of Shakespeare's Sonnets was given by Colonel Bernard R. Ward, in his book, *The Mystery of 'Mr W. H.'* (Cecil Palmer, 1923). He argued that a certain William Hall acquired the Sonnets in 1609 at the time when Oxford's widow removed the family's household belongings from Hackney. Ward suggested the disruption caused by packing the household contents together, prior to transporting them to Castle Hedingham, allowed some unknown person to 'liberate' the Sonnets, and, possibly *Troilus and Cressida*, too, for this was published in the same year as the Sonnets. This is the play with its interesting Preface referring to its escape —

> ... the Epistle [to the reader] strongly implies that the play had never been acted in a public theatre, and (in order to appear in print) had made some kind of 'escape', since the 'grand possessors' would have prevented publication of it (together with other comedies [sic] by the same author) had they been able. (Palmer, 2)

From this, it is a simple matter to speculate that the Sonnets also 'escaped' their 'grand possessors' at the same time. It would also explain why the furtive removal of these manuscripts occasioned no outcry. To have done so would have drawn attention to the Oxford household, and the family's connection to the authorship of the manuscripts.

This allows a further possibility to arise. Was it Oxford's son Henry who passed his father's sonnets over to Hall? At the time of their publication, the 18th Earl was sixteen years of age, short of money, and undergoing a period of teenage rebellion.

> Managing young Henry's estate was one thing, but managing "a young nobleman neither of years nor judgement to advise himself, wanting the guidance of a father and past the government of a mother ...", in the words of countess Elizabeth, [it] was evidently quite another once the sixteen year old Henry had fallen into the wayward company of his second cousin John Hunt. (Crick, 29)

It is not difficult to imagine the headstrong young man believing he was fulfilling his father's wish for publication by passing the Sonnets over for printing. And, if he knew they had been forbidden to the public, then so much the better for satisfying his rebellious nature. Like father, like son, one could say.

Ward's argument for William Hall as the Mr W. H., to whom Thorpe was beholden, extended beyond the circumstance of just location. Amongst the entries in the parish church register for Hackney, he found that: *'William Hall and Margery Gryffyn were joined in matrymonye on the 4th Aug. 1608.'* (Michell, 180). It was an event that coincided both in time and in detail to the reference made by Thorpe in his dedicatory preface to the Sonnets, in which he wished the *'begetter Mr. W. H. All Happinesse ... In Setting Forth':* an apt expression for someone embarking upon married life.

William Hall was also Sir Sidney Lee's choice for Mr W. H. This was for a different reason. Hall had already earned a reputation for obtaining manuscripts and then either selling them on to interested publishers, or occasionally publishing them himself. He also had connections with both Thorpe, who was one of his *'occasional collaborators'*, and with George Eld who printed the Sonnets for Thorpe.

In 1606, Eld had published *A Foure-fold Meditation*. This was a poem believed written by Father Robert Southwell, a Catholic priest who was betrayed in June 1592, and arrested by Richard Topcliffe, the recently made head of Elizabeth's secret police. After undergoing torture, Southwell was executed in February 1595 at Tyburn.

When writing about the poems he had acquired, W. H. informed his readers: *'A mere accident conveyed them into my hands'*. Lee identified W. H. as William Hall, and likewise assumed some other 'mere accident' had placed the Sonnets in his hands.

The sudden emergence of the Sonnets after a decade of silence – they were first brought to public notice in *Wits Treasury* – and the failure of Shakspere to stay their publication or seek legal redress, or take any interest at all in what was happening to them, is understandable only if their author was the Earl of Oxford. His position at Court forbade him being identified as a common playwright, or making public his most intimate thoughts in verse. Moreover, the proximity of William Hall's residence in the village of Hackney, close to the Countess of Oxford and her errant son, the eighteenth earl, made manuscript copies of the Sonnets potentially accessible. It required only a misdemeanour on the part of someone in the Oxford household to supply the missing link, and a connection between the Sonnets and Mr. W. H. would be established. Thomas Thorpe seemed aware of what had happened and the rush to print them is evident from the number of typographical errors that appear in the pages. But Thorpe went further. He wrote an introduction to the sonnets that is full of curiosities. Most obviously, his introductory remarks are asyntactic, with each word separated by a point. While it was not unusual for an introduction to be set out in the form of a triangle, Thorpe has instead employed three trapeziform shapes, which contain six, two and four lines respectively. Was it just coincidence that Oxford's name, Edward de Vere, happened to have the same 6-2-4 combination of letters? Dr John Rollett of Ipswich was curious, and by noting the sixth, second and fourth word in succession, Thorpe's contrived syntax revealed a statement equivalent to the headlines one encounters in media reports of today: THESE SONNETS ALL BY EVER THE FORTH.

Although at the time Rollett failed to understand the significance of THE FORTH, when he realised that the authorship of Shakespeare's plays and poems were being claimed for Vere, and that EVER could be read E VER or as an anagram of Vere, he began devoting time to testing the probability

> TO.THE.ONLIE.BEGETTER.OF.
> THESE.INSVING.SONNETS.
> Mr. W. H. ALL.HAPPINESSE.
> AND.THAT.ETERNITIE.
> PROMISED.
>
> BY.
> OVR.EVER-LIVING.POET.
>
> WISHETH.
>
> THE.WELL-WISHING.
> ADVENTVRER.IN.
> SETTING.
> FORTH.
>
> T. T.

that the statement had occurred by chance. As he later remarked: after having examined *'many thousands of paragraphs, probably well over 20,000 I have only ever found one sentence that even remotely made sense at all ... 'London was not built before.' It comes out of Boswell's Life of Johnson (an abridged version, I hasten to add).'* (Rollett, 265).

The lack of discovering any comparable phrase eventually led Rollett to conclude that the statistic for the hidden statement occurring by chance was approximately *'1 in 100 million',* which, he said, coincided with the required level suggested by the professional cryptologists, William and Elizebeth Friedman.

It is comparatively easy to doubt Thorpe's apparent encryption of the identity of the poet who wrote Shake-speare's Sonnets (Thorpe hyphenated the name Shake-speare on the title page). What is not an easy matter, as Rollett discovered, is to justify that doubt by demonstrating such phrases are sufficiently commonplace as to be within the realm of chance. After all, Thorpe's revelation is only possible because his dedication was, in the words of J. L. Hotson, so *'preposterous'*, it could only be *'a cryptogram'* (Mr W. H. London, 1964).

There are other features about Thorpe's introductory address to the reader that are noteworthy. The first of these refers to THE FORTH. This, as it has since been discovered (*Proving Shakespeare*, p.182), applies to Oxford's status as the *fourth* signatory on decrees passed by King James's Privy Council. The first three signatures were those of *ex officio* officers: the Archbishop of Canterbury, the Lord Keeper, and the Lord Treasurer. After these came members of the nobility according to rank. Oxford, as the senior earl and Lord Great Chamberlain, was first amongst the rest of the nobility, and always fourth on the list of signatories. The difference in spelling between 'forth' and 'fourth' is of little or no consequence. Elizabethan spelling was idiosyncratic: words were spelt as they were pronounced.

The second note of interest was remarked upon by Professor Gervinus, who drew attention to the singular instance of Thorpe having written the dedication himself. It was not that this was unusual: it was actually unique. But with Oxford five years in his tomb and Shakspere retired to his native Stratford for a similar length of time, and completely disinterested in what was happening to the Sonnets, Thorpe's dedication is readily explained.

The third peculiarity, which is also unique, is that Thorpe described the author as OUR EVER-LIVING POET. Such descriptions are, and always have been, reserved for those who are deceased: that after death they may continue to live through their work. The pronoun OUR also assumes a collective ownership of the poet, and this too points to a deceased person. All of this is appropriate to Oxford, who had been dead for the past five years. But his dissenters still insist the phrase was intended for Shakspere. The problem with this is that he was undoubtedly *living* at the time, and eagerly pursuing Hornby to recover the £6 plus costs, owed to him by the absconder, Addenbrooke.

Although Shakspere took no more interest in Shake-speare's Sonnets, than he took in the publication of 'his' *"stolen and maimed"* plays that were frequently pirated for another's profit, he did maintain an interest in his financial investments. In 1598 he had joined with the Burbage brothers, Richard and Cuthbert, John Heminge, Will Kempe, Augustine Philipps and Thomas Pope, in dismantling the Theatre in Shoreditch and re-assembling it as the Globe on the Southwark bankside of the Thames. The Burbage brothers were the main shareholders in this enterprise, with fifty-percent of the investment. The other five members of the consortium each held a ten-percent share.

This arrangement continued up until 1610, although the shareholders changed. Kempe left in acrimonious circumstances in 1599, within months of buying into the company. It seems he had been profiting from the sale of Shakespeare's plays to pirate publishers; because, coincidentally or not, after he left the Chamberlain's Men, all references to his entrances on stage, which had appeared in pirated editions, ceased. In 1605, Philipps died. In his will, he bequeathed *"amongst the hired men of the company which I am of the sum of five pounds to be equally distributed amongst them.'* He also bequeathed *"to my fellow William Shakespeare a thirty shilling piece in gold,'* (Wilson, 310). Lest this should be seen as something special, he also named *Beeston, Fletcher, Armin, Cowley, Cooke, Tooley, Gilbourne,* and *Sands,* as beneficiaries.

Then, in 1610, the shareholders increased in number to allow Henry Condell to invest. This meant that the five 10% shareholders were now six, each holding one twelfth of the total share (8⅓ %), but with a lower liability for the annual ground rent payable to the owner of the land.

In the spring of 1611, Heminge's sixteen-year-old daughter Thomasina married William Osteler. And on 20 May, Richard Burbage gave the bridegroom the one seventh share in the Blackfriars theatre that he had been holding ever since Will Slye's death, five years earlier.

On 21 February 1612, Osteler was also allowed to become a shareholder in the Globe. Thomasina was pregnant, and this would ensure extra income for the family which, by the spring, had increased to three. But it also caused the number of investors holding one sixth of the capital to become seven, thus reducing Shakspere's interest in the Globe to one fourteenth (7¹/₇ %), with the Burbage brothers still retaining 50%.

On 10 March 1613, Shakspere purchased the Blackfriars Gate House for £140.

> The next day he mortgaged it back to its previous owner for £60 [£30,000]. The device barred inheritance of any part of the property by his wife, who would otherwise have been entitled to her dower right of a third of its value. (Ogburn, 33)

The building stood by the side of the river Thames, with a hidden passage leading to the waterside. It also contained several secret hiding places that had once been used as priest holes. Was this coincidental to the purchase or the reason for it? Either way, it was Shakspere's first investment in a London property, but there is nothing to suggest he ever lived there.

Shakspere was, in fact, one of four investors who put up the money for the Gatehouse, the other three men involved in the purchase were John Jackson, *'a Hull shipping magnate'*, William Johnson, *'citizen and vintner of London'*, and John Heminge. Shakspere's signature appears on the deed as "*William Shakspē*" and this is repeated on the indenture as "*Wᵐ Shakspē*". Jackson, Johnson, and Heminge signed their names in the normal manner.

This house, with its several hiding places and a secret passage leading to the Thames, sounds dangerously as if it was used for smuggling wine etc. into England; especially when two of the investors were a vintner and a ship owner. Why else should a vintner and a ship owner join forces with a third man, who had previous connections with the underworld, and invest in such a house? Heminge, the fourth investor, was a grocer; his trade made him a convenient outlet for smuggled goods. Further doubt as to Heminge's true character will emerge below.

An alternative suggestion is that the house was intended for human trafficking; that is to say, Catholic sympathisers. The tenant installed in the house was John Robinson. He was the *"son of a Catholic recusant who had harboured priests in Blackfriars and brother of a priest who was lodged at the English College in Rome."* (Ackroyd, 468). Another suggestion is that Robinson *"acted as a 'recruiting agent' for the Jesuit College at St. Omer.'* (ibid). If the house was used for trafficking Catholic priests into and out of England, the motive of the investors would have been the same as for all traffickers, financial gain.

Three weeks after purchasing the Gate House, the steward to the 6th Earl of Rutland, Francis Manners, paid £1. 2s. 0d *"to Mr Shakespeare in gold about my Lord's impresa,'* and the same amount to *"Richard Burbadge for painting and making it."* (Wilson, 371). Rutland's home was at Belvoir Castle in Lincolnshire. It would therefore appear that *Mr Shakespeare* was someone other than the new owner of the Blackfriars Gate House. He may have been related to Matthew Shakespeare, George Peele's brother-in-law, or he may have been a local man who assisted 'Burbadge' during a visit to the area by the King's Men. In any event, *"Sir Henry Wotton record[ed] that none of the emblems was a success except the two carried by the Earl of Pembroke and his brother."* (Wilson 371). The rest, apparently were so confused *"that their meaning is not yet understood."* (ibid). Pembroke and his brother would have had the benefit of Jonson's classical education for their success.

On 29 June 1613, the Globe caught fire and burned to the ground. In the following year plans were already in place for it to be rebuilt at a cost of £1400. Since Shakspere held one fourteenth of the shares, he was required to pay £100 towards its reconstruction. But, later, in 1613, another tragedy hit the company when, in December, Osteler died leaving Thomasina a widow with their baby son to bring up. Osteler's death was to have a most unexpected consequence for Shakspere.

> When her husband died, Thomasina procured from the Archbishop of Canterbury letters of administration. On the day of receiving these letters, Dec. 22, 1614, she also delivered to her father John Hemynges, two leases to be held in trust for her. These leases were for certain shares in the Globe and Blackfriars Theatres acquired by her late husband. (Wallace)

It appears that Heminge and Thomasina argued about the future of the shares, and that her father really wanted them for himself, although making promises to his daughter if she would agree to his conditions. What followed was a mighty row between the two that caused Thomasina to part from her father, and later have him arrested for trespass, at the common law. In making her case at court, Heminge was described before the judge as: *"craftily and cunningly plotting to deceive and defraud her,'* (ibid). Heminge never forgave Thomasina and she was the only member of his family to be excluded from his will.

This is not the picture that biographers paint of Heminge. They need to show him as the benevolent man of theatre life who joined Condell in giving up a huge amount of his time (literally years), as well as large sums of his own money to seek out old manuscripts of Shakespeare's plays, and edit them for the enormously expensive publication of the First Folio. *"Though scholars mayhap oft believe, / It never is they self-deceive.'* Which is never truer than with Shakspere's non-career as a playwright.

Essentially, Thomasina was making her case against the shareholders, which included Shakspere. This was because Heminge was *"the acting business manager and agent of the company."* (ibid). The case eventually went to trial in February 1616; at precisely the time Shakspere was in the midst of making out his last will and testament. Two months later, although still reportedly in good health, he died. The trial involving Heminge and his daughter had some bearing upon the life of Shakspere. In his will, which had been changed so many times during its drafting that it finally emerged on three different types of paper, and even these were marked with changes and interlineations, there is no longer any mention of the shares he held in the Globe and the Blackfriars. Yet, the case Thomasina brought against her father was precisely because these shares were highly valued. Shakspere's beneficiaries would have greatly benefited from holding them, but holding them would have linked the holders to these theatres, where the truth about Shakspere's background and his literary association with 'Shakespeare' would have been in danger of becoming discussed. As a consequence of this eventuality, there seems to have been a decided effort by someone in authority to prevent the shares, and their association with the life Shakspere had been leading in London, from reaching his family.

This included his investment in the Blackfriars Gatehouse, which was referred to in his will as: *"that messuage or tenement with thappurtenaunces wherein one John Robinson dwelleth, scituat lyeing and being in the Blackfriers in London nere the Wardrobe.'* (Laroque, 134). Shakspere had taken steps to prevent his wife from inheriting the property; he also seems to have made a private agreement for the transfer of the property away from Susanna and Dr John Hall in the event of his death.

> In 1618, two years after his death, the trustees did in fact convey the gatehouse to John Greene of Clement's Inn and to Matthew Morrys of Stratford 'in performance of the confidence and trust in them reposed by William Shakespeare deceased, late of Stretford aforesaid gent., ... and according to the true intent and meaning of the last will and testament of the said William Shakespeare'. (Ackroyd, 467)

The gatehouse therefore poses another mystery. Why should four investors buy this house, if it was just to accommodate one man? And why did Shakspere take precautionary measures to prevent his family from retaining ownership of the house, by adding some hidden sub-clause to indicate his *true intent and meaning*?

The final document referring to Shakspere, before his death, was found amongst the Chamberlain's accounts at Stratford-upon-Avon. It alluded to his penny-pinching attitude towards money. This has been a frequent and vexatious part of his character, entirely at odds with the reports made about Shakespeare the poet and playwright.

In 1614, Shakspere apparently received a request to entertain a preacher on behalf of the Stratford-upon-Avon Council. He complied, and then promptly applied for reimbursement of the twenty pennies it had cost him, in serving wine.

> Item, for on quart of sack and on quart of clarrett winne, geven to a preacher at the Newe Place           xx.d.

The Council would have been wiser to have requested their resident poet to have written a sonnet of welcome for their visitor. Judging by his pecuniary disinterest in accepting payment for his sonnets, it would have cost the Council nothing.

# 18

# THE RIVAL POET

It is a feature often seen in Shake-speare's Sonnets but rarely observed that the poet is more apt to address his subject as *thou* than to use the alternative form of *you*. Because past commentators have ploughed the wrong field when seeking to dig up reliable facts concerning Shakespeare's literary connections, they have never been able to discover as a certainty, either the identity of the rival poet, or for that matter the poetry which caused the rivalry in the first place. A little attention to the different forms of address in Elizabethan England would have shed light upon the problem.

> In Old English, thou was singular and you was plural; but during the thirteenth century, you started to be used as a polite form of the singular – probably because people copied the French way of talking, where vous was used in that way. English then became like French, which has tu and vous both possible for singulars. So in early Modern English, when Shakespeare was writing, there was a choice: (Crystal, 13).

| Opener | Situation | Normal reply |
|---|---|---|
| you | upper classes talking to each other, even when closely related | you |
| thou | lower classes talking to each other | thou |
| thou | superiors to inferiors, such as: | |
| | • parents to children | you |
| | • masters to servants | you |
| thou | special intimacy, such as | |
| | • talking to a lover | thou |
| thou | • addressing God or a god (e.g. Jupiter) | you |
| thou | character talks to someone absent | |

It will be noticed that there is no opener for an inferior addressing a superior. This is because an inferior addressed a superior as your lordship, or your honour; see the letters that prefix *Venus and Adonis* and *Lucrece*. Only after this courtesy had been performed would it then be appropriate to use 'you'. This said: attention can now be focussed upon the poet's use of *you*. According to the opener in the situation described above, Shakespeare was a member of the upper class and he was addressing a person of the same class, although not necessarily always the same person. The context of the sonnet provides the clues as to which member of the nobility it was intended for. The answer to the rival poet therefore lies with the nobility. But first it is necessary to dismiss Sonnet 79, which uses *thou* and also speaks of rivalry. In this particular case, it is noted that the poet is addressing the so-called *fair youth*, whom he calls, *"sweet love"*. This would appear to come under *special intimacy*, such as talking to a lover (see above). But it does not preclude Southampton being addressed as *you*, as different occasions may have required.

> Whilst I alone did call upon thy aid,
> My verse alone had all thy gentle grace;
> But now my gracious numbers are decay'd,
> And my sick Muse doth give another place.
> I grant, sweet love, thy lovely argument
> Deserves the travail of a worthier pen;
> ...

Thomas Nashe dedicated *The Choice of Valentines* to the 3rd Earl of Southampton in late 1593. The work was inspired by *Venus and Adonis*, but more sexually explicit; this may have been why it remained unpublished until much later. In the same year, Barnabe Barnes dedicated a sonnet to Southampton. Nashe then sought better success with *The Unfortunate Traveller*, (1594), which he also dedicated to the Earl, declaring it to be, *'a cleane different vaine from other my former courses of writing.'* (Drabble, 687).

> [Southampton] was early the patron of all scholars; the excellent Chapman calls him in his Iliad 'the choice of all our country's noblest spirits;' Nash, in speaking of him, says: 'Incomprehensible is the height of his spirit, both in heroical resolution and matters of conceit.' Beaumont asks, who lives on England's stage and knows him not? All poets and writers vied with each other in dedicating their works to him. (Gervinus, 446)

This presumably was the reason behind the composition of Sonnet 78.

> So oft have I invok'd thee for my Muse,
> And found such fair assistance in my verse,
> As every alien pen has got my use,

> And under thee their poesy disperse.
> ...

'Shakespeare' was talking about rival poets in the plural. He also continued to address the youth as *thee*. However, when Shakespeare used *you*, the alternate form of the second person singular, he need no longer have been talking to the *fair youth*, as we shall discover.

After Oxford's return from Italy, he turned his knowledge into good effect by attending to the Queen's entertainment at Court. The sudden appearance of so many anonymous plays that became identified as those of Shakespeare during the 1590s, many reflecting life in renaissance Italy, is indicative of their composition by Oxford after his return. *Titus Andronicus*, *The Taming of a Shrew*, *King Lear*, and *Hamlet*, which appear as entries in Henslowe's daybook dated 1594, support this inference, as well as *The Comedy of Errors, Henry V, Love's Labour's Lost*, and *Twelfth Night*.

It was in the midst of this early period of creativity that a new poet appeared at Court; this was Walter Raleigh. Sir Robert Naunton (1563-1635) observed the effect this had upon the Queen:

> True it is, he had gotten the Queen's ear in a trice, and she began to be taken with his elocution, and loved to hear his reasons to her demands. And the truth is, she took him for a kind of oracle, which nettled them all. (Williams, 1962, 49)

To add to the Queen's delight with Raleigh, he began plying her with poetry.

> Now we have present made
> To Cynthia, Phoebe, Flora,
> Diana and Aurora,
> Beauty that cannot fade.
> ...
> So her celestial frame
> And quintessential mind,
> Which heavens together bind,
> Shall ever be the same.
>
> Then to her servants leave her,
> Love, nature and perfection,
> Princess of world's affection,
> Our praises but deceive her.

In another poem, Raleigh confided: *'In heaven Queen she is among the spheres:'* and in another: *'Those eyes that hold the hand of every heart,'* and yet one other: *'Those eyes which set my fancy on a fire.'* To these laudations, he added: *"Praised be Diana's fair and harmless light,"* followed by *"Wrong not, dear Empress of my heart, / The merit of true passion"*. And the Queen loved it.

This affectionate display of words was quickly recognized by watchers at Court as an attempt by Raleigh to play court to Elizabeth. Indeed, his ambitious enterprise even found its way into Spenser's *Faerie Queen* (Book III canto 5; Book IV canto 7). There, he is portrayed as *Timias*, the lowborn squire who loves *Belphoebe*: a thin disguise for Elizabeth in her virginal role.

It was at this time that Raleigh completed a long sequence of verses entitled: *The Ocean's Love to Cynthia*, which he addressed to Elizabeth. In fact, her nickname for Raleigh was *'Water'*, and since she was his *'Cynthia'*, the title speaks for itself.

Oxford could not help but be aware of Elizabeth's new favourite and the love Raleigh was expressing in his poetic overtures addressed to her, for he admitted as much in Sonnet 80. Note, therefore, how he addresses the Queen as *you*, without preamble, as one member of the upper class would address another.

> O, how I faint when I of you do write,
> Knowing a better spirit doth use your name
> And in the praise thereof spends all his might
> To make me tongue-tied, speaking of your fame!
> But since your worth, wide as the ocean is,
> The humble as the proudest sail doth bear,
> My saucy bark, inferior far to his,
> On your broad main doth wilfully appear,
> Your shallowest help will hold me up afloat,
> Whilst he upon your soundless deep doth ride;
> Or, being wreck'd, I am a worthless boat,
> He of tall building and of goodly pride. ...

The poem is flooded with allusions to the sea, and by inference to Raleigh: he having identified himself with *the Ocean* in his love for *Cynthia of the Sea*.

Reference to the rival poet's superior ship also appears in the poem, as confirmed by the 800-ton *Ark Raleigh*, launched at Deptford in June 1587. The vessel was subsequently sold to the Queen for £5000 to become the first *Ark Royal*. Oxford's own ship, the *Edward Bonaventure*—his *saucy bark*—was inferior in build, and less expensive, as he admitted in the sonnet.

Oxford then refers to his rival's *tall building*. Raleigh had tried several times to get possession of Sherborne Castle in Dorset, with its impressive, four, huge, Norman towers. He had wanted to make this his family home, but it was not until 1592 that Elizabeth was able to acquire it for him as a present. In return, Raleigh became her new Admiral, *'in full command of an expedition of thirteen ships to attack the silver fleet and sack Panama.'* (Williams, 1962, 106).

Shakespeare's rival poet, we are told, was also a man of *goodly pride*. John Aubrey, in *Brief Lives* ascribed this same word to Raleigh: *'His naeve was that he was damnably proud.'* (ibid, 73). It was a sentiment expressed, too, by an anonymous epigram writer: *'Raleigh doth time bestride ... For all his bloody pride.'* Charles Cavendish, in a letter written to the Countess of Shrewsbury, was another who remarked upon Raleigh's pride (ibid, 79). A similar accusation was made by the correspondent, known only as *'A. B'*. In a letter of protest written to Lord Burghley (7 July 1586), he maintained: *'His pride is intolerable, without regard to any, as the world knows ... '* (ibid 70).

In the same verse, Oxford also managed to compare his current low estate with that of his rival. In this, he would have had in mind the aid he received from the Queen six years earlier, when she had given him an annuity of £1000 to add to her gift of the Manor of Rysing in Norfolk. *Your shallowest help will hold me up afloat*, he wrote.

Raleigh, by comparison, fared very much better. Apart from Sherborne Castle, a knighthood in 1584, several leases from All Souls College at Oxford, and a monopoly on wine, he was also given the lease of a manor formerly owned by the Bishop of Bath and Wells, and appointed, firstly, Lord Warden of the Stannaries, and secondly, Vice-Admiral of Cornwall and Devon. This joint position made him the most powerful man in the west of England, with charge over the lucrative tin industry and control of both the army and navy in Cornwall. In addition he also held the licence to export cloth. In Ireland he received 42,000 acres of land in Cork and Waterford: previously the property of the Earl of Desmond; and to this bounty were added the land and manors of the Babington Estate in the Midlands. As Oxford acknowledged – *Whilst he upon your soundless deep doth ride.*

*The Ocean's Love to Cynthia* is now lost, which may have something to do with its author having impregnated Elizabeth Throgmorton, while perhaps dreaming of a different Elizabeth. The Queen was understandably not impressed. Raleigh did the honourable thing, eventually, and married the pregnant Bess. And for his deceitful protestations of love to Cynthia, Cynthia sent him and his wife to the Tower. *'Ma sœur s'en alla à la Tour, et Sir W. Raleigh.'* (Williams, 1962, 109).

The Queen's reaction to the loss of Raleigh's attention was to turn once more to Oxford, demanding from him the reason why he had remained silent for so long, thus allowing Raleigh to gain such a huge advantage in her affections.

Her complaint echoed that made by Edmund Spenser in *Teares of the Muses* – *"Our pleasant Willy, ah! is dead of late."* Spenser's poem was published in 1591, shortly after *The Faerie Queen*, which parodied Raleigh's *amour* for Elizabeth. Spenser then complained that Willy, *"from whose Pen / Large Streams of Honey and sweet Nectar flow ... Doth rather choose to sit in idle Cell."*

Oxford's awakening at the Queen's rebuke, if not Spenser's protest, may be judged by the sonnets he wrote referring to his rival at Court, and which, as dignity required, continue to address the Queen as *you*.

>   ...
> I found, or thought I found, you did exceed
> The barren tender of a poet's debt;
> And therefore have I slept in your report
> That you yourself, being extant, well might show
> How far a modern quill doth come too short,
> Speaking of worth, what worth in you do grow.
> This silence for my sin you did impute,
> Which shall be most my glory, being dumb;
> For I impair nor beauty, being mute,
> When others would give life, and bring a tomb.
>   There lives more life in one of your fair eyes
>   Than both your poets can in praise devise.     (83)

Raleigh, it will be recalled, had written several poems in praise of the Queen's eyes. Oxford's response was an attempt to exceed his rival in disseminating praise. The opening two lines to this sonnet are also revealing. They begin: *'I never saw that you did painting need, / And therefore to your fair no painting set'.* Elizabeth was noted for her daily application of face paint: *'Her face paint was a mixture of white-of-egg, powdered egg-shell, alum, borax and poppy-seeds moistened with mill water.'* (Williams, 1972, 197)

Needless to say, the thought of Will Shakspere referring to the Queen's personal use of cosmetics is too ludicrous to even contemplate. It is also noteworthy that Oxford has used the words, *you yourself*. This appears to hark back to the speech made by Elizabeth at Tilbury, when she appeared there on horseback to rally her troops in preparation for the arrival of Spain's armada.

> I know I have only the body of a weak and feeble woman; but I have the heart and courage of a king, and even of a king of England, and think foul scorn that Parma, or Spain, or any prince of Europe, should dare invade the border of my realms; to which rather than any dishonour shall grow by me, I myself will take up arms, I myself will be your general, judge and rewarder of every one of your virtues in the field. (Montague, vol. ii: 68).

For the Queen to repeatedly refer to herself as *I myself* was at that time a novel form of expression. Did Oxford write her speeches, one wonders? In any case, Oxford's reference to *you yourself* captures the subjectivity of the Queen's reference to herself at Tilbury, by making it objective.

Shortly before his disgrace, Raleigh had sailed from England to lead a fleet of thirteen ships; his purpose was to intercept a silver fleet and to sack Panama. But during the voyage he heard from a Spanish informer that no treasure ships were to sail that year, he therefore ordered Martin Frobisher to alter course and intercept Portuguese carracks returning from the East Indies. He then turned his own ship about and returned to London.

It was therefore left to Sir John Burroughs in the *Roebuck*, although still under Raleigh's command, to seize one of the prize vessels making for the Iberian coast. This was the *Madre de Dios*, which was escorted under arms into the port at Dartmouth.

> She was the largest ship that had ever entered an English port, seven decks high, the most valuable single prize ever taken, with 537 tons of pepper, cloves, cinnamon, cochineal, mace and nutmegs, and as well jewels, gold ebony, carpets and oriental silks.
> (Williams, 1962, 113)

> The crewmen who boarded it had immediately begun stuffing their pockets, and the pillaging resumed when the ship reached Dartmouth harbour. The lure of spices and gems attracted merchants, jewellers and goldsmiths, who descended on the port to purchase plunder from sailors at a bargain ... The queen claimed as her share ... far more than her actual investment. Some of what she garnered came at Raleigh's expense, who though nominally entitled to at least two-thirds of the loot, had to settle for about one fourth.
> (Jones, 144)

The reason for Elizabeth's indifference to Raleigh was because she had by then discovered his secret marriage. As punishment for deceiving her, she confined him first to Durham House, and then to the Tower. Oxford's response to this sudden downfall of his rival at Court is remarkably apt, and not without a few of those poisonous barbs for which he was noted. Observe too, his use of *you* when addressing the Queen.

> Was it the proud full sail of his great verse,
> Bound for the prize of all-too-precious you.   (86)

In the opening line, Raleigh's *pride* is again mentioned: coupled, firstly, with his *full sail*; apt enough, since he was a seaman, privateer, and latterly Admiral of the fleet. Secondly, there is the remark about his *great verse*: his lengthy declaration in poetry for the love he felt for Elizabeth, which was contained in the *Ocean's Love to Cynthia*.

In the second line 'Shakespeare' draws upon the capture of the prize ship, *Madre de Dios* for a further allegory. In this, the Queen is the precious prize and Raleigh is the nautical versifier windward bound to make the capture.

The sonnet then resumes with the reason for Oxford's silence.

> That did my ripe thoughts in my brain inhearse,
> Making their tomb the womb wherein they grew?

By these words he continues to excuse himself for his recent silence, offering several possible explanations. His thoughts, he admits, were enclosed as in a tomb. But now, with Raleigh in prison, the tomb inside his brain has become a womb, wherein new thoughts are able to develop. Note, especially, that Oxford has coined his own word for this recent burial: it is *inhearse*. One does not have to look far for the reason. In Raleigh's postscript to *The Ocean's Love to Cynthia*, written while in prison, these lines occur:

> But my loue's wounds, my fancy in the hearse,
> The Idea but restinge, of a wasted minde,           (Latham, 25).

Raleigh's *fancy*; that is, his mental imagery, like Oxford's thoughts, lay *in the hearse*, entombed, or as the sonneteer coined his new verb: *inhearse*. One might pass this off as coincidence, except that Oxford has deliberately drawn upon his rival's own expression for a similar entombment. Further allusions to Raleigh follow as the sonnet progresses.

> Was it his spirit, by spirits taught to write
> Above a mortal pitch, that struck me dead?

Oxford once again questions his recent silence, but now with a note of sarcasm. Raleigh was known to have been conducting séances at Durham House, hence the reference to *spirits*. As historian, Norman Williams remarked: *'It is widely held that a free-speculating group around Raleigh was known by the name of 'the School of Night'.'* (Williams, 1962, 115 fn.)

In 1592, a pamphleteer referred to this assemblage of persons as, *'Sir Walter Rauley's Schoole of Atheisme.'* Chapman even composed a poem, *The*

*Shadow of Night*, to honour the circle of mathematicians and philosophers who attended Raleigh's meetings. The poem was entered in the Stationers' Register in December 1593 and published the following year.

By 1593, Raleigh's nocturnal activities had come under the surveillance of Lord Burghley —

> ... he was looking askance at the activities of a loose club or gathering of scientists, mathematicians, astrologers, astronomers and writers, who met under the joint aegis of Sir Walter Raleigh, and Henry Percy, Earl of Northumberland, nicknamed "the Wizard Earl". It was known as the School of Night. (Cook, 64)

Robert Parsons, an Oxford University educated Jesuit, living in exile in Augsburg, was aware of Raleigh's occult practices. *'Certainly if the school of atheism of Sir Walter Raleigh flourishes a little longer—which he is well known to hold in his house, with a certain necromantic astrologer as teach.'* (Cook, 105). Parsons went on to voice his fear that Raleigh might be appointed to the Council, where he could be influenced to draw up *'a proclamation by that Magus and Epicurus, Raleigh's teacher, and [get it] published in the name of the Queen"*(ibid).

As the sonnet continues, Oxford refers again to his recent silence, but now, with an air of defiance, he delivers a stinging blow at his rival, and to what Parsons called Raleigh's *Magus and Epicurus*.

> No, neither he, nor his compeers by night
> Giving him aid, my verse astonished.
> He, nor that affable familiar ghost
> Which nightly gulls him with intelligence,
> As victors, of my silence cannot boast:

Amongst Raleigh's *compeers* were the mathematicians, Thomas Harriot, Walter Warner and Thomas Hughes. Marlowe, Chapman, and the minor poet Matthew Roydon also attended. It was later revealed that —

> Marlowe had boasted he had 'read the atheist lecture to Sir Walter Raleigh and others', and had said 'that Moses was but a juggler, that one Harriot, being Sir Walter Raleigh's man, can do more than he.' (Cook, 118-19).

Sonnet 86 reveals how well informed Oxford was regarding the spiritualist practices that were taking place inside Durham House. The *familiar ghost*, for example, would be what is now called a spirit guide, but in earlier language was called *a familiar*.

It can be seen from this how sceptical Oxford was towards the séances held by Raleigh at his School of Night, for he dismissed them as being no more than something that *gulls him with intelligence*; in other words, Raleigh was being deceived by the information he received, or so Oxford believed.

The evidence supporting Raleigh as the rival poet is impossible to deny. Every line focuses upon this man, either through his activities, his poetry, his possessions, or his known character. In each instance, the descriptive passages employed by Oxford are amply supported by history.

The implications for this are shattering. The rivalry mentioned in the sonnets is about obtaining Queen Elizabeth's favour, and the competition for this was between Oxford and Raleigh, using poetry. In which case, the authorship controversy must be considered proven. The 17th Earl of Oxford was William Shakespeare. Only Oxford could, by right of protocol, address Queen Elizabeth as *you*. Shakspere would have had to address the Queen as *your majesty* or similar. In any case, it is unimaginable that Shakspere would have written to the Queen apologising for his silence while Raleigh enjoyed first place in her affection.

How might Shakespeare experts respond, apart from ignoring the evidence altogether? The obvious move is to draw attention to what academics are pleased to call a 'proof' that Shakspere was Shakespeare. The reader should, however, be aware that if any such 'proof' existed, there would be no authorship question. For a proof to be valid, it must be both necessary and sufficient. Evidence that is *necessary* for Shakspere to be Shakespeare can be proposed, but this *per se* is not enough. For evidence to be sufficient there can be no alternative explanation.

Consider the present case. If Oxford wrote the 'rival poet' sonnets to the Queen, then it would be *necessary* that he addressed her as *you*; that his references to her accorded with her position as Queen of England; that another poet had been writing verse addressed to her; that this poet could be reliably identified by the terms used in the sonnet; that historical records confirmed the content of the sonnets wherever possible; that there were no contradictions in the sonneteer's verse.

It seems reasonable to conclude that these *necessary* conditions have been met. But are they also sufficient? To prove they are insufficient, it requires that an alternative rival poet be named: a person who satisfies the criteria of necessity in equal measure to that provided by Raleigh. If this proves impossible, then the evidence identifying Oxford, Raleigh and Elizabeth has been shown to be both *necessary* and *sufficient*. In short, it proves that Oxford wrote the 'rival poet' sonnets. In which case, he wrote the complete set of *Shake-speares Sonnets*, published by Thorpe in 1609.

Nevertheless, alternative poets have been considered for the status of 'rival', but because Shakspere has always been thought to be the poet experiencing rivalry, the suggestions made have never been more than an advocate's fancy: unsubstantiated by sufficient evidence to withstand doubt. Christopher Marlowe is one of the more obvious candidates proposed – in fact, by both sides of the authorship debate.

The basis for this belief rests almost entirely upon Sonnet 80 being either Oxford's, or Shakspere's response to Marlowe's intervention in their personal and intimate relationship with 'Shakespeare's fair youth'

In the autumn of 1592, Southampton was included as a member of Elizabeth's progress to Oxford University. He had become a rising star at Court, and had caught the eye of the Earl of Essex, which was to subsequently bring him into contact with his coterie. But to suppose that Southampton gave intimate time to Marlowe, with his tradesman-class upbringing and belligerent reputation, or that he divided his affections between this man and Lord Oxford, or for that matter, Shakspere, is to completely misunderstand the class structures that had been put in place in Tudor England. Projecting liberal, western, democratic values back through the centuries to 16th century England is a *faux pas*. *"The past is a foreign country; they do things differently there."* (L. P. Hartley, 1895-1972).

The little support there is for advocating Marlowe as 'Shakespeare's' rival poet is found in *Hero and Leander*. It was an unfinished poem, perhaps cut short by Marlowe's death, although it was licensed for publication in 1593, the year he died. This poem is believed to possess similar words to those found in Sonnet 80. But, there may be a problem with this. Sonnet 80 consists of 14 lines and 116 words, whereas Marlowe's poem has 818 lines and 6319 words. Both poems also refer in part to the sea; hence, the chance of finding the same word appearing in *Hero and Leander* as appears in the sonnet is not really remarkable, since there are 109 words to choose from in Marlowe's poem for every 2 in 'Shakespeare's'.

Consider, for example, when 'Shakespeare' writes: *"Or, being wreck'd, I am a worthless boat,"* he was referring, in metaphor, to his ship sailing on the *"broad main"* of the Queen's benevolence, for which he has correctly addressed her majesty as 'You'. Contrary opinion ignores the significance of this aristocratic courtesy, and likens the phrase to Hero's *"treasure suffered wrack*'. But the *treasure* Marlowe is referring to is Hero's virginity, whose *wreck* she has *suffered* through Leander's seduction. The poets are talking about unrelated matters. This is further exemplified when 'Shakespeare' writes: *"He of tall building and of goodly pride."* In Marlowe's poem, it is she, Hero, who dwells in a tall tower. As for his (her?) pride, Marlowe's only mention of pride is when he refers to *"proud Adonis"*. Again, what is to be made of 'Shakespeare's' *"saucy bark, inferior far to his"*? According to the Oxford English Dictionary, the definition of 'saucy' is: – 'd. Applied to a ship or boat: (*a*) In early use (with figurative context): Presumptuous, rashly-venturing (*obs.*)'. For Oxford, *his rashly-venturing ship [Edward Bonaventure], inferior far to his [Ark Raleigh]* was historically accurate. Leander, on the other hand, possessed no ship. Instead, he nightly swam across the Hellespont, guided by the lantern Hero had lit for him.

Further division between the sense of Shakespeare's references to his rival, and Marlowe's story of Leander's first night in the bed of Hero are as easily made, and tedious to recount. And although it may be said that 'Shakespeare' was picking on some of Marlowe's words for his own purpose, this could also be said to be true of almost anyone writing about the sea.

From what has been said, it can be seen how Shakespeare's 'Rival Poet' has encumbered the faithful with yet another imponderable problem, which centuries of research have failed to solve. It is yet one more case of searching for non-existent records in the desolate archives of William Shakspere's past. To meet the challenge of this vacancy, many Shakespeare experts have attempted to fill the void by using their imagination, but with no appreciable success. In 1944, H. E. Rollins examined the candidates that had been proposed, dismissed the lot, and concluded that the 'Rival Poet' was a piece of fiction.

Advocates for Oxford's authorship of the Shakespeare canon are much better placed; they now have at hand the historical evidence to solve the problem of the rival poet's identity. It is therefore without question, that were this same historically backed evidence applicable to Shakspere, it would be Oxford's supporters, instead, who were faced with an insoluble problem.

# 19

# THE DARK LADY

In Sonnet 144, published in 1599 by William Jaggard, 'Shakespeare' had confessed to having two loves. In the following extract it will be noticed that there is no thought within these lines of any love for his wife, but there is for his male friend.

> Two loves I have, of comfort and despair,
> Which like two spirits do suggest me still;
> The better angel is a man right fair,
> The worser spirit a woman colour'd ill.

The story of Oxford's shame, and his separation from the plays and poetry he had written, seem bound up within these four lines. But as the sonnet progresses, the story told becomes even more sensational. His mistress has, or so he believes, seduced his male friend and both are now betraying him.

> To win me soon to hell, my female evil
> Tempteth my better angel from my side
> And would corrupt my saint to be a devil,
> Wooing his purity with her foul pride.

Even though the poet suspects this has occurred, he remains uncertain that the seduction has yet been accomplished.

> Yet this shall I ne'er know, but live in doubt
> Till my bad angel fire my good one out.

So the poet must wait until the passion between his two friends is spent, and confessions are made. It cannot pass notice that there is an obvious similarity between the subject referred to by Oxford, and that described in *Willobie His Avisa*, which, suspiciously, was called in as soon as this sonnet was published.

> H.W. being suddenly infected with the contagion of a fantastical fit, at the first sight of A, pineth a while in secret grief, at length not able any longer to endure the burning heat of so fervent a humour, bewrayeth the secrecy of his disease unto his familiar friend W.S. who not long before had tried the courtesy of the passion. (Ogburn, 669)

Past commentators of this passage, notably Schoenbaum and Chambers are agreed that H.W. and W.S. refer to Henry Wriothesley and William Shakespeare, respectively. But who is A.?

At the commencement of 1592, Oxford was forty-one years of age, Southampton was eighteen, and Anne Vavasour was twenty-six; for several years after first joining the Court at the age of fifteen, she had been Oxford's mistress, and had subsequently given birth to his illegitimate son as a result of their liaison.

> Anne Vavasor had a keen wit and a caustic tongue; she was a musician, a graceful dancer, a writer of verse, an adept at repartee. A list of the men who were attracted to her during the seventy years that followed her arrival in London is like a Who's Who of the court. She lived to be well over ninety. Before she was thirty-four, she had borne two illegitimate sons (both of whom were to have distinguished careers). She had several husbands (two of them at one time) and was faithful to none. She has been identified as the Rosalind of Edmund Spenser, who was one of her admirers, and she certainly is the celebrated "Dark Lady" of the *Sonnets*. For at sixteen, when Oxford met her, she had very dark hair and black eyes, a pink-and-cream complexion, and rosy-red cheeks, hence her nickname of "Rose". (Benezet, 55)

The question this now poses is whether Oxford renewed his affair with the mother of his son after the death of his first wife in 1588, as Professor Benezet believed, or did he take a new mistress? The author of *Willobie* has certainly provided the correct initial for Anne, but are there other clues to be had?

In Sonnet 138, the age difference between Oxford and his mistress is exposed and this corroborates what is known about Anne Vavasour and Oxford in 1591.

> When my love swears that she is made of truth,
> I do believe her, though I know she lies,
> That she might think me some untutor'd youth,
> Unlearned in the world's false subtleties.
> Thus vainly thinking that she thinks me young,
> Although she knows my days are past the best.

Further clues supporting the proposition that Vavasour is the mistress are forthcoming in Sonnet 152, where the poet's conscience now becomes a factor in the action that is taking place. Note, too, that Oxford has reverted to *thou* when addressing his subject.

> In loving thee thou know'st I am foresworn.

Oxford's marriage to Elizabeth Trentham occurred sometime near the end of 1591. It would also appear the marriage was one of convenience, and not the result of a love tryst. Mistress Trentham was Queen Elizabeth's maid of honour, already about thirty years of age, and far beneath Oxford in social status. In addition to which, Oxford was heavily in debt, and in no wise able to support a new wife's financial requirements.

The next line to the sonnet provides further damning evidence. He accuses his mistress of *swearing love to me* as well as to her husband. The second line confirms her adultery, which also implies his own adultery.

> But thou art twice forsworn, to me love swearing;
> In act thy bed-vow broke,

As Gwynneth Bowen discovered:

> [Anne Vavasour] after a succession of illicit love affairs had married a sea captain named John Finche, but left him about 1589 for the redoubtable Queen's champion, Sir Henry Lee, then nearly 60 years old and on the point of retiring. Nevertheless, with Sir Henry Lee she continued to live, steadfastly if not faithfully, to his dying day, 21 years later. (Ogburn, 661)

By piecing together this evidence, it can be inferred that the poet may well be referring to John Finche and Sir Henry Lee; for by Anne swearing her love to Oxford, she was also renouncing whatever vows of love she had made to these other two men. In this sense, she is *twice forsworn*. And her *bed-vow broke*.

Oxford pursues this dishonesty with a question.

> But why of two oaths' breach do I accuse thee,
> When I break twenty? I am perjur'd most;

This is a plain admission of guilt on Oxford's part for his many sins when set against the *two breaches of oath* committed by his mistress. He then goes on to explain why he has lost faith in what she says.

> And all my honest faith in thee is lost,
> For I have sworn deep oaths of thy deep kindness,
> Oaths of thy love, thy truth, thy constancy;

There is so much here that Oxford is referring to, and to have discovered that it is actually false, implies the affair between the two had had a long and troubled history. Once again, Oxford's affair with Anne Vavasour, which began in 1580, is right on target.

Oxford concludes with a neat couplet that summed up his feelings.

> For I have sworn thee fair—more perjur'd I,
> To swear against the truth so foul a lie.

Anne Vavasour left her husband to live as Lee's mistress because Lee had made her pregnant. '*Their son, Thomas Vavasour, (later known as Thomas Freeman), was born in 1589 when his half brother, Edward Vere, was eight years old.*" (Ogburn, 661). Presumably, John Finche had been away at sea when the child was conceived, therefore the mother was unable to pass it off as his.

Oxford alludes to an illegitimate birth in Sonnet 127. The opening lines of the verse also introduce the colour black as a new definition for beauty: the poet claiming it to be the successor of fair.

> But now is black beauty's successive heir,
> And beauty slander'd with a bastard shame:

Both of Anne's children were bastards, but equally, she herself was illegitimate (Haynes, 39). In describing his mistress, Oxford has provided a brief pen picture of her features. And this bears a marked resemblance to the portrait of Anne Vavasour owned by the Master and Wardens of the Armourers & Brasiers' Company in London.

> Therefore my mistress' brows are raven black,
> Her eyes so suited, and they mourners seem
> At such who, not born fair, no beauty lack,
> Sland'ring creation with a false esteem.
>   Yet so they mourn, becoming of their woe,
>   That every tongue says beauty should look so.   (127)

This conflict between black and fair is resumed in Sonnet 131. The poet, although confessing love for his mistress, begins to question the reason.

> ...
> For well thou know'st to my dear doting heart
> Thou art the fairest and most precious jewel,
> Yet, in good faith, some say that thee behold
> Thy face hath not the power to make love groan,
> To say they err I dare not be so bold,
> Although I swear it to myself alone.

In the concluding couplet, the poet wraps up his dilemma in a single sentence. He is under the dark spell of a woman he cannot resist, even though he knows her motives are sinful. Also, it was because of her past immorality, so he maintains, others have defamed her looks.

> In nothing art thou black save in thy deeds,
> And thence this slander, as I think proceeds.

Evidence of Anne Vavasour's immoral behaviour has already been given above; for instance, her taking Sir Henry Lee as a lover despite the fact he was married; while, at the same time being married herself to John Finche. Then, after giving birth to Lee's son, transferring her affections to

Oxford, whose illegitimate son she had given birth to while in the Queen's service.

There is also further reference in the sonnets to her illicit affairs, which occurred between her having given birth to her first illegitimate son and her marriage to Finche. But in addition to this part of her history, she is also reported as having turned her attention to Oxford's friend; and, as it would appear, successfully seduced him. An explanation for this occurs in Sonnet 135.

> Whoever hath her wish, thou hast thy Will,
> And Will to boot, and Will in over-plus;

The word 'will' had a double meaning at the time, in that it referred to both desire and the object through which it was achieved. In short, the poet is implying that his mistress was insatiable, a nymphomaniac.

By allowing Oxford to have been Shakespeare and his young friend to have been the 3rd Earl of Southampton, who had played the role of patron to 'Shakespeare', so that *Venus and Adonis* and *Lucrece* could be published, the third person in this *ménage à trois* must be Anne Vavasour.

In 1592, Anne was twenty-seven, Henry was nineteen, and an object of temptation too urgent for her to resist. Oxford had already suspected what was happening behind his back, and his suspicion is made plain in Sonnet 144, published by Jaggard in 1599. The misgivings, which Oxford had first weighed in the balance, were finally justified, as can be seen from Sonnet 42. This is addressed to his male friend, using *thou*.

> That thou hast her, it is not all my grief,
> And yet it may be said I lov'd her dearly;
> That she hath thee is of my wailing chief,
> A loss in love that touches me more nearly.
> Loving offenders, thus I will excuse thee:   (42)

There is in this verse a weary resignation concerning what has befallen the poet. In danger of losing both his loves, he concedes defeat to preserve what he still cherishes. The poet's fiery youth of former years has been mellowed by age and bitter experience. This change was to prove dramatic, and its effect soon came to reveal itself in the revisions he made to his plays during the 1590s, which have come down to us in a more polished form than when they were first penned.

Once again, as was found when investigating the identity of the Rival Poet, it is with Oxford's personal history that a fit can be made with Anne

Vavasour as the *Dark Lady*. This being true, the publication of Sonnet 144, within a year of Meres having publicly announced Shakespeare as the playwright of a dozen plays that had previously appeared anonymously, was political dynamite. The sonnet suggested the bisexuality of the author, implying both homosexuality and adultery. While this might be looked down upon at the time, as being typically reprehensible amongst the type of low class hack who wrote for the theatre, and who dwelt amongst the whores on the Southwark bank of the Thames, it was an entirely different matter when it involved a member of Lord Burghley's family. It can therefore be no coincidence that *Willobie His Avisa*, which had been licensed for publication on 3 September 1594, was suddenly called in after five years of being freely available on bookstalls. The connection between the threesome in Sonnet 144 and a similar threesome with the initials W.S., H.W. and A., in *Willobie*, if not immediately apparent to members of the public, would certainly have been obvious to those in authority.

With both the rival poet and the dark lady identified, attention must now turn to the relationship between Oxford and Southampton. For it is in this that the seeds of the authorship controversy, with its attendant doubt that Will Shakspere wrote the works of Shakespeare, are sprung. This was always evident from the events of 1599, with the publication of Sonnet 144 and the calling in of *Willobie His Avisa*.

Strangely, for one would think it so, Professor James Shapiro who wrote a 414-page prize-winning book with the title *1599 A Year In The Life Of William Shakespeare*, somehow managed to avoid mentioning even once *Willobie His Avisa*, and the three embarrassing sets of initials that contradict his advocacy that Shakspere was Shakespeare.

In his next book, *Contested Will*, Shapiro explained his reasons for accepting that Shakspere wrote the works of Shakespeare. The problem with this is that anyone can justify their belief with a set of reasons, even that the Earth is flat: but this only works if the evidence contradicting those reasons is omitted from the debate. Shapiro has used the same strategy. At the time he was writing *Contested Will*, he was contacted by a scholar who was conversant with the strengths contained in *Proving Shakespeare*, and who suggested Shapiro's book would benefit by referring to the evidence it contained. Shapiro wrote back declining.

The information Shapiro refused to read is repeated in these chapters, and it completely destroys the explanations he cites in support of his belief.

This raises a disturbing question. Was Shapiro's commission to explore the authorship question as a scholar, or was it to support Shakspere with whatever arguments seemed sufficiently persuasive on the pro-Shakspere side while referring only to dissuasive arguments on the pro-Oxford side?

**ANNE VAVASOUR**

# 20

# A Scandalous Affair

Pro-Shakspere academics, like biographers are in a dither when forced to come to terms with *Shake-speares Sonnets*. If they are not, as many will claim, then they have blocked out the many problems and unanswered questions that are manifest. What follows is a list of difficulties that have never been satisfactorily dealt with. Indeed, for the Shakespeare expert to pick and choose, here and there, from the list and give possible answers is itself unsatisfactory. What is required is a single solution to the entire set of problems.

[1] Who was the youth that is so lovingly addressed? [2] Who was the dark lady? [3] Who was the rival poet? [4] Where are the poems that caused the rivalry? [5] Are the poems biographical? [6] If they are biographical, why do the details not match Shakspere? [7] Why did the author expect to be forgotten after his death, yet also believing his words would live on? [8] If they are merely exercises in poetry, why did the author not publish them earlier when interest in *Venus and Adonis* and *Lucrece,* and in sonnets generally, was at its greatest? [9] Why did thirty years pass by before a second edition was published? [10] Why was the first printed draft not corrected so as to eliminate the errors and misprints? [11] Why did the author not write his own dedication? [12] Why is Thorpe's dedication ungrammatical? [13] Why did Thorpe end the dedication with his initials, T.T. instead of his name? [14] Why did Thorpe refer to Shake-speare as ever-living: a phrase reserved for those who were deceased? [15] Who was Mr W.H.? [15] Who were Shakespeare's *private friends,* referred to by Meres, amongst whom manuscript copies were circulating? [16] If his private friends were players, why did they not sell them to a willing publisher, as was the case with his plays? [17] If they were business colleagues, what interest was it to them, other than as a marketable

piece of literature? [18] Why did the author sometimes address his subject as *you* in place of *thou*?

An answer to every one of these questions is contained in what follows. Moreover, these solutions, when combined, form a coherent and consistent explanation that is in agreement with the many problems that beset the authorship controversy.

In confronting some of the problems listed above, Professor Jonathan Bate wrote in the *New York Times*, which was copied by Shapiro in *Contested Will*: *"Don't be drawn into the trap of supposing that they are autobiographical: that is an illusion of Shakespeare's art."* (301). Bate admitted to having tried to identify the rival poet and the dark lady, but had now abandoned the task; as did the fox who tried to reach the grapes before declaring them to be sour. Bate's failure to achieve his aim was because he worked on the premise that Shakspere wrote the Sonnets. His efforts were bound to fail.

As referred to in the previous chapter, after Meres advertised the existence of Shakespeare's Sonnets in 1598, Jaggard managed to get hold of two, which he published a year later in *The Passionate Pilgrim*. The content of Sonnet 144 was potentially devastating, should it ever be connected to the extract appearing in *Willobie His Avisa*; for this, too, described a similar situation involving three persons, one of whom had the same initials as William Shakespeare. Seemingly, because of this connection, *Willobie His Avisa* was suddenly called in, although it had already been on the market for the past five years.

Given that the connection between these two publications is valid, then the reference made to W.S. the *old player*, H. W. the *new actor*, and A. can be read as William Shakespeare, Henry Wriothesley, and Anne. Those who object by saying that A. stands for Avisa should bear in mind that much of the art of satire lies in the ambiguity of its phrases, and *Willobie* was indeed written as a piece of satire.

At the beginning of 1594, the year that *Avisa* was published, William Shakspere was aged twenty-nine and therefore disqualified by age from being the *old player*. The Earl of Oxford, however, was forty-three, Henry Wriothesley was twenty, and Anne Vavasour eight years his senior. Yet, in Sonnet 144, despite the age difference between the two men, the poet refers to the young man as 'his love' – *"Two loves I have"*. This might be excused as poetic licence except that many of the accompanying sonnets addressed to this young man are considered to be homo-erotic. This would certainly explain why the sonnets were kept away from the public gaze. If the Earl of Oxford was identified as the 3rd Earl of Southampton's lover, and the affair dated back to the early 1590s, or even earlier, not only was this unlawful, but it also implicated Lord Burghley, who had been the boy's legal guardian at that time. Burghley would therefore be culpable in the affair.

This raises the question as to exactly when Sonnet 144 was written. The fact that it was liberated for publication in 1599 proves only that it had been written before then. Whereas, the publication of *Willobie* in 1594 suggests that the facts relating to this threesome affair was, at the time, recent history. But, if the dark lady interfered with the love between the poet and the youth in, say, 1593, then Oxford's love for Southampton must predate this. There exists circumstantial support for this inference, based upon well documented events.

In the middle of July, 1590, when Henry Wriothesley was still sixteen years of age, Lord Burghley resolved to wed him to his granddaughter who, on the 2nd July, had just celebrated her fifteenth birthday. Burghley's own daughter, Anne, had married a fortnight after her fifteenth birthday; but her wedding to Oxford had been fraught with unhappiness. Burghley had written, even before the wedding, confessing that he thought fifteen was too young an age for his daughter to marry. He had been proved right. Why, then, did he suddenly have a change of heart? It was not as if Southampton wanted to marry: he clearly did not. But measures were put in place to persuade him otherwise; these were the carrot and the stick.

In 1593, against all precedence, and having done nothing to warrant such an honour, Southampton received the promise of nominations for Knight of the Garter, presumably as a sweetener. It did not work. Instead, he was levied with a crippling £5000 fine (2·5 million pounds by today's reckoning) for breaching his engagement to Lady Elizabeth. As reported in chapter 5, Lady Bridget Manners did not believe Southampton was yet eligible as a husband, because she said, he was *'so fantastical and would be so carried away."* *'Fantastical'* was the same word used in *Willobie His Avisa* when describing H.W.

The question must therefore be urged: Why was Burghley so desperate to see Southampton safely married, when the youth had neither the wish for wedlock nor the outward show of one who was yet ready for that responsibility? It can only have been through sheer desperation that the Lord High Treasurer prepared his own granddaughter for marriage, which in different circumstances he would have avoided. And then, as an equal act of desperation, he had first tried to bribe and then punish Southampton. The 'bribe' and the fine were both out of proportion, considering the youth of the prospective bridegroom, and make sense only when intended as a means of enforcing the marriage to take place.

The reason for Burghley's anxiety will be understood by parents with the same religious background as that of people living in England at the time of Elizabeth I. Upon discovering that a son's development into manhood has become arrested, and unlikely to proceed to a point where an interest in the female sex occurs, a solution may be sought, where possible, through an arranged marriage. This appears to have been Burghley's method of finding a way out of his predicament; which, if not quickly resolved, could end in scandal with untold consequences.

In the sixteenth century, acts of male homosexuality were taken with deadly seriousness. The Elizabethan and Jacobean periods were times of devout religious observance. The Bible was seen as the unquestionable Word of God and a doorway to eternal salvation. The Book of Corinthians in the Geneva Bible of that period was unequivocal upon the issue of homosexuality.

> 9 Knowe ye not that the vnrighteous shal not inherite the kingdome of God? Be not deceiued: nether fornicatours, nor idolaters, nor adulterers, nor wantons, nor bouggerers. (Nelson, 214)

In 1563, Elizabeth had decreed by statute that sodomy was a crime punishable by death (Crompton, 362-6). A case at that time involving the buggery of a boy throws light upon the crime of male intercourse, with possible ramifications for Oxford. *'Humphrey Stafford was tried by the Court of the King's Bench (1607-8) for just such a crime and executed.'* (Haynes, 107-8). As the astrologer, Simon Forman later remarked: *'his mistake was to choose a sixteen-year-old.'* Oxford's relationship with Southampton covered the same age group. Burghley's anxiety at the thought of his grandchildren and the memory of his own daughter being tarnished by the public shame of her husband was sufficient motive for his frantic attempt to prevent the situation developing further, and causing a public scandal.

But what evidence connects Southampton with homosexuality in 1590? It happens that evidence does exist. This came to light at the end of the twentieth-century, when a portrait of Henry Wriothesley was discovered. This had lain neglected in the Cobbe household for three centuries, until a chance inspection identified the sitter as the 3rd Earl of Southampton at the age of about seventeen. The Cobbes were seventeenth century neighbours of the Earls of Southampton, and it is presumed that the 4th Earl, who died childless, passed the portrait on to the Cobbes. Prior to this discovery, the picture was mistakenly labelled as a likeness of Lady Norton, daughter of the Bishop of Winton. That Southampton's face should be mistaken for a woman's does remind one of Shakespeare's words describing the fair youth: *'A woman's face with Nature's own hand painted.* (Sonnet 20).

Art expert, Alastair Laing, who studied the portrait of Southampton, declared: *'The provenance of the picture is now entirely convincing.'*

> Experts who have studied the facts now agree that the portrait is undoubtedly the earliest known image of the third Earl of Southampton–Shakespeare's patron, the 'fair youth' addressed in his sonnets–somewhere between the age of 17 and 20 and painted exactly the time those first few sonnets were written. (Holden)

Apart from the femininity of Southampton's features, it should also be emphasised that the portrait has been painted to show the sitter wearing make-up. He is clearly wearing lipstick, and rouge colours his cheeks. The eyebrows have been plucked with a careful precision and the eyes are bright, possibly from the effects of belladonna. He is also wearing double earrings and a Venetian lace collar that was in vogue between 1590 and 1593. The curling tongs have been carefully applied to his hair, which has been styled to give the same appearance as that of Juno, the Roman queen of heaven and of womanhood; a long tress dangles down one side to his left breast and this is held in place by the slender delicate fingers of his right hand. (Roper, 203). *"He was known as 'Rose' to those who dared."*

In Sonnet 82, which refers to the words used in dedications, the poet almost unobtrusively slips in a reference that would certainly apply to the youth in the portrait. Addressing his subject as 'thou', in contrast to Sonnet 83, which addresses the Queen as 'you' (see chapter 18), 'Shakespeare' wrote: *'Where cheeks need blood; in thee it is abus'd.'*

Southampton's portrait cannot have escaped Burghley's notice, and it can only have added to the urgency he must have felt as the boy's legal guardian, with its attendant responsibility for his moral welfare. But the situation was made awkward by the fact that he was Oxford's father-in-law, and former legal guardian. Also, despite being Lord High Treasure, Oxford's earldom outranked him in the hierarchy of the nobility.

There was also the fact that any scandalous damage to Oxford was likely to embarrass his daughters and stain their reputation; they were also Burghley's grandchildren. Burghley's plight was indeed desperate. To add to this, his political position would be placed in danger by the threatened scandal, since the office he held would come under threat from his enemies once the affair became public knowledge. He therefore saw the relationship between Oxford and Southampton as a threat to national security, at a time when the country was at war and the Church divided. There can be no doubt that the Queen was advised of the situation and that she gave her consent to what followed. *"Henry's mother was equally anxious to bring it about, and her letters to her son on the subject are also numerous."* (Benezet, 77).

Marriage by the offending parties was only the first part of the solution; it would divert attention away from the scandal of Southampton's portrait and any rumours that were surrounding his effeminacy. Those familiar with Shakespeare's sugared sonnets, said to be circulating amongst his private friends, would have been in no doubt as to the identity of his male lover. Any notion that this could be Shakspere is foolhardy. In 1590, he was still an unknown person, having newly arrived from the midlands. He had published nothing, nor had he a letter of introduction to any person of importance in the capital. His own story told to Davenant, possibly while in his cups, confirmed that he began life in London as a horse waiter at Shoreditch. Apart from which, as Peter Ackroyd explained —

> The 'lovely boy'and object of the poet's passion has been identified with the earl of Southampton. In the late sixteenth century, however, the impropriety of addressing a young earl in that manner would have been quite apparent; to accuse him of dissoluteness and infidelity, as Shakespeare accuses the unnamed recipient, would have been unthinkable.
> (Ackroyd, 288)

According to Ackroyd, Southampton could not have been the 'lovely boy' that Shakespeare addressed. On the other hand, he not only could have been, but was that person; accepting that Shakespeare was Oxford's pseudonym.

What evidence is there for this? Again, by going back two years another portrait, a miniature dated 1588, appears to answer this very question. This is the picture with the title, *Unknown Man Clasping a Hand from a Cloud*, and is owned by the Victoria and Albert Museum; a copy also exists at Castle Howard, which shows the colours in greater detail.

**Female hand reaching down from Heaven to save a bereaved man from pederasty.**

Although the subject of the portrait is not named, it is known to have been painted by the Queen's artist Nicholas Hilliard. The picture shows a man dressed in mourning black, implying recent bereavement, and who has been captivated by *Attic love* (a euphemism for pederasty), for the artist has actually inscribed these words in Latin onto the picture as a reason for its commission. The outstretched hand of a woman reaches down through the clouds from heaven, to clasp the man's right hand, as though the soul of his dead wife was trying to lift him from his sorrowful plight. In every respect, the facts fit Oxford as the subject of Hilliard's composition.

The painting has been suitably inscribed with the reason for its composition *'Attici amoris ergo'* – 'Because of Attic Love'. (*Attici* is an adjective in the genitive case for *Atticus*, the ancient district of east central Greece whose chief city was Athens; *amoris* is the genitive case for the noun, *amor*, meaning love or great desire; *ergo*, if accompanied by the genitive, as it is in this present case, means *because of* or *for the sake of*). Also, the date is written *'Ano Dm 1588'* – 'In the Year of the Lord 1588': *Domini* being a reminder of the religious symbolism in the painting, for it is often omitted from other works of art, being merely implied.

In 1588, Oxford celebrated his thirty-eighth birthday. The portrait shows a man of similar age, with hazel eyes and curly auburn hair: features that describe Oxford. Moreover, he had also lost his wife in the summer of that year, hence the black mourning attire. The hand reaching down through the clouds has its precedent on the *Bayeux Tapestry*, where the hand of God also drops beneath the clouds to offer assistance. The same artistic device was later adopted by Henry Peacham who drew a hand reaching down from the clouds to present the Crown of England to James I. (*Minerva Britanna*, 1612).

Hand reaching down from Heaven to give the Crown of England to James I

Oxford's wife was known for her angelic spirit, and her forbearance at the wayward behaviour of her husband, even when he denied paternity of their daughter Elizabeth. For her to be depicted in heaven, while still reaching out for her husband below, would be easily recognized by those who knew her circumstances. As poet Wilfred Samonde wrote: *'Who as she liv'd an Angel on the earth, / So like an Angel doth she sit on high, / On his right hand ... '* (Nelson, 310). It is to his right hand that the Lady in Hilliard's portrait offers her own.

The picture has never been officially identified as that of the 17th Earl of Oxford. The Latin epigraph would have been an early deterrent to making this a positive identification. Yet, logically, the facts available are without exception those belonging to Oxford. Understandably, the very idea that England's beloved Shakespeare should possess such a slur to blight his fame is a complete anathema to admirers of his plays and poetry. Even those persuaded that Oxford was Shakespeare baulk at the suggestion his love for Southampton was other than pure.

But consider: Oxford never once in his lifetime received sufficient votes to be nominated for the much prized Order of the Garter. Support for him wavered yearly up and down until 1590, when it ceased altogether. From then onwards, up until his death in 1604, he received zero nominations. Only at the time of his approaching death, almost as a consolation and in memory of his deceased sister Anne, did Thomas Cecil cast a vote in his brother-in-law's favour. Why did all support cease at the time Burghley was so desperately trying to persuade Southampton to marry? The stain of homosexuality, or worse still, paedophilia provides the likely answer.

This blight on Oxford has caused a theory to develop that Southampton was really Oxford's illegitimate son by Queen Elizabeth. It removes the crime of paedophilia, but is devoid of any substantive evidence. It exists not so much as a theory, but more as an act of faith, especially amongst those, who, for understandable reasons, cannot accept the alternative.

Unfortunately, Oxford already had a previous charge against him for paedophilia. Upon his return from Italy in 1576, he was accompanied by Orazio Coquo, a sixteen-year-old choir boy, whom he engaged as his page. The boy's service was short-lived, for after just eleven months he escaped the Oxford household and fled back to his native Venice. Its significance became apparent at the tribunal hearing which followed, when Coquo *'complained howe horribly my Lord had abusid him, and yet wold not giue him any thinge:'* (Nelson, 141). This 'thing' in question, is presumed to have been a salve to ease his anal discomfort. Apart from this incident, Oxford had other enemies willing to condemn him for sexually abusing boys.

> Howard and Arundel were bent on having Oxford tried for the specific crime of pederasty. To this end they offered testimony from nearly a dozen victims, near victims, and non-victim witnesses. They charged Oxford with the sexual abuse of 'so many boyes that it must nedes come out' especially of pages (LIB-3.6.1/3). (Nelson, 215)

But the charges levelled against Oxford by Howard and Arundel were not subjected to prolonged scrutiny, and he was never brought to trial. Was Oxford entirely innocent of these accusations? Had it not been for his infatuation with the teenaged Southampton and the homo-erotic verses it inspired, or the condemnatory epigraph inscribed on Hilliard's miniature, it might be easier to set the matter aside. But then again, Southampton's intimacy with Captain Piers Edmund, when they were alone in his tent and while on duty in Ireland, does nothing to diminish suspicion that the relationship which developed between Oxford and Southampton extended beyond polite verbal intercourse.

As the matter stands, there is a continuous chain of evidence that when taken in sequence, points to a homosexual relationship having occurred between Southampton and Oxford. This inference seems to be further compounded by Oxford having apparently been pressured into accepting the same remedy as that designed for Southampton. He, too, must marry with immediate effect. Queen Elizabeth was implicated in arriving at this decision.

The wedding took place quietly during the final weeks of 1591 — about five months after their engagement in July when property rights were being negotiated for the benefit of Oxford's wife in the event of his death. (Crick, 24-35). His bride, Elizabeth Trentham, being untitled was far below the dignity and expectations of Oxford's high birth, and would have been judged entirely unworthy of his family name had circumstances been different. One must therefore suppose that pressure was exerted from the highest position in the land. Only the Queen could have applied the force necessary to impel the insolvent Lord Oxford towards another period of matrimony, following the failure of his previous marriage.

The Queen's intervention may be concluded from her lack of objection to Oxford's new wife, and the release of one of her ladies-in-waiting for that responsibility. In fact she gave the pair a wedding present. Elizabeth Trentham was then about twenty-nine years of age, and the Queen's goddaughter as well as being one of her Maids of Honour. That the Queen should so willingly agree to the marriage of one of her maids was quite exceptional, and indicated just how seriously she viewed the threat of scandal. Previously, an aspiring bridegroom had been forced to elope with his bride, if she was attached to the Queen's service, and then spend a penitent period in the Tower with his wife as punishment. Oxford was the exception.

With Oxford's marriage diffusing the threat of scandal involving his illicit relationship with Southampton, there was still the problem of his confessed love for this youth in the many sonnets that were circulating amongst his private friends. These posed a problem; they could never be published.

Consequently, when it is wondered why 'Shakespeare' did not publish his sonnets, we have an answer. The risk that Oxford and Southampton would be identified through them was too great. It would also lead to Burghley having been involved in covering-up the affair to protect his reputation and his position at the head of government. When the outcome of this potential chain of events was made known to the Queen, and the threat it posed to her, she would have realised that the danger to Burghley could also extend to herself. A woman's hold on power was secured only be the men she had around her, as Lady Jane Grey had discovered to the cost of her life.

How could the scandal in the sonnets be prevented from coming out? Solution! Divorce Oxford from their authorship; engage another from the lower classes to accept responsibility for having been their author. This would also include Oxford's plays. They, too, would have to be assigned to the same person. The choice of William Shakspere for this role was relatively simple. He had played it before in 1593, when he agreed to be the poet who wrote *Venus and Adonis* and then *Lucrece*. It was therefore onto the life of this man that the entire work of a literary genius was grafted in 1598, when Meres formerly identified William Shakespeare as the author of twelve plays whose author had previously been unnamed.

It was a brilliant solution, and could not have been made without the Queen's knowledge. The public had already accepted William Shakespeare as the author of two popular narrative poems; hence, it was no great surprise to discover he also wrote popular plays. Strict censorship, and the knowledge that Oxford had agreed to this ban, ensured that those close to him, who knew the secret, would respect his wishes and refer only to 'Shakespeare' when discussing his work.

Sure enough, in *Sonnet 72*, we discover Oxford bewailing his fate to the youth, and the reason for what had happened —

> My name be buried where my body is,
> And live no more to shame nor me nor you!

Oxford understood that his desire to cheat death by empowering his name to live on through his writing had been defeated. He repeats the same forlorn realisation in Sonnet 81 —

> ... I, once gone, to all the world must die;
> The earth can yield me but a common grave.

This misapplication of Lord Oxford's literary output, by transferring it to another person, and by maintaining a firm grip on the censorship of what was published, has meant that succeeding ages have had no reason not to accept William Shakespeare as historical fact. It is also what William Camden meant when he wrote that *present powers intended to extinguish the memory from future generations*. This has caused biographies of Shakespeare to be constructed by interpolating Oxford's plays into his allonym's life. A ramification of which, has been that a rural figure with no recorded education, born of illiterate and uneducated parents and with two illiterate daughters, has been given the status of England's literary genius.

To support this contrived 'historical fact', a very blank and ordinary life has been infilled with a must-have-had education; must-have-read books in classical and modern languages; must-have-obtained knowledge of the law, and of the nobility, and of the internal politics of England, and France. So the list goes on with his 'knowledge' of botany, the sea, and the army added to hawking, hunting, sport and music. Without even realising it, biographers have added so much to this man's life that they have provided him with the upbringing of an educated, privileged nobleman; when, in fact, the documented life of Shakspere affirms the very opposite to be true.

It is not an idle thought to suppose that the powers that began this conspiracy of silence would be astounded to see the result, four centuries later. Experts in the critical acclaim of Shakespeare's plays and poetry have long been claiming to be experts in the life of the man who wrote them. But this is only made possible by interpolating the plays and poetry into the years when Shakspere was in London, and drawing whatever conclusion they can from this. Books therefore yearly fall from the press, discussing the works and the biography that have been concluded from this sixteenth-century conspiracy (see Chapter 16); but it is all smoke.

When censorship obstructs truth, truth has a way of emerging through the diligent use of cryptology. This must have been in the mind of Thomas Thorpe when he acquired Oxford's collection of sonnets.

Thorpe's first move was to refuse to print Shakespeare's name as it appeared in *Venus and Adonis* and *Lucrece*; instead, he hyphenated it.

His next move was to compose a suitable dedication. The problem Thorpe faced was one that is well known to cryptographers who have chosen to conceal hidden words within a piece of text. The cipher language, in this case the dedication, needs to be repeatedly adjusted in order that the plain-text, the secret that is being encrypted, can be read. For this reason, Thorpe's dedication has resulted in such incondite language that it has mystified readers ever since. Yet the fact is that this *'preposterous'* language reveals the existence of a secret that Thorpe wished to conceal in the hope that it would be uncovered in the future.

Hotson realised this when he announced that it was *"a cryptogram"*. But his attempt at a solution, based upon his belief that Shakspere was Shakespeare, was bound to fail. Others, no doubt, have reached the same dead end. The pity of it is that for anyone committed to accepting that Shakspere wrote Shakespeare, no reason exists for any concealment: especially in such an elaborate manner.

It was left to Dr John Rollett to confirm the existence of Hotson's cryptogram, and he did so with his 6-2-4 decryption of the dedication: THESE SONNETS ALL BY EVER THE FORTH. Rollett also discovered the name HENRY WRIOTHESLEY had been encrypted into the dedication to reveal the name of *the fair youth*.

```
                                              T  O  T  H  E
O  N  L  I  E  B  E  G  E  T  T  E  R  O  F  T  H  E
S  E  I  N  S  V  I  N  G  S  O  N  N  E  T  S  M  R
W  H  A  L  L  H  A  P  P  I  N  E  S  S  E  A  N  D
T  H  A  T  E  T  E  R  N  I  T  I  E  P  R  O  M  I
S  E  D  B  Y  O  V  R  E  V  E  R  L  I  V  I  N  G
P  O  E  T  W  I  S  H  E  T  H  T  H  E  W  E  L  L
W  I  S  H  I  N  G  A  D  V  E  N  T  V  R  E  R  I
N  S  E  T  T  I  N  G  F  O  R  T  H
```

Attention is drawn to the initials T.T. that are in alignment with the vertical and diagonal representation of Southampton's family name. The reason why Thorpe chose to initial his dedication rather than identifying himself by name is because he wished these initials to signal the validity of what a future investigation would reveal.

Some have cast doubt upon Wriothesley's name because it is broken into three parts. However, professional cryptologist William Friedman, when considering the validity of acrostics – of which this is a special type – stated that any run of five letters or more should be seriously considered. ESLEY has five letters and is adjacent to IOTH. This clustering effect, which is considered by cryptologists to signal intelligent design, greatly increases the probability that it was deliberately encoded. By using the same method of calculating probabilities as that employed by Friedman, the respective statistics for the two main parts of Wriothesley's name having occurred by chance, are: IOTH = 0.000,03 and ESLEY = 0.000,000,8. Since these two parts are adjacent, and considered to be independent of each other, their joint probability is in the order of 0.000,000,000,024, and well outside the probability of a chance occurrence.

Thorpe must have been aware that the sonnets did not name the youth who had been both the inspiration and cause of their censorship, so he encrypted it into his dedication. This caused Sir Sidney Lee to remark how the words were: *'fantastically arranged and in odd grammatical order.'* (Michell, 181).

In fact, they conceal a third secret.

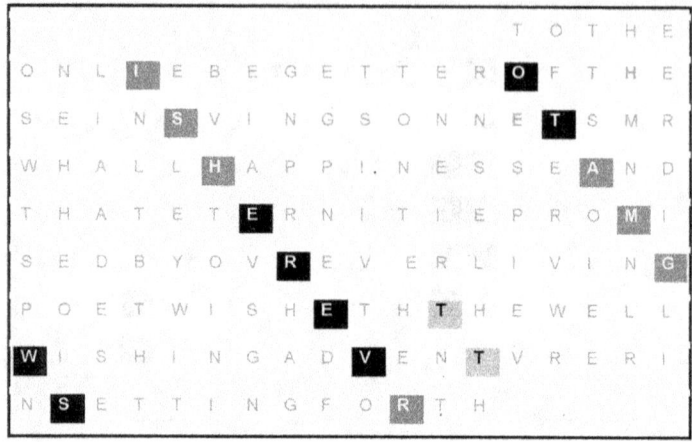

The mathematics of probability had not been developed when Thorpe published Shake-speare's Sonnets, and in order to guard against the challenge of coincidence, a second encryption indicating the same secret was deemed to be an adequate means of overcoming doubt. Thorpe's 6-2-4 encryption naming Vere was discussed on page 209. His second encrypted reference, that Vere was the author of the sonnets, occurs in an alternating 9-10 letter sequence that spells out To Vere His W.S. Gram.

Once again, note the appearance of Thomas Thorpe's initials, which have been aligned with the message. Let us therefore take a closer look at how this new tribute to Vere has been formed.

There is a perfectly acceptable objection to treating a string of letters as an anagram, and then deriving from them a phrase, or set of words that serve a set purpose. That objection does not apply in the present case. Of the 15 letters, 9 have already been positioned correctly, (TO VERE H_ _ _ _ G_A_). After H, a simple transposition of S I for I S was necessitated by Thorpe having encrypted the E **S** L E Y part of Southampton's surname. To get S into the correct position, it required that he transpose the letters I S in the word HIS, and that is why it reads HSI instead of HIS.

The transposed initials S.W. instead of W.S. are of no consequence, since either way they carry the same meaning: i.e., William Shakespeare.

Thus, of the fifteen letters in Thorpe's phrase, only 2 letters, R and M, require repositioning. Added to this, when we take into account the fact that these fifteen letters actually conform to an alternating sequence of 9 and 10 without interruption, right across the grille, the argument for coincidence is outweighed by the numerical probability in favour of the letters being there by design. And, let it be observed, the initials T.T. once again accompany the decrypted statement, as would be required of a genuine encryption.

To further explore the possibility of chance, we can again employ the percentage statistics for letter frequencies published by Beker and Piper (Singh, 19), and set them against the letters revealed by the 9-10 sequencing contained in the dedication.

**T** (9.1); **O** (7.5); **V** (1.0); **E** (12.7); **R** (6.0); **E** (12.7); **H** (6.1); **I** (7.0); **S** (6.3); **W** (2.4); **S** (6.3); **G** (2.0); **R** (6.0); **A** (8.2); **M** (2.4).

The product of these percentage frequencies is $6.3 \times 10^{-20}$ (2 significant figures), which converts to approximately 6 chances in a hundred-million-trillion trials.

Yet again, this value far exceeds anything that could reasonably be ascribed to coincidence. And when placed alongside Jonson's declaration asserting Oxford's authorship of the Shakespeare canon (see back cover: this subject will be dealt with in the penultimate chapter) with its own probability value of exceeding chance, a sound, scientific resolution of the authorship question is established, and to which future scholarship must eventually defer.

Cryptology can now be seen as a coherent response to the censorship of Oxford's work, and the attribution of his plays and poetry to William Shakspere of Stratford-upon-Avon. There were also other effects caused by this false attribution. For example, Shakspere could never intervene when *his* plays were pirated for publication. He could never be seen to write anything, as Aubrey noted, when he jotted in his notebook, that *when asked to write, he was in pain*. Nor could Shakspere tell his secret to anyone amongst his home community, for they would know at once the falsity of his claim. This would explain why his death went unremarked by the local community, and why it was ignored by the literary and theatrical world of writers and actors. It also explains the original monument erected c.1623, which showed Shakspere as a merchant (see back cover). And it explains why he was unable to bequeath any plays or books to his descendents. The future generation was in the process of having its memory extinguished, in as far as the plays and poetry of Oxford was concerned.

The merest contemplation of this having occurred is sufficient to begin providing answers to many of the questions surrounding the enigma of Shakspere's sudden emergence in London from a *'provincial nobody'* to a literary genius. It explains the insignificance of his family's illiteracy, his lack of any recorded education, the absence of any letters written or received by him, his failure to own any books at this death, the absence of any major biographical details in his plays and sonnets, his disinterest in the *stolen and surreptitious copies maimed and deformed by the frauds who exposed them*; all these, and many other problems vanish. In their place is a better understanding of the true author: a gifted writer for whom the slings and arrows of outrageous fortune led to the most marvellous outpouring of verse the world has ever known.

Consider, too, the scholastic benefit of accepting Oxford as the author of *Hamlet*. Immediately, very many biographical details fall into place. Lord Burghley had been Oxford's guardian from the age of twelve and his father-in-law from the age of twenty-one. Burghley is often recognized as Shakespeare's *Polonius*. The name is actually an epenthesis of POLUS; that is, POL-oni-US. *'Polus is thrice applied to him [Lord Burghley] in Gabriel Harvey's address at Audley End of 1578."* (Jolly, 173). Originally, Shakespeare had named the play's character *Corambis*. Burghley's motto was COR UNUM, VIA UNA (one heart, one way), whereas Corambis translates as *"double-hearted"*, A complaint must have been made, causing Oxford to choose Polonius instead. Also, the name of Polonius's servant Montano was changed to Reynaldo. Burghley's son, Robert, who was being trained by his father for later office, was a hunchback; *montano* (L. Given a mountain) seems to have been an unkind reference to this. Elizabeth's penchant for nicknames was no better: she called him *"Pygmy"*.

As a more informed class of scholarship amongst independent thinkers and scholars begins to veer towards Oxford having been Shakespeare, the pro-Shakspere lobby become more affirmative with their commentaries. Bate, for example, is adamant —

> ... it is absurd to suppose that any Elizabethan play might contain satiric references to particular aristocrats of the day. Polonius cannot be a satirical portrait of Lord Burghley for the simple reason that if it were, the author of the portrait would have found himself in prison before he could turn around. (Bate, 90)

Bravo! But untrue if the author was Burghley's noble son-in-law.

Before doubts began to surface with regard to Shakspere's credentials as a playwright and poet, scholarly opinion was more open and honest.

> "In his proper person," Froude stated in 1865, "Polonius burlesqued Sir William Cecil." The latest biographer of Cecil, Conyers Read, confirms the opinion of Froude. An eminent editor of Shakespeare, Dover Wilson, observes that "the figure of Polonius is almost without doubt intended as a caricature of Burleigh." (Feldman, 10)

To continue the analogy, it was to his son Robert that Burghley directed *Certaine Precepts, or Directions,* which were intended to guide him safely through life.

> Let thy hospitality be moderate ... Beware thou spendest not more than three of four parts of thy revenue ... Beware of being surety for thy best friends ... Be sure to keep some great man thy friend ... Towards thy superiors be humble yet generous; with thy equals familiar yet respective; ... Trust not any man with thy life, credit or estate. (Londré, 23)

Felicia Londré pointed out that these directions were not published until two years after Shakspere's death. Dr. Louis Wright, former director of the Folger Shakespeare Library admitted that it is unlikely Burghley's maxims would have been available to a commoner of Shakspere's class, prior to their publication. Yet, in *Hamlet* a similar set of *Certain Precepts and Directions* are given voice —

> Do not dull thy palm with entertainment ... Costly thy habit as thy purse can buy. ... Neither a borrower nor a lender be; For a loan oft loses both itself and friend ... those friends thou hast, and their adoption tried, Grapple them to thy soul with hoops of steel ... Be thou familiar, but by no means vulgar ... This above all: to thine ownself be true. (Act 3: sc.i).

Burghley's daughter Anne fell in love with Oxford, and they were subsequently married. The Queen approved the match. But a letter from Burghley revealed he had cherished thoughts of a different husband for his daughter. His foresight was commendable. Oxford's life style, and his distrust of Burghley soon became the cause of Anne's unhappiness, which her devotion to religion helped to assuage. She died young. In *Hamlet,* Polonius's daughter Ophelia falls in love with Prince Hamlet, and he with her. Queen Gertrude approves the match, but Polonius and Laertes try to dissuade Ophelia. After Hamlet encounters his father's ghost, his entire mood changes, and he advises Ophelia to *'get thee to a nunnery.'* Thereafter, his subsequent annoyance with her father, leads to her death.

The play also contains phrases that directly call to mind events in Oxford's life, and to which other authors have also drawn attention. On one occasion *Hamlet* cries out *'I am but mad north-north-west'.* Oxford had invested heavily in Frobisher's north-westerly voyage to Baffin Island in Canada, for which he lost a significant part of his fortune. On another occasion, the Prince confesses: *'I could accuse me of such things that it were better my mother had not borne me'* (Act 3, Scene 1). In 1581, Oxford had indeed been accused of crimes that warranted Hamlet's outburst.

> Arundell and Howard – and to a lesser extent the more subdued Southwell – churned out nearly one hundred pages of invective against de Vere, accusing him of being a liar, a murderer, an atheist, a pederast, a homosexual, an alcoholic, a practitioner of bestiality and necromancy, a traitor, a vile and unredeemable creature, and a "monstrous adversary ... who would drink my blood rather than wine." (Anderson, 167)

Elsewhere in the play, while on a voyage to England, Hamlet's ship is boarded by pirates and he is made captive before being returned to Denmark. Oxford, too, whilst crossing the English Channel, had twice shared the same experience: on one occasion, his ship was boarded by pirates, and: *'the young Earl of Oxford ... had been stripped to his shirt only six miles from Dover.'* (Williams, 1972, 252).

These are some of the noticeable parallels between Hamlet and Oxford. Academics and pro-Shakspere biographers refuse to acknowledge them as having any part in the play. What is extraordinary about this dissent is that it implicitly suggests Lord Burghley to have been too obtuse to notice what other academics have seen as patently obvious.

Apart from the name Corambis, which apparently was recognised for its satirical connotation, because it was later changed to Polonius, there were his moral maxims. Commentators have often drawn attention to these, since similar moral maxims occur in *Hamlet*. Also in *Hamlet*, Polonius is Lord Chamberlain; Burghley was Lord Treasurer. Polonius sends a servant to spy on his son Laertes in Paris; Burghley sent a servant to spy on his son Thomas in Paris. Polonius is called a *"fishmonger'*; Burghley was called *"the Fishmonger Secretary of State'* by Professor John Dover Wilson (1881-1969), because he had drafted a bill decreeing Wednesday to be an additional meatless day as well as Friday; this was intended as a means of assisting the fishing industry. Polonius's daughter Ophelia is destroyed by her love for Hamlet; Burghley's daughter Anne was ruined by her love for Oxford. The character of Polonius is described by Marchette Chute as *"a pompous talkative old man.'* (Chute, 159). In his long career, Burghley had been Principal Secretary to the Queen, Lord Treasurer and Chief Minister; his verbosity is evident in his letters, and he died a month short of his seventy-eighth birthday. Hamlet described the death of Polonius as: *"a certain convocation of politic worms are e'en at him. / Your worm is your only emperor for diet.'* (Act 4: sc. iii). This sentence is also appropriate to Burghley: 'convocation'; 'politic'; 'worms'; 'emperor', and 'diet' being the important words. Burghley was born 13 September 1520. One month later, Charles V was crowned King at Aachen and made *emperor*-elect. Charles then proceeded to Worms to attend the *convocation* that had been arranged for the purpose of confronting Martin Luther in a specially prepared *Diet*: one of the most important religious and political events of the century. Oxford was mocking Burghley with that sentence.

Ophelia's funeral is also connected to Oxford. The account of a similar funeral is described in Marguerite de Valois' *Memoirs*, which were not published until 1628, twelve years after Shakspere's death.

> Hélène de Tournon, daughter of one of the ladies in waiting on Marguerite, Queen of Navarre, died of love for a young nobleman, the Marquis de Varembon. The Marquis was not in Liége, where the death occurred, at the time of the event, and only learned of it when, returning, he met the funeral procession. ... Hélène died in 1577, but in the previous year, when Oxford was in France, she was living with her mother at the Castle of Roussillon.
> (Clark, 121)

At that particular time, the Château Tournon belonged to the Comte de Rousillon, who also held land and property in the nearby town.

For Oxford, travelling up from the south of France, this would have been an obvious choice of where best to break his journey before reaching Lyons, since Tournon lies thirty kilometres downstream from that city, and the castle of Roussillon would have provided him with the hospitality of a titled family.

Had William Shakspere been the author of *Hamlet*, the play would first have had to undergo an audition procedure before the Master of Revels, to test if it met the standard required for performance at Court. It was not left for the Chamberlain's Men to decide the form and content of plays they were to perform before the Queen. Plays were specially chosen only if they were appropriate for Her Majesty's entertainment. To have included dialogue considered offensive to religion, or to the State and its officers, would be cut out to ensure the play met with royal approval. Oxford's plays were largely the exception. Corambis had, however, been changed to Polonius to make the connection with Burghley less obvious and less offensive. For Shakspere to have been the author of *Hamlet*, the Master of Revels would have necessarily been complicit in licensing and approving it. Burghley would have noticed how he had been slighted by Shakspere, and responded by throwing him into prison. The Master of Revels, too, would have been called to account.

But given that Oxford wrote *Hamlet*, his position at Court and his favour with the Queen would have bypassed the need for much censure. Elizabeth may also be thought to have taken satisfaction at recognising herself and her courtiers in his plays. As a woman alone in a man's world, and ruler of the nation, it is an attractive thought that the occasional wry smile crossed her face at seeing her ministers caricatured: the more especially if she discerned their discomfort when recognising themselves.

First mention of *Hamlet* occurred in 1589, and was made by Thomas Nashe. The date is interesting because it was one year after Oxford's bereavement and his descent into poverty. The possibility of his having suicidal thoughts at that time is not improbable; Hamlet's character may well be voicing his actual thoughts at the time. Indeed, the tragic theme that runs through this drama could reasonably be said to reflect the emotional state in which Oxford found himself, shortly after his wife's death. *Hamlet* is an object lesson in: *"Writer, write about what you know!"*

In the *Preface to Greene's Menaphon*, entered in the Stationers' Register on 23 August 1589, which Nashe addressed directly to 'The Gentlemen Students of Both Universities', he laid the ground for modern scholars to misrepresent him: as they do, when claiming that Nashe was praising Thomas Kyd for having written *Hamlet*, or *Ur-Hamlet*, as it is referred to, so that confusion may be averted when referring to Shakespeare's *Hamlet*. Nashe's controversial phrase follows a flow of criticisms.

> It is a common practise now a dayes amongst a sort of shifting companions, that runne through euery Art and thriue by none, to leaue the trade of *Nouerint*, whereto they were borne, and busie themselues with the indeuours of Art, that could scarcely Latinize their neck verse if they should haue neede; yet English *Seneca* read by Candlelight yeelds many good sentences, as *Blood is a begger*, and so forth; and if you intreate him faire in a frostie morning, hee will affoord you whole Hamlets, I should say handfuls of Tragicall speeches. But O griefe! ... The Sea exhaled by droppes will in continuance bee drie, and *Seneca*, let blood line by line and page by page, at length must needes die to our Stage; which makes his famished followers to imitate the Kid in *Æsop*, who, enamoured with the Foxes new fangles, forsooke all hopes of life to leape into a newe occupation.

It seems perfectly clear that Nashe was praising an author who he refers to as *English Seneca*, for he twice mentions him. *"Senecan drama was familiar in the 16th cent. At a time when Greek tragedies were scarcely known; all the nine plays were translated (1559-1581)."* (Drabble, 884). Since a revised version of *Titus Andronicus* was performed in the 1580s, with its excess of bloodletting, and *Hamlet* too, at the end of the decade, Nashe's reference to Seneca: an author who *"dwells habitually on bloodthirsty details and introduces ghosts"* (ibid), seems apt.

There is also Nashe's reference to *the Kid in Æsop* to be explained. The fable refers to a thirsty goat who is persuaded by a fox's lavish praise to drink from the well in which he has become trapped. The goat enters, and the fox uses the goat to climb out of the well, leaving the goat trapped in the place he had vacated. Nashe deliberately calls the goat a 'Kid', thus alluding to Thomas Kyd. Had Nashe thought of Kyd as the *English Seneca*, he would not have ridiculed him as the silly goat in Æsop's fable.

It was Bronson Feldman who explained Nashe's reference to Kyd and his *leap into a new occupation*. It refers to the *'translation of Torquato Tasso, The Householder's Philosophy ... registered at Stationers' Hall on February 6, 1588.'* (Feldman, 5). According to Nashe, and explained by Feldman, it was through agreeing to do this translation that Kyd, like Æsop's goat, had leapt into a situation for which he was not prepared, and was then *trapped* and made to suffer the consequences.

Oxford was therefore Nashe's *English Seneca*: he having written by 1589 *Titus Andronicus* and *Hamlet*, with much bloodletting and a ghost. Kyd was the goat in Æsop's fable. But why did Kyd depart from playwriting to do translations, when his *Spanish Tragedie* had been repeatedly played to huge audiences? A clue to understanding this can be discerned in the answer he gave under torture at Bridewell. In 1593 he was arrested, and accused of having written and circulated *'divers lewd and mutinous libels.'* It was then that he confessed to having lost *'the favors of my Lord, whom I haue servd almost theis vi yeres nowe.'* But this does not answer the question of why it should have caused him to do translations instead of writing plays. That answer must surely reside with the *Lord* he served. And for this, attention turns to Lord Oxford in residence at Fishers Folly: a huge house that once occupied the site that is now Devonshire Square.

Fishers Folly, with its collegiate atmosphere, had been Oxford's home since 1580, but with the death of his wife in 1588, he was compelled to part with it. The house was huge and had proved to be an excellent dwelling place for the occupant to continue with his literary school. Oxford first began this idea at the Savoy in 1573, where he leased two *"tenements"*, and where *"deserving university students and writers could obtain lodging through an influential acquaintance. Lyly, by 1577 at the latest, was living at least part of the time at the Savoy."* (Ogburn, quoting R. W. Bond, 567).

By purchasing Fishers Folly, Oxford was able to expand upon the Renaissance idea of a master conducting the work of promising pupils, while adding the occasional master-touch. It is no coincidence, therefore, to find echoes of Shakespeare in the work of Lyly, Marlowe and Lodge: all three, according to pro-Shakspere writers, 'instructed' Shakespeare in some way or other; whereas, in fact, it was the other way round. Robert Greene, in particular, may be thought to have paid tribute to Oxford in his *Menaphon*, published the year after the Spanish Armada was defeated. In his work, Greene gave his best poetry to Melicert, the god of harbours, thus recalling Oxford's role in the defence of the harbours at Harwich, one year earlier.

To this elite group must be added the name of Kyd, who was sharing lodgings with Marlowe in 1590. His connection with Oxford throws some light upon the composition and singular popularity of *The Spanish Tragedie*. For this drama was not only performed throughout the reign of Elizabeth, but its appeal extended well into the seventeenth century; and for this, it has been *"styled the most popular of all old English plays."* It is noteworthy that *'Titus Andronicus presents and exaggerates so many of his characteristics that Mr. Sidney Lee and others have supposed that tragedy to be a work of Kyd's, touched up by Shakespeare.'* (Encyclopaedia Britannica, 11th Ed., vol. XV).

*The Spanish Tragedie* would have been written during Kyd's attendance at either the Savoy or Fishers Folly. It could also explain that without Oxford's help, Kyd was compelled to turn his attention to the translation of *Padre di Famiglia*; although without a university education, he was likely to be ill-equipped for the task; this would explain Nashe's biting comments aimed at translators —

> ... and these men, renouncing all possibilities of credite or estimation, to intermeddle with Italian Translations: Wherein how poorely they haue plodded, (as those that are neither prouenzall men, nor are able to distinguish of Articles,) let all indifferent Gentlemen that haue trauelled in that tongue discerne by their two-pennie Pamphlets.

Since *The Householder's Philosophy* was entered for publication in February 1588, it must have been worked upon in the previous year, when Oxford was in the throes of selling Fishers Folly. One may discern from this that a falling-out between Oxford and Kyd had occurred sometime previously, unless the split came when Oxford ran out of money.

Kyd never regained the popularity won by his single triumph with *The Spanish Tragedie,* and his life ended in utter destitution. He died in 1594, aged thirty-six, with his parents refusing to oversee the administration of his belongings.

*Hamlet* therefore has no place amongst Kyd's literary works. Instead, the play is a biographical sketch of Oxford's life at the time of his greatest emotional torment: a catharsis for his troubled state of mind.

# 21

## WILL. SHAKSPERE GENT. DECEASED

Faced with the very many facts that support Oxford's authorship of the Shakespeare canon, it seems almost unnecessary to continue with the life of Shakspere; for which, by contrast, the evidence is at best minimal. But his supporters are not so easily dissuaded from their beliefs.

From 1609, when Shake-speare's Sonnets were published, up until 1616, the date of his death, Shakspere is found almost entirely in Stratford. During this time a number of local records have been uncovered that provide some insight into his business activities. Nothing in these records indicates that he was otherwise engaged with writing plays or poetry. Instead they deal with what appears to be the fulltime occupation of a man of business. There are references to property, to surveys, to tithes, to freehold, to leases, to land, to a Highway bill and more, but nothing that would lead to the belief that he was writing; that is, allegedly writing *Cymbeline*, *A Winter's Tale* and *The Tempest*; of such things are dreams made on.

It will be recalled, however, that in 1612, Shakspere was summoned to appear in London to give evidence in the *Belott-Mountjoy* case (see Chapter 13). The court report does nothing to inspire confidence that this was the same man who had supposedly only recently written the aforementioned plays. His evidence was practically worthless because he was unable to remember the details that he had been called upon to give as witness. In fact, he was not even able to recall his exact age, since the recorder entered an approximation: *"William Shakespeare of Stratford upon Aven in the Countye of Warwicke gentleman of the age of xlviij yeres or thereabouts,"* (Laroque, 131).

There is one other reference to Shakspere's involvement with London during these later years, referred to in Chapter 17.

> On 10 March 1613, 'William Shakespeare of Stratford upon Avon ... gentleman' bought a house in Blackfriars ... for £140, obviously as an investment, since he never occupied it. The next day he mortgaged the property back to its previous owner for £60. (Ogburn, 33).

As pointed out, a number of curiosities exist relating to the purchase of the Gate House. Why did Shakspere purchase a house in London, when for the entire time he was active in the capital, he had lived as a lodger? The previous owner is described by Ian Wilson as Henry Walker *"citizen and minstrel of London"*, *and its "now or late" tenant one William Ireland, who gave his name to Ireland Yard."* (Wilson, 373). It may be recalled there was another Henry Walker living in Stratford at the same time, whose son William was Shakspere's godson. However, his occupation was described as a mercer.

A duplication of names occurs for a second time regarding the Gate House, when John Robinson's name appears on Shakspere's will as its resident. On the same document, the witnesses to the will, who are named at the end of the document, include John Robinson: *"Witnes to the publishing hereof, — Fra: Collyns: Julius Shawe; John Robinson; Hamnet Sadler; Robert Whattcott.'* (ibid).

None of these names are represented in the literary world of that time, nor the theatre. It must therefore be assumed that the purchase of the Gate House had been a very special investment, the reasons for which lie in the shadowy world of Shakspere's London life. Since it is accepted that the Robinson who resided in Blackfriars is the same person who witnessed Shakspere's will in Stratford, then one may surmise that the purchase of the Blackfriars property gave him an address from which to operate from. But how that benefitted Shakspere, who committed a hefty sum of money for the property, more than twice what he paid for New Place, is unlikely ever to be known.

Three years after investing in this London property, Shakspere was dead. In an age, noted for men of property writing their will upon learning that death was imminent, Shakspere is among the exceptions. Three months were to pass before his will was finalised. As Wilson admitted: *"it is still very unusual among legal documents for its large number of alterations, substitutions and interpolations.'* (Wilson, 386). One of these interpolations is the famous bequest of £5 to be shared between Heminge, Condell and Burbage. Why should this have been a last minute insertion?

Since the will took far longer than normal to complete, and because Shakspere admitted to being *"I William Shackspeare, of Stratford upon Avon in the countie of Warr. Gent., in perfect health and memorie, God be praysed,"* (Laroque, 133), it must be concluded that he did not consider his death was imminent. In which case, his advocates should at least wonder why this master of the written word did not write it himself? The misspelling of 'Shackspeare' indicates another hand was at work: one who was quite unfamiliar with the legacy of literature that this man was about to leave to the world. On the other hand, since there is nothing in the will that suggests such a legacy ever existed, the lawyer who drafted the document can be excused.

On 25 March 1616, Shakspere added some new amendments to his final testament. One month later, to the day, he was laid to rest inside the parish church of the Holy Trinity. Was his death from natural causes? One thing is certain, given that Oxford wrote the works of Shakespeare, his allonym living in retirement in Stratford upon Avon was an obstacle to publication of the First Folio. Until his death, there could be no Folio of Shakespeare's Comedies, Histories, and Tragedies. It was therefore fortuitous that in the spring of 1616, the way at last became clear for this massive enterprise to begin.

Shakspere's death caused no outside interest beyond his immediate family. He was interred beneath the chapel of the Holy Trinity Church in a plain wooden coffin. A ledger stone covered his grave, onto which four lines of absurd rhyme were later inscribed, but without identifying who lay beneath. The marvel is that this lack of interest concerning a man feted to be the greatest poet of the English language has not sown more seeds of doubt amongst the faithful. Yet, so strong is the belief that this really was the great William Shakespeare, it has overcome every logical obstacle placed in its path. Consequently, it is useless to point out that *"Francis Beaumont died suddenly of a fever in 1616 and was mourned by many, not least by his closest friend, Fletcher.* ([www.luminarium.org](www.luminarium.org)). *Beaumont was buried in Westminster Abbey.'*

It was a little more than a month before Shakspere died that Beaumont, too, had died. Though less talented than Shakespeare, he was a recognised collaborator with Fletcher. His body was brought to London and interred inside Westminster Abbey, where he was *'mourned by many, not least by his closest friend, Fletcher.'* But where was Fletcher, the recent 'collaborator' with 'Shakespeare', at Shakspere's death? Like every other writer of that time, he, took no interest in this man's death. Not one single person, poet, or actor came forward to mourn Shakspere at his passing.

Edmund Spenser was another literary giant whose last resting place is inside Westminster Abbey. At his burial, poets gathered around the coffin and cast their quills into his open grave. Ben Jonson even made plans in advance for his burial inside Westminster Abbey, where he would join the other great men of literature. And when that day came, *"his funeral procession included all of the nobility and gentry then in the town*.*'* (Ackroyd, 487, quoting Fripp). In the year following his death, *Jonsonus Viribus* was published, which included many tributes to Jonson written by his circle of friends.

Three great poets, Spenser, allegedly 'Shakespeare', and Jonson died in 1599, 1616 and 1637, respectively. Of these three, 'Shakespeare' was undoubtedly the greatest, and yet the only one of this trio to be totally ignored. David Kathman claims it was not unusual. And to back his case he names Henry Chettle (d. 1603); John Webster (d. 1625); Thomas Middleton (d. 1627); John Marston (d. 1634); John Ford (d. 1639), and Thomas Heywood (d. 1641): asserting that none of these writers attracted eulogies either. What is Kathman thinking about? Why does he believe they should have attracted the same eulogising as Spenser, 'Shakespeare', and Jonson? The men he names were satellites of these great men. They are mentioned today only because they lived at the time of Shakespeare. By naming these writers, Kathman is implicitly suggesting they were on an equal footing with Shakespeare, and because they received no tributes at their deaths, it was perfectly natural that Shakespeare should receive none either.

Kathman's argument fails on logical grounds, because he does not compare like with like. 'Shakespeare' was immensely popular at Court, and in public. Immensely poets such as he were celebrated at the time of their death, but only under normal circumstances. 'Shakespeare's'; that is, Oxford's circumstances were far from being normal.

Other pro-Shakspere scholars have a different answer; they point out that William Basse, although a lone voice amongst a throng of able writers, did acknowledge the death of Shakspere, albeit six years after his burial. That is to say, Basse refers to the *"carved marble of thine owne'* monument, which did not exist before 1622/3. He therefore could not have written about it until it existed.

In his poem, Basse pleaded that Shakespeare should be interred inside Westminster Abbey alongside the other great men of literature. But he also made sure there would be no mistaking the Shakespeare to whom he was referring, by quite unnecessarily naming the month and year in which this man died. The purpose behind this additional information was to ensure that his plea would never be mistakenly applied to the real poet who had used 'Shakespeare' as his pseudonym. As we shall now discover, Basse's verse was a deliberate ploy to achieve the very opposite effect of what it seemed to intend.

> On Mr Wm Shakespeare
> he dyed in Aprill 1616
>
> Renowned Spenser lye a thought more nye
> To learned Chaucer, & rare Beaumont lye
> A little neerer Spenser to make roome
> For Shakespeare in your threefold, fowerfold Tomb.
> . . .
>
> (Nelson, TLR: 155-6)

This was the signal that Ben Jonson was waiting for. He immediately refuted Basse's request, even though Basse's poem was unpublished; and he placed his retort in the First Folio, at the head of Shakespeare's plays, where it would be seen for all time.

> My Shakespeare rise; I will not lodge thee by
> Chaucer, or Spenser, or bid Beaumont lye
> A little further, to make thee a roome:
> Thou art a Moniment, without a tombe, (Alexander, 13)

This counter argument to Basse's plea for Shakspere to be re-interred in Westminster Abbey, and which was inserted at the front of the First Folio, as part of Jonson's personal dedication to the poet, was designed to prevent an impostor being given this burial right. The transfer of authorship had done its job, but the law of unintended consequences now meant that the man attributed with false authorship should also be honoured like other great writers, with a burial in Westminster Abbey.

This was a step too far, and Jonson must have received support from higher authority, otherwise his denial would have been ignored. In modern parlance, it was a put-up job, contrived between Jonson and Basse. Basse was acting as the *feed* so that Jonson could use his authority by responding with a measured rebuttal. There is even a suggestion that Basse only lent his name to the poem, and that Jonson wrote both verses to ensure that the rebuttal could be entered in the First Folio before it went to print.

In either case, the timing proved perfect. In 1622, by which time both verses had been written, *"The Workes of William Shakespeare'* were about to be published in what would later become known as the First Folio. These exquisitely written Histories, Comedies and Tragedies, would undoubtedly revive public interest in his work. But it was feared this would lead to calls from the masses that the author should be buried alongside the other immortals of literature; that is, in what is now known as Poets' Corner in Westminster Abbey.

Those who had known Oxford's secret life as Shakespeare were aghast at this prospect, fearing the public voice would be impossible to resist without the truth being exposed. The Jonson-Basse strategy was designed to pre-empt any anticipated clamour by pointing out beforehand that Shakespeare was too great a person for this lesser honour: he was himself a *moniment*, and in no need for stone or marble inside Westminster Abbey to make this known. Actually, if in 1623 he was such a monument, as Jonson proposed, then why had no one from the world of literature given a single thought to this 'monument' of literature in 1616?

The strategy succeeded, at least for a time; it was not until 1740 that the public got their way. In defiance of Jonson's plea, and swayed by the fawning nonsense of *Bardolatry*, the statue of a figure in the likeness of the imagined author (there are no portraits of Shakespeare, because as a flesh and blood person, he never existed) was commissioned by public subscription, and given its place inside the Abbey. And there it now stands; the imagined likeness of a man invented by 17th Earl of Oxford.

A connection between Basse and Jonson can be traced back to Lord Oxford's daughter, Bridget. In 1599, she married Francis Norris, Baron of Rycote. Among their family's retainers was William Basse. It would appear from research conducted by Ruth Loyd Miller that shortly before Norris's death in 1623, Basse had dedicated his poem *Polyhymnia* to Lady Bridget. This is likely to have drawn attention to him as a poet, and for him to have been seen as a man apt to prove compliant in Jonson's projected plan. It is conceivable that Basse was persuaded to further serve his employers by participating in an arranged poetic exchange with Jonson; an exchange of words designed to prevent the illiterate and undeserving Shakspere from becoming commemorated in Westminster Abbey through public acclaim.

Shakspere's descendents lived on, mostly in the vicinity of Stratford-upon-Avon. Anne, née Hathaway, died on 6 August 1623, three months before the First Folio was entered in the Stationers' Register. Susanna died on 11 July 1649, having lived through the English Civil War. Her husband, John Hall, had left her a widow fourteen years earlier, departing this world on 25 November 1635. Their daughter Elizabeth died childless, despite marrying twice and she was buried at Abingdon on 17 February 1670.

Shakspere's other daughter Judith, who married Thomas Quiney, gave birth to three sons; none survived beyond the age of twenty-one. Judith died in 1661 and was buried on 9 February in the same church where her mother and father were laid to rest.

Despite the passage of years and the reprinting of the 1623 First Folio in 1632, 1663, 1664, 1665 and 1685, none of Shakspere's descendants ever came forward to identify themselves with Shakespeare. Similarly, neither did the place of his birth acknowledge anything special about the man until 1769, when David Garrick arrived in Stratford to organise a three-day jubilee in memory of Shakespeare, and to present the town with a bust of their famous son to fill a niche in the new town hall.

The Jubilee included *"a masked ball, fireworks, concerts, processions and a horse race. ... [But] no performance of a Shakespeare play.'* (Holland, 90). It ended with a poetic speech from the organiser, and the first openly recorded voice of dissent that Stratford's Shakspere was not William Shakespeare.

> Garrick's ode ... spoke of Shakespeare's immortality and national significance, his exploration of nature, and his local roots. The success of the ode which praised Shakespeare as 'The bard of all bards' ... 'The god of our idolatry' ... did much to establish, if not to create, the notion of Shakespeare as a bard to be worshipped by bardolators." (ibid)

It was during the oration of this ode, the crowning moment of the Jubilee, that Garrick received a dramatic interruption: one that will be all too familiar with authorship doubters. Garrick was heckled by a person from amongst the crowd. Someone in Stratford-upon-Avon had finally spoken out to add to the dissent first voiced more than forty years earlier in 1728. *"Shakespeare,'* so the man maintained, *"was a provincial nobody.'* And in heckling mood, repeatedly contradicted Garrick with a speech of his own, which told some home truths about Stratford's former resident. (ibid).

In an effort to explain away this barracking by an onlooker during the Jubilee's closing speech, it has been claimed that the heckler was planted in the audience by David Garrick so that his *"complaining"* could be countered by the content of Garrick's ode. Not only have I yet to see a politician making a major speech that welcomed the interruptions of a heckler (in the UK they are forcibly ejected from the hall), but who in their right mind would engage a heckler to interrupt the recital of a poem?

Then again, 'Shakespeare' was a world famous figure in 1769, his statue had just recently been erected in the midst of Poets' Corner at Westminster Abbey, his plays were being performed across Europe, and the complete set of his *Comedies, Histories and Tragedies* had been published in Folio editions on six occasions.

> More than seventy issues and editions of his work appeared in his lifetime. By 1660 no fewer than nineteen of his plays had been published, and by 1680 there had been three editions of his collected plays. Theatrical reports suggest that in hard times the King's Men supported themselves by replaying Shakespeare's 'old' dramas. Other playwrights, including Massinger and Middleton, Ford and Webster, Beaumont and Fletcher, were drawn to imitate him ... Shakespeare also seems almost single-handedly to have maintained the status of the revenge tragedy and the romance. He was a hard writer to ignore. (Ackroyd, 487)

From where then did this idea that Shakspere was *a provincial nobody* arise? It arose within Stratford-upon-Avon; the place where he was born, and where the story of his secret success in London had been passed down from one family to the next. Several generations of families within the community had always known this, as the initial lack of recognition and respect at his death testified. But honesty and lack of actual evidence, other than what they had been told, governed their silence on this matter.

Only after Garrick's arrival did the burghers of Stratford-upon-Avon finally decide to join the rest of the world and accept what was commonly believed about their former neighbour. First, the Shakespeare Club was formed; then a theatre was built. But it was not until 1869 that the Theatre Royal was adapted from the Shakespearean Rooms. This was later replaced in 1879 by the Victorian Memorial Theatre.

Today, Stratford-upon-Avon is a thriving tourist town that welcomes visitors from every country in the world. It is a delightful place to visit. Understandably, residents, and those concerned with the conventional story of Shakespeare, are desperate to see that this should remain so.

## 22

## THE STRATFORD MONUMENT

Shakspere left no money for a monument of remembrance to be placed over his grave, and for six or seven years the ledger stone was all that marked his final resting place. But this dramatically changed when the First Folio was ready to go to print. The complete set of his Comedies, Histories and Tragedies would no doubt attract visitors, curious to know where this greatly admired author grew to manhood. A focal point to meet the interested visitors' expectations was therefore essential. And since visitors to Stratford would be drawn to stand by the poet's graveside, a fitting tribute in the parish church was needed. It can therefore be no coincidence that the wall monument set above Shakspere's grave was erected at approximately the same time that the First Folio was published.

The completed monument had to serve two requirements. It must meet the nodding agreement of the congregation who knew Shakspere from recent memory. It must also satisfy the outsider who knew 'Shakespeare' from the recent publication of his plays, or who had seen some of them performed on stage. The result was the monument that appears on the back cover of this book. It is the first of several that were separately drawn and engraved at different times over a period of more than a hundred years.

The figure's outward show was intended to satisfy local parishioners, who cast their eyes upon the bust as they passed by; as such, it quite clearly showed a man who had formerly been involved in commerce. Shakspere died a very wealthy man with business interests in property, wool and agriculture; hence the curiosity of the congregation would not be disturbed by what they saw.

Outsiders visiting the church would be more inclined to look at the face of the man rather than the woolsack with its four knotted corners, and their attention would quickly turn to the inscription beneath, with its Latin distich and the English sixaine that follows on from it. What they would have made of it is likely to be neither more nor less than what is made of it

## THE STRATFORD MONUMENT 267

by tourists in the present day. Why should the inscription challenge those reading it, in the way that it does? It is facile to excuse it as being similar to those found on other inscriptions. This is supposed to be an epitaph to a playwright and poet that was already acknowledged by Jonson to be a monument to the nation. Where are similar challenges to be found on the monuments of other men of greatness? There are none. In fact, almost one half of the six lines beneath the Latin distich is needed just to issue this challenge, and it has been inserted in place of the subject's biographical details, which are entirely missing from the monument.

A closer inspection of the inscription reveals a number of anomalies. Carelessness might excuse one, but to find seven is beyond any normal reasoning.

- WHOM in line 2 is spelt differently to WHOME in line 3.
- THIS in line 3 is written in full, but in line 4 it is abbreviated to Y$^S$.
- THAT is abbreviated to Y$^T$ in line 5.
- The words, SHAKSPEARE MONVMENT, have been inverted in line 3 to read, MONVMENT SHAKSPEARE.
- The name SHAKESPEARE has been spelt SHAKSPEARE
- The German word, SIEH, has been used in line 5 instead of SEE.
- WRITT has been completed with an additional 'T'.

> IVDICIO PYLIVM GENIO SOCRATEM ARTE MARONEM,
> TERRA TEGIT, POPVLVS MÆRET, OLYMPVS HABET
>
> STAY PASSENGER, WHY GOEST THOV BY SO FAST,
> READ IF THOV CANST, WHOM ENVIOVS DEATH HATH PLAST
> WITH IN THIS MONVMENT SHAKSPEARE: WITH WHOME,
> QVICK NATVRE DIDE WHOSE NAME DOTH DECK Y$^S$ TOMBE,
> FAR MORE, THEN COST: SIEH ALL, Y$^T$ HE HATH WRITT,
> LEAVES LIVING ART, BVT PAGE, TO SERVE HIS WITT.
>     OBIIT ANO DO 1616
>     ÆTATIS 53 DIE 23 AP.

The rationale for changing words in a piece of text, as explained when decrypting Thorpe's dedication at the front of Shake-speares Sonnets, is one of necessity. That is to say, sentences that conceal a hidden meaning need to be tailored to accommodate the encrypted words and phrases, but without attracting too much attention. This presents a difficulty that can only be overcome by the word-power and ingenuity of the encoder. Inevitably, with a long message, this entails certain liberties being taken with the cipher-text: a fact long recognized where decryption processes are studied. Dr David Kahn, an authority on the history of cryptology, noted this in his reference to ELS encryptions: – *'the method's chief defect, of course, is that awkwardness in phrasing may betray the very secret that that phrasing should guard: the existence of a hidden message.'* (Kahn, 879). Equidistant Letter Sequencing is the method of encoding a secret by embedding it within a piece of text, referred to as cipher-text, so that the selected letters are an equal distance apart. When these letters are placed together, they form a meaningful sentence. A similar example was briefly cited on *Foyle's War* (25/4/10), a UK, ITV drama in which a letter from an espionage agent in occupied France used every sixth and seventh word to convey a message sent back to England. The key was given by inverting the date.

This was essentially the same method employed by Thorpe, who used a sequence of each sixth, then second, then fourth word in his dedication, in order to conceal his message: these numbers coinciding with the number of letters in 'Edward de Vere', the subject of the plain text; which read: *These Sonnets All By E Ver The Fourth.*

The method dates from 1550, and was invented by Girolamo Cardano, from which the name 'Cardano Grille' was derived. It *"was certainly widely used in diplomatic correspondence for hundreds of years after its invention."* (Callery, 53).

> Small holes were punched in an irregular pattern in a piece of card, which was used as an overlay on top of a letter. This method allows for reading only single letters at a time, but it can be adapted to use larger holes so that syllables or whole words appear in the window. ... The system also requires there to be two identical copies of the stencil, or that it be sent to the receiver in some guise. (ibid 52-30)

An alternative method for creating a Cardano Grille requires that a message be composed of units forming an arithmetical sequence of letters or words. This method was used in *Foyle's War* (see above). With Thorpe's encryption, the words were equally spaced at regular intervals of 6, 2 and 4. In both cases cited above, a stencil overlay was impossible, therefore an arithmetical sequence was employed. This provided the same service, but without the risk of a stencil falling into the wrong hands.

The six-lined verse on the Stratford monument, with its suspicious inclusion of seven variations in the text, accompanied by a challenge to every passer-by: *read if you can who is placed within this monument*, implies the concealment of a name; for what else can be *read* to answer the author's challenge?

Any attempt to decrypt the sixaine is susceptible to two approaches; one of which is by observation, and the other by arithmetical methodology. The credit for discovering the first method belongs to Dr Bruce Spittle. He observed how the second line of the Latin distich has been inset. Of the eight lines making up the inscription, the second stands alone as being out of alignment with the seven remaining lines. It also leads directly onto the three couplets that follow. By counting the letters in this inset line, Spittle arrived at a total of 34. This was made possible because the author of the distich had written the Latin word, MAERET as MÆRET using the digraph Æ in place of AE, Consequently, since this inset line leads directly onto the sixaine, it is reasonable to suspect a connection may exist between them.

The inscription is also susceptible to a scientific approach. In Appendix A, a simple arithmetical method for decrypting *any* piece of cipher-text involving equidistant letter sequencing (ELS) is described. This method was recently employed to search the inscription for concealment of a name; thus seeking to answer the challenge issued by the opening words on the sixaine.

The attempt, using what cryptologists refer to as a *crib*, in this case VERE, proved to be successful, for it revealed the existence of E VERE, occurring with an Equidistant Letter Sequence of 34: the same number Dr Spittle discovered by counting the letters in the inset line.

> Once ... the code breaker has a crib: a word or piece of text that they know is already repeated somewhere in the encrypted message ... the code breaker can then search for patterns that relate to it. (Callery, 115)

Since it is known that E VERE occurs with an ELS of 34, the search for words to accompany this name can be simplified by firstly, constructing a 34-column grille containing the sixaine set out in word order. The second, logical step is to examine the seven variations in the text, which have been listed above, to discover if, or how, they affect what appears on the grille. And thirdly, to piece together any grammatical formation of words that may arise from this exercise, especially it these appear in clusters.

The result of this exercise is the following sentence.

**SO TEST HIM I VOW HE IS E DE VERE AS HE SHAKSPEARE: ME B I**

A CARDANO GRILLE, INVENTED BY GIROLAMO CARDANO IN 1550

```
S T A Y P A S S E N G E R W H Y G O E S T T H O V B Y S O F A S T R
E A D I F T H O V C A N S T W H O M E N V I O V S D E A T H H A T H
P L A S T W I T H I N T H I S M O N V M E N T  SHAKSPEARE W
I T H W H O M E Q V I C K N A T U R E D I D E W H O S E N A M E D O
T H D E C K Y S T O M B E F A R M O R E T H E N C O S T S I E H A L
L Y T H E H A T H W R I T T L E A V E S L I V I N G A R T B V T P A
G E T O S E R V E H I S W I T T
```

It is now possible to see why the words appearing vertically on the grille have been selected. They emerge as a result of the variant spelling made to the cipher text. Had this variant spelling not been present, the message would have been non-existent.

> The additional E added to WHOME has provided the E in the word TEST.
> The change of the word THIS to its abbreviated form Y$^s$ has provided the S in the word TEST.
> The abbreviation Y$^T$ has ensured the letters T, H, W, and I, each fall into their correct position.
> The transposition of SHAKSPEARE MONVMENT has provided the V in VERE,
> By omitting E from SHAK(E)SPEARE, the letters, S and E correctly align with A and H to produce AS HE.
> The letters, I and E in SIEH provide an I for the initial of Ionson's surname, and an E for the word ME.
> By adding an extra T to WRIT(T), the final E in VERE and the initial B for Jonson's first name each fall into position.

Importantly, the result of attending to these variant words has been to produce three clusters. Clusters are an affirmative sign to the cryptologist that the decrypted words are there by intent. When encoding a message of this sort, the cryptologist aims to keep the words used in the encryption as close together as possible. It is this that creates the clusters. At the same time, the encoder tries to keep extraneous words formed by coincidence as far from the clusters as possible. This 'extraneous chatter' is impossible to eliminate completely, except in the case where a stencil has been used to cover unnecessary words. Since this has not been possible in the present case, it is essential to focus solely upon the clusters created by the word variations that were responsible for their existence.

This clustering effect also allows the plain-text message to be read one cluster at a time, from left to right, in the numerical order of the leading cell; for this would have been the manner in which the plain-text was inserted.

Hence, proceeding from cell [8] **So Test** [41] **Him** [78] **I Vow** [179] **He** [182] **Is**; the second cluster begins at [53] **E Vere** [122] **de**, and the third cluster starts at [62] **As** [64] **He** [92] **Shakspeare** [133] **Me** [166] **I B**.

The initials I. B. Are the same as those that occur in the First Folio and belong to Ben Jonson who frequently wrote his surname commencing with 'I' as in the Latin alphabet in which 'J' is absent. It also seems to have been the habit at the time to identify one's self by writing 'me'. Those familiar with Shakspere's will, may recall his use of *'me William Shakspeare'*.

It will also be noticed that there is insufficient space for E DE VERE to appear in sequence, causing 'DE' to be set alongside E VERE on the Grille. Nevertheless, it is perfectly acceptable to write the name correctly. A slight adjustment to the plain-text was endorsed as permissible by the celebrated cryptologist William F. Friedman: from whom we shall hear more, further down.

> ... exceptions are made to the rules, and these permit the 'right' kind of messages to be extracted. This tactic is acceptable to the professional cryptologist only if the exceptions do not exceed a certain maximum. (Friedman, 280)

Ben Jonson's Cardano Grille, for such it may be called, confirms what has been said in the preceding chapters. Edward de Vere was Shakespeare. It also does more. It confirms that the transfer of Oxford's plays and poetry to Shakspeare of Stratford-upon-Avon was so secret: and a secret guarded just as much by Oxford, that no one dared expose it, although there were several sly and cryptic references made to it by writers of that era.

Jonson was known for his wish to be recognised by posterity as honest. And since it fell to him to write an introductory poem to the First Folio, extolling Shakespeare to the world, he soothed his conscience by using the Stratford monument as a means of revealing to some future generation the truth about Oxford's role as Shakespeare. This exonerated him from the mischief caused by the tributes that were to appear in the First Folio, and with which he was associated. An examination of these is deferred until the next chapter.

Despite the clarity and underlying logic with which the Cardano grille is presented, the avowal by Ben Jonson that Oxford was the celebrated William Shakespeare has proved too much for some. For these dissenters, it has to be incorrect: for otherwise it would they who were wrong; and to their mind, that is quite unthinkable. Objections have therefore been raised against it, but none have been anything more than off-the-cuff comments, and of no appreciable value. Several objectors adopted an ostrich pose by burying their heads in the sand and declaring they would have nothing to do with ciphers. This response may be taken as an admission of their level of intelligence: it being short of the requirement for understanding what is involved. But by far, the most frequently heard response was that the matter should be left for a cryptology journal or a professional cryptologist, in order to determine the grille's validity.

Academic protocol refuses to adopt this suggestion. Universities worldwide have accepted the English-led paradigm that Shakespeare was the man born in Stratford-upon-Avon, who ultimately became the great poet and author of that name. Consequently, no professional cryptologist or cryptology journal is willing to give time to opposing the official view. It would also render the editors or the cryptologist a target for attack by those defending Shakespearean scholarship, either on quasi-historical grounds or from literary studies. For this reason there is an unwillingness to concede that a proof could exist to overturn such a widely held opinion. And the concomitant belief that the authorship of Shakespeare's work has already been settled acts as a barrier to anyone offering contradictory evidence.

In point of fact, modern cryptology is directed towards developments made in cyberspace, the digital world, and factoring prime numbers composed of fifty and more digits. The Cardano Grille belongs to an earlier era. Before the outbreak of the Second World War – *'British cryptanalysts had traditionally been an 'old boy' and 'old girl' network of linguists and classicists chosen for their ability to solve crosswords.'* (Callery, 125). Mathematicians did not join this group until their need was realised by the intelligence centre at Bletchley Park during WWII. Fortunately, two US cryptanalysts who rose to prominence during this war have left their input concerning what is acceptable for a decoded message to be considered valid.

William F. Friedman and his wife Elizabeth S. worked together during the Second World War for the Signals Intelligence Service. At the time, the Japanese were using a code known as PURPLE. Friedman's department broke the PURPLE CODE, which enabled American Intelligence to read a decoded message breaking off diplomatic relations before the attack on Pearl Harbor commenced.

In the middle of the 20th century, fresh from being decorated by a grateful American government for his work in breaking the Japanese code, Friedman joined forces with his wife Elizebeth, to confront, and dispose of the arguments from cryptology proposed by those claiming Francis Bacon was William Shakespeare (*The Shakespeare Ciphers Examined*, Cambridge, 1957). For this, a grateful Folger Shakespeare Library rewarded the author with their annual prize.

In pursuit of their objective, the Friedman pair also laid the ground for what a valid decryption must display for it to be accepted by a professional cryptologist.

> Anti-Shakespearean "claims based on cryptography can be scientifically examined, and proved or disproved." Because of this certainty, they agreed, unconditionally, [to] accept as valid any cipher that fulfils two conditions: that its plaintext makes sense, and that this plaintext be unique and unambiguous—that, in other words, it not be one of several possible results. (Kahn, 879)

Note that Kahn states only *two conditions* are required: both of which, were confirmed by William and Elizebeth Friedman in their prize-winning book, *The Shakespearean Ciphers Examined*. So certain were the pair that these two criteria were sufficient to cover all cases, that they appended their personal assurance to that effect.

> [Providing that] independent investigation shows the answer to be unique, and to have been reached by valid means, we shall accept it, however much we shock the learned world by doing so.

So let us take the first criterion proposed by the Friedmans – the plain-text must make sense. SO TEST HIM I VOW HE IS E DE VERE AS HE SHAKSPEARE ME I B. Does this make sense? Is it grammatically correct? If both be answered in the affirmative, then it does not require the services of a professional cryptologist to give a verdict; unless, that is, those voicing doubt do not trust their own judgement concerning what is grammatical and what is not.

The second criterion states that the plain-text must be unique; it must not be one of several possible results. It is an easy matter to suppose that an inspection of alternative grilles will display some other message: one that has no bearing upon the authorship of Shakespeare's writing. However,

Professor Albert Burgstahler has proved the uniqueness of this grille by publishing the alternative grilles on his website. It is with his permission that a selection of these grilles is displayed in Appendix B. The doubting reader is advised to inspect these, to be better advised of the uniqueness which the 34-column grille displays.

From this, the conclusion is straightforward. No alternative messages lay hidden within grilles formed from the inscription on the Stratford monument. Jonson's avowal that Edward de Vere was Shakespeare is therefore unique to these grilles.

For neither of the Friedmans' two criteria did it require a professional cryptologist to observe (i) that the plain-text is both grammatical and meaningful, and (ii) that it is unique. The Friedmans' criteria have therefore been successfully met. Those persisting with their disagreement are placing themselves in opposition to the Friedmans, for they are implying that their dissent overrides the criteria laid down by a man considered to be the greatest cryptanalyst of the American people.

Nevertheless, because Johnson's avowal is of such importance, it is worth considering what else Friedman said.

> [A] valid or authentic cryptanalytic solution cannot be considered as being merely what the cryptanalyst thinks or says he thinks the cryptogram means, nor does the solution represent an opinion of the cryptanalyst. Solutions are valid only insofar as they are objective and susceptible of demonstration or proof employing scientifically acceptable methods or procedures. Namely ... observation, hypothesis, deduction, induction, and confirmatory experiment. (Sources in Cryptologic History No. 3, 'The Friedman Legacy: A Tribute to William and Elizebeth Friedman' NSA, 1992, page 22)

The Cardano Grille is a valid means for conveying important, secretive information. The plain-text message was revealed using a mathematical (that is, scientific) method that can be applied to any cipher-text in which an ELS encryption is suspected. In addition, a *crib* was used. In this same respect, Friedman also used a *crib* when he broke the Japanese Purple Code (Callery, 130). Finally, observation and deduction were both employed to note down the variant words, and their effect upon the letters that spelt out the plain-text. All of which meets the requirements that Friedman said were necessary for a decrypted message, if it is to be considered genuine. And we must not forget that Dr Spittle also found the key to the Grille in the line above the sixaine.

It is also important to understand, when referring to the Friedmans and their denunciation of the cryptology associated with claims made on behalf of Francis Bacon, that at no time then, or since, did either he or his wife attempt to investigate Thorpe's asyntactic dedication to the Sonnets; nor did they seek to answer the challenge on the Stratford monument; nor did Friedman in any of his recorded work ever add to, or discuss, the work of previous cryptologists who had written extensively upon the Cardano Grille. Yet, he was an avid gatherer of articles concerning Shakespeare's authorship, especially those referring to Oxford, as well as collecting all things cryptographic. It is therefore futile to refer to Friedman in the context of his being opposed to Cardano grilles, for he said nothing about them. Nor did he refer to Equidistant Letter Sequences.

Some interest has also been shown concerning the probability value of Jonson's avowal being due to chance. Using Friedman's method for dealing with acrostics, it is possible to compute some meaningful statistics. Taking for example, So Test, which occurs in a straight run of six letters, and E Vere which has a run of five letters, the following probabilities occur.

S (0.063), O (0.075), T (0.091), E (0.127), S (0.063), T (0.091) = 0.000,000,313

E (0.127), V (0.01), E (0.127), R (0.06), E (0.127) = 0.000,001,23

(Statistics by Beker and Piper: Singh, 19)

In layman's terms, the probability that So Test will occur randomly is in the region of 3 chances in ten million; and that of E Vere, one chance in a million. However, the one place wherein both are found is Jonson's grille, and this is without computing probabilities for the remaining words, which together comprise the plain-text message.

Closer attention to the message, *So Test Him, I Vow He Is E De Vere As He Shakspeare: Me B.I.* suggests that the author of this plain-text is referring to something that was said earlier. This implies there may be another reference to Edward de Vere concealed in the cipher text, to which this message has responded. It will be recalled that Thorpe cryptically twice embedded the name Vere in his asyntactic dedication to the Sonnets, as a means of overcoming the accusation of coincidence.

Attention is therefore drawn to the three clusters comprising the plain-text. These are joined by the words, QVICK NATVRE DIDE. The significance of this can be found within the subtle world of word play, in which words used for concealing secrets are allowed to die; that is to say, they are allowed to fade away leaving behind their first syllables. When these remaining letters are joined together, they form a meaningful phrase or sentence. Take for example, the crossword clue that appeared in the *Today* newspaper: it read: *'Diane and Edward faded away.'* The answer to which, was *Died*, since this word is produced by joining together the remaining letters of the two names, *Diane* and *Edward* after their second syllables, 'ane' and 'ward' have died or faded away.

> Late sixteenth century England was a country that provided a ready audience for dissident codes: its people were addicted to hidden meanings. Codes, devices, and punning allusions were everywhere—in street songs and ballads, conversation, poems, plays, woodcuts, portraits, jewellery, costumes. Entire buildings were constructed in the form of riddles.
>
> (Asquith, 20)

By treating QVICK NATVRE DIDE as a potential source of concealment, and translating it into one of its Latin equivalents, since Latin was the language of scholars, and Latin grammar is indicated by the previous inversion of noun and adjective; that is, 'MONVMENT SHAKSPEARE' the translation reads: SUMMA DE VELOCIUM RERUM NATURA. This reference to 'Nature' is derived from Titus Lucretius's much acclaimed work on Nature, *De Rerum Natura*, which was very popular at that time. The poem, printed in six books, described the universe according to the atomic theory proposed by Epicurus, who viewed Nature as the sum (Latin – *Summa*) of its working parts, and operating without divine intervention. Consequently, by taking the title of Lucretius's poem on Nature, and adding to it the Latin for 'Quick', it becomes *De Velocium Rerum Natura*. Next, by adding 'Summa' to qualify the insertion of 'Quick', we obtain *Summa De Velocium Rerum Natura*. Now, if these Latin words are viewed after they have 'DIED', or faded away, as with the Diane-Edward example, we obtain: SUM DE VE RE NATU, which combines to form, SUM DE VERE NATU: or, in English, **I AM DE VERE BY BIRTH**. This provides the perfect antecedent to Jonson's avowal; thereby confirming the name of the person he identified as HIM. It also provides the opportunity for the following response: **SO TEST HIM I VOW HE IS E DE VERE AS HE SHAKSPEARE: ME B.I.**

By repeating the encrypted name VERE, but using a different method of encryption, Jonson has employed a strategy of repetition: this stratagem was intended to overcome objections that the message was coincidental. Even so, more than one person has objected to this message on the dubious ground that it requires the decoder to insert punctuation and to separate adjoining words. Since website addresses are written in a similar fashion, and require no more than a modicum of intelligence to understand their construction, it is left to the reader to wonder why that same modicum of intelligence was missing from the dissenters, when confronted by evidence that Oxford was Shakespeare. Is this some form of defence mechanism against accepting a truth, in which they had no part?

In point of fact, Ben Jonson, for it was undoubtedly he who wrote the Latin distich and the three couplets of cipher-text, anticipated that doubts and objections would soon ensue, once the monument's decrypted secret became public knowledge: so great had been the suppression of de Vere's authorship. Realising this would be difficult to overcome, despite his personal avowal that it was true, he issued his challenge – SO TEST HIM if you still don't believe me.

The foregoing chapters have done exactly that; they have tested Oxford to see if the claim that he was the author of Shakespeare's plays and poetry holds true. For this exercise, Oxford has been tested to see if his plays contain incidents that he had personally experienced. – They do. He has been tested to see if the Sonnets bear any relationship to the shame and censorship attached to his having been their author. – They do. He has been tested to see if any fellow writers indicated, however covertly, that they were aware he was Shakespeare. – Some did. He has been tested to see if Thorpe's enigmatic dedication to the Sonnets refers to him – It does. He has been tested to see if Greene's Groatsworth of Wit applies to him. – It does. He has been tested to see if one half of the ambiguities that occur in the First Folio refer to him. – They do, as will be demonstrated in the next chapter. He has been tested to see if Sweet Swan of Avon applies to him. – It does. He has been tested to see if the plays allegedly written, or co-written, after his death can be dated before his decease. – They can. He has been tested to see if the Stratford monument, that iconic symbol of his allonym's claim to authorship, conceals the truth about his having been the immortal Shakespeare – It does. In fact, it actually adds to the revelation already made above by means of the Latin distich.

The Latin distich, with its references to three figures from antiquity, was designed so that each of the three named persons confirm a part of the myth relating to the sack-bearing figure that Dugdale and others drew and etched for publication in the 17th and 18th centuries (see back cover).

Jonson's first choice, Nestor King of Pylos, was the mythical character described by Homer as having fought at Troy. This same individual also makes a rather lame appearance in Shakespeare's *Troilus and Cressida*. In the play, Thersites refers to him as: *'old Nestor, whose wit was mouldy ere your grandsires had nails on their toes,'* [act 2 sc. i, 106-7]. And again: *'that stale old mouse-eaten dry cheese Nestor ... is not proved worth a blackberry'* [act 5 sc. iv, 10-12]. Jonson eagerly seized upon this 'JUDGMENT OF NESTOR', from Shakespeare's own pen, and used it to form the first line of his Latin tribute, *viz.* IVDICIO PYLIVM.

This comparison can scarcely have been intended as a compliment to Shakespeare; for, by comparing Nestor to the bust situated immediately above the distich, the myths surrounding the Pylosian King automatically become associated with the figure of Shakspere. It is just the first step to what follows.

Jonson's next names Socrates. But, whoever thinks that Shakespeare was another Socrates either knows nothing about this philosopher, or nothing about Shakespeare. The 'GENIUS OF SOCRATES' has nothing remotely in common with the genius of Shakespeare. Nevertheless, Jonson has deliberately used this philosopher for the purpose of finding a comparison, *viz.* GENIO SOCRATEM.

What, then, has Socrates in common with Shakspere? From what we know of Socrates, the one thing that defined him, apart from his reasoning ability via inductive arguments, was the *fame attributed to him by others*. This was necessary because *he wrote nothing himself*. Socrates's wisdom only became known when Plato published impressive dialogues that described in detail Socrates's powerful ability to analyse problems in order to arrive at the truth. This was achieved by Socrates adopting a probing question and answer process; it had nothing remotely to do with the prose, poetry, or drama of Shakespeare.

Consequently, the picture being built up by this Latin distich is one of Shakspere being likened firstly to the mythical figure of *Nestor*, and then to *Socrates*, who wrote nothing but achieved undying fame through the report of others.

The third figure from antiquity is Virgil. But, by comparing the 'ART OF MARO' (Maro was Virgil's surname) with that of Shakespeare, Jonson was ignoring the fact that this Roman's *'influence on the dramatist was negligible.'* (Price, 145)

> L. P. Wilkinson, in the best book we have on Ovid, reminds us that Shakespeare echoes him about four times as often as he echoes Virgil, that he draws on every book of the Metamorphosis, and that there is scarcely a play untouched by his influence.
>
> (Nims, introduction)

Jonson was a classical scholar and would have been aware of this fact. He would have also known that in the sixteenth century, a biography of Virgil had been published in Holland, claiming that a spirit, whose identity was kept a carefully guarded secret, had been forced to transfer its gift of poetry to Virgil. *Een Schone Historie Van Vergilius*, 1552. (Brewer, 1276-77).

The reason behind this unlikely tale was religious. Virgil was a pagan, having been born before Jesus Christ. To make his work acceptable reading for Christians, a story was invented that described his personal triumph over the forces of darkness, and this proved very popular in continental Europe.

This tale also bears a striking resemblance to Shakspere's sudden emergence from obscurity to one of literary acclaim; from having a history divorced from poetry to a future in which his name resounded through the fame of 'his' verse. The story associated with Virgil therefore allows anti-Stratford scholars to claim that Shakspere too received a 'poetic gift', which quickly elevated him to his place of honour. And, in line with Virgil's biography, Shakspere kept the identity of his benefactor a closely guarded secret, so that he could be acknowledged as an author.

Jonson's Latin distich therefore complements his Cardano grille by covertly signalling the truth about the man in the monument. It confirms Shakspere to have been in every possible respect the merchant figure that was portrayed in books about Shakespeare during the seventeenth and eighteenth centuries.

By the nineteenth century, William Shakespeare had become such an icon for the British people that it was impossible to allow *'the Curious Original Monument and Bust'* (Matus, 200) to continue in its original though renovated form. This engraving by Reynolds Grignion (d. 1787) shows the monument as it appeared after major restoration work was carried out from funds raised in 1746. Note that the features have been *'beautified'* in line with instructions given to the restorer. This was when John Ward's band of players visiting Stratford-upon-Avon were so appalled at seeing the monument's decay (cf. Rowe's print) that they put on a special performance of *Othello* to raise the money needed for its repair. Grignion's plate was copied for a volume of Shakespeare's plays by John Bell in 1786 (Price, 176), although Bell's first volume appeared as early as 1774. The words below the central corbel identify the artist by name. The caption beneath the picture reads: *"Shakspere's Monument in the Church at Stratford upon Avon'*. This, therefore, represents a genuine declaration of its veracity.

The monument, now ravaged by time and having suffered damage, was eventually replaced in the mid 19th century with money raised by public subscription, and this has resulted in the statuary presently on display. It is currently described as a fine —

> ... polychrome sculptured monument set on the chancel's north wall, within a few feet of his grave. Set against a background of white marble, with black marble Corinthian columns, and black touchstone panels, surmounted by the earliest surviving example of usage of the Shakespeare arms, appears a painted bust of Shakespeare, made of Cotswold limestone.
> (Wilson, 397)

The need for its replacement had become apparent by 1814, when an attempt to remove it for a plaster cast to be made, revealed that it was in such a decayed and dangerous state that to remove it again would threaten its destruction. This raises the question – whatever happened to this plaster cast? A genuine copy of that *curious monument*, after it had been *beautified*, would settle many questions concerning what the original looked like. But nothing has been heard of it since that report. Like all evidence capable of challenging the Shakespeare paradigm, this, too, has disappeared.

In 1849 plans went ahead for a public subscription. *'The King subscribed £50, the Borough of Stratford the same. Many sent their subscriptions 'only for the restoration and preservation of the Monument.'* (Stopes, 121). At its close, the total raised was £5,000. But, *'The cost of restoring both the Shakespeare Monument and the Chancel'* was initially estimated to be only £1,210. 12s.

Some commentators, for example Professor Alan Nelson, maintain that the present monument is the original one. This ignores the restoration work that was needed in the 18th century, and the £5000 collected from King and country for its repair a century later. It is totally absurd to suppose that the Stratford committee embezzled the money donated for the monument. Moreover, with such an excess of money available, and the monument risking destruction just by moving it, the logical conclusion to draw is that the present monument dates from the middle of the 19th century.

The design for the new monument was chosen to resemble the idealised drawing made by George Vertue in 1723. He arrived in Stratford-upon-Avon to sketch the monument for its inclusion in Alexander Pope's edition of Shakespeare's plays. But his engraving, which appeared two years later, shows the frustration he must have experienced at seeing the decaying remnants that Nicholas Rowe had faithfully reproduced in his edition of Shakespeare's plays sixteen years earlier, and which Sir Thomas Hanmer would repeat nineteen years later when compiling his own eight volume edition of *Shakespeare*. All of Hanmer's thirty-six plates were engraved by Hubert Gravelot (1699-1773). Sandwiched between these two editions, and in obvious protest, Vertue designed his own ideal monument, which some people desperately wish to believe was the only real copy of the original ever drawn.

> George Vertue was enchanted by the Chandos portrait and when he was commissioned to provide a drawing of the Stratford monument for Pope, he took the liberty of substituting the Chandos head for the one on the monument ... in every other respect, Vertue's illustration depicts the monument we see today. (Matus, 204)

Vertue's illustration showing the figure holding a quill and paper was in all likelihood based upon a similar monument inside the Tudor church of St. Andrew Undershaft in the City of London. This shows the historian John Stow (1525–1605) at his desk, with quill in hand, penning his *Survey of London*, (1598).

Vertue's engraving was to become *the blueprint* for a new monument which, by 1814, had become so fragile that to even remove it would *threaten its destruction*. Unfortunately, the folly of idolatry is that it is insensitive to reason. Professor Alan Nelson, writing 380 years after its emplacement, was still able to declare it to be as good as new, save for a new coat of paint: *'the Stratford Moniment ... which survives unchanged from the original except for its surface paint.'* (Nelson, 156). Diana Price was another similarly affected. In her 1997 article, *Shakespeare's Monument Reconsidered*, she discussed the different monuments that appeared in print between 1656 and 1786, and concluded that Dugdale had made very serious errors, and these were repeated thereafter by artists who copied from his original. Once again the quickness of the word deceives the mind. By digging deeper, an entirely different picture emerges.

> Dr Whitaker has told us that Dugdale's 'scrupulous accuracy united with stubborn integrity' has elevated his Antiquities of Warwickshire 'to the rank of legal evidence.' (Greenwood, 9)

The Encyclopaedia Britannica (1973) took a similar view:

> Sir William Dugdale ... one of the most distinguished antiquaries ... He was a pioneer in the technique of historical research and his works display an accuracy and insight of unusual order for this period.

Thomas Betterton, the foremost actor of his day and a man especially distinguished in society for his integrity, visited Stratford purposefully to gain what information he could for Rowe's edition of Shakespeare's *Life*. For Price, or indeed anyone, to then infer that Betterton, having supposedly seen the monument Vertue would later draw, nevertheless affirmed to Rowe that it was the same as Dugdale's picture, while knowing that Rowe was having a new plate engraved for his book, is a negation of reason in favour of pure imagination.

MONUMENT ENGRAVED FOR ROWE IN 1709

MONUMENT DRAWN BY VERTUE IN 1723

The Reverend William Thomas was a doctor of divinity and the rector of St. Nicholas Church, Worcester. His parish was within easy reach of Stratford-upon-Avon. It was Thomas who was responsible for the second edition of Dugdale's *Antiquities* published in 1765, which is notable for the corrections he made to the first edition.

The Antiquities of Warwickshire Illustrated; from Records, Leiger-Books ... Tombes ... The second edition ... printed from a copy corrected by the author himself, and with the original copper plates. The whole revised, augmented, and continued down to this present time; by W. Thomas, D.D. (British Library Catalogue)

Thomas actually admitted having *'visited all the churches'* prior to editing the reprint of Dugdale's *Antiquities* (Title page, ix). He had therefore witnessed the same monument that Vertue drew earlier, and which was published in Pope's edition of Shakespeare's plays in 1725; yet he accepted Dugdale's version, after having visited the church and seen it personally.

The original Stratford monument was designed as a cryptic structure. As such, it had a unique function. To members of the congregation, it was seen as a curious reminder of the man they had known for his wealth and his business dealings. To visitors seeking the grave of 'Shakespeare' the inscription offered some satisfaction. But concealed beneath this facade was a hidden motive for its emplacement. It told the truth about the man to a third section of people: those who would one day challenge the received opinion that this was the bust and memorial of William Shakespeare.

Because of the appearance of the original monument, conventionalists believe it to be inaccurate; it is natural they would, but they are misguided. It is also incorrect to suppose it was ordered by Shakspere's wife, although she died shortly before it was put in place. The obscure Latin references defeat the suggestion that Shakspere's family had anything to do with it. Pylos, Socrates and Maro would be expected to defeat the understanding of even a moderately educated person of that age. Greek culture did not become available in England until the sixteenth century. It is also interesting to note that no objection was ever raised concerning these supposedly inaccurate pictures of the monument that appeared in the 18th century. Three were printed from different plates. It is unreasonable to believe that pictures of William Shakespeare in merchant pose would have ever been commissioned and published had they not conformed to the existing bust at Stratford-upon-Avon. Admirers of Shakespeare's genius would have rebelled, as they rebel now, at what they saw, and ensured that Dugdale's error was never repeated.

## 23

## THE FIRST FOLIO

The First Folio was published in 1623 and is noticeable for the tributes that precede the plays. Amongst these is one by Leonard Digges.

> Leonard Digges ... was an Oxford scholar; he was the stepson of Thomas Russell whom Shakespeare made the overseer of his will. Leonard Digges and his elder brother Sir Dudley Digges must have known Shakespeare, as Dr Hotson has shown, on familiar terms.
> (Alexander, Vol. 4: 9)

Hotson was correct, but for the wrong reason. In his poetic tribute, Digges began by addressing his subject as 'SHAKE-SPEARE', capitalised, and in its hyphenated form. This was in contrast to the title of his tribute in the line above, where the heading reads, MAISTER W. SHAKESPEARE. Why did Digges write the name in two different forms on adjacent lines? The answer must be to draw attention to it, for that is what it achieves. It does not prove that Shakespeare was a pseudonym, but its hyphenated form adds to what has already been shown previously: it was a penname.

Particular note should also be made of Digges's archaic use of 'Maister'. The reason for this was because Digges required equally archaic meanings to be applied to his poem as a whole, especially to the third line, which reads: *'And Time dissolues thy Stratford Moniment.'* By writing 'Moniment' – the archaic spelling for 'monument' [*Chambers English Dictionary*, 1989 p.928] – Digges was adopting the use of an older form of English for which the word had an alternative meaning.

    b. "Something serving to identify;"

    3.a. "An indication, evidence, or token (of some fact). Now *rare*."    (OED)

Through Digges's use of 'moniment' with its archaic definition, he was also able to create a link with the Shake-speare monument at Stratford. So that when he employed the verb, 'dissolve', also with its archaic definition, *'to resolve (as doubts, riddles; arch.)'* [*Chambers* p.112], he had in mind a time when the *moniment* would *serve as a sign*, and its *riddle* would *resolve doubts* about the true identity of the man he referred to as Shake-speare. It will not have passed notice that Shakespeare experts are apt to cite Digges's reference to the *Stratford Moniment* as proof positive that he was referring to Shakespeare's Stratford origin. It is equally clear now that this was not so.

Digges's subtle duplicity in writing firstly SHAKESPEARE and on the next line SHAKE—SPEARE suggests that what Hotson called *his being on familiar terms* with Shakspere had more to do with persuading him to write out his will than any conviviality between them.

It will likely have been Digges who called upon his stepfather to become involved as an overseer to Shakspere's will. It also appears that some form of coercion was used to persuade Shakspere to make out his will. Perhaps he had been reassured that he could always rewrite it at a later date. Since, judging by the time it took to finalise his list of bequests, it does not appear he had given much thought to the subject before then. And why should he have done? The writing of a will was usually left to the days when ill-health compelled the reluctant testator that there was no further time for delay. Shakspere, however, declared himself to be in *"perfect health ... God be praysed"*.

It is a little known fact that the tribute written by Digges was not his first choice for inclusion in the First Folio. He had actually written a much lengthier poem that he intended should appear in place of the one written by Ben Jonson. But it was rejected, and it did not appear until 1640, five years after his death, when it was printed in a publication containing Shakespeare's Sonnets.

> To complete the historical picture presented to us by the contributors to the First Folio, it is necessary to reproduce the following lines which were designed for a place in that publication, but rejected for reasons we can well understand. (Alexander, vol. 4: 20)

> > Poets are borne not made, when I would prove
> > This truth, the glad rememberance I must love
> > Of never dying Shakespeare, who alone,
> > Is argument enough to make that one.
> > First, that he was a Poet none would doubt,

Arthur Neuendorffer's untiring search for possible encryptions, which add to those presently discovered, has revealed one by Digges that can now be added to those made by Thorpe and Jonson. His discovery was that ME E VERE is present in the seventeenth column of an ELS of 18, and that it commences with the very first sentence of Digges's dedication, which was intended for inclusion in the First Folio.

Because of the media used to convey the truth about Edward de Vere, "Shake-speares Sonnets", the Stratford Monument and Digges's poem intended for the First Folio, they were each in their own special way, time capsules, and likely, to survive destruction; with the expectation that one day they would reveal the truth to an astonished and doubting people.

```
P O E T S A R E B O R N E N O T M A
D E W H E N I W O U L D P R O V E T
H I S T R U T H T H E G L A D R E M
E M B E R A N C E I M U S T L O V E
O F N E V E R D Y I N G S H A K E S
P E A R E W H O A L O N E I S A R G
U M E N T E N O U G H T O M A K E T
H A T O N E F I R S T T H A T H E W
A S A P O E T N O N E W O U L D O
U B T
```

**ME E VERE**  or quite possibly  **ME E DE VERE**

Since de Vere's name emerges as a possible encryption within the very first sentence of his poem, it greatly enhances its authenticity. The first line is also about proving the truth of Shakespeare, albeit that he was born not made. And, recall, this was intended for inclusion in the First Folio. Added to which, there is the fact that the plain-text message occupies the 17th column, which was also the number of de Vere's earldom. As to whether the additional ED was intended to be transposed into the name, it is not possible to say with absolute certainty, and this is left for the reader's judgement.

With regard to the probability of ME E VERE being present due to a random occurrence; then, were it an acrostic, and according to Friedman's method of assessment, its value would be: 0.000,000,003,749,04 ; that is, approximately 4 chances in a billion trials. But, as it is an ELS covering 132 letters, discounting the part that refers to ED, the probability is reduced. This is because the 7-cell sequence could occur in any column of grilles composed between 7 rows by 19 columns and 61 rows by 2 columns. Effectively, this means there is an increased possibility of it occurring by chance in any one of approximately 1200 seven-cell spaces. However, by placing the encrypted phrase in the opening sentence, with an ELS of 17, Digges has made this a leading consideration, with what we now know is an extremely high probability against it being a chance occurrence.

Digges was not the only contributor to the First Folio who addressed Shakespeare by hyphenating his name. Another who did so, identified by the initials, I. M., is assumed to be James Mabbe, a fellow of Magdalen College. This may be doubted; Cambridge University was already well represented by Hugh Holland of Trinity. John Marston, representing the world of the theatre would seem a more likely choice. In fact, Marston's name had previously appeared alongside that of Holland's when commending Jonson's publication of *Sejanus*; added to which, he had once before used the hyphenated form of Shake–speare in a title; viz. *To the Memorie of M. W. SHAKE-SPEARE*, it would therefore be natural for him to re-use it in the First Folio, where, once again, it was directed at Oxford's pseudonym: *'We wondered (Shake–speare) that thou went'st so soone… "*

The plaudits appearing in the First Folio seem to follow a logical pattern. Leonard Digges and Hugh Holland represent the two great English universities Oxford and Cambridge, and John Marston, who like Ben Jonson, gave only his initials, presented his tribute on behalf of the theatre. Indeed, his poem is all about the theatre and its response to the author's death.

Marston had also written *Scourge of Villainy*, which definitely includes a coded aside to Oxford. Recall: *'Most, most of me beloved, whose silent name / One letter bounds. Thy true judicial style / I ever honour.'* Marston then referred to this unnamed poet as *'my love'*; which, all told, makes him better qualified to be the I. M. of the First Folio than James Mabbe. Mabbe seems to have played no part of any consequence whatever in the biographical accounts of Shakespeare, and is excluded from the majority of indices.

Jonson was the man closest to Oxford, as both a poet and a playwright, and it fell to him to act as the director and master of ceremonies when writing a leading tribute for the prefatory material in the First Folio. In this capacity, he began by penning ten lines of verse beneath the engraving of William Shakespeare's *imagined* face, drawn by Martin Droeshout, and it is this that confronts the reader upon opening the volume of plays. But Jonson's words cut both ways.

Jonson had been taught by bitter experience to temper his style of writing after spending two terms of imprisonment for his part in penning *The Isle of Dogs* (1597), and *Eastward Ho* (1605).

> In the Isle of Dogs affair, he paid for his indiscretion with seven weeks' imprisonment, an experience that led him to 'temper' his style thereafter so that his targets were more ambiguous ... [that is] by blending allusions ... that could not be identified exclusively with specific victims. (Kay, 20)

What, then, are these ambiguities and anomalies that occur in the tributes made to 'Shakespeare'? And are there not, at the same time, to be found many straightforward expressions of fact that apply to Shakspere and that could apply to no one else but he? A careful analysis of the letters and poems that precede the thirty-six plays in the First Folio answers these questions. But first there is Jonson's verse to be considered. This occurs beneath the Droeshout engraving of Shakespeare, although he refers to it rather dismissively by exclaiming: *'Reader, looke / Not on his Picture but his Booke.'*

Another curious expression occurs when Jonson admits, *'This figure, that thou here seest ... was for gentle Shakespeare cut.'* In other words, it was *for* Shakespeare, not *of* him. The difference between the usages of these two words is one of truth; 'for' in the present case is ambiguous, but 'of' is specific, and has been avoided.

To this, we may also add Jonson's use of the word 'brass', which he employs twice in the space of three lines.

> O, could he but haue drawne his wit
> As well in brasse, as he hath hit
> His face; the Print would then surpasse
> All, that was euer vvrit in brasse.

What is Jonson alluding to that has been *written in brass*? Engravings, such as that made by Droeshout, were *etched* on copper. However, if Jonson was using the word 'brass' as a synonym for 'effrontery', then *writ in brass* does make sense, *if* applied to Will Shakspere, since he had adopted the role as the face of Shakespeare with shameless, effrontery.

In which case, Jonson has used *brass* in the same context that Oxford used the word in *Love's Labour's Lost*.

Berowne:   Can any face of brass hold longer out ?   (Act 5, sc.ii)

This passage is given in the *O.E.D.* as being the first example of the expression, where it is defined as, *'insensibility to shame: hence, Effrontery.'*

It is with this that we come to the Droeshout drawing that so dismayed Jonson, although the numbers are legion that have also been dismayed by it. Martin Droeshout was the son of Flemish immigrants living in Southwark, close to the Globe. He had yet to obtain a reputation in society when the drawing of Shakespeare was completed, and this seems to have been the reason for his commission. No artist of repute would have wished to give their name to what was being asked of the artist.

But, given that Shakespeare was Oxford's penname, this proved to be a decided advantage, because it was never intended that the figure at the front of the First Folio should be identified as either William Shakspere or Edward de Vere. Had Droeshout portrayed either of these two men, then on the one hand, it would have eventually alerted residents in Stratford-upon-Avon, who knew this man to be the father of two illiterate and uneducated daughters, as well as being the son of John Shakspere and Mary Arden, neither of whom could read or write: although this was a common enough feature in those days. On the other hand, for Droeshout to portray Oxford would be to give reality to the satirical joke mentioned in the Parnassus Plays, in which Gullio says, *'O sweet Master Shakspeare! I'll have his picture in my study at the court.'* Identifying Shakespeare in a portrait, as a live person was therefore impossible. It will be noted that there are no known portraits of this man, contrary to other writers and actors who lived during the Jacobean age.

Droeshout was simply another tool in the ongoing plan to leave a consistent trail of misrepresentation wherever Shakspere was concerned. And his drawing achieves that goal admirably.

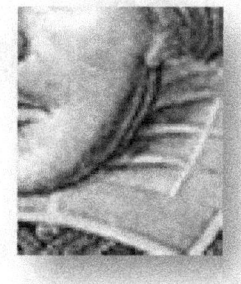

In the past, several commentators have drawn specific attention to the unnatural line that extends from beneath the chin of the figure upwards to the lobe of the left ear. It has been suggested that this was intended to represent the outline of a mask. Its visage would then belong to Will Shakspere, with Oxford's face concealed behind it. But the face Droeshout has drawn is not that of Shakspere. The face known to his family must be accepted as having a close resemblance to that which appeared on the Stratford monument, and the face drawn by Droeshout is quite different. Apart from which, Shakspere's face would have been too easily recognizable by the local community where he grew up, had any one of them seen it in the First Folio.

Since the visage is not that of Shakspere, and it cannot have been that of Oxford: whose face is it? The answer is William Shakespeare's; the man Oxford called *"my invention'* when he wrote the dedication for *Venus and Adonis*, and whose *persona* was assumed by the previously unknown Shakspere. In short, it is a symbolic cartoon. It was intended to represent a person that never actually existed in flesh and blood. Despite this, the figure definitely lends itself to a number of symbolic features.

To begin with, Oxford, using the penname William Shakespeare, and operating in secret behind the façade of Will Shakspere, fits the Droeshout drawing quite well, with the evidence for this interpretation occurring on the portrait. Principally, it is the doublet that the figure is wearing, which commands most attention. For apart from the fact that the garment is expensively embroidered and of a type worn only by gentlemen of the upper classes, to which Shakspere did not belong, the right sleeve is without doubt the rear view of the left arm. In reality, this would be attached to the left side of the back panel of the same garment, which is actually the case in the Droeshout drawing. Consequently, one half of the figure's attire appears to have its back turned to the viewer, while the other half of the figure is facing forward, as one would expect in a picture of this type.

The factual aspect of the divided doublet was confirmed by expert opinion and published in two trade journals, *The Taylor and Cutter* (March, 1911), and the *Gentleman's Taylor* (April, 1911). Both agreed the figure of Shakespeare was drawn from a composition of the front and back halves of the same doublet.

> Gentlemen's Taylor, as long ago as 1911, had commented that the tunic "is so strangely illustrated that the right-hand side of the forepart is obviously the left-hand side of the back

part and so gives a harlequin appearance to the figure which it is not u nnatural to suppose was intentional, and done with express object and purpose." (Ogburn, 173)

In other words, the doublet is displaying the Janus effect. One half is intended for the figure facing forward, the other half is there to suggest what would be seen if its back was turned away from the observer.

The collar, too, is of interest. Until quite recently, it was believed to be a unique example. However, research conducted by Derran Charlton at Wentworth House, resulted in the discovery of a portrait found in a two-centuries-old book referring to the Wentworth family. It showed Thomas Wentworth, 1st Earl of Strafford (1593 – 1641), wearing a starched, pleated collar that is virtually identical to the one drawn by Droeshout; the obvious difference being that Shakespeare's collar shows no observable means of fastening. By contrast, a ribbon tied in a bow secures that worn by Lord Wentworth. The strange lack of any means for securing the collar in Droeshout's picture therefore gives it the impression of being a shield. Presumably, this was intended to send a signal to the more intellectually aware that the subject was indeed being protected. And since it is the head

that is held by the shield, seemingly detached from the body, it suggests the role played by 'Shakespeare', was separated from the protection he was receiving from the bodily form of Will Shakspere.

To pursue this line of thought further, attention is drawn to the fact that the head of the figure is too large for the body. Art connoisseurs have had no difficulty in arriving at the same conclusion. The result gives the figure's head an appearance of detachment, and this allows it to be seen floating above the torso, as if these two parts were separated.

This previous reference to the Janus effect, as suggested by the divided doublet, directs attention back to the thick unnatural line beneath the chin. It, too, suggests a dividing line, as with the two faces of Janus. In that case, the forward-looking face represents the public image of Shakespeare; the hidden face is that belonging to Oxford: turned away to conceal his identity from the public. Sufficient evidence taken from the drawing does indicate that the two faces of Janus was Droeshout's model, especially since: *'Janus, a dual-faced god, presided over all that is double-edged in life;* "(Gray, 56); exactly right for portraying the dual faces of Oxford and Shakespeare.

An opportunity to correct this impression was certainly available to the editors and producers of the *Poems Written by Wil. Shake-speare, Gent.* and published in 1640. The book contained William Marshall's reproduction of the Droeshout engraving (see front cover). But with the artist having  declined to alter either the Earl of Strafford's collar, or the shield-like effect it gave. The doublet, however, was altered so as to give the figure a more conventional appearance; but to this, the engraver added a shoulder cape, typically worn by gentlemen of nobility, and a sprig of hyssop, which was then popular, because of its fragrance in combating the stench of London's streets. Oxford can be seen wearing a similar cape in a picture showing him holding the *great dagger* that Nashe had mentioned to Harvey, to confirm who was meant by his anagram of 'Will Monox'. But most interestingly, both the 1623 and 1640 pictures of 'Shakespeare' break the Sumptuary Laws governing dress code in England during the sixteenth and early seventeenth centuries.

> In Elizabethan and Jacobean England, strict dress codes known as Sumptuary laws were well known by all the people. The penalties for violating sumptuary laws could be harsh. Heavy fines could be imposed for dressing out of one's class. The Renaissance culture required that everyone dress according to their status. ... Noblemen were allowed to wear a doublet of embroidered cloth ... According to Tarnya Cooper, curator of sixteenth-century portraits at the National Gallery in London, "the clothing a person wore was seen as a true reflection of his social status ... Only men above the rank of gentlemen could wear a cape over their clothing." (Cooper, 114); (Hamill, 20)

The strategy of both artists is most apparent. Martin Droeshout has shown his 'Shakespeare' in the *embroidered cloth* worn by a nobleman, while William Marshall, in the edition of 1640, depicts his 'Shakespeare' as being *above the rank of a gentleman* by adding a cape to his figure's apparel (see front cover). In their own particular ways, each artist has confirmed the silence that surrounded Oxford's authorship of the Shakespeare plays and poems, by revealing sufficient clues to indicate their subject belonged  to the rank of a nobleman in the Court of Queen Elizabeth and subsequently King James.

One feature of Marshall's drawing remains unanswered. Why did he think that the sprig of hyssop was necessary? There is no indication in the picture that this was required, since the portrait is devoid of any suggestion of an open air background, where this would be more natural to a sensitive nobleman unused to the smell of the city. The answer lies in the interesting fact that in the sixteenth century and before, hyssop was a similar shrub to what was called in the French language, 'belvedere'; viz. *'belvedere is a shrub that grows to a man's height ... full of pleasant green boughs resembling branches of Hysope.'* (Dictionary of the French and English Tongues, Randle Cotgrave, 1611). The word, bel – ve – de – re, with one very simple transposition, and when written in English, becomes 'Noble de Vere', thus identifying the extravagantly caped figure.

Marshall may have been acting under the guidance of Leonard Digges's friends when he redrew the picture of Droeshout's Shakespeare. Digges was *'a perfect understander of the French and Spanish, a good poet, and no mean orator.'* (James Mabbe, Wikipedia). Digges's poem with its encrypted ELS of 18, was also designed to reveal 'ME E. VERE' or even 'ME E. DE VERE', in the opening line (as referred to above), and this follows on from the caped figure of 'Shakespeare', for such is the encrypted form of Oxford's family name appearing in: *Poems Written by Wil. Shake-speare, Gent.*

The 1640 book also rearranged the order of the sonnets, setting them into groups, so that they appeared as complete poems. John Benson, the owner of the copyright, which he somehow acquired after Thorpe's death, also altered the pronouns in a number of sonnets to make it appear that Shakespeare's 'fair youth' was really a woman. However, it is again to the frontispiece of this book that we return. Beneath Marshall's drawing is a poem, as there is in the First Folio: but curiously, it begins by repeating phrases from Jonson's opening tribute to Shakespeare (*Soule of the Age! / The applause! Delight! The wonder of our Stage!*): and then changes two of the exclamation marks to question marks, while also adding a third to Shakespeare's name. Elsewhere, the lines also borrow heavily from Jonson's poem.

> This Shadowe is renowned Shakespeare's? Soule of th'age
> The applause ? delight ? the wonder of the Stage.
> Nature her selfe, was proud of his designes
> And joy'd to weare the dressinge of his lines.
> The learned will Confess, his works are such,
> As neither man, nor Muse, can prayse to much.
> For ever live thy fame, the world to tell,
> Thy like, no age, shall ever paralell.

The question marks are specific to just these three declarations. The first occurrence suggests questioning Marshall's figure of Shakespeare, which the poet calls a 'shadow'. The same word occurs in *Measure for Measure*. And we can see, again, how faithfully Digges has followed Jonson in presenting this edition. Where Jonson used the word 'brass', in order to connect with its same meaning of effrontery, as occurs in *Love's Labour's Lost*, Digges follows with a connection of his own:

Duke: Go you to Angelo; answer his requiring with a plausible
obedience ... that the time may have all shadow and silence in it;
and the place answer to convenience: this being granted in
course, now follows all. (Act 3: sc.i)

Given that Digges knew Shakspere was Oxford's allonym, then he would have been aware that *plausible obedience* was *required* when *answering* questions about Shakespeare; *that the present time* was *shadow and silence* regarding the truth of what had been concealed, *and the place*, Stratford-upon-Avon, *answered to convenience*. From which, *in the course* of events, *all follows* from this: — which, seems fair comment regarding the switch that occurred when Shakspere assumed responsibility for Oxford's poetry.

The second and third question marks cast doubt, respectively, on the 'applause' and the 'delight' attributed to Shakespeare. Digges has again hit the mark. Oxford was looked at with disdain by his fellow peers, because of his attachment to the stage. Audiences may well have applauded his work and taken delight at his poetry, but it was not to Oxford that they directed their admiration; it was to Shakspere, hence the question marks.

With the Droeshout and Marshall pictures each showing Shakespeare attired as a member of the nobility, it is time to take a sceptical view of the prefatory material in the First Folio. To do otherwise would be to deny the evidence that justifies this.

It is with this in mind that we encounter the letters allegedly written by Heminge and Condell. Heminge was a grocer, an actor and a business manager for the King's Men; Condell was an actor. Biographers willingly inform readers that these two men, alone, were responsible for discovering the whereabouts of old plays going back thirty years, as well as more recent ones over the past twenty years, and then acquiring recent ones: some of which had never before been published, and some that had never even been heard of before 1623. This would have been a time consuming occupation. Trained scholars with financial freedom have spent large parts of their lifetime engaged in similar pursuits. Heminge and Condell had families to feed, and an income to maintain. Where did they find the time? From where did they obtain plays that were unknown until they appeared in the First Folio? If the King's Men owned them, why were these plays not performed first, before being published?

All such problems are brushed aside by biographers, and the bald fact is presented to the reader that thirty-six plays were gathered together by Heminge and Condell. They then edited them. In fact they admit to this when they say:

> ... we pray you do not envie his Friends, the office of their care, and paine, to haue collected & publish'd them; and so to haue publish'd them, as where (before) you were abus'd with diuers stolne, and surreptitious copies, maimed, and deformed by the frauds and stealthes of iniurious impostors, that expos'd them: euen those, are now offer'd to your view cur'd, and perfect of their limbes; and all the rest, absolute in their numbers, as he conceiued them. (Alexander, 12)

Editing thirty-six plays would be intellectually demanding, and very time consuming. From where did they obtain this unpaid time? Moreover, neither man had any previous experience of what was required to edit a play and restore missing parts. As far as it is known, their education had been rudimentary. Heminge's ability lay in account books, not in editing play books. Acting lines written by another while under direction does not confer editing ability.

An equally pertinent question that is never asked, presumably because there is no answer is — If Heminge and Condell had this ability, then why did they not publish some of the plays earlier? Why did they allow these plays to be *stolen, maimed* and profitably *published* by *the frauds of injurious imposters*? The answer to this, but ignored by Shakespeare experts who refuse to admit the plays were written by the Earl of Oxford, is that he could do nothing about the theft of his plays without identifying himself as their author. As a result, Shakespearean scholarship becomes burdened by yet another unlikely event: the existence of which, among so many others, would normally inform a reasonably intelligent person that the increasing number of questions involving Shakespeare, with unsatisfactory answers, must be the result of some crucial error in the reasoning leading to them.

Turning again to the letters signed by Heminge and Condell, the following statement stands out: *'he not having the fate, common with some, to be exequutor to his owne writings.'* Ben Jonson was executor to his own writings, which he published midway through his career. Had Shakspere been the author Shakespeare, then he would most certainly have been at leisure after his retirement to Stratford-upon-Avon, to have accomplished this task. The sentence does not prove Shakespeare was the penname of Oxford, but its presence adds to the cumulative evidence that this was so.

Interestingly, in the second of their letters, Heminge and Condell emphasise the same sentiment by repeating it. Those doubting Shakspere's authorship may see this as a covert signal to contradict belief that it was Shakspere they were talking about. *'It had bene a thing, we confesse, worthie to haue bene wished, that the Author himselfe had liu'd to haue set forth, and ouerseene his owne writings.'*

The third problem with accepting that Heminge and Condell were responsible for collecting and editing the thirty-six plays attributed to Shakespeare is one of finance. Both men had families to provide for. Between them, their wives gave birth to twenty-four children, although not all survived. Publishing the First Folio was such a huge undertaking that the financial outlay would have been beyond their means. It was also a venture fraught with difficulties from the beginning, and apt to fail at any time before completion. The loss suffered from this publication is estimated to have been between £2340 and £5340. (In today's money, this averages at nearly two million pounds). Heminge and Condell could not have sustained this loss; therefore they were not responsible for the publication of the First Folio. The wills of Condell who died in 1627, and of Heminge, in 1630, give no indication of any absence of wealth. They were untouched by this massive loss. If money talks, then it emphatically states that Heminge and Condell were merely following their trade as actors, or role players, in an enterprise funded and organised by wealthy sponsors, eager to ensure that this literary gift to the world would survive into the future.

> Four master printers and their men worked for two years setting up the type for the First Folio. The total cost of this edition has been estimated at between three and six thousand pounds. Only six hundred copies were sold, at twenty-two shillings each, hence someone took a staggering loss. (Benezet, 108)

There is also the problem of editorial practice. Both men were in charge of this publication. Yet, they allowed those contributing to the memory of Shakespeare to repeatedly hyphenate his name. Why did they not edit it? They allowed Droeshout to produce a picture of Shakespeare that bears no likeness to the one inside the Holy Trinity Church: the appearance of which must have received the nodding assent of his family and neighbours; they did nothing to correct Droeshout's divided doublet; yet they allegedly exercised enough power to reject the poem submitted by Digges: a man who came from such a highly respected and titled family that it is difficult to understand how this lower class pair of actors could have exercised their authority over him. In summary, the evidence for Oxford having been Shakespeare is now so compelling that extreme doubt is called for when arguments are proposed to contradict this.

Foremost in importance amongst the tributes paid to Shakespeare is Ben Jonson's praise. It consists of forty couplets, but without divulging a single biographical fact that is attributable to Shakspere; ambiguities are another matter.

Jonson's tribute commences with nine couplets: each serving as an introduction to what follows. The tenth quickly refutes the plea made by William Basse that Shakespeare be allowed to share a tomb at Westminster with Chaucer, Spenser, and Beaumont.

Basse's poem, it will be recalled, was strategically written shortly before the First Folio was published, and it gave Jonson just the time needed to make his reply public, and thus pre-empt any future attempt made by the popular voice, urging that Will Shakspere be interred amongst the great men of literature. Perhaps Jonson also had in mind his own death one day, and had no wish to share eternity with an impostor whom he had once ridiculed as the clown, Sogliardo (*Every Man Out of His Humour*).

A little further down, Jonson writes several curious lines.

> For, if I thought my judgement were of yeeres,
> I should commit thee surely with thy peeres,
> And tell, how farre thou didst our Lily out-shine,
> Or sporting Kid, or Marlowes mighty line.

This is to admit that had Jonson's judgement been conditional upon time (why should it not have been?) he would have placed Shakespeare amongst the men of literature who had once been his peer group; he named these men as Lyly, Kyd and Marlowe.

John Lyly (c.1554 – 1606) was for many years a secretary to Oxford, and subsequently his theatre manager. While lodging at the Savoy, a tenement that seems to have been funded by Oxford for the benefit of promising writers, Lyly produced the much acclaimed *Euphues The Anatomy of Wit* (1578), followed by *Euphues and his England* (1580); this second book was dedicated to Oxford. Both works gave rise to a style of expression known as 'Euphuism', for which, Oxford became its leading exponent.

It was while in his position as Oxford's secretary that Lyly wrote a number of plays for boy actors to perform at Court. Amongst which are counted: *Alexander, Campaspe and Diogenes, Sapho and Phao*. But note! *"The attractive songs in the plays, including such well known lyrics as 'Cupid and my Campaspe played' ... it is doubtful to what extent they are the work of Lyly."* (Drabble, 595). When one calls to mind the equally *'attractive songs in the plays'* of Shakespeare-Oxford, the connection becomes obvious.

Thomas Kyd's single triumph, *The Spanish Tragedie*, written during the first half of the 1580s has already been examined, and its composition at Fishers Folly under the guiding hand of Oxford is referred to above. Kyd's relationship to Marlowe, the third person named by Jonson, was admitted during his arrest, when he confessed: *"My first acquaintance with this Marlowe, rose from his bearing name to serve my Lord, although his Lordship never knew his service, but in writing for his players."* Here again is an oblique reference to a nobleman, a Lord, and to his writers, of which Marlowe was one amongst several.

One suspects it was Lyly who first arranged for Marlowe to meet Oxford. Both he and Lyly were from Canterbury. It would therefore be natural to suppose that upon arriving in London, Marlowe made contact with his fellow countryman in the hope of finding suitable employment. An introduction to Oxford's writing group at Fishers Folly may therefore be inferred. This would satisfy Kyd's remark that Marlowe was writing for the players of an unnamed Lord.

Let it also not be forgotten that Marlowe was a guest of Oxford in company with Nashe and Greene when they dined together at a banquet held in the late summer of 1592, prior to 'William Shakespeare' being launched as the author of *Venus and Adonis*. Marlowe was therefore a close member of Oxford's group of writers and confidants.

Jonson's reference to Lyly, Kyd and Marlowe being the natural peers of Shakespeare now makes better sense, because it can be understood as a reference to Oxford. And it is this that takes us to the next part of Jonson's verse.

> And though thou hadst small Latine and lesse Greeke,
>   From thence to honour thee, I would not seeke
> For names; but call forth thund'ring Æschylus,
>   Euripides, and Sophocles to vs,

The opening remark is ambiguous. It can be read, firstly, as: 'And *although* you had very little Latin and even less Greek...' thus seeming to imply Jonson's superiority in recognizing that 'Shakespeare's' early education had been inadequate to prepare him for the plays he was to later write. Most pro-Shakspere writers prefer this interpretation, for it allows them to cock a snoop at Jonson, and protest their own man's command of the classics, which they then point to in Shakespeare's plays and poetry.

The alternative interpretation is to read the phrase with the word *though* as 'Shakespeare' used it, meaning *if* in *As You Like It*. In the play, Rosalind remarks: *"Leander, he would have lived many a fair year, / Though Hero had turned nun."* (Act 4: sc.i). Jonson's line then reads 'And *if* thou hadst small Latin and less Greek…' thus allowing the poet to have had an education on a par with that of Jonson. This makes uncomfortable reading for Shakspere's advocates, since Jonson's education at Westminster School is well documented, whereas Shakspere's schooldays in Stratford-upon-Avon require very special pleading to overcome his father's descent into poverty, and a need for William to help with the family business.

Professor Gervinus who wrote a scholarly account of Shakespeare's erudition believed that Jonson certainly intended his comment to be a tribute to the poet's command of the classics.

> This poem consists throughout of such boundless, well-nigh extravagant praise of Shakespeare that I do not believe that the line, 'And though thou hadst small Latine and lesse Greeke,' can be interpreted as detracting from his merits. The spirit of the whole passage is this: 'And even though thou hadst small Latin and less Greek, yet is there in that bygone age no lack of tongues to sound thy praise; for even Æschylus, Sophocles, and the rest would render a tribute of admiration to the power of thy words.' (Gervinus, 939)

Towards the end of Jonson's dedication, and with nothing biographical to precisely identify the man vaunted as the supreme genius of the written word, these oft-repeated lines occur; which, we are told, fill the void.

> Sweet Swan of Auon! What a sight it were
> To see thee in our waters yet appeare,
> And make those flights vpon the bankes of Thames
> That so did take Eliza and our Iames !

William Shakspere, being a native of Stratford-upon-Avon, is naturally the principal contender for the intended meaning of this expression. If this were the only truth behind Jonson's meaning, then little more could be said. But Jonson has gone to extraordinary lengths to be ambiguous in whatever could be construed as applying to Shakespeare. Moreover, as explained earlier, The Avon, to which this line refers when Oxford is its intended recipient, is then seen as the river Avon in Wiltshire, whose waters still flow past Wilton House, reviving distant memories of Oxford and his compositions while staying as a guest of Lady Pembroke.

In summary, although the First Folio dedications are part of several mainstays supporting Shakspere as William Shakespeare, the foundation upon which this support stands is logically insecure. The ambiguities in Jonson's choice of words are frequent, and together with the lack of any uniquely applicable details relevant solely to Shakspere, these attenuate the force of argument supporting the conventionalist view. Also to be considered are the number of instances in which the hyphenated form of Shakespeare's name occurs, and by whom they were made. There are also the comments made by Heminge and Condell, which, more realistically, are applicable to Oxford. Altogether, these shift emphasis away from the man popularly thought of as Shakespeare, and onto Edward de Vere, for whom proof of authorship has already been set out in several different forms.

# AFTERWORD

Since writing *Proving Shakespeare*, for which this is in part a sequel, a summary, and an opportunity to expand upon what was previously put forward, the authorship controversy has continued to move on. Like all proofs that counter former 'certainties', this too has been no different in dividing those already certain in the knowledge of Shakespeare's identity.

Despite the fact that *Proving Shakespeare*, as with this book, includes four different proofs that pertain either to Shakespeare's true identity or the impossibility that the man born to John and Mary Shakspere wrote the works he has been credited with, attention has concentrated upon just one: the Cardano grille. Many wrote congratulating me upon the discovery. These, I was able to ascertain were professional people: usually with a background in the sciences. They easily recognised the improbability of the clustering formation of the message having occurred by chance alone, especially when comparative grilles were examined, showing a buckshot splattering of disconnected words spread randomly across each surface.

What intrigued these correspondents was the lack of acknowledgement from Oxford support groups that had been formed to establish precisely what Ben Jonson was avowing to be true. More than one dissenting voice mumbled the name Friedman, as though calling up his spirit offered protection against cryptographic solutions. Presumably, it was the dissenters' opinion that if the Friedmans were still alive, they would dispose of Jonson's avowal that Edward de Vere was Shakespeare. The ignorance behind this nonsense resides in the fact that the Friedmans wrote nothing about Cardano grilles, or about equidistant letter sequencing. It is therefore a pointless exercise to call upon their name, unless it is to adopt the criteria they laid down for the acceptance of a genuine decryption. In which case, Ben Jonson's enciphered avowal passes the test they proposed with consumate ease.

The response from conventionalist thinking was predictable. Leopards do not change their spots, and a lifetime of uncritical acceptance of the man the 'faithful' were taught to believe was William Shakespeare, coupled with enjoying the rich pickings to be had from adding to the speculative myths about the man, required no effort at all on their part in ignoring anything that contradicted this comfortable world of make-believe.

Unfortunately, since peer-reviewed journals are populated by the same people, the opportunity to spread the news to a wider audience becomes stifled at birth. Professor James Shapiro acknowledged this as fact when referring to – *"Those who would deny Shakespeare's authorship, long excluded from publishing their work in academic journals or through university presses, are now taking advantage of the level playing field provided by the Web, especially such widely consulted and democratic sites as Wikipedia.'* (Shapiro, 2010: p.7).

This, I discovered, does not only apply to literature and Shakespeare studies, but infects the sciences as well. Dr Michael Brooks reported that *"biologists suppress reports of homosexual behaviours in the natural world. ... Others admitted documenting homosexual behaviour in animals but not publishing until they had tenure.'* (Brooks, 148). The dispute concerning the fluoridation of the public water supply is another example. Again, it concerns how easy it is for vested interests to exercise control over the publication of research data, whenever it draws attention to the harmful effects of fluoride. Nobel Prize winner, Brian Josephson, met with the same obstacle when attempting to publicize research results that seemed to contradict our understanding of physical law. He advised – *"You have to look properly at the evidence typically blocked from publications ... and few people are willing to do that ... it's also hard to change how people think. People have vested interests, and their projects and reputations would be threatened if certain things were shown to be true.'*

Riding upon the crest of this trend, Professor Shapiro, a Shakespeare expert teaching at Columbia University in New York, published *Contested Will*. His purpose was, as he announced to the Shakespeare Guild in New York – *"to shut them up once and for all"* and *"show how they don't know how to evaluate evidence.'* That, at least, was his intention when he began writing his apologia for Will Shakspere's right to be seen as the immortal Shakespeare. This was to be combined with a joint attack on the claims made for Bacon and Oxford. The idea had apparently originated at a get-together with Stephen Greenblatt and several others, at which it was decided that a book should be written to finally settle the authorship 'conspiracy'.

Did Shapiro succeed? Quite the reverse, his book revealed the shallow level of scholarship that supports (his) belief in Shakspere as having been William Shakespeare. His evaluation of evidence amounted to no more than accepting specious statements without investigating further to see if there was a hidden depth to them. This kind of unquestioning acceptance was precisely what was expected of people in Tudor England, when the *conspiracy* that William Camden declined to write about, had already begun to operate.

Attention has previously been drawn to errors that appear in Shapiro's book, where his desire to *show they don't know how to evaluate evidence* had the unfortunate effect of seeing him hoist by his own petard. It was remarked in Chapter 5, how Shapiro had asserted that the hyphenated form Shake-speare, was necessitated by the printer's need to separate the 'k' from the long 's' when typeset in *italic* font. It was then pointed out, apart from the obvious fact that an 'e' already separates these two letters, that printers used a 'spacer' for this purpose. Moreover, the hyphenated form of Shake-speare is not limited to italic font; it also occurs in Roman font and in capitals; e.g. SHAKE-SPEARES SONNETS.

Shapiro's second error was to wrongly assert that it was Shakespeare who first wrote his name in its hyphenated form, when he appended his name to the dedication addressed to the 3rd Earl of Southampton in *Venus and Adonis*. This assertion is false. The name William Shakespeare appears beneath the dedication, un-hyphenated and in non-italic font. Were it not for the fact that Shapiro is a perfectly honourable man, it would be easy to suppose that he had been inventing evidence to support his apologia for Shakspere's authorship.

It was remarked in Chapter 19 that it is possible to 'prove' anything by omitting evidence that contradicts the 'proof'. When Shapiro wrongly cited *Venus and Adonis* as a means of contesting the hyphenation of Shake-speare, and allowed this to weigh on the side of his evidence for Shakspere, he omitted to mention that *Venus and Adonis* has the inexplicable feature of being *'the first heir of [Shakespeare's] invention'* – a Warwickshire man – that contains not a single word in the Warwickshire dialect; as was ascertained by Appleton Morgan in *A Study in the Warwickshire Dialect*.

> "William Shakespeare had been, up to his eighteenth year, a resident of Stratford-upon-Avon, a Warwickshire village, where were spoken a dialect and a patois quite as distinguishable from other British dialects [sic] as from the urban English. For this Warwickshire boy to have achieved the plays was one thing, the most miraculous miracle of genius heaven has vouchsafed mankind. To have written the poem *Venus and Adonis*, however inferior to the plays, genius itself would have been inadequate without the absorption of certain arbitrary rules of composition and the learning by rote of the existence of certain arbitrary trammels and limitations of diction, vocabulary and prosody ... it is absolutely impossible that the lad Shakespeare acquired or used any other dialect than the Warwickshire he was born to, and that his father, mother and neighbours spoke."
>
> (G. Goldstein quoting Appleton Morgan)

This leads to further peculiarities that may also have been omitted, and which could erroneously support those claiming that the Warwickshire lad was William Shakespeare. Especially since his earliest poem (if it were his), extends to just short of 1200 lines, yet contains not one single word in the dialect he spoke at the time of its composition. This must be something that Shapiro desperately needs to explain, if his apologia is to have any sort of credibility amongst an intelligent readership.

Shapiro was also aware that the composition of *Hamlet* is often cited by Oxford's advocates for its portrayal of certain characters, as though they had been modelled on Lord Burghley and his family. Shapiro's response to this is similar to that of others, who have been forced to defend Shakspere against Oxford's authorship of *Hamlet*, and he uses J. T. Looney to make his case.

> Looney didn't understand that Edmund Tilney, the Master of the Revels, whose job it was to read and approve all dramatic scripts before they were publicly performed, would have lost his job – and most likely his nose and ears, if not his head – had he approved a play that so transparently ridiculed privy councillors, past and present. Looney's scheme also defies common sense, for Lord Burghley was dead by the time *Hamlet* was written, and nothing could have been in poorer taste, or more dangerous, than mocking Elizabeth's most beloved councillor soon after his death, on stage or in print. (Shapiro, 201)

This argument is popular within Shakespeare cacodoxy, and likely to receive instant agreement from those of that persuasion. It also highlights the difference between Professor Shapiro, whose excellence in the field of teaching the work of Shakespeare is undoubted, and Professor Shapiro the authorship dilettante. In the latter case, his account is once again riddled with logical error.

To begin with, he begs the question regarding the date when *Hamlet* was written. Oxford's supporters, whom he is criticising, accept that both internal and external evidence suggests the play was written c. 1587-88, when Oxford's emotional plight was at its lowest ebb and likely to have been similar to that of Hamlet's.

Shapiro is forced to concede that *Hamlet* is recorded in Henslowe's diary for a performance given on 9 June 1594, alongside *Titus Andronicus* and *The Taming of A Shrew*, also in the month of June. And that even before then, a reference to *Hamlet* was made by Thomas Nashe in 1589, when he referred to – *"whole Hamlets, I should say handfuls of Tragicall speeches"*. Shapiro's only response to this is to lamely beg acceptance for a second play of the same name, written by an unknown author, and it was this to which Henslowe's entry referred. Shapiro has added to this presumption by implicitly agreeing that this other *Hamlet* must also have contained *handfuls of tragical speeches*. As a conjecture, everything about it rests upon Shakespeare not being Oxford, or anyone else other than Shakspere; it also has no basis in fact. It is an invention by 'experts' to defend their belief. But in doing so, yet another inexplicable fact becomes added to those that abound when factual evidence contradicts a 'required fact'.

Shapiro's further error is to assume that the Master of Revels failed to see the connection between Burghley and Polonius, when every scholar since then, with a competent awareness of Burghley's biography, has mentioned this similarity without hesitation. Even a dissenting voice like that of Alan Nelson, in his bilious treatment of Oxford's documented life, could not avoid quoting historian Lawrence Stone (*Crisis of the Aristocracy 1558-1641* Oxford, 1965, p.582), thus implying that he too recognised the truth of what Stone said.

> A personal recklessness of behaviour ... grew up [amongst] a whole new generation of high-spirited young aristocrats in open rebellion against the conservative establishment in general and Lord Burghley [i.e., Cecil] in particular. Very many, like Oxford, Rutland, Southampton, Bedford, and Essex, had been wards of the old man and were reacting violently against his counsels of worldly prudence. Such a development is hardly surprising. To listen to Polonius for a few moments in a theatre is one thing; to have to put up with him pontificating at every meal-time for years on end is another. (Nelson, 35)

Is it reasonable to suppose that Edmund Tilney was blind to this, when it was his job to be hawk-eyed in ensuring that such caricatures were never made public? Of course not, and this leads to Shapiro's next oversight. Tilney would never have ventured to censor anything Oxford wrote for the Queen's entertainment. If he did cast his eye over the plays Oxford wrote, as suspected, then the most he would have done would be to question a piece of dialogue that might invite the Queen's disapproval; or that of an important courtier. Since Oxford and Burghley were family, and titled, Tilney would have had to tread very carefully. Quite likely this happened when the name Corambis was changed to Polonius; and again in the *Henry* plays, when Oldcastle was changed to Falstaff.

Shapiro's next error is to misunderstand the class system that operated in Tudor England. Oxford's seventeenth earldom outranked Burghley's baronetcy; moreover, Burghley could never take action against his former son-in-law without also disgracing the father of his favourite daughter's three children, who had been placed under his care since the death of their mother. His only recourse would therefore be to complain to the Queen. But Elizabeth had a fondness for Oxford's poetry, witness the sonnets addressed to her as *you* instead of *thou*, and she enjoyed his entertainment: especially if it brought discomfort to members of her all male counsel when they recognised themselves as characters in one of his plays. To maintain favour, Oxford always ensured the Queen would recognise herself as the heroine.

Shapiro's arguments against Oxford's authorship of *Hamlet* reside in their superficiality. If the extract is read quickly, the reasons given appear sound, but dig deeper and they fall apart. Nor is this a unique example. It is a failing of minds quite brilliant at working on the artistic content of Shakespeare's plays, but much less adept when that same talent is directed at a different and much deeper level of reasoning. A gold medal won for show jumping does not mean the rider would make a champion jockey. When Shapiro writes about Shakespeare's art, he is a prize winner; when he writes about the authorship problem his errors are embarrassing.

One of the problems for this disparity is that conventionalist thinking never sees the need to remain up-to-date with the latest findings in authorship studies, preferring to believe that the position they hold in academia is sufficient to authenticate what they have to say. While this may be true for literary studies, it is very far from being correct where authorship research is concerned. The two activities are separate, and being separate they are distinguishable, with each requiring different skills.

In a more positive light, since writing *Proving Shakespeare*, Professor Albert Burgstahler, who attended a convention in China in 2007, was given the opportunity of lecturing to audiences at several universities on the subject of William Shakespeare and the controversy in the west over his alleged authorship. His own researches into the theory first advanced by Ralph L. Tweedale (1904 – 1977), together with the evidence from Jonson's Cardano grille, were met with enthusiasm. As a result of this presentation, the International and Academician Forum of Shanxi Agricultural University published the Burgstahler lecture in full, as part of its centennial celebrations. The English version is currently available on Google via "KU ScholarWorks – Shakespeare Authorship".

In Germany, Kurt Kreiher published *Der Mann, der Shakespeare erfand: Edward de Vere, Earl of Oxford*, which was met with considerable academic acclaim, and was favourably reviewed on the continent. The book included the proof, but only in part that I had first advanced, based upon Henry Peacham's date of 1574, as it appears on the Titus manuscript. Sadly, the author's attempt to justify this proof using different reasoning was marred by an error concerning Greek numbers.

In March 2010, after a period of 57 years, the Cambridge University Press advertised its republication of *The Shakespeare Ciphers Examined*, by the celebrated cryptographers, William and Elizabeth Friedman. In the last century, this book had been responsible for putting an end to the Bacon Society' s hope of proving that the plays of Shakespeare contained hidden codes identifying Bacon, as Shakespeare. The Friedmans' book examined the Society's claims and demolished them, one by one.

The Folger Shakespeare Library, clearly pained at being upstaged by the Bacon codes, had been instrumental in encouraging the Friedmans to inspect these codes, following a lecture given by Friedman at the Folger in 1951 (*A Cryptanalyst Looks At Literature*). As a result of the Friedmans' efforts, William was awarded the Folger prize of $1000 for his contribution to literature.

All of which raises the question why, after more than half a century, has the Friedmans' book been reissued? The answer can only be that in the space of the last few years, a number of alleged codes have appeared purporting to establish the Earl of Oxford as Shakespeare; one of these is the Cardano grille, asserting that Edward de Vere was Shakespeare, and which has been certified with Ben Jonson's initials. The Cardano grille also conforms to the criteria that the Friedmans said were imperative for the validity of a genuine cipher.

It must therefore have been the belief of whatever moving force lay behind the reissue of Friedmans' book, that with a suitable preface by a well qualified person of distinction, the threat posed to conventionalist belief by the appearance of this new wave of alleged ciphers would share the same fate as befell the Bacon Society, and that the Oxford ciphers would be delivered a *coup de grâce*.

But there was no book in March 2010. Instead, it was promised for April. April came and April went: still no book. The new date for its publication was to be May. But May passed, and any hope of seeing the book went with it. In June, the publishers promised the book would be available by the 16th of the month. It was another false hope, the date was later cancelled. July has now become the promised month as this book goes to print. But with one week left, and again nothing, August now beckons.

The republication of an existing book for a company with the resources of Cambridge University Press is less than a week's work; writing a suitable preface seems to have been the stumbling block. The possibility exists that Ben Jonson's Cardano grille has proved to be an insurmountable obstacle, which is quite understandable, because it meets the Friedmans' criteria for a genuine encryption. Coincidentally, following the aborted June date for publication, the military wing of the Pentagon began taking an interest in Ben Jonson's Cardano grille. One wonders if a cryptologist from their department had been called upon for assistance.

It is therefore not unexpected that a probability result may be contrived to persuade the general reader that the statement on the Cardano grille falls within accepted limits for this type of problem. Do not be misled!

The true probability can only be assessed using Bernoulli's theorem. To discover the value of this probability, it is required that a large number of independently written pieces of text, comprising 220 letters, be consigned to grilles of different dimensions. The target is to discover how many grilles succeed in producing a grammatical, meaningful, statement of 14 vertical words (omitting the initials of a name), arranged into three (or less) clusters, and which, when read, comments upon the text from which the statement has been derived.

In Appendix B, the answer is zero successes divided by 13 trials, which equals zero. As the number of different texts employed increases, so the number of successes recorded will contribute to the probability value. However, zero successes means the task is impossible. Employment of Bernoulli's theorem will undoubtedly show this as the correct value, despite the number of trials attempted. If, conceivably, a success was to be recorded within the first, say, trillion trials: Bernoulli's theorem indicates no more than that the true probability tends to a value so close to zero, as to make no significant difference.

And there, for the moment, the matter ends as this book goes to print. It was originally intended to delay publication so that specific arguments aimed against Jonson's Cardano grille could be dealt with and quickly disposed of. For example, that it can be opposed by arguments used against the Bible Code. The Cardano grill was invented in 1550 and widely used for the next hundred years in Europe, for sensitive diplomatic information. It is therefore distinguishable from the modern-day controversy surrounding the alleged code found in the Pentateuch.

In 2016, the fourth centennial of the death of Oxford's allonym will be celebrated. The question is – How much by then will have changed?

# APPENDIX A

Equidistant Letter Sequencing is a valid method for encrypting a secret inside a piece of ostensibly innocent text. The encoder simply takes the letters of the intended secret and ensures that each of these letters occur at equal intervals within a piece of text, which is then called the cipher text. The key to decoding the secret is the number of spaces between each letter. Once the decoder receives the cipher text, and with prior knowledge of the key, he or she can transfer the cipher text to a grille with the number of the columns equal to the number of the key, and the secret will appear spelt vertically downward.

Let us now introduce a level of difficulty; the decoder does not know the key, but is awaiting secret instructions concerning the code word 'Dawn'. The decoder can easily discover the key from whatever text is received. The letters of the alphabet are placed across the top of 26 vacant columns. Under each of these letters, a number is entered that coincides with the position each letter occupies within the text. In this particular paragraph, 1 would be placed in the 'L' column; 2 would be placed in the 'E' column; 3 would be placed in the 'T' column, and so on, to the end of the text under examination.

When the columns under the letters of the alphabet are complete with numbers, the next operation can be conducted. Since 'Dawn' is expected to occur in the message, the columns under 'D' and 'W' are chosen, since they are likely to have less members than appear under 'A'and 'N', thereby shortening the number of calculations. The task is to calculate all the possible differences that occur between the numbers in the 'D' column and the numbers in the 'W' column, eliminating all results that involve an odd number. If all differences involve an odd number, then we can safely say that the text does not contain the word 'Dawn' as part of an equidistant letter sequence. This is because there must be an equal space between 'D' and 'A', and between 'A' and 'W'. But if the number of spaces between 'D' and 'W' is an odd number, this is impossible. It is therefore only the differences that involve even numbers that need to be considered. The decoder therefore collects all the even numbers resulting from having differenced the numbers in the 'D' and 'W' columns, and halves each one. Each of these numbered halves is then examined to determine if it appears in the 'A' column. This exercise will greatly reduce the number of positive results. It will also provide a potential key, since the difference between 'D' and 'A' and 'A' and 'W' will now be the same number for all positive results; that is to say, an equidistant letter sequence will have occurred between 'D', 'A', and 'W'.

Armed with a potential key, the next task is to add this number to the number representing 'W' in order to determine if the result appears in the 'N' column. Where this occurs, it is then possible to construct a grille with the number of columns equal to that of the key. The word 'Dawn' will than appear vertically alongside any other words that the encoder intended to send to the decoder, and the ELS message can then be read vertically in what is a version of the Cardano Grille.

The Cardano Grille was first proposed in 1550 by Girolamo Cardano, from whom it acquired its name. The original model involved a carefully written missive in which the letters that spelt the secret message were exposed by laying a template over the cipher-text. The template had windows the size of a letter cut out so that these openings exposed only those letters that made up the message. The missive would arrive in a diplomatic box and the template by a separate courier. It was highly popular during the late 16th and early 17th centuries, especially in diplomatic correspondences where confidential exchanges were necessary.

An equidistant letter cipher, as contained by the cipher-text on the Stratford monument, is the equivalent of a simple Cardano Grille. The line of Latin text above the inscription, which has been uniquely inset to indicate its difference from the other lines, contains 34 characters. And 34 is the exact number of columns required for the plain-text message to be read that refers to Edward de Vere's secret identity as William Shakespeare

# APPENDIX B

The following grilles are reproduced by kind permission of Professor Albert W. Burgstahler: http://www2.chem.ku.edu/aburgstahler/stratmon/ Attention is drawn to the spread of disconnected words across the surface of each grille. This is in direct contrast to the 34-column grille, in which three separate clusters form a continuous sentence of 15 words, which also occur in response to a prior encryption: – **I AM DE VERE BY BIRTH**.

```
33
S T A Y P A S S E N G E R W H Y G O E S T T H O V B Y S O F A S T
R E A D I F T H O V C A N S T W H O M E N V I C V S D E A T H H A
T H P L A S T W I T H I N T H I S M O N V M E N T S H A K S P E A
R E W I T H W H O M E Q V I C K N A T V R E D I D E W H O S E N A
M E D C T H D E C K Y S T O M B E F A R M O R E T H E N C O S T S
I E H A L L Y T H E H A T H W R I T T L E A V E S L I V I N G A R
T B V T P A G E T O S E R V E H I S W I T T
```

```
32
S T A Y P A S S E N G E R W H Y G O E S T T H O V B Y S O F A S
T R E A D I F T H O V C A N S T W H O M E N V I O V S D E A T H
H A T H P L A S T W I T H I N T H I S M O N V M E N T S H A K S
P E A R E W I T H W H O M E Q V I C K N A T V R E D I D E W H O
S E N A M E D C T H D E C K Y S T O M B E F A R M O R E T H E N
C O S T S I E H A L L Y T H E H A T H W R I T T L E A V E S L I
V I N G A R T B V T P A G E T O S E R V E H I S W I T T
```

```
31
S T A Y P A S S E N G E R W H Y G O E S T T H O V B Y S O F A
S T R E A D I F T H O V C A N S T W H O M E N V I O V S D E A
T H H A T H P L A S T W I T H I N T H I S M O N V M E N T S H
A K S P E A R E W I T H W H O M E Q V I C K N A T V R E D I D
E W H O S E N A M E D C T H L E C K Y S T O M B E F A R M O R
E T H E N C O S T S I E H A L L Y T H E H A T H W R I T T L E
A V E S L I V I N G A R T B V T P A G E T O S E R V E H I S W
I T T
```

```
30
S T A Y P A S S E N G E R W H Y G O E S T T H O V B Y S O F
A S T R E A D I F T H O V C A N S T W H O M E N V I O V S D
E A T H H A T H P L A S T W I T H I N T H I S M O N V M E N
T S H A K S P E A R E W I T H W H O M E Q V I C K N A T V R
E D I D E W H O S E N A M E D O T H D E C K Y S T O M B E F
A R M O R E T H E N C O S T S I E H A L L Y T H E H A T H W
R I T T L E A V E S L I V I N G A R T B V T P A G E T O S E
R V E H I S W I T T
```

## 29

```
S T A Y P A S S E N G E R W H Y G O E S T T H O V B Y S O
F A S T R E A D I F T H O V C A N S T W H O M E N V I O V
S D E A T H H A T H P L A S T W I T H I N T H I S M O N V
M E N T S H A K S P E A R E W I T H W H O M E Q V I C K N
A T V R E D I D E W H O S E N A M E D O T H D E C K Y S T
O M B E F A R M O R E T H E N C O S T S I E H A L L Y T H
E H A T H W R I T T L E A V E S L I V I N G A R T B V T P
A G E T O S E R V E H I S W I T T
```

## 28

```
S T A Y P A S S E N G E R W H Y G O E S T T H O V B Y S
O F A S T R E A D I F T H O V C A N S T W H O M E N V I
O V S D E A T H H A T H P L A S T W I T H I N T H I S M
O N V M E N T S H A K S P E A R E W I T H W H O M E Q V
I C K N A T V R E D I D E W H O S E N A M E D O T H D E
C K Y S T O M B E F A R M O R E T H E N C O S T S I E H
A L L Y T H E H A T H W R I T T L E A V E S L I V I N G
A R T B V T P A G E T O S E R V E H I S W I T T
```

## 27

```
S T A Y P A S S E N G E R W H Y G O E S T T H O V B Y
S O F A S T R E A D I F T H O V C A N S T W H O M E N
V I O V S D E A T H H A T H P L A S T W I T H I N T H
I S M O N V M E N T S H A K S P E A R E W I T H W H O
M E Q V I C K N A T V R E D I D E W H O S E N A M E D
O T H D E C K Y S T O M B E F A R M O R E T H E N C O
S T S I E H A L L Y T H E H A T H W R I T T L E A V E
S L I V I N G A R T B V T P A G E T O S E R V E H I S
W I T T
```

## 26

```
S T A Y P A S S E N G E R W H Y G O E S T T H O V B
Y S O F A S T R E A D I F T H O V C A N S T W H O M
E N V I O V S D E A T H H A T H P L A S T W I T H I
N T H I S M O N V M E N T S H A K S P E A R E W I T
H W H O M E Q V I C K N A T V R E D I D E W H O S E
N A M E D O T H D E C K Y S T O M B E F A R M O R E
T H E N C O S T S I E H A L L Y T H E H A T H W R I
T T L E A V E S L I V I N G A R T B V T P A G E T O
S E R V E H I S W I T T
```

## 25

```
S T A Y P A S S E N G E R W H Y G O E S T T H O V
B Y S O F A S T R E A D I F T H O V C A N S T W H
O M E N V I O V S D E A T H H A T H P L A S T W I
T H I N T H I S M O N V M E N T S H A K S P E A R
E W I T H W H O M E Q V I C K N A T V R E D I D E
W H O S E N A M E D O T H D E C K Y S T O M B E F
A R M O R E T H E N C O S T S I E H A L L Y T H E
H A T H W R I T T L E A V E S L I V I N G A R T B
V T P A G E T O S E R V E H I S W I T T
```

APPENDIX B    313

24
```
S T A Y P A S S E N G E R W H Y G O E S T T H O
V B Y S O F A S T R E A D I F T H O V C A N S T
W H O M E N V I O V S D E A T H H A T H P L A S
T W I T H I N T H I S M O N V M E N T S H A K S
P E A R E W I T H W H O M E Q V I C K N A T V R
E D I D E W H O S E N A M E D O T H D E C K Y S
T O M B E F A R M O R E T H E N C O S T S I E H
A L L Y T H E H A T H W R I T T L E A V E S L I
V I N G A R T B V T P A G E T O S E R V E H I S
W I T T
```

23
```
S T A Y P A S S E N G E R W H Y G O E S T T H
O V B Y S O F A S T R E A D I F T H O V C A N
S T W H O M E N V I O V S D E A T H H A T H P
L A S T W I T H I N T H I S M O N V M E N T S
H A K S P E A R E W I T H W H O M E Q V I C K
N A T V R E D I D E W H O S E N A M E D O T H
D E C K Y S T O M B E F A R M O R E T H E N C
O S T S I E H A L L Y T H E H A T H W R I T T
L E A V E S L I V I N G A R T B V T P A G E T
O S E R V E H I S W I T T
```

22
```
S T A Y P A S S E N G E R W H Y G O E S T T
H O V B Y S O F A S T R E A D I F T H O V C
A N S T W H O M E N V I O V S D E A T H H A
T H P L A S T W I T H I N T H I S M O N V M
E N T S H A K S P E A R E W I T H W H O M E
Q V I C K N A T V R E D I D E W H O S E N A
M E D O T H D E C K Y S T O M B E F A R M O
R E T H E N C O S T S I E H A L L Y T H E H
A T H W R I T T L E A V E S L I V I N G A R
T B V T P A G E T O S E R V E H I S W I T T
```

21
```
S T A Y P A S S E N G E R W H Y G O E S T
T H O V B Y S O F A S T R E A D I F T H O
V C A N S T W H O M E N V I O V S D E A T
H H A T H P L A S T W I T H I N T H I S M
O N V M E N T S H A K S P E A R E W I T H
W H O M E Q V I C K N A T V R E D I D E W
H O S E N A M E D O T H D E C K Y S T O M
B E F A R M O R E T H E N C O S T S I E H
A L L Y T H E H A T H W R I T T L E A V E
S L I V I N G A R T B V T P A G E T O S E
R V E H I S W I T T
```

# BIBLIOGRAPHY

Ackroyd, Peter: *Shakespeare The Biography*, London, 2006
Adams, J. Q. ed. *Shakespeare's Titus Andronicus*, London, 1936
Alexander, Peter: ed. *Histories -William Shakespeare*, London, 1988
——————— *Tragedies and Poems -William Shakespeare*, London, 1988
Anderson, Mark: *Shake-speare By Another Name*, New York, 2005
Asquith, Claire: *Shadowplay*, New York, 2006
Bate, Jonathan: *The Genius of Shakespeare*, London, 1998
——————— ed. *Titus Andronicus*, London, 1995
Benezet, Louis P. *The Six Loves of Shake-Speare*, New York, 1958
Bentley, R. *The Shakespeare Oxford Newsletter*, vol.30: No.2A, spring 1994
Berry, H. *Shakespeare Bulletin*, spring 1999
Brewer E. Cobham: ed. *The Dictionary of Phrase and Fable*, classic edition, n.d.
Brooks, Michael: *13 Things That Don't Make Sense*, London, 2010
Bryson, Bill: *Shakespeare*, London, 2007
Callery, Sean: *Codes and Ciphers*, London, 2006
Capelli, Adriano: *Dizionario De Abbreviature Latine*, Italy, 1961
Carroll, D. *Tennessee Law Review*, Vol. 72 No.1, Knoxville, 2004
Chambers, E. K. *William Shakespeare*, 2 vols. 1931
Chute, Marchette: *Stories From Shakespeare*, London, 1996
Cibber, Theophilus: *The Lives of the Poets of Great Britain and Ireland*, London, 1753
Clark, Eva Turner: *Hidden Allusions in Shakespeare's Plays*, New York, 1931
Collier, J. P. *Works of William Shakespeare*, London, 1844
Compton Mackenzie, Faith: *William Cory*, London, 1950
Cook, Judith: *Dr Simon Forman*, London, 2001
Cooper, Tarnya: *Searching for Shakespeare*, London, 2006
Cotterell, A. & Storm, R. *The Encyclopedia of World Mythology*, London, 2006,
Cox, Jane: *Shakespeare in the Public Records*, London, 1964
Crick, J. *De Vere Society Newsletter,* February 2007
Crompton, L. *Homosexuality and Civilization*, Harvard, 2003
Crystal, D. & B. *The Shakespeare Miscellany*, London, 2005
David, R. ed. *Love's Labour's Lost*, New York, 1981,
Dawson, G. E. & Kennedy-Skipton, L. *Elizabethan Handwriting*, London, 1966
Detobel, R. *De Vere Society Newsletter*, April/May 2001
——————— *The Oxfordian*, vol.4.
Doran, Gregory: *The Shakespeare Almanac*, London, 2009
Drabble, Margaret: ed. *Oxford Companion to English Literature*, Oxford, 1989
Duncan Jones, K. *Ungentle Shakespeare*, London, 2001
Dunton-Downer, L. & Riding, A. *Essential Shakespeare Handbook*, London, 2004
Encyclopaedia Britannica, 11th edition
Feldman, Bronson: *Secrets of Shakespeare*, Philadelphia, 1972
——————— *Hamlet Himself*, Philadelphia, 1977

Feuillerat, A. *John Lyly*, Cambridge, 1910
Fido, Martin: *Shakespeare*, London, 1988
Foakes, R. A. ed. *Henslowe's Diary*, Cambridge, 2002
―――――― ed. *King Henry VIII*, London, 1986
Fowell, Frank: *Censorship In England*, London, 1913
Fox, Levi: *The Shakespeare Handbook*, London, 1988
Friedman, W. F. & E. S. *The Shakespeare Ciphers Examined*, Cambridge, 1957
―――――― *Philological Quarterly*, Vol. XXXVIII: No.1, 1959
Gervinus, G. *Shakespeare Commentaries*, transl. Bunnett, F.E., London, 1883
Goldstein, G. *Shakespeare's Native Tongue:* De Vere Society Newsletter, vol, 16/3, 2009
Gray, Emma: ed. *Encyclopedia of World Mythology*, London, 2006
Greene, R. http://www2.prestel.co.uk/rey/groats.htm
Greenwood, Sir G. *Oxford Shakespeare Newsletter*, Vol. 30 No, 1: 1994
Halliwell-Phillipps, J. O. *The Life of William Shakespeare*, London, 1848
Hamill, John: *Shakespeare Oxford Newsletter*, Vol. 45: No. 3, 2009
Haynes, Alan: *Sex In Elizabethan England*, Stroud, 1997
Holden, Anthony: *Shakespeare's True Love*? 'The Observer': 21 April 2002
Holland, Peter: *William Shakespeare*, Oxford, 2007
Honan, Park: *Shakespeare: A Life*, Oxford, 1998
Humphreys, A. R. ed. *Much Ado About Nothing*, London, 1991
Jolly, E. *Great Oxford*, ed. Richard Malim, Tunbridge Wells, 2004
Jones, E. & Guy, R. *The Shakespeare Companion*, London, 2005
Jones, Norman, *What Was Life Like in the Realm of Elizabeth*, (Time-Life), London. n.d.
Kahn, David: *The Codebreakers The Story of Secret Writing*, New York, 1996
Kermode, Frank: ed. *The Tempest*, London, 1992
Kay, W. David: *Ben Jonson A Literary Life*, Basingstoke, 1995
Knecht, Robert J. *The French Religious Wars 1562 – 1598*, Botley, Oxford, 2002
Knowles, Richard: ed. *New Variorum Edition of Shakespeare*, 1977
Kreiler, Kurt: *Der Mann, der Shakespeare erfand*, Frankfurt am Main, 2009
Laroque, François: *Shakespeare, Court, Crowd and Playhouse*, London, 1993
Latham, Agnes: ed. *As You Like It*, London, 1993
―――――― ed. *The Poems of Sir Walter Raleigh*, London, 1951
Looney, J. T. *Shake-spear Identified*, London, 1920
Malim, Richard: *Great Oxford*, Tunbridge Wells, 2004
Matus, Irwin: *Shakespeare In Fact*, New York, 1994
Michael, W. *History of Wilton House*, Westbury, Wilts. 1873
Michell, John: *Who Wrote Shakespeare?* London, 1996
Miller, Ruth L. *Oxfordian Vistas*, Jennings, 1975
Montague, W. H. *A New and Universal History of England:* Vol. II, London, 1798
Moore, Peter: *Shakespeare Oxford Society Newsletter*, Vol. 32: 3
Morgan, James Appleton: *A Study in the Warwickshire Dialect*, New York, 1900
Nashe, T. http://www.oxford-shakespeare.com/NasheStrange_News.pdf
Nelson, Alan: *Monstrous Adversary*, Liverpool, 2003
―――――― *Tennessee Law Review*, Vol. 72 No.1, Knoxville, 2004
Nims, J. *Metamorphosis*, (Arthur Golding's translation) New York, 1965
Ogburn, Charlton: *The Mystery of William Shakespeare*, London, 1988
Oliver, H. J. ed. *The Merry Wives of Windsor*, London, 1987
Palmer, Cecil: *The Mystery of 'Mr W. H'*, London, 1923
Price, D. *Shakespeare's Unorthodox Biography*, Westport, 2001

———— *The Review of English Studies*, New Series, Vol. 48, No. 190: 1997
Reese, M. M. *Shakespeare: His World and His Work*, London, 1980
Rollett, John: *Great Oxford*, ed. Richard Malim, Tunbridge Wells, 2004
Roper, David L. *Proving Shakespeare*, Virginia, 2008
Rose, Edward: *Illustrated London News*, August 6th 1887
Rowe, N. *Some Account of the Life &c. of Mr. William Shakespeare*, 1709
Rowse, A .J. *Shakespeare The Man*, London, 1988
Schlueter, June: Shakespeare Quarterly (50:2) 1999
Schoenbaum, Samuel: *Shakespeare's Lives*, Oxford, 1991
Shakespeare Birthplace Trust Record Office and Library: Stratford-upon-Avon
Shapiro, James: *Contested Will*, London, 2010
Sobran, Joseph: *Alias Shakespeare*, New York, 1997
Stokes, Francis G. *Who's Who in Shakespeare*, New York, 2007
Stone, L. *The Crisis of the Aristocracy, 1558 – 1641*, Oxford, 1965
Stopes, C. *Shakespeare's Environment*, London, 1918
Stritmatter, Roger: *The Scandinavian Psychological Review,* 2009
———————— *Shakespeare Oxford Society Newsletter*, vol. 36 No .2
Trow, M. J. *Who Killed Kit Marlowe?* Sutton, 2002
Vaughan, Virginia M. & Alden T. eds. *The Tempest*, London, 2007
Waith, Eugene M. ed. *Titus Andronicus*, Oxford, 1998
Wallace, Charles W. *New York Times*, 3 October 1909
Waugaman, Richard M. *The Scandinavian Psychological Review,* 2009
Williams, E. N. *Dictionary of English and European History 1487-1789*, 1986
Williams, Neville: *The Life and Times of Elizabeth I*, London, 1972
Williams, Norman Lloyd: *Sir Walter Raleigh*, London, 1962
Wilson, Ian: *Shakespeare: The Evidence*, London, 1993
Wilson, Mona: *Sir Philip Sidney*, London, 1931
Woolley, Benjamin: *The Queen's Conjuror*, London, 2001

## Illustrations

1. Globe theatre xiv
2. Marks of John and Mary Shakspere 2
3. Greene's Groats-worth of Wit 35
4. New Place 60
5. Henry Peacham's signature and date 95
6. Enlargement of Peacham's letter 'q' 96
7. Henry Peacham's handwriting 99
8. Handwriting on the *Titus Manuscript* 99
9. Title page of 'Minerva Britanna' 103
10. Juliet's balcony in Verona 126
11. William Shakspere's signature 145
12. Shakespeare's House at Wilton 174
13. Judith Shakspere's mark 203
14. Thomas Thorpe's dedication in the Sonnets 209
15. Anne Vavasour 234
16. Hand of Anne Cecil supporting Edward de Vere 241
17. Hand of God offering the Crown to James I 242
18. Grille revealing the name Henry Wriothesley 247
19. Grille revealing the name Vere 248
20. Ben Jonson's Cardano grille 270
21. Stratford monument for Bell 279
22. Stratford monument for Rowe 282
23. Stratford monument for Pope 282
24. Grille revealing the name Vere 286
25. Dividing mark on Shakespeare's neck 289
26. Droeshout's picture of Shakespeare 290
27. Thomas Wentworth, Earl of Strafford 291
28. Oxford, with cloak and 'dagger' 292
29. Shakespeare's sprig of belvedere 292

Basilicon Doron, © British Library Board. All Rights Reserved Harley 6855, 13. Titus Manuscript, reproduced by permission of the Marquess of Bath. Nicholas Hilliard miniature of Lord Oxford: reproduced by permission of the Victoria and Albert Museum. Portrait of Anne Vavsour, by courtesy of the Armourers & Brasiers Company of London.

While every possible effort has been made to communicate with owners of some material contained in this book, or to discover its provenance, this has not always been possible.

# INDEX

## 1

1599 A Year In The Life Of William Shakespeare, 233

## A

Ackroyd, Peter, 4, 9, 24, 42, 45, 207, 212, 214, 240
Addenbrooke, John, 206, 211
Admiral's Men, 61, 92, 110
Aesop, 29, 255
Alençon, duc d', 83, 117, 118
Alexander, 298
Alexander, Peter, 21, 31, 71
*All Is True,* 200, 201
*All's Well That Ends Well,* xii, 178
*Amends for Ladies,* 110
Anagram, 102, 103, 104, 105, 139, 248
Anderson, Mark, 184
*Anthony and Cleopatra,* 192
*Antiquities of Warwickshire,* 181, 282, 283
*Apis Lapis,* 171, 172, 173
Aquitaine, 118
Ark Raleigh, 219
*Arte of English Poesie,* 67, 79
Arundel, Earl (Philip Howard), 243
*As You Like It,* 34, 62, 158, 160, 167, 183, 188, 299
Aspley, William, 183
Asquith, Clare, 68
*Astrophel and Stella,* 84, 115
Athene, 107
Aubrey, John, 16, 17, 142, 150, 159, 162, 220, 249
Austen, Jane, xiii
Ayrer, Jakob, 196

## B

Babington, Anthony, 166, 220
Bacon Society, 307
Bacon, Sir Edmund, 200
Bacon, Sir Francis, 104, 273, 275, 302, 307
Baffin Island, 252
Barnes, Barnabe, 217
Barnfield, Richard, 135, 136
*Bartholomew Fair,* 90
Basse, William, 261, 262, 263, 297
Bate, Jonathan, 33, 34, 59, 98, 108, 185, 187, 199, 200, 236, 250
Beaumont, Francis, 260, 297
Beker and Piper, 249, 275
Bell, John, 280
Belott, Stephen, 146, 147, 148
Benezet, Louis P., 229, 296
Benson, John, 293
Bermuda, 194, 196, 197, 198
Bernoulli's theorem, 308
Berry, Herbert, 96, 97, 98
Betterton, Thomas, 4, 5, 6, 7, 8, 28, 180, 282
Beverley, Peter, 164
*Bible,* 238
Bible Code, 308
Blackfriars Gate House, 212, 213, 214, 259
Blackfriars Playhouse, 112, 143, 205, 206, 211, 214
Bodenham, John, 139
Bond, R. W., 165
Bott, William, 60
Bourchier, Sir Henry, 109
Bowen, Gwynneth, 230
Brend, Nicholas, 137, 182
Brend, Thomas, 137
Bretchgirdle, Rev. John, 1
Breton, Nicholas, 75
*Brief Lives,* 220
Britton, John, 180, 181
Brooke, Arthur, 123, 124, 126
Brooke, John, 114
Brooks, Michael, 302
Browne, Lady Mary, 44, 105
Bryson, Bill, 3, 4, 8, 15, 141
Buc, Sir George, 190, 191
Burbage, Cuthbert, 149, 205, 206, 211
Burbage, James, 149
Burbage, Richard, 53, 54, 140, 141, 149, 178, 185, 205, 211, 212, 259
Burby, Cuthbert, 182
Burghley, Lady Mildred, 131
Burghley, Lord, 25, 41, 42, 43, 44, 45, 49, 80, 81, 121, 127, 128, 131, 166,

INDEX 319

167, 176, 187, 220, 224, 233, 237,
238, 239, 240, 242, 244, 250, 251,
252, 305
 Characterised, 250, 251, 252, 253,
 304, 305
Burgstahler, Albert W., ix, xiv, 274, 306, 311
Burroughs, Sir John, 222
Busby, John, 184

## C

Caesar, Julius (Emperor), 29
Calais, 152
Cambridge University Press, 307
Camden, William, xi, 176, 187, 245, 303
*Campaspe and Diogenes*, 298
Cardano grille, 268, 271, 272, 274, 275, 279, 301, 306, 307, 308, 310
Cardano, Girolamo, 268, 310
Carey, H., 54
Cavendish, Charles, 220
Cecil, Anne, 41, 80, 112, 113, 115, 131, 198, 229, 237, 242, 251, 305
 Characterised, xii, 123, 251, 252
Cecil, Elizabeth, 113
Cecil, Sir Robert, 188, 199, 250, 251
Cecil, Thomas, 242, 252
Chamberlain's Men, 66, 92, 211, 253
Chambers, Sir Edmund K., 96, 112, 160, 229
Chapman, George, 52, 75, 141, 184, 187, 223, 224
Charles IX of France, 118, 123
Charles V, 253
Charlton, Derran, 291
Chaucer, Geoffrey, xiii, 297
Chester, Robert, 75, 183
Chettle, Henry, 15, 20, 22, 23, 24, 27, 29, 30, 31, 32, 34, 50, 51, 52, 151, 152, 153, 185, 261
 Groats-worth of Wit, 31
Children of the Queen's Revels, 205
*Choice of Valentines*, 217
Churchyard, Thomas, 81
Chute, Marchette, 35, 54, 130, 252
Cicero, 29, 97
Clark, Eva T., 103, 108, 112, 164
Clayton, John, 182
Clopton, Sir Hugh, 60
Cobbe portrait, 42, 238, 239, 240
Cobham, Lord, 109, 110
Colet, John, 172
Collier, John P., 3, 12, 13, 16, 121, 161

Combe, John, 17, 184
Combe, William, 184
*Comedy of Errors*, 16, 49, 50, 112, 113, 115, 190, 218
*Comical Gallant, The*, 168
*Complaint of Poetry for the Death of Liberality*, 135
*Compleat Gentleman*, 101
Condell, Henry, 49, 137, 141, 148, 149, 150, 178, 179, 205, 206, 211, 213, 259, 294, 295, 296, 300
*Contention Between the Two Famous Houses of Yorke and Lancaster*, 51, 52, 71, 72, 107, 203
*Contested Will*, 233, 236, 302
Cook, Robert, 64
Cooke, James, 204
Cooper, Tarnya, 292
Coquo, Orazio, 243
*Corinthians*, 238
*Coriolanus*, 178
Corniche, 19
Cory, William, 159, 160, 161
Cotgrave, Randle, 139, 293
Cox, Jane, 143
Creede, Thomas, 184
*Crisis of the Aristocracy* 1558-1641, 305
Croft, Peter, 99
Cryptology, 246, 249, 268, 270, 272, 273, 274, 275, 276, 309
Curtain, 28
*Cymbeline*, 258
*Cynthia of the Sea*, 219
*Cynthia's Revels*, 90

## D

Daniel, Samuel, 184
Danter, John, 90, 92
Davenant, John, 28
Davenant, Sir William, 28, 240
Davies, John, 185
Day, John, 52
*De Rerum Natura*, 276
Dee, John, 70
Dekker, Thomas, 52
Dennis, John, 168
Derby, 5th Earl, 49
Desmond, Earl of, 220
Dethick, W., 64
Dethick, William, 64, 65
Devereux, Penelope, 84
*Diaphantus and the Passions of Love*, 189

Dickens, Charles, xiii
*Dictionary of the French and English Tongues*, 139, 293
*Die Schöne Sidea*, 196
Digges, Leonard, ix, 76, 126, 284, 285, 287, 293, 294, 296
Donne, John, 36
Doran, Gregory, 91, 92
Dowdall, 16, 28
Dowden, Edward, 168
Drayton, Michael, 46, 52, 184
Droeshout, Martin, 287, 288, 289, 290, 291, 292, 293, 294, 296
Dryden, John, 79
Dugdale, Sir William, 180, 181, 277, 281, 282, 283, 289
Duncan-Jones, Katherine, 160
Durham House, 222, 223, 224

## 𝓔

*Eastward Ho*, 288
Edict of Beaulieu, 118
Edmund, Piers, 243
Edward Bonaventure, 219
Edward VI, 172
*Een Schone Historie Van Vergilius*, 279
Eld, George, 208
Elizabeth I, 24, 25, 26, 41, 42, 43, 45, 53, 70, 80, 81, 83, 99, 101, 105, 106, 109, 115, 116, 122, 141, 151, 152, 153, 154, 155, 164, 167, 171, 177, 185, 188, 218, 219, 220, 221, 222, 223, 224, 225, 226, 229, 238, 239, 240, 242, 243, 244, 245, 250, 251, 253, 254, 256, 292, 305
ELS encryption, 268, 269, 274, 287, 301, 309, 310
*Encomion of Lady Pecunia*, 135
*Endymion*, 164, 165
*England's Parnassus*, 116
English Civil War, 35
Epicurus, 276
*Epigrammes in the oldest cut and newest fashions*, 136, 182
Essex, 2nd Earl (Robert Devereux), 63, 153, 226
*Euphues and his England*, 114, 297
*Euphues The Anatomy of Wit*, 297
Evans, Henry, 205
Evans, Norman, 143
Evans, Thomas, 205
*Every Man In His Humour*, 57, 63, 66, 187, 188, 190

*Every Man Out of His Humour*, 65, 187, 190, 297

## 𝓕

*Faerie Queen*, 78, 219, 221
*Famous Victories of Henry the Fift*, 51, 52, 72, 107, 108, 109, 110, 111, 112
Faunt, William, 108
Feldman, Bronson, 205, 255
Feuillerat, Albert, 112
Field, Nathaniel, 110
Field, Richard, 46
Finche, John, 230, 231, 232
First Folio, xvi, 4, 6, 33, 38, 46, 49, 71, 76, 78, 90, 101, 104, 126, 130, 162, 163, 169, 170, 178, 179, 183, 187, 193, 194, 200, 201, 206, 214, 260, 262, 263, 264, 266, 271, 277, 284, 285, 286, 287, 288, 289, 290, 293, 294, 295, 296, 297, 300
Fishers Folly, 30, 80, 81, 114, 255, 256, 298
Fitzgeffrey, Rev. Charles, 184
Fletcher, John, 143, 150, 201, 202, 260
Fletcher, Lawrence, 186
Florio, John, 128
Fluoridation, 302
Foakes, R. A., 200
Folger Shakespeare Library, 104, 251, 273, 307
Ford, John, 261
Forest of Ardennes, 167
Forman, Simon, 238
*Foure-fold Meditation*, 208
Fox, Levi, 18
*Foyle's War*, 268
Friedman, W. & E., 210, 272, 273, 274, 301, 307, 308
Friedman, William F., 104, 247, 271, 272, 274, 275, 286, 301, 307
Frobisher, Sir Martin, 222, 252

## 𝓖

Gads Hill, 108, 110, 111
Gamage, Barbara, 84
*Garden of Eloquence*, 100
Gardiner, James, 55, 56, 60
Garrick, David, 192, 264, 265
Gates, Geoffrey, 114
*Geneva Bible*, 238
*Gentleman's Taylor*, 290

*George a Greene,* 190
Gervinus, G. G., 116, 119, 167, 210, 299
Gildon, 168
Globe, 137, 138, 143, 148, 149, 179, 182, 186, 200, 205, 211, 212, 213, 214, 289
Goldstein, G., 303
Goulding, Captain, 59
Granville, George, 168
Gravelot, Hubert, 281
Greenblatt, Stephen, 302
Greene, Robert, 15, 20, 21, 22, 23, 24, 25, 26, 27, 29, 30, 31, 32, 33, 34, 50, 51, 52, 56, 150, 151, 152, 163, 171, 256, 277, 298
Grey, Catherine, 84
Grey, Lady Jane, 84, 244
*Grief of Mind,* 115
Grignion, Reynolds, 180, 279, 280
Grimston, H., 80

## ℋ

Hakluyt, Richard, 194, 195
Hall, Dr John, 177, 203, 204, 214, 263
Hall, Elizabeth, 205, 263
Hall, William, 207, 208, 209
Halliwell-Phillipps, James, 12, 54, 162
*Hamlet,* 50, 51, 52, 62, 183, 185, 191, 202, 218, 250, 251, 252, 253, 254, 255, 257, 304, 306
Hampton Court Palace, 112, 115
Hanmer, Sir Thomas, 281
Harriot, Thomas, 224
Harrison, John, 48
Hart, Joan, 4
Hartley, L. P., 226
Harvey, Gabriel, 24, 25, 33, 112, 114, 133, 150, 162, 165, 170, 183, 250, 292
Harwich, 80, 152, 256
Hatfield House, 99
Hathaway, Agnes, 13
Hathaway, Anne, 9, 10, 12, 13, 14, 15, 18, 149, 150, 161, 263, 283
Hathaway, Bartholomew, 13
Hathaway, Catherine, 13
Hathaway, Elizabeth, 13
Hathaway, Joan, 13
Hathaway, Joan (daughter), 13
Hathaway, John, 13
Hathaway, Richard, 10, 11, 13
Hathaway, Thomas, 13
Hathaway, William, 13

Hazlitt, William, 125
Hedingham Castle, 49, 80, 207
Heminge, John, 49, 137, 141, 143, 148, 149, 158, 178, 179, 205, 206, 211, 212, 213, 214, 259, 294, 295, 296, 300
Heminge, Thomasina, 211, 212, 213, 214
Henri III of France, 116, 117, 118, 120
Henri IV of France, 116, 117, 118, 120
*Henry IV,* 62, 72, 107, 108, 110, 111, 130, 167, 168, 173
*Henry V,* 33, 62, 72, 107, 168, 173, 183, 190, 218
*Henry VI,* 16, 21, 22, 26, 27, 29, 30, 50, 51, 61, 71, 72, 107, 130, 199, 202, 203, 305
Henry VII, 64, 65
*Henry VIII,* 100, 143, 199, 200, 201
Henslowe, Philip, 21, 48, 50, 51, 52, 53, 60, 61, 92, 93, 141, 190, 201, 202, 218, 304
*Hero and Leander,* 226
Heyes, Thomas, 131, 183
Heywood, Thomas, 261
Hicks, Michael, 81, 100
*Hidden Allusions to Shakespeare's Plays,* 164
Hilliard, Nicholas, 241, 242, 243
*Histoire du Roy d'Angleterre Richard,* 70
*Historie of Ariodante and Genevora,* 164
*History of Error,* 112
Holland, Hubert H., 124, 164
Holland, Hugh, 287
Hollywood, 308
Homer, 277
Homosexuality, 233, 238, 242, 243, 252, 302
Honan, Park, 158
Horace, 140
Hornby, T., 206, 211
Hotson, Leslie, 56, 210, 246, 284, 285
*Householder's Philosophy,* 256
Howard, Lord, 169
Howard, Lord Henry, 169, 243
Howard, Philip, 81
Hoy, Cyrus, 201
Hughes, Charles, 38
Hughes, Thomas, 224
Hume, Noël, 195
Humphries, A. R., 165
Hunter, Joseph, 119, 124, 198

## I

Ignoto, 75, 78
*Illustrated London News,* 161
Isam, 33
*Isle of Dogs,* 52, 288
Ivan the Terrible, 120

## J

Jackson, John, 143, 212
Jackson, Roger, 48
Jaggard, William, 38, 39, 137, 182, 228, 232, 236
James I, 74, 141, 153, 155, 158, 159, 160, 162, 177, 186, 188, 189, 190, 191, 205, 241, 292
James, Richard, 109
Janus, 291
Jesus Christ, 279
Johnson, Arthur, 184
Johnson, Joan, 146
Johnson, Philip, 164
Johnson, William, 143, 212
Jones, Inigo, 163
Jonson, Ben, 52, 56, 57, 63, 65, 66, 74, 75, 76, 78, 90, 91, 126, 140, 141, 150, 163, 174, 176, 179, 184, 187, 190, 196, 213, 249, 261, 262, 263, 267, 270, 271, 272, 274, 275, 276, 277, 278, 279, 285, 287, 288, 294, 295, 297, 298, 299, 301, 306, 307, 308
   First Folio, 285, 287, 288, 289, 293, 294, 297, 298, 299, 300
Josephson, Brian, 302
Jove, 173
*Julius Caesar,* 62
Juvenal, 23, 24, 27, 93

## K

Kahn, David, 268, 273
Kathman, David, 261
Kempe, William, 53, 54, 137, 140, 149, 211
*Kind-Harts Dreame,* 31, 151
*King John,* 50, 51, 62, 70, 71, 72, 107
*King Lear,* 50, 51, 52, 202, 218
King's Men, 158, 159, 178, 179, 186, 188, 189, 190, 191, 213, 295
*Knack to Know A Knave,* 90
Knell, Rebecca, 148
Knell, William, 148
Knollys, Elizabeth, 122
Kyd, Thomas, 90, 114, 202, 254, 255, 256, 257, 297, 298

## L

*La Chronicque de la Traison et Mort de Richart Deux roy Dengleterre,* 70
Laing, Alstair, 239
Lambert, Edmund, 16, 19
Lampedusa, 198
Langley, Francis, 56, 59
Lawrence, Herbert, 59
Leake, William, 48, 136
Lee, Sir Henry, 230, 231
Lee, Sir Sidney, 159, 208, 247
Lefranc, Abel, 117, 118
Leftwich, R., 144
Leicester, (Robert Dudley), 80, 152
Leveson, William, 137
Lilly, William, 172
Lodge, Thomas, 114, 150, 256
Londré, Felicity H., 251
Looney, J. Thomas, xiii, 82, 84, 86, 115, 304
Lord Chamberlain's Men, 54, 61, 62, 137, 140
Lord Strange's Men, 61, 148
Lord Sussex's Men, 61
*Love's Labour's Lost,* 38, 50, 62, 71, 87, 116, 117, 118, 120, 122, 131, 190, 218, 288, 294
*Love's Labour's Won,* 129
*Love's Martyr,* 75, 183
*Lucrece,* 35, 36, 37, 38, 40, 44, 45, 46, 48, 50, 54, 56, 62, 68, 76, 92, 93, 127, 131, 135, 136, 146, 152, 153, 175, 183, 217, 232, 235, 244, 246
Lucretius, Titus, 276
Lucy, Sir Thomas, 17
Luther, Martin, 253
Lyly, John, 112, 114, 164, 165, 256, 297, 298

## M

Mabbe, James, 76, 287
Mackenzie, Faith Compton, 160
Madre de Dios, 222, 223
*Malcontent, The,* 74
Malim, Richard, 190
*Man Who Was Shakespeare,* 103
Manners, Francis, 213

# INDEX

Manners, Lady Bridget, 42, 237
Manningham, John, 121
Marlowe, Christopher, 23, 25, 27, 30, 31, 32, 34, 52, 114, 150, 163, 169, 171, 224, 226, 227, 256, 297, 298
Marshall, William, 292, 293, 294
Marston, John, 52, 74, 75, 76, 184, 187, 261, 287
Master of Revels, 253, 305
Matus, Irvin, 63
Mayenne, duc de, 120
*Measure for Measure,* 294
Medici, Catherine de', 118, 123
Melicertes, 152
*Menaphon,* 256
*Merchant of Venice,* 62, 129, 131, 183, 190
Meres, Francis, 71, 93, 107, 128, 129, 131, 133, 134, 135, 136, 137, 138, 139, 141, 146, 175, 176, 186, 233, 235, 236, 245
*Merry Wives of Windsor,* xii, 62, 167, 168, 170, 172, 173, 174, 184, 190
Michael, W., 160
Middleton, Thomas, 52, 261
*Midsummer Night's Dream,* 49, 50, 62, 183
Miller, Ruth L., 263
Millington, Thomas, 92
*Minerva Britanna,* 102, 241
*Mirrour of Mutabilitie,* 114
Monox, Will, *(see Will Monox)*
Montgomery, Earl (Philip Herbert), 49, 162, 174, 179, 205, 206
Moore, Peter, 194
Morgan, Appleton, 303
Mountjoy, Christopher, 146, 147, 148, 151, 156
Mountjoy, Mary, 146
*Mourneful Dittie,* 185
Mozart, W. A., 123, 191, 202
*Much Ado About Nothing,* 62, 163, 164, 165, 166, 167, 174, 183
Mümpelgart, Count, 169, 170, 171
Munday, Anthony, 52, 114
Munro, J., 123
Mussum, Walter, 3
*Mystery of Mr W. H,* 207

## N

Nashe, Thomas, 21, 22, 23, 24, 25, 26, 27, 30, 31, 32, 50, 52, 56, 150, 162, 163, 170, 171, 172, 173, 174, 184, 217, 254, 255, 256, 292, 298, 304
*Nashes Lenten Stuffe,* 170
Naunton, Sir Robert, 218
Nelson, Alan, 133, 134, 144, 176, 181, 280, 281, 305
Neuendorffer, Arthur, 285
*Never Too Late,* 29
New Place, 60, 62, 130, 131, 177, 179, 184, 195, 204, 259
*New York Times,* 236
Norris, Francis (Baron Rycote), 263
Northern Rebellion, 49
Northumberland, 9th Earl (Henry Percy), 224

## O

*Ocean's Love to Cynthia,* 154, 219, 220, 223
Ogburn, Charlton, 123, 125, 165, 206
Oldcastle, Sir John, 108, 109, 110
Order of the Garter, 167, 171, 242
Osteler, William, 211, 212, 213
*Othello,* 280
Oxford, 11th Earl, 108
Oxford, 17th Earl, 24, 25, 27, 29, 47, 49, 68, 70, 72, 79, 80, 81, 93, 96, 111, 112, 113, 114, 121, 123, 133, 144, 152, 153, 156, 162, 163, 167, 171, 172, 186, 188, 189, 190, 199, 210, 211, 220, 222, 224, 225, 229, 236, 239, 241, 242, 243, 255, 256, 290, 291, 292, 294, 297, 298, 304, 305
  Burghley, 41, 113, 166, 176, 187
  Characterised, xii, 107, 125, 191, 251, 252, 254
  Insolvency, 80, 81
  Italy, 116, 118, 119, 218, 243, 253
  Marriage, 237, 243, 244, 251
  Mistress, 229, 230, 231, 232
  Plays, *(see Shakespeare)*
  Playwright, 33, 34, 36, 47, 52, 62, 71, 85, 87, 89, 95, 100, 101, 105, 111, 112, 115, 120, 121, 122, 125, 126, 128, 133, 134, 135, 165, 167, 171, 188, 193, 196, 200, 202, 218, 245, 249, 250, 253, 254, 255, 256, 271, 277, 295, 297, 298, 300, 304, 305, 306
  Poet, 38, 67, 68, 69, 75, 76, 78, 79, 84, 85, 87, 88, 115, 129, 135, 136, 152, 153, 154, 156, 163, 173, 185,

193, 209, 221, 223, 228, 245, 287, 294, 305
Portrait, 241, 242, 292
Pseudonym, xi, xiii, 29, 32, 34, 35, 36 38, 39, 45,46, 52, 53, 54, 58, 69, 73, 74, 76, 88, 93, 101, 105, 109, 111, 126, 128, 133, 140, 141, 149, 152, 157, 160, 162, 163, 176, 183, 185, 187, 190, 225, 232, 240, 245, 250, 260, 261, 263, 271, 277, 287, 289, 290, 292, 296, 297, 298, 302, 305, 307, 308,
Rival Poet, 219, 221, 222, 223, 224, 225, 232
Southampton, 37, 39, 40, 43, 45, 153, 156, 226, 229, 233, 237, 238, 240, 242, 243, 244
Venus & Adonis, 30, 31, 32, 39, 40
Wilton, 49, 158, 160, 162, 163, 171, 174, 299
Oxford, 18th Earl, 208, 209
Oxford's Men, 80

## ℘

*Padre di Famiglia*, 256
*Palladis Tamia, Wit's Treasury*, 90, 107, 128, 129, 130, 131, 132, 135, 136, 137, 141, 175, 176, 182, 186, 209
Panama, 220, 222
*Paradise of Dainty Devices*, 69
*Parnassus Plays*, 153, 182, 289
Parsons, Robert, 224
*Passionate Pilgrim*, 38, 137, 182, 236
Peacham, Henry, 94, 99, 101, 102, 103, 104, 105, 241
Peacham, Rev. Henry, 94, 95, 97, 98, 99, 100, 101, 306
Peacham's chronogram, 95, 96, 98
Peele, George, 24, 29, 205, 213
Peele, Isabel, 205
Pembroke, 2nd Earl, 84
Pembroke, 3rd Earl (William Herbert), 49, 159, 160, 162, 174, 179, 205, 206, 213
Pembroke, Lady Mary, (see Sidney)
Penn, Julia, 81
*Pentateuch*, 308
Peyton, Sir John, 188
Philip II, 71, 156
Phillips, Augustine, 70, 137, 149, 179, 205, 211
Phillips, Sir Thomas, 8
*Phoenix and the Turtle*, 75, 183

*Pierce Pennilesse*, 162, 163
Plaistow House, 81
Plato, 77, 134, 152, 278
Plautus Titus, 113
*Poems in Divers Humours*, 135, 136
*Poems Written by Wil. Shake-speare, Gent*, 293, 293
*Poetaster*, 140
*Polyhymnia*, 263
Pope, Alexander, 281, 283
Pope, Thomas, 137, 149, 211
Porter, Henry, 52
*Preface to Greene's Menaphon*, 254
Price, Diana, 281, 282
*Principal Navigations, Voyages*, 194
Priscian, 172
Privy Council, 23, 63
*Proving Shakespeare*, 203, 233, 301
Ptah, 173
Purchas, Samuel, 195
Puttenham, George, 36, 67, 72, 73, 74, 76, 79, 85, 133
Pythagoras, 122

## 𝒬

Queen's Men, 148
Quiney, Adrian, 132
Quiney, Judith, 264
Quiney, Richard, 63, 64, 130, 131, 132
Quiney, Thomas, 64

## ℛ

Raleigh, Sir Walter, 113, 121, 122, 159, 218, 219, 220, 221, 222, 223, 224, 225
Rival Poet, 154, 218, 219, 221, 223, 225, 232
School of Night, 223, 224
Reese, Max, 187
*Remembrance of some English Poets*, 135
*Return From Parnassus*, 140
Rich, Lord, 84
*Richard II*, 50, 62, 69, 70, 136
*Richard III*, 16, 26, 50, 72, 75
Richardson, John, 8, 9, 10, 11
Roberts, James, 131, 183, 185
Robinson, John, 212, 259
Roebuck, 222
Rogers, Philip, 189
Rollett, John, 209, 210, 246

# INDEX

Rollins, H. E., 227
*Romeo and Juliet*, 50, 62, 123, 124, 125, 136, 182
Roscius, 29
Rose theatre, 61, 90
Rose, Edward, 161
Ross, Terry, 102, 105
Rousillon, Comte de, 253
Roussillon, 253
Rowe, Nicholas, 4, 5, 28, 57, 79, 93, 109, 120, 122, 168, 180, 188, 280, 281, 282
Royal Shakespeare Company, 91
Roydon, Matthew, 224
Russell, Thomas, 284
Rutland, 6th Earl, 213

## S

Sadler, Hamnet, 15
Sadler, Judith, 15
Sadler, Roger, 19
Samonde, Wilfred, 242
Sandells, Fulke, 8, 9, 10, 11
*Sapho and Phao*, 298
Savage, Thomas, 137, 148
Savoy, 30, 114, 255, 256, 297
Schoenbaum, Samuel, 229
School of Night, 122, 223, 224
Scoloker, Anthony, 189
*Scourge of Villainy*, 74, 75, 287
Sea Venture, 193, 195, 196
*Second Folio*, 104
Second World War, 272
*Secrets of Shakespeare*, 205
*Sejanus*, 187, 196, 287
Seneca, 90, 95, 254, 255
*Seven Deadly Sins*, 148
*Shadow of Night*, 224
Shakespeare
  Authorship, xi, xii, xiii, 6, 27, 30, 66, 89, 101, 102, 109, 121, 133, 134, 141, 144, 149, 163, 181, 192, 193, 199, 225, 227, 233, 258, 271, 272, 286, 296, 297, 301, 303, 306
  Plays, xiii, 6, 27, 29, 32, 34, 38, 50, 51, 52, 53, 55, 59, 61, 66, 70, 71, 73, 77, 78, 87, 90, 91, 93, 94, 100, 101, 102, 104, 106, 107, 108, 128, 129, 130, 135, 138, 139, 141, 143, 146, 154, 168, 173, 174, 175, 176, 182, 183, 186, 190, 193, 195, 197, 200, 202, 206, 209, 211, 213, 216, 218, 245, 246, 249, 256, 260, 262, 278,
  280, 281, 283, 292, 296, 299, 302, 304, 306, 308
  Portraits, 179, 180, 181, 263, 287, 288, 289, 290, 291, 292, 293, 294, 296
  Rival Poet, 218, 220, 223, 226, 227
Shake-speare, 20, 37, 39, 62, 65, 67, 68, 69, 72, 76, 92, 128, 182, 183, 184, 185, 187, 190, 210, 211, 216, 235, 248, 258, 284, 287, 296, 303
*Shakespeare Ciphers Examined*, 273, 307
Shakespeare, Edmund, 205
Shakespeare, Edward, 205
Shakespeare experts, 46, 47, 59, 72, 144, 149, 167, 203, 225, 227, 235, 246, 285, 295, 302, 305
Shakespeare Guild, 302
*Shakespeare Identified*, 82
*Shakespeare In Love*, 308
Shakespeare, Matthew, 205, 213
*Shakespeare, Oxford and Elizabethan Times*, 164
*Shakespeare Through Oxford Glasses*, 124
Shakespeare, William, 12, 16, 18, 19, 27, 29, 30, 31, 32, 34, 35, 44, 46, 48, 50, 52, 66, 69, 70, 75, 76, 79, 81, 86, 87, 89, 92, 99, 115, 127, 128, 133, 140, 142, 146, 151, 159, 161, 173, 177, 178, 182, 185, 188, 191, 215, 217, 229, 236, 242, 248, 264, 274, 278, 279, 283, 287, 288, 290, 297, 298, 307
Shakespeare's House, 160, 161
Shakspere, Anne, 2
Shakspere, Edmund, 2, 15, 19, 204
Shakspere, Gilbert, 2, 15, 19, 184
Shakspere, Hamnet, 15, 18, 19, 55, 62, 150, 205
Shakspere, Joan, 2, 15, 19
Shakspere, John, 1, 2, 3, 5, 7, 15, 16, 18, 19, 64, 65, 91, 140, 185, 204, 289, 299, 301
Shakspere, Judith, 15, 18, 19, 199, 203, 264
Shakspere, Margaret, 2
Shakspere, Mary, 1, 2, 15, 204, 289, 301
Shakspere, Richard, 2, 15, 19
Shakspere, Susanna, 15, 19, 91, 177, 199, 203, 204, 205, 214, 263
Shakspere, William
  Allonym, xi, 15, 19, 27, 29, 30, 35, 36, 53, 54, 58, 59, 65, 69, 85, 105, 126, 128, 130, 133, 134, 135, 136, 149,

150, 153, 157, 163, 183, 187, 188, 190, 240, 245, 249, 260, 290, 294, 298, 305, 308
As Shakespeare, 32, 33, 34, 35, 36, 38, 45, 46, 47, 51, 52, 53, 54, 56, 57, 58, 59, 61, 65, 67, 68, 69, 70, 72, 79, 87, 91, 93, 95, 98, 100, 101, 104, 105, 106, 107, 110, 111, 112, 116, 119, 130, 132, 133, 136, 137, 140, 141, 142, 151, 152, 156, 157, 159, 163, 166, 167, 168, 169, 173, 175, 182, 183, 185, 187, 188, 189, 192, 193, 194, 195, 199, 201, 202, 203, 206, 209, 211, 214, 221, 225, 226, 227, 228, 233, 234, 235, 236, 240, 244, 245, 246, 251, 253, 256, 258, 260, 261, 263, 264, 266, 271, 272, 278, 279, 283, 288, 289, 291, 294, 295, 297, 298, 299, 300, 301, 302, 303, 304, 305, 308, 310
Last will and testament, 148, 178, 179, 214, 259, 260, 266, 271, 285
London, 19, 28, 55, 56, 57, 58, 59, 60, 62, 63, 64, 65, 107, 130, 131, 132, 138, 143, 146, 147, 148, 150, 151, 182, 185, 188, 205, 212, 214, 246, 250, 258, 259
Lost Years, 15, 17, 18, 19
Marriage, 8, 9, 11, 12, 13, 14, 15, 161
Signatures, 142, 143, 147, 212
Stratford, 1, 2, 4, 5, 6, 7, 15, 16, 17, 18, 27, 28, 47, 55, 56, 59, 60, 63, 64, 66, 89, 93, 96, 109, 119, 131, 132, 138, 140, 147, 150, 152, 161, 177, 180, 184, 187, 189, 190, 191, 193, 195, 199, 203, 204, 206, 210, 215, 246, 251, 258, 260, 263, 265, 266, 279, 285, 299
Theatre, 17, 20, 53, 54, 55, 62, 66, 131, 137, 138, 149, 159, 178, 179, 185, 186, 189, 205, 206, 211, 212, 213, 214
Shanxi Agricultural University, 306
Shapiro, James, xii, xiii, 37, 59, 68, 92, 150, 233, 234, 236, 302, 303, 304, 305, 306
*Shepheardes Calender*, 82, 83, 86, 87, 88
Sherborne Castle, 219, 220
Shrewsbury, Countess, 220
Sidney, Mary, 49, 84, 159, 160, 161, 162, 163, 171, 188, 190, 299
Sidney, Philip, 49, 83, 84, 85, 101, 115
Simonides, 152
Slye, William, 149, 205, 211

Smart, Elizabeth, 149
Smith, William, 7
Socrates, 278
Somers, Sir George, 197
*Sonnet 10:* 43
*Sonnet 20:* 239
*Sonnet 42:* 232
*Sonnet 55:* 73
*Sonnet 72:* 73, 75, 245
*Sonnet 78:* 217
*Sonnet 80,* 219, 226
*Sonnet 81:* 73, 245
*Sonnet 82:* 239
*Sonnet 83:* 221, 239
*Sonnet 86:* 222, 224
*Sonnet 107:* 153, 157
*Sonnet 127:* 231
*Sonnet 131:* 231
*Sonnet 135:* 232
*Sonnet 136:* 85
*Sonnet 138:* 137, 229
*Sonnet 144:* 137, 228, 232, 233, 236, 237
*Sonnet 152:* 229
Sonnets, 27, 43, 44, 45, 62, 72, 73, 75, 85, 130, 137, 157, 206, 207, 208, 209, 210, 211, 216, 221, 235, 236, 240, 244, 248, 258, 275, 277, 285, 286, 293, 303, 305
*Sonnett upon the pitiful burneing of the Globe playhouse*, 201
Southampton, 2nd Earl, 105
Southampton, 3rd Earl
  Life, 41, 42, 43, 44, 45, 106, 128, 153, 156, 157, 217, 226, 237, 238, 239
  Marriage, 42, 44, 237, 242, 243
  Oxford, 37, 39, 44, 45, 105, 156, 229, 233, 237, 238, 240, 243, 244
  Role as Patron, 16, 31, 35, 37, 40, 56, 127, 128, 129, 153, 157, 229, 232, 303
  Sonnets, 43, 45, 61, 153, 156, 217, 236, 248
Southampton, 4th Earl, 239
Southwell, Edward, 16
Southwell, Fr. Robert, 208
Spanish Armada, 71, 152, 154, 256
*Spanish Maze,* 190
*Spanish Tragedie,* 90, 255, 256, 257, 298
*Speculum Tuscanismi,* 24
Spenser, Edmund, 78, 79, 81, 82, 84, 85, 86, 87, 88, 101, 133, 184, 219, 221, 260, 261, 297
Spittle, Bruce, 269, 274

St Bartholomew's Eve Massacre, 83
St Martin's Church, 9, 12
St Mary at Aldermanbury,, 149
Stafford, H., 238
Stone, Lawrence, 305
*Story of the Learned Pig,* 57
Stow, John, 70, 281
Strachey, William, 193, 194, 195, 196, 197
*Strange News,* 24, 162, 163, 170, 171, 173
Stratford monument, xiv, ix, 104, 150, 181, 268, 271, 274, 275, 277, 280, 281, 283, 284, 285, 286, 289, 310
Street, Peter, 137
*Study in the Warwickshire Dialect,* 303
Sturley, Abraham, 63, 64, 130, 132
Süssmayr, Franz, 202
Sumptuary laws, 292
Surrey, Earl of (Henry Howard), 124
Sussex, 3rd Earl, 49
Sussex, 4th Earl, 49
Sussex's Men, 92
Swan theatre, 60

## *T*

Talbot, Lady Catherine, 84
*Taming of A Shrew,* 16, 51, 202, 218, 304
*Taming of The Shrew,* 26, 50, 51, 52, 62, 129
Tarleton, Richard, 107, 149
*Taylor and Cutter,* 290
Taylor, John, 179
*Teares of the Muses,* 78, 79, 85, 88, 221
*Tempest, The,* 100, 190, 194, 195, 196, 198, 199, 258
Theatre, the, 28, 54, 137, 211
Thomas, Rev. Dr William, 180, 282
Thorpe, Thomas, 85, 104, 126, 208, 209, 210, 226, 235, 246, 247, 248, 249, 267, 268, 275, 277, 285, 293
Throgmorten, Elizabeth, 220
Tilney, Edmund, 190, 304, 305
*Timon of Athens,* 178
*Titus and Vespasian,* 90
*Titus Andronicus,* 16, 48, 49, 50, 61, 62, 89, 90, 91, 92, 93, 94, 95, 99, 100, 112, 193, 202, 218, 255, 256, 304
*Titus Manuscript,* 93, 94, 95, *98*, 99, 100, 101
*Today* (newspaper), 276
Tofte, Robert, 117

Tomson, Robert, 194, 195
Topcliffe, Richard, 208
Tower of London, 222, 244
*Tragical History of Romeus and Juliet,* 123
Transmigratus, 57
Treaty of London, 156
Trentham, Elizabeth, 207, 209, 229, 243, 244
*Troilus and Cressida,* 62, 185, 207, 277
*Troublesome Reign of King John,* 51, 52, 70, 71, 107, 202
*True Tragedy of Richard Duke of Yorke,* 51, 52, 71, 72, 107, 203
Turberville, George, 123
Twain, Mark, xiii, 183
Tweedale, Ralph L., 306
*Twelfth Night,* 62, 86, 121, 122, 218
*Two Gentlemen of Verona,* 50, 62
*Two Noble Kinsmen,* 100, 143, 201

## *U*

Ulloa, Francis de, 194, 195
Underhill, Fulke, 60
Underhill, Hercules, 60
Underhill, William, 60
*Unfortunate Traveller,* 217
*Unknown Man Clasping a Hand from a Cloud,* 240
*Ur-Hamlet,* 254

## *V*

Valois, Marguerite de, 118, 119, 253
Vavasour, Anne, 113, 121, 122, 229, 230, 231, 232, 233, 236
*Venus and Adonis,* xv, 16, 30, 35, 36, 37, 39, 44, 45, 46, 47, 48, 50, 56, 68, 76, 92, 93, 127, 131, 135, 136, 146, 152, 153, 163, 173, 174, 175, 183, 217, 232, 235, 244, 246, 290, 298, 303
Vere House, 80
Vere, Aubrey de, 72
Vere, Bridget, 49, 162, 174, 263
Vere, Elizabeth, 42, 49, 105, 128, 237, 242
Vere, John de, 72
Vere, Susan, 49, 162, 198
Vertue, George, 179, 180, 181, 281, 282, 283
Virgil, 278, 279

## W

Walker, Henry, 259
Walsingham, Sir Francis, 25, 80, 83, 152, 166
Ward, Bernard R., 108, 207, 208
Ward, John, 279
Ward, Rev. Dr. John, 177
Warner, Walter, 224
Wayte, William, 55, 56, 59
Webbe, William, 36
Webster, John, 52, 261
Weever, John, 136, 182
Wekes, Henry, 164
Wentworth House, 291
Wentworth, Thomas (Earl of Strafford), 291, 292
Westminster Abbey, 5, 131, 260, 261, 262, 263, 264
Whateley, Anne, 8, 9, 10, 11, 12, 161
White, Edward, 92
Whitgift, John (Archbishop of Canterbury), 44, 127
Wilkins, George, 59, 146, 147, 148, 156
Will Monox, 24, 25, 26, 27, 29, 163, 292
Williams, Norman, 223
*Willobie His Avisa*, 30, 37, 38, 39, 43, 44, 46, 50, 92, 128, 152, 153, 186, 228, 229, 233, 236, 237
Wilson, Ian, 1, 46, 158, 259
Wilson, J. Dover, 252
Wilson, William, 13
Wilton House, 49, 158, 159, 160, 161, 162, 163, 167, 171, 174, 188, 191, 299
Winchester, Bishop of, 138
Windet, John, 50
*Winter's Tale,* 258
*Witts Recreations Selected from the Finest Fancies of Modern Muses,* 67
Worcester, Bishop of, 9, 10, 11
Wotton, John, 108
Wotton, Sir Henry, 200, 213
Wright, Louis, 251
Wyse, Andrew, 183

## Z

Zeus, 107, 173

DAVID L. ROPER has a thorough background in Shakespeare Authorship studies. In recent times he has appeared on national television, and been a much quoted contributor to current journals concerning the mysteries tht surround Shakespeare's life.
He has also been an invited speaker on both sides of the Atlantic.

It was his prowess as a mathematician, with more than twenty years experience in the field of teaching that enabled him to construct a valid means for decrypting secrets embedded in passages of text. This had been a strategy used in diplomatic circles for concealing confidential information, first introduced by Girolamo Cardano in 1550. It was the discovery of this decrypting process that led to a valid means for unlocking information that had lain hidden for more than four centuries on the wall monument at Stratford-upon-Avon. It certifed that the court poet and playwright Edward de Vere, 17th Earl of Oxford, was the true genius known to the world as William Shakespeare.

www.ingramcontent.com/pod-product-compliance
Lightning Source LLC
Chambersburg PA
CBHW052050230426
43671CB00011B/1862